Kabuki heroes

on the Osaka stage
1780–1830

kabuki heroes

on the Osaka stage
1780–1830

C. Andrew Gerstle

with
Timothy Clark
Akiko Yano

THE BRITISH MUSEUM PRESS

© 2005 The Trustees of the British Museum

C. Andrew Gerstle has asserted the right
to be identified as the author of this work

First published in 2005 by The British Museum Press
A division of The British Museum Company Ltd
38 Russell Square, London WC1B 3QQ

www.britishmuseum.co.uk

A catalogue record for this book
is available from the British Library

ISBN-13:   978-0-7141-2430-8

ISBN-10:   0-7141-2430-3

Designed by Harry Green
Printed in Spain by Grafos SA, Barcelona

DEDICATION

To Matsudaira Susumu (1933–2000),
who devoted his life to the study
of Osaka Kabuki and Bunraku culture

contents

PREFACE

The relationship between Kabuki popular theatre in Kyoto–Osaka and Edo (modern Tokyo) in the eighteenth and nineteenth centuries was perhaps a bit like the relations between Broadway and Hollywood in the twentieth century. The industry in a brash frontier town (Los Angeles/Edo) mushroomed to dwarf the venerable home of theatre (New York City/Kyoto–Osaka) in terms of money and size, and never ceased trying to lure away its leading talent. Osaka actor Nakamura Utaemon III (Shikan), one of the heroes of this exhibition, succumbed and went to Edo for three prolonged tours. His great Osaka rival Arashi Kichisaburō II (Rikan) steadfastly stayed at home. All of the great female role specialists (onnagata) of the eighteenth century originated from Kyoto–Osaka, no matter where they ultimately performed.

Colour woodblock printing in late eighteenth-century Japan was the motion picture of its day, capturing magical performances and promoting reputations. Unlike the divide between performers and audience created by the mechanical medium of the movies, however, in pre-modern Japan Kabuki actors inhabited the same world as their fans; and nowhere more so than in Osaka. This exhibition presents the inter-connected social networks that linked actors, patrons and audience in Kabuki fan clubs, and poetry and painting salons. All were expected to turn a haiku poem in praise of a performance – or in modest gratitude, when basking in the fans' praise. Remarkably, those who in day-to-day life were the businessmen who captained Osaka's mercantile powerhouse were also the semi-professional artists of 'likeness' (nigao-e) portraits of Kabuki stars, published as commercial sheet prints or in illustrated books.

It is true to say that the vibrant 'Kabuki culture' of eighteenth- and nineteenth-century Osaka, home of the great dramatist Chikamatsu Monzaemon (1653–1724) and the puppet theatre he first wrote for, has been relatively neglected by later generations. We are particularly gratified, therefore, to bring together a rich and unprecedented array of paintings, prints and books that reveal this fascinating world, building on the achievements of the late Matsudaira Susumu (1933–2000), who organized the last great exhibition of Osaka Kabuki art in 1975 and to whose memory the current project is dedicated. And it is particularly appropriate that, after its debut in the Japanese Gallery at the British Museum, the exhibition travels on to be shown first at the Osaka Museum of History, not very far from the Dōtonbori theatre district where most of the works were created; and subsequently to that great centre for theatre studies in Japan, the Tsubouchi Memorial Theatre Museum at Waseda University in Tokyo.

Our warm thanks go first to Professor Andrew Gerstle of the School of Oriental and African Studies, University of London, for his vision in creating the central concept of the exhibition and for his boundless energy in bringing the project to fruition. In this he has been most ably assisted by a large group of scholars, whose names appear in the list of contributors: we thank them for their expertise, so freely given. Research for the project has been funded by a substantial grant from the Arts and Humanities Research Council and it is gratifying that the results can now be shared with a wide public, by means of this exhibition and catalogue. In addition, research at Waseda University Theatre Museum was supported by a grant from the Japanese MEXT's 'Academic Frontier' Project (2003–2008). The beauty and superb craftsmanship of Osaka actor prints has led them to become scattered in collections the world over, and we also thank the many public and private lenders in the UK, Japan, Europe and USA who have given the project such generous approbation and support. The works are generally light in weight and relatively easily transported, nevertheless it has required considerable resources to bring them together and to present them in an appropriate manner. We are especially grateful to the family of foundations and other supporters who have made this possible, in particular The Japan Foundation, The Daiwa Anglo-Japanese Foundation, The Tōshiba International Foundation, The Great Britain–Sasakawa Foundation, The Japan Foundation Endowment Committee, The Sainsbury Institute for Japanese Arts and Cultures, Dr Willem Dreesman, The Sankei Newspaper, All Nippon Airways and Shōchiku Co. Ltd. The Art Research Centre at Ritsumeikan University, Kyoto, has made a particularly special contribution with the creation of very appealing, state-of-the-art digital displays.

It is a great and fitting honour that 'Living National Treasure' Kabuki actor and star Osaka performer Nakamura Ganjirō III has contributed a preface to this volume, and also that he has found time in his hectic schedule this year to present performances at the British Museum in early September. Ganjirō is descended artistically directly from Nakamura Utaemon III, featured in the exhibition, and we wish him well with his taking of the name Sakata Tōjūrō IV in December of this year.

We hope that the exhibition will contribute to an evermore thriving Kabuki culture in Osaka and beyond, and invite your enthusiastic participation in that culture.

Neil MacGregor, Director, The British Museum

Osamu Wakita, Director, Osaka Museum of History

Mikio Takemoto, Director, The Tsubouchi Memorial Theatre Museum, Waseda University, Tokyo

PREFACE

Kabuki has had two major streams since the late seventeenth century: Kyoto–Osaka (Kamigata) and Edo (Tokyo). Like the two wheels of a cart these have carried Kabuki along its path of development. The two traditions have many aspects in common, of course, but also have many fundamental differences.

Edo Kabuki is characterized by the term *aragoto*, describing a rough, flamboyant style in which the superhero overcomes villains or evil supernatural forces. This style is surely related to the fact that Edo itself was a relatively new city, with an overabundance of samurai and filled with raw popular energy. The predominant warrior culture had a fascination with religious ritual and spiritual power, and mixed with the samurai's natural interest in physical and political power, this produced the *aragoto* style of acting. The aesthetics of formal acting, statue-like poses and an obsession with continuation of the actor's family line gave Edo Kabuki its particular character.

Kyoto–Osaka Kabuki, on the other hand, reflected the urban cultures of those two cities, which had longer and more mature traditions. Its plays were more developed dramatically, with complex plots, compared to the simpler ones in Edo. The aesthetic term *wagoto* (gentle, realistic) came to characterize Kyoto–Osaka Kabuki, epitomized in the role of the male lover. Passionate love stories were a common theme, with deep and realistic, often humorous depiction of human emotions.

Kyoto–Osaka Kabuki drew from the courtier culture of Kyoto and the vibrant merchant culture of Osaka from early on in the seventeenth century, and combined them into a thriving theatrical form. The gentle style of *wagoto* was perfected by the actor Sakata Tōjūrō (1647–1709), known for the deeply searching nature of his acting technique (*gei*). We are fortunate to have a substantial record of his ideas and attitudes to acting included in *The Actors' Analects* (*Yakusha rongo*; trans. Dunn and Torigoe, 1969).

One incident describes a scene in a drama where Tōjūrō plays a man who comes to the pleasure quarter late at night and knocks at the gate. The porter asks, 'Who's there?' Tōjūrō, as head of the troupe, also had the role of director. He didn't like the way the actor responded, 'That was not the voice of a porter in the middle of the night!' He kept correcting him, complaining, 'Now it sounds like a voice at dawn!', until after five or six times he got it right. We can see from this episode how deeply interested Tōjūrō was in the essence of realistic acting. Even for one line of a minor character, he demanded that it sound natural to the situation. This passion for detail led to the creation of the *wagoto* style.

Tōjūrō was fortunate to have worked with the great playwright Chikamatsu Monzaemon (1653–1724). Chikamatsu was stimulated by Tōjūrō's acting skills and together they created many masterpieces for the stage. In 1953 my father and I revived the Chikamatsu play *Love Suicides at Sonezaki* and I have since played the lead female role Ohatsu in more than 1,200 performances, including in London and Manchester in 2001, and in Moscow and St Petersburg in 2003. We were overwhelmed at receiving a standing ovation after each performance. I was very impressed that, although the language, culture and religion may be different, Chikamatsu's play has retained its power to move audiences.

Since the time of Tōjūrō, Kyoto–Osaka Kabuki has continued to produce star actors who have each created distinctive acting styles. A particular characteristic of Kyoto–Osaka Kabuki is that rather than the obsession with maintaining family tradition common to Edo, it has spurred individuality in acting styles (*geifū*).

Since the Pacific War, Tokyo has dramatically absorbed Japan's economy and culture, coming to dominate the whole nation. This has led to a crisis in Kyoto–Osaka Kabuki. Kabuki needs competition between the two styles of Kyoto–Osaka and Edo to maintain a healthy and vibrant future. I was born and bred in Kyoto–Osaka culture, and am working with others to restore Kyoto–Osaka Kabuki in the twenty-first century.

This coming December at Kyoto's Minami-za Theatre I will accede to the acting name Sakata Tōjūrō IV, restoring the Tōjūrō name to the stage after a 231-year hiatus. I hope that this will be a first step towards ensuring a flourishing future for the two wheels of Kyoto–Osaka and Edo Kabuki that have created our tradition.

This exhibition *Kabuki Heroes on the Osaka Stage: 1780–1830* will show the brilliant heritage of Kyoto–Osaka Kabuki and the magnificence of its past star actors. I hope that it will enjoy a tremendous success in London, Osaka and Tokyo.

Nakamura Ganjirō III

FOREWORD

The Russian film director Sergei Eisenstein saw the first foreign tour of a professional Kabuki troupe in Moscow in 1928 and was totally fascinated by its power of theatricality. It was a crucial moment for Eisenstein when he was struggling with the complex problem of how to incorporate 'sound' into hitherto silent films. He later wrote on this moment of epiphany for him, the impact of a star Kabuki actor at a climactic moment of intensity:

> The Japanese have shown us another extremely interesting form of ensemble – the *monistic ensemble*. Sound–movement–space–voice here do not accompany (nor even parallel) each other, but function as elements of equal significance. . . . Directing himself to the various organs of sensation, he [the actor] builds his summation to a grand total provocation of the human brain; without taking any notice which of these several paths he is following. (*Film Form*, 1959, pp. 20–21)

Eisenstein's 'grand total provocation of the human brain' was the intense moment in a Kabuki play when movement of the actor, accompanied by music and voice, culminates in a histrionic pose (*mie*) that the actor holds for a brief kinetic moment (*ma*). These are the points of Kabuki's greatest impact, the moments when cries of delight emerge from the audience electrifying the magical ties of unity between actor and audience. These poses of kinetic intensity are essential to the art of Kabuki – first and foremost an actor-centred theatre. Master actors achieve magnificent tableaux moments of intense emotion that set a tingle of excitement reverberating through the audience. Such moments linger enticingly in the memory. The many prints here show how artists devised a range of techniques to capture these magical moments and to portray the fascinating personalities of the actors behind the characters. The catalogue also presents the actors at the centre of a vibrant popular urban culture, and shows them interacting with fans, poets and artists.

Exactly two hundred years ago in 1805 one of the stars of this show, Arashi Kichisaburō II (Rikan), became the head of one of the two professional Kabuki troupes in Osaka, the acknowledged superstar among his peers and a favourite of women fans. Kabuki fans are particular, they love their favourite actor and tend to idolize them above all others. Our catalogue too is actor-centred; we hope that their personalities come alive on the page and that readers will come to have their own favourites among Tomijūrō, Hinasuke, Rikan, Shikan and the others.

A Japanese-language edition of the catalogue will be published to accompany the exhibitions held in Osaka and Tokyo. Transcriptions of the texts on the prints will be included in this Japanese-language version.

Andrew Gerstle

ACKNOWLEDGEMENTS

In 1929 and 1931 two important studies on Osaka (Kamigata) actor prints appeared, based primarily on the theatre-related materials owned by Osaka collector OKADA Isajirō. These studies by KURODA Genji and HARUYAMA Takematsu were the first attempts to document the range of Kabuki prints produced not in Edo but in Osaka and Kyoto. Haruyama in his acknowledgements at the end of his 1931 article dedicated it to the city of Osaka, adding that Okada had suddenly died on 25 May 1931 at the age of fifty-two. The Okada collection was subsequently lost from sight, remaining unseen by any scholar after that time. It was a mystery even to MATSUDAIRA Susumu, the leading authority on the subject, who had heard that the collection had survived the Pacific War but could not locate it. During the planning for this exhibition, this lost collection discretely began to appear on the art market in Japan in small groups of 100 or 150 items at a time. Only after dealers and collectors noticed this steady stream of material flowing month by month into dealer auctions did they realize the source. It has been estimated that during 2002–2003 as many as 10,000 items were sold from this one collection. Many of these have gone to collectors outside Japan, in Europe and the USA. Quite a few of the items in this exhibition are known from illustrations and references in pre-War publications to be from this source, and others are suspected to have an Okada provenance. We are fortunate to be able to showcase many items neither previously seen in public nor published in colour, particularly many works by the early Osaka master Ryūkōsai and his successor Shōkōsai.

This catalogue and the exhibition it documents would not have been possible without the help of many individuals. Like the Kabuki culture we are documenting, the project has developed out of passion and collective effort, and we are lucky to have had the friendly co-operation of so many specialists and enthusiasts. The subject is relatively young, and we wish to acknowledge and thank the many who have been involved. First and foremost is the late MATSUDAIRA Susumu, whose passion for Osaka Kabuki prints developed while teaching in London at the School of Oriental and African Studies (SOAS) from 1970 to 1974, and to whom we dedicate this volume. The British Museum and the Victoria & Albert Museum collections encouraged his first systematic explorations of Osaka prints, which had largely been ignored by scholars in Japan. Matsudaira's later work back in Japan – organizing the first major exhibition of Osaka prints in 1975, and systematically documenting several major collections at Waseda University, Ikeda Bunko Library and Kōnan Women's University – provided the foundation for all later research. His modesty, warmth of spirit and co-operative attitude towards all those who came with queries, from both inside Japan and out, is legendary and a model to us all. Matsudaira always acknowledged the pioneering work and support of Roger Keyes, who with his late wife MIZUSHIMA Keiko catalogued the important Osaka print collection of the Philadelphia Museum of Art, and who has revealed to us all the beauty and significance of the art of *surimono*. Keyes' *The Theatrical World of Osaka Prints* (1973) remains a model study of the subject, to be read alongside the current catalogue. KITAGAWA Hiroko worked with Professor Matsudaira for many years and has enthusiastically assisted this project, particularly in documenting items. Her experience in dating materials related to Kyoto–Osaka Kabuki is unparalleled.

IWATA Hideyuki has been an unflappable source of knowledge on all aspects of Kabuki, the transcription of difficult calligraphy, and the interpretation of poetry. AKAMA Ryō has helped in many ways, taking thousands of quality photographs, creating digital archives and websites for research and videos and digital displays for the exhibition, and exploring the rich cultural production that surrounds Kabuki. His enthusiasm and drive to make available this vast material culture of Kabuki has changed the way we research the subject, and opened it to scholars everywhere.

KOBAYASHI Fumiko, during a six-month stay at SOAS, helped greatly in transcribing the texts of many *surimono*, together with Barbara Cross, TSUCHIDA Makiko and MUTŌ Junko. Osaka theatre specialists HAYASHI Fumiko, KAGURAOKA Yōko and KURAHASHI Masae helped with transcription, interpretation and documentation during an intensive summer workshop in London in 2004. HANYŪ Noriko during her two years at SOAS 2002–2004 and then back in Japan always helped with queries and problems relating to Kabuki, poetry circles and publishers. SAKAGUCHI Hiroyuki and NISHIJIMA Atsuya have helped the project all along through their related research centre activities. The Osaka Museum of History and in particular Director WAKITA Osamu, TAKAI Kenji and SAWAI Kōichi have worked enthusiastically to enlist the co-operation of many lenders and to help organize the overall exhibition. In Tokyo, the Waseda University Theatre Museum staff, in particular Director TAKEMOTO Mikio, former Director TORIGOE Bunzō, KIRA Sueo, WADA Osamu, ŌE Yoshiko, UCHIDA Yōko and TAGUSAGAWA Mizuki have wholeheartedly supported the project. AKEO Keizō, MIZUNO Kayano and NAKATANI Nobuo have helped with particular queries. Peter Ujlaki and Israel Goldman have provided constant information on Osaka prints and the whereabouts of excellent impressions. SAKOMOTO Jun'ichi has led the co-operation given by Shōchiku Company, with all their wonderful Kabuki resources. MIURA Katsuhiro of Sankei Shinbun believed in the project from the outset and has helped to make it possible.

We thank most warmly collectors in Japan, Europe and the USA who have so generously loaned to the exhibition precious prints, illustrated books and paintings: Ed Freis, Scott Johnson, HIDA Kōzō, KATŌ Sadahiko, Hendrick Lühl, Gerhard Pulverer, Ellis Tinios, Peter Ujlaki, and John Weber.

In the UK we have received unstinting help from Alan Cummings, Rupert Faulkner and his colleagues at the Victoria & Albert Museum, Gillian Hudson, Peter Kornicki, David Newman, Kate Newnham, Sheila O'Connell, Glenn Ratcliffe, Hamish Todd, UCHIDA Hiromi, WATANABE Mitsuko, YASUMURA Yoshiko and others, as well as from many supportive colleagues in the various departments of the British Museum. Mavis Pilbeam read and commented on all our writings, which have been most ably translated into a beautiful catalogue by Laura Brockbank and Sarah Levesley at British Museum Press, and designer Harry Green.

Andrew Gerstle
Timothy Clark
YANO Akiko

KABUKI CULTURE AND COLLECTIVE CREATIVITY

C. ANDREW GERSTLE

Celebrity and fame

We are obsessed today with celebrity and fame. The grip of this obsession on the print and electronic media is tenacious, and it is of course the power of the media, particularly photography, that feeds the frenzy. Commercial profit is a main driving force: celebrity sells magazines, books, TV programmes, news, films and music. We simply love the glamour of the spotlight, either to gaze upon or to bask within. Young or old, we all worship our favourite musicians, our film and television stars, and our sports heroes, sometimes in private, sometimes in a crowd – at concerts, theatres and sports grounds.

This obsession with celebrity has been driven in large measure by the technological advances of the last century. Its rise was most dramatically evident during the golden era of Hollywood in the 1920s and 1930s, when films made in a dusty town in southern California came to be shown in darkened theatres all over the globe, on silver screens that conjured up a seductive dream-world of glamorous heroes and heroines.

We need our celebrities to be up on the stage or on the screen. Distance makes the glamorous more beautiful and exciting. At the same time, however, we chase the illusion of intimacy by attending performances in person and by collecting photographs (bromides), magazines, autographs and anything else associated with them. We want to know about their daily lives, their 'real' lives off screen. We want to emulate their styles, their voices and, as in the case of Elvis, walk in their boots.

The rise of electronic media ushered in an age in which celebrity became a commodity, passively consumed, far from the actual players – the musicians, actors or sportspeople. Recently, however, the Internet and 'reality' TV have added new, more participatory dimensions to the construction and uses of fame, and we have yet to know the full consequences.

An obsession with celebrity is not, however, only a modern phenomenon. London in the eighteenth century, for example, promoted the celebrity of its courtesans and actors in prints. A print of the famous actor David Garrick shows him at his histrionic best (fig. 19). It is fascinating to witness many of the same elements that characterize our contemporary obsessions in a relatively remote Japanese society of two hundred years ago, long before modern technologies had their impact. The example offers us an interesting perspective on our own times. Technological innovation is, in fact, crucial to our story. The Japanese obsession with celebrity was fanned by exploitation of the potential of full-colour woodblock printing, which burst upon the commercial publishing scene in the late 1760s and ushered in a golden age of what is termed here 'Kabuki culture'. An early masterpiece in the lineage of coloured portraits of actors is the illustrated book *Ehon butai ōgi* (*Picture Book: Actor Fans*, 1770; cat. 9).

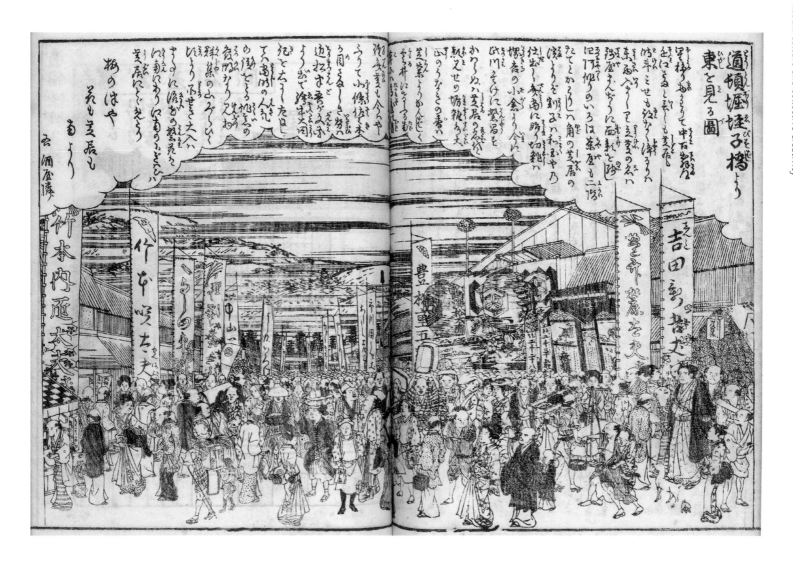

1 Osaka Dōtonbori Theatre District, viewed from the western side. The signs mark both Kabuki and Bunraku puppet theatres. From *Shibai gakuya zue* (*Backstage at the Theatre: An Illustrated Guide*), 1800 (see cat. 70). (Cambridge University Library)

One very appealing and intriguing dimension of this Kabuki culture was its interactive nature. Actors, all the while worshipped as heroes of the stage, were also active participants in other cultural forums, such as poetry salons. Conversely, members of Kabuki fan clubs (*hiiki-ren*) performed rituals at the theatre (Kaguraoka essay; cats 276, 277 and 278), and individual fans created or sponsored actor prints to support their favourites and promote their fame.

The system was indeed driven by certain commercial imperatives, not dissimilar to those we see in action today. Nevertheless, it becomes clear as we investigate further that there was also an opposing ethos of playful amateurism; of participation in the arts as a life-long hobby (*yūgei*) that many found enriching. Amateur groups for poetry, art, theatre, dance and music constituted artificial 'utopian spaces' (*za*)[1] for social interaction, in which each person took a turn at contributing creatively to a performance. With the production of an actor print, a memorial print with poetry (*surimono*), or a parody flybill (*mitate banzuke*; an ephemeral, comic printed sheet that impersonated

functional genres) even the ordinary enthusiast could see their name in the public arena, albeit under the guise of a fictional pen name (*haimyō*). Publishers, too, were part of these same networks, and products of the cultural salons were often issued from small, 'boutique' firms. The parallels with contemporary Internet publishing are intriguing, and it is easy to see, too, why it was Japan that created and successfully marketed karaoke. Two ephemeral prints in this catalogue illustrate how average townsmen and women dreamed of being like their stage idols (cats 58 and 59).

Such salon arts illustrate how playful spaces for cultural interaction are often created against the grain of officially accepted ideology or practice. Although they never aspired to be (and certainly were never permitted to be) politically active, Japanese salons were inherently culturally and socially subversive: their egalitarian ethos ran contrary to government-sponsored ideology based on strict and legal segregation by class, profession and region. The role of the arts, therefore, was as a vital catalyst for social intercourse and development.

The work of Henri Lefebvre has stimulated many to

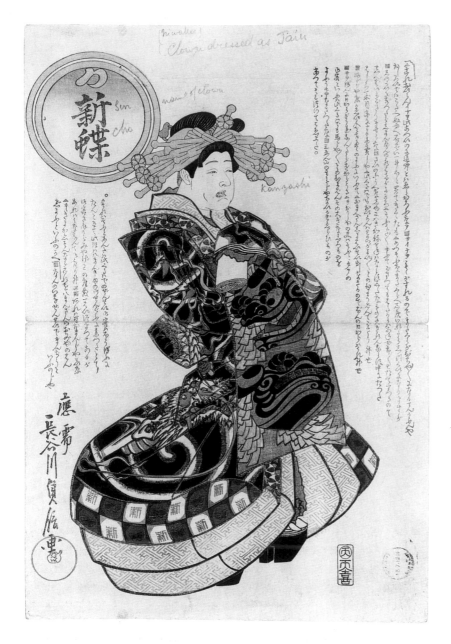

2 An amateur performs a skit (*niwaka*) as a courtesan with the name of Shinchō, *c.* 1835, by Hasegawa Sadanobu (see also cat. 280). (Bodleian Library, Oxford University)

examine how societies construct their cultural spaces.[2] The network of inter-linked real and imagined spaces around Kabuki culture is a fascinating example of how the construction and control of space was negotiated at all levels of society, from the Shogun at the top down to the actors who were outcasts at the bottom. Kabuki culture was a delicious and subversive fantasy space for entertainment, officially kept within the bounds of licensed theatres, but effectively reaching out through printed media into all corners of the land. At its best it was an interaction of artists, writers and enthusiasts who used performance as the stimulant for creativity and social interaction. It demonstrates to us how performance and celebrity can be catalysts for artistic production.

The erotic actor

Many art exhibitions tend to focus on the brilliance of an individual artist. Our narrative here, however, is about collective genius stimulated by performance – on the stage, in poetry salons and fan clubs. Participation is a key term. Large numbers of individuals, in most cases ordinary townsmen, but samurai and courtiers as well, contributed to the phenomenon of 'Kabuki culture' in Osaka and Kyoto around the period 1780–1830. This catalogue documents the vibrancy and creativity of a society in which theatre, art and poetry were essential elements of social and cultural life, where the arts were the medium for interaction across class, gender and region. It is a fascinating story of the passionate worship of actor heroes, with fans vigorously participating in the creation of celebrity and fame for their idols, thereby gaining their own moments of glory and glamour in the spotlight. This desire for dynamic and playful participation in culture is epitomized by a set of prints (cat. 280) by Sadanobu which depicts four townsmen enthusiasts in elaborate 'drag' as Edo courtesans, performing a Kabuki-style skit (*niwaka*, also called *chaban* in Edo). There was a *niwaka* festival in the Edo Yoshiwara Pleasure Quarter in the eighth month each year, with costume parades; the four Osaka gentlemen may have been imitating this. Figure 2, for example, shows the self-styled 'courtesan' Shinchō in his/her finest moment of glory!

Kabuki was (and is) quintessentially urban, popular, commercial theatre, deemed by successive governments until after World War II to be as dangerous to public morals as prostitution. 'Two sides of the roll of a dice' was a phrase used to describe the artificially constructed 'dangerous spaces' (*akusho*) of the floating world (*ukiyo*) of urban pleasures: brothels and theatres. They were zoned entertainment districts, licensed urban festival spaces where fantasies were given rein to run free outside the strictures of everyday working life. Whereas women (and some young men) were the objects and men the consumers in the brothels, with Kabuki the situation was somewhat reversed; from 1629 the actors, even of female roles, were always men (see below), and female fans were easily as numerous as male.

Kabuki actors have traditionally formed a segregated, relatively closed social group, clannish and guild-like. From early on, the perpetuation of a lineage (by blood line or adoption) from a great star became an important vehicle for the manufacture of celebrity and fame. Some of these actor lines continue today: for example, Nakamura Utaemon, Nakamura Tomijūrō, Ichikawa Danjūrō and Kataoka Nizaemon; others died out only recently in the twentieth century. This catalogue shows how visual representation of actors across generations was a key technique for promoting a younger actor in the mould of his namesake forebear. Good examples

3 *Yakusha hama no masago* (*Myriad Actors, Like Sand on a Beach*), 1803. The poem celebrates Yoshizawa Hakō (Iroha I, later Ayame V, 1755–1810) in the role of the courtesan Hana-tachibana (see cat. 83).

salacious dance in the early seventeenth century Kabuki was always flamboyant and 'bent' – the literal early meaning of the word *kabuki*.[4] It was outlandish and socially rebellious, with a love of the playboy, the outlaw, the prostitute and the trickster. The actor's physical body was the focus, and only superstars mattered. Little has changed today: fans still go to Kabuki to see their favourite actors in dashing, heroic roles that show them at their histrionic best. Actor worship remains essential to Kabuki.

This focus on the actor's sensual voice and body was already apparent from Kabuki's origins as an all-female troupe that performed dances and skits in the city of Kyoto from around 1600. Prostitution was inextricably linked to this theatre, and subsequently women were banned from the stage in 1629 because of public disturbances surrounding both their performances and their offstage activities. The star role for the legendary actress Okuni was to play Nagoya Sanza, a swaggering masterless samurai (*rōnin*) who visits the pleasure quarter to meet his courtesan lover. This 'prostitute Kabuki' (*yūjo kabuki*) was followed by 'youth Kabuki' (*wakashu kabuki*). But these all-boy troupes were also considered too licentious and presently banned in 1652 for reasons similar to the all-women troupes. From that time onward Kabuki has been an all-male 'adult' theatre with female roles played by male specialists (*onnagata*). The element of eroticism has remained a constant beneath the veneer of greater respectability, however. As in good theatre anywhere, the best lead actors must create an irresistible presence. Add the elements of cross-dressing and gender-impersonation – the necessity for a man to create the image of a seductive woman onstage – and we can understand the potential for eroticism, charged with intrigue and ambiguity, which would be enticing for both men and women. A 'crazy verse' (*kyōka*) by the artist Shōkōsai that accompanies a portrait in the illustrated play book *Yakusha hama no masago* (*Myriad Actors, Like Sand on a Beach*, 1803, cat. 83) gives a sense of this erotic excitement and fascinating sexual allure of the *onnagata* onstage (fig. 3). The poem celebrates Yoshizawa Hakō (Iroha I, later Ayame V, 1755–1810) in the role of the courtesan Hana-tachibana:

> *Koyoi koso / shubi yoshizawa to / hatsukoi no /*
> *kao ni momiji no / iroha somekeri*
> Tonight especially
> Things will go well
> First love with Yoshizawa
> Cheeks glowing, colour deep
> As autumn leaves swirling about Iroha
> SHŌKŌSAI

The poem turns on double meanings for the sounds of the actor's name: *yoshi* ('good') and *iroha* ('tinged leaves').

are seen in cats 197 and 245, which portray Arashi Rikan I and Arashi Rikan II almost as lookalikes, the only distinction being the drawing of a single versus a double eyelid. The two men were in fact completely unrelated: artists often portrayed the younger actor as looking similar to his predecessor even when there was no actual blood tie, as was often the case. Compare also the representation of Rikan II (cat. 244) by Kunisada to see how differently an Edo artist portrayed him. The revival of a famous acting name still occurs occasionally today. In December 2005 the current Nakamura Ganjirō III will revive the name of the great Sakata Tōjūrō I (1647–1709), held to be the founder of the Kyoto–Osaka 'gentle' (*wagoto*) acting style (see below), to become Tōjūrō IV. The name will be revived after a considerable hiatus since the death of Tōjūrō III in 1774. Only a top actor with the backing of other stars can create a new name or revive the name of a legendary predecessor.

Actors and courtesans, however highly revered by the public as celebrities or even deities, were legally considered to be outside and beneath the class system of four hierarchical rankings: samurai, farmer, artisan and merchant. They were officially registered as 'non-persons' (*hinin*).[3] Sometimes referred to in official documents as 'dry-riverbed beggars' (*kawaramono*), they had many restrictions over aspects of their daily lives, although these were strictly enforced only rarely in the case of actors.

There were, of course, concrete reasons for this disdain by the Confucianist samurai government. From its beginnings in

Kyoto–Osaka versus Edo

Japan was relatively closed off from outside contact from the late 1630s to the mid-nineteenth century, but it also developed some of the largest and most vibrant cities in the world during that period. In 1800 Edo (modern Tokyo), with a population of about 1 million, and Kyoto and Osaka, each with about 350–400,000, were major urban centres by global standards of the time. Each city was acutely conscious of its differences from the others, and it was common to compose 'three-city comparisons' (san-ka-tsu or santo-kurabe) for all sorts of things, from food to women, from manners to theatre and language. Edo, the administrative capital of the Shogun, was new, brash and over-populated with low-level samurai males from the provinces; Kyoto was the seat of the imperial court and home to tradition and the arts; Osaka was the commercial centre, proud of its mercantile, self-reliant verve. A sense of competition among these three, and other smaller centres, was crucial for cultural stimulation at a time when there was relatively little contact with the outside world.

Kabuki theatre, too, was different in each region. In general, Edo Kabuki was described as 'rough' (aragoto) – brash, bombastic, flamboyant and cheeky.[5] Kyoto–Osaka Kabuki, on the other hand, was 'gentle' (wagoto) – smooth, realistic, passionate, and more interested in the lover than the fighter. A further difference was that Osaka was home to the Bunraku (Jōruri) puppet drama and its great playwrights, such as Chikamatsu Monzaemon (1651–1725), Takeda Izumo II (1691–1756), Namiki Sōsuke (Senryū, 1695–1751) and Chikamatsu Hanji (1725–83). Plays that originated in the Osaka puppet theatre (maruhon-mono) still today comprise the core of the Kabuki repertoire. The puppet theatre, with its origins in narrative storytelling, was a decisive influence on the progressive development of Kabuki from dance into sophisticated drama. Its texts were the models for all aspiring playwrights, whether in Edo or Osaka. Many who went on to be successful Kabuki authors, such as Namiki Shōzō (1730–73) and Namiki Gohei (1747–1808), were first nurtured in the world of Bunraku.

Edo was not a major centre of literary publishing until the second half of the eighteenth century, but it took the lead in the production of imagery related to Kabuki and the pleasure quarters from the late seventeenth century onwards, with the so-called 'pictures of the floating world' (ukiyo-e).[6] From the late 1690s the Torii line of specialist theatre artists painted 'picture sign-boards' (e-kanban) to hang outside the theatre buildings. They also designed an increasing stream of actor prints, initially hand-coloured, then from the 1740s with one or two printed colours, and finally from the late 1760s printed in full colour. The Torii were followed by other artist-lineages in Edo who specialized in the theatre, most notably the Katsukawa (Shunshō, Shunkō and Shun'ei) and the Utagawa (Toyokuni and Kunisada). They all worked as part of a commercial network of artists, publishers and theatres to promote Kabuki's bi-monthly programmes. Kyoto and Osaka did not have such a system. The large Kyoto–Osaka publishing firm Hachimonjiya produced actor critiques (yakusha hyōbanki) comparing performances in the three cities at least once a year,[7] as well as other books on actors and the theatre. Large numbers of Jōruri puppet-play texts and books on Kabuki were also issued regularly by other publishers, but a tradition of single-sheet colour actor prints did not start in Kyoto or Osaka until the 1790s, with the work of the artist Ryūkōsai Jokei (worked 1777–1809).

Performance and creativity

Theatre has been central to Japanese social and cultural life since at least the fifteenth century. Audiences have never been just passive observers, however. It was common from early on for fans to participate as amateur performers, and thereby to contribute to cultural life. As a consequence Japan has a long tradition, beginning in the early 1600s, of publishing playbooks. Texts of both the Noh and Jōruri (Bunraku) theatres were regularly published under the names of famous troupes or individuals. These usually contained the complete musical notation used by the professionals, and were 'official' authentic performance texts (shōhon, maruhon), though normally without illustration. From around 1700 illustrated play summaries were also published. Thousands of original shōhon plays were published in this way and many hundreds remained in print over the centuries. The primary audience for these books were amateur performers, and the market extended to cover the whole country, finally peaking in the 1920s. One rarely just 'read' a play; it was common to learn to chant Noh or Gidayū (Bunraku chanting) as a hobby and then to perform in recitals regularly over a lifetime.

Kabuki, too, encouraged participation. It was a common hobby to perform Kabuki-style dance (buyō), or to learn to imitate the declamatory styles of favourite actors (kowa-iro). Professional actors often taught dance; even today some actors are also the heads of dance schools. Kabuki differed fundamentally from Noh and Bunraku, however, in two important respects. First, Kabuki troupes have never published complete 'official' playbooks. And second, unlike Noh and Bunraku, Kabuki professionals have never taught acting to amateurs.

Kabuki plays were written afresh for each programme. This was the case even when the play was famous and an established part of the repertoire. Staff playwrights always rewrote a story to suit the particular cast of the moment, with the straightforward aim of creating a vehicle for the star actors to shine in. Therefore even though there are large numbers of extant manuscripts of Kabuki plays it will never be possible to find the definitive edition. Kabuki remained essentially an oral tradition without fixed texts for centuries. As a consequence, the only true 'text' is a particular performance by the actors, which by definition dissipates with the closing of the curtain. The passionate desire to anticipate or to remember these moments of magic was a tremendous catalyst for artistic production. The range of publications around Kabuki was (and is) vast. The following are some of the main genres, most of which are represented in this catalogue:

- *yakusha hyōbanki* (actor critiques, cat. 192)
- *e-iri kyōgen-bon* (illustrated plot summaries with considerable text)
- *e-zukushi kyōgen-bon* (illustrated plot summaries with minimal text)
- *yakusha ehon* (illustrated books about actors, many examples included)
- *gekisho* (illustrated books about the theatre, cats 70, 71 and 72)

- *yakusha-e* (single-sheet actor prints)
- *yakusha nendaiki* (accounts of individual actors' careers, cats 64–7)
- *kaomise banzuke* (opening-of-the-season playbills, with a list of actors contracted for the coming year, cats 168 and 169)
- *yakuwari banzuke* (playbills listing actors in their various roles in the programme)
- *ehon* (or *ezukushi*) *banzuke* (illustrated pamphlets of all the scenes of the play with the actors and roles listed, cat. 61)
- *surimono* (single-sheet, privately commissioned prints combining poetry and images, often produced as memorials)
- *e-iri nehon* (illustrated playbooks, a genre unique to Osaka, cats 83, 96, 140–4 and 193)
- *mitate banzuke* (parody flybills, ephemeral, comic printed sheets that impersonate functional genres, cats 55–60, 170–1).[7]

Kabuki may not have been popular with the government, but it continuously generated mountains of publications for its adoring fans (fig. 4).

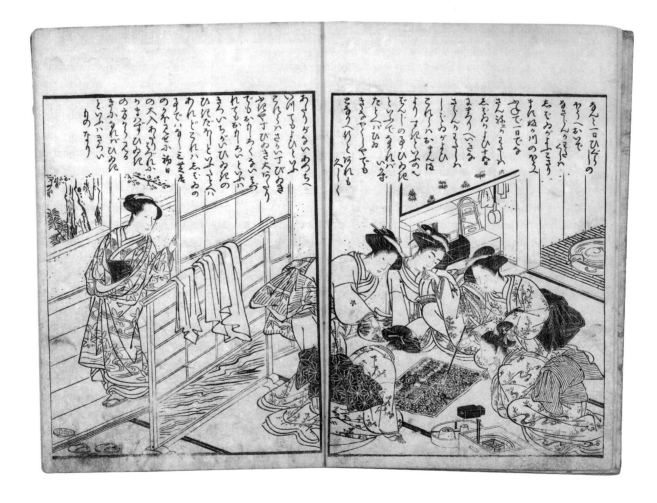

4 *Yakusha natsu no Fuji* (*Actors Without Makeup, Like Mt Fuji in Summer*), 1780, by Katsukawa Shunshō. Young women looking at a *kaomise* playbill point out their favourite actors (see cat. 11). (The British Museum)

of blind-printing/embossing (*karazuri*), and printing with mica (*kira*), metallic pigments (primarily tin and brass) and even mother-of-pearl.

Kabuki fan clubs and other obsessions

Matsudaira Susumu, pre-eminent scholar of Osaka actor prints, explored the fascinating world of Osaka's Kabuki fan clubs (*hiiki-renchū* or *hiiki-renjū*; see also Kaguraoka essay).[11] Their members, mostly businessmen, were known for their passionate participation and for their group rituals on special occasions, such as parading on stage to welcome actors at the opening-of-the-season (*kaomise*) performances held in the eleventh or twelfth month of each year (fig. 6). Cat. 150, for example, is a depiction of actors being welcomed for the new season. Another aspect of their activities very pertinent here was the production by literati and amateur members of various types of theatre-related materials, such as actor critiques (*yakusha hyōbanki*), theatre books and single-sheet actor prints. Many of these artist-enthusiasts and theatre patrons were also prolific

haiku or *kyōka* poets, sometimes leaders of poetry circles, such as Yoshikuni with his Jukōdō haiku group or members of the Maruha *kyōka* group.

The Osaka Kabuki playwright and writer Nishizawa Ippōken (1801–52) commented in his *Denki sakusho* (*Biographies and Happenings*, 1851) on patron–amateurs of the late eighteenth and early nineteenth centuries:

In Kyoto and Osaka, book and single-sheet print publishing relating to the theatre is different from Edo, where there is a considerable group of professional artists and writers. In Osaka wealthy businessmen pursue various activities such as frequenting Kabuki and the pleasure quarters, and enjoy being patrons of actors, sumo wrestlers and courtesans. They are called *suijin* [masters of the elegant pursuit of aesthetic pleasure] and are somewhat akin to the *daitsū* [grand connoisseurs] of Edo. They contribute poems and writings in various fields but are known to be proud of their amateur status and do not usually reveal their individual names. Such theatrical books are simply issued under the publisher's name Hachimonjiya.[12]

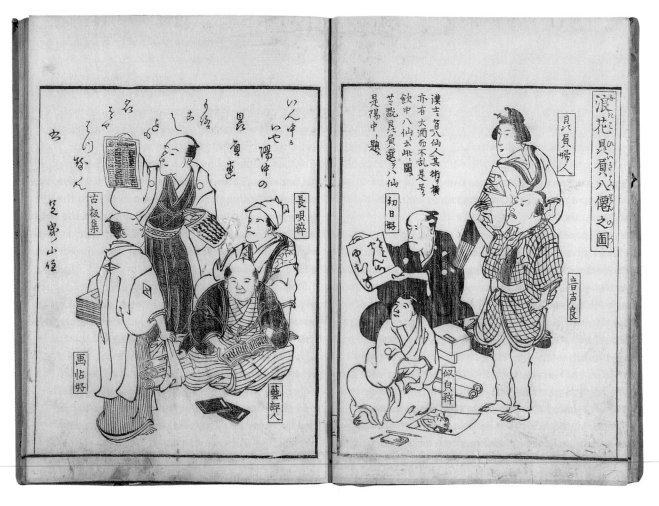

6 (*Shikan-miyage*) *Kokkei dōchū Kumosuke-banashi* (*Shikan Souvenir: Kumosuke's Comic Road-Tales*), 1820, by Akatsuki Kanenari. Woodblock book, 3 vols, 22.5 x 15.8 cm (covers). A group image of various types of fans of Osaka Kabuki (from right to left): 'Female fan', 'Good at imitations', 'Likes opening performances', 'Amateur artist of actor portraits', 'Amateur chanter', 'Critic', 'Collector of old prints' and, finally, 'Likes making scrapbooks'. (Kansai University Library, Osaka, 22.913.171/172)

He describes the production of Osaka actor critique books in some detail:

> Between about 1790 and 1820, in order to produce actor critiques, the amateur *suijin* such as Teiga, Doran, Rokitsu and Nitoan would gather in a restaurant after seeing the play and write the critique together. In those days there were such people with wide experience and knowledge. Many fellows came from various fan clubs (Ōzasa, Ōte, Fuji-ishi, Sakura, Zakoba and Kōbai), and as a group they were able to determine rankings and write the critiques.[13]

The dedication and passion of Kabuki fans is renowned, but in Kyoto and Osaka this was elevated to a high art. *Temae miso* (*Singing my Praises*, 1873), the diary of the Edo actor Nakamura Nakazō III (1809–86), describes his experiences in Kyoto and Osaka. In 1830 the young Nakazō III performed in Kyoto at the opening-of-the-season (*kaomise*) production in the eleventh month:

> Ōzasa or Sasaki fan-club members assembled in groups every day, each with an extravagant costume, and a scarf covering their head and part of their face. With an air of 'look at us' they would saunter boldly down the walkway [*hanamichi*] from the front of the stage to the seats in the centre. Then when all were assembled they would send word to the dressing room that everything was ready. And with this announcement the curtain would open.[14]

It is clear from this extract that the fans were part of the show (cats 276–8).

Actors as artists and poets

Many actors participated in the poetry and other performing art (*yūgei*) networks, and some gained fame as poets and artists. Literati patrons of Kabuki without doubt encouraged the development of actors as sophisticated artists and poets. The stars that are featured in this volume were all tremendously active within the broader cultural life around them. Brief biographies of some of the main players follow below.

Kabuki actors used several names during their careers. Their principal acting name was ceremoniously changed at key points in a progressing career, generally to inherit a more illustrious, established name; new names were occasionally created. Each man also had a *yago*, a family or acting-clan sobriquet ending in *-ya*. Even today this is often called out by fans during performances. In addition, actors had at least one poetry pen name (*haimyō*) and sometimes also an art name (*gō*).

Nakamura TOMIJŪRŌ I (1719–86) was well known also as a painter, using his pen name KEISHI; indeed, the book that chronicles his career is entitled *Keishi gafu* (*Keishi's Painting Album*, 1786), which has three volumes containing twenty-seven illustrations by Keishi, and seventy-seven poems by Keishi and other actors from the three main cities. Another art name was Kinreisha, and his clan sobriquet (*yago*) was Tennōjiya. Keishi, one of the most famous female role specialists (*onnagata*) in Kabuki history, was the fourth son of the legendary Kyoto *onnagata* Yoshizawa Ayame I (1637–1729), and he regularly performed in Kyoto, Osaka and Edo over a fifty-year career. He began his career as a youth prostitute (*iroko*) and first performed on the stage at sixteen. Elegant and good-looking, he was a master of all types of female role, in both dramatic and dance pieces. His particular genius was for playing strong samurai women, and late in life Keishi even performed some male lead roles (*tachiyaku*). At the end of his career he was ranked as the top *onnagata* in the country. He is also known to have been talented at music, tea ceremony and haiku poetry. Cats 16 and 17 are examples of pictures by him.

Arashi HINASUKE I (1741–96) was the star of his generation, recognized as such also in Edo even though he performed there only in the eleventh month, 1780. He also used the acting family name Kanō and had at least two pen names, MINSHI and Koshichi. He succeeded to the name Koroku III in the eleventh month, 1793, and was known familiarly as 'Koroku-tama' ('jewel of the Koroku line'). His clan sobriquet (*yago*) was Yoshidaya. Hinasuke's career began in 1751, and he was a female role specialist (*onnagata*) until 1775, after which he switched to male leads (*tachiyaku*). Unusually able at a wide range of roles, he was also outstanding in portraying evil courtiers. His equal success in both male and female roles is rare in Kabuki. In 1794 he was ranked as the top actor in all of Japan. Physically, Hinasuke was quite large and stocky. Nonetheless, he was noted for his Kabuki dance and as a dance teacher. He was influential in the development of both Arashi Kichisaburō II (Rikan) and Nakamura Utaemon III (Shikan).

Arashi SANGORŌ II (1732–1803) was known for his portrayal of aristocratic male roles. He was from Kyoto and was active in poetry circles using the pen name RAISHI. His clan sobriquet (*yago*) was Kyōya. He retired in 1797 and took the Buddhist

[Ehon] Butai ōgi is sensually beautiful [jōen], it does not have enough pure resonance [seiin]. As for [Ehon] Mizu ya sora, although it is fine – plain and aloof – it is also too light and frivolous. The current book appeared later, and is rich, beautiful, elegant and plain. It has combined what is appropriate in every aspect, and can be called theatre drawings in the proper style. He has not deigned to apply colour, but shows off the marvels of his methods of plain outlining. This is the brushwork of a cultivated gentleman [bunshi] roaming in the realm of art, and there are few in this world who can equal him. Even if we were to bring Zhao Songxue [Zhao Mengfu, 1254–1322] back to life today, or rely on Li Boshi [Li Gonglin, 1049–1106] of past times, I am afraid they would not be able to surpass this. It is regrettable that Suifutei, with his marvellous skill, gave up on [the better things in life] and placed himself in this situation, and, with all his fine qualities, grew old in the world of the theatre. Could it be because he could not help it? I cannot be free of regrets. Here, because I have the same excessive fondness, I simply write down what I feel. Readers should not laugh at my pedantry.

Alert Immortal from the Realm of Drama (Giiki Kassen)[19]

9 Portrait of Asao Tamejūrō I from *Suifutei gigafu* (*Album of Actor Caricatures by Suifutei*), 1782 (see cat. 14). (The British Museum)

Suifutei gigafu is a mystery book by an anonymous artist, privately printed to an exquisite standard and with anonymous prefaces and postscripts (fig. 9). This work fits perfectly with Nishizawa Ippōken's ideal of the literati (suijin), one who is passionate about the subject, devotes tremendous energy, but then is modest about his achievement, maintaining his anonymous status.

The preface to Yakusha mono iwai, published two years later, again takes up the theme of amateurs, continuing from the two previous books. The allusion to the Confucian Analects reappears: 'In painting, one begins with the white [shiro] background and after that applies the colour. In all the arts, the heart of the amateur [shirōto] comes first: being an amateur, he takes his time to observe and to express the image better.' Ryūkōsai is consciously placed within a tradition of independent artistic expression, free from commercial demands.

The painters Ryūkōsai and Nichōsai were both also part of a wide network of haiku and kyōka poetry circles. They jointly contributed actor portrait paintings to Rien shoga (1788, cat. 19 and fig. 10), an album that includes, in addition, many poems contibuted by the actors portrayed. Ryūkōsai, like others around him, presented the actors as men of letters. It is surely significant that in Yakusha mono iwai none of the actor portraits actually includes the acting name. The primary name listed is their pen name (haimyō), accompanied by their actor-clan sobriquet (yago), and each actor is awarded a haiku verse in celebration of his performance. The connections between artists, poetry and Kabuki had already become evident in the first colour-printed actor book Ehon butai ōgi (Illustrated Book: Actor Fans; cat. 9), published in Edo in 1770. At the end of this book are listed the actors' pen names, followed by a series of haiku by famous poets such as Bashō; also haiku by Katsukawa Shunshō and Ippitsusai Bunchō, the two Edo artists of the work. These literary-artistic trends escalated from the 1790s onwards, with the production of theatre-related colour-printed books, prints and surimono in ever-increasing numbers.

Poetry salons and cultural networks

One of the aims of this catalogue is to show how Kabuki actors circulated among a broad cross-section of the population, via extensive cultural networks formed for the composition of haiku and kyōka poetry. Surimono – single-sheet, privately commissioned prints with text, poetry and (often) an image – are our primary record of these poetry gatherings.

Japanese poetry is distinctive for its brevity, with the two main genres waka (traditional 'court' poetry; also including the lighter, sometimes comic-parodic version, kyōka) and haiku

10 Nakamura
Tomijūrō I by
Ryūkōsai in the
album *Rien shoga*,
1788 (see cat. 19).
(Osaka Museum
of History)

(including the comic version, *senryū*), respectively just thirty-one and seventeen syllables in length. Another characteristic is the poetry's interactive, social function. Most poems were composed and presented originally either for a public context – a competition (*uta-awase*), a recitation on a topic at a banquet (*dai'ei*) – or, more privately, to accompany a letter. The brevity of the form must also have encouraged the flourishing of linked verse (*renga*), in which each participant took up the theme of the previous verse, according to set rules. This became an essential method of haiku composition for Bashō, Saikaku and later poets. It is clear that a romantic notion of the lonely poet interacting with his muse to compose verse was not at all the ideal for Japanese poetry. Rather poetry was from its origins expressly democratic, in the sense that everyone had the potential to cast a verse inspired by their feelings. Ogata Tsutomu and Haruo Shirane have shown how important a communal context was for the production of haiku poetry in the seventeenth and eighteenth centuries.[20]

Performance is the key stage in the composition process, leading from the individual's heart and mind to the printed page. Poetry was usually composed and presented orally within a group. This performance was, then, the raw material from which an editor created a text for printing in a book or on a *surimono* print.

Surimono literally means 'printed thing', but it has come to refer to a single-sheet print that includes an image and poems.

The first examples date from the early eighteenth century; those printed in full colour using the woodblock technique date from around 1773.[21] Their popularity continued well into the early twentieth century. *Surimono* have been popular with Western collectors since the late nineteenth century, and there are significant numbers in museums around the world. U.S. scholar Roger Keyes and others have provided much insight into these magnificent artworks, often printed as they are to an exquisite standard with embossing and metallic printing. More recently in Japan *surimono* have come to be the focus of haiku and *kyōka* poetry research.[22]

As we learn more about *surimono* we are beginning to sense how integrated cultural networks were around the country. These networks were indispensable for Kabuki actors, offering them contact with literati and wealthy patrons. A simple, text-only *surimono* that records a gathering in the spring of 1787 well illustrates the function of poetry circles for social interaction.[23] The host was a certain Tanaka Fushū (d. 1808) from Takasago (modern Hyōgo Prefecture), who published a collection of poems entitled *Kurimotoshū* in 1790. He first offers an auspicious greeting, welcoming the cherry blossoms. The poems of three actors then follow in unbroken sequence, by Kitō (Sawamura Kunitarō I, 1739–1818), Raishi (Arashi Sangorō II, 1732–1803) and Fujaku (Onoe Shinshichi I, 1745–1809), each in the prime of his career. Next come verses by six other well-known literati figures from various parts of the country: Hisamura Gyōtai (1741–92) from Nagoya; Nishimura Teiga (1744–1826) from Kyoto; Miya Shigyō from Kyoto; Matsumura Gekkei (better known by his art name Go Shun, 1752–1811), who lived in both Kyoto and Ikeda; Takakuwa Rankō (1726–98) from Kanazawa, who also lived in Kyoto; finally Takai Kitō (1741–89) from Kyoto, who was a close collaborator of the poet–artist Yosa Buson. This is a highly illustrious group of artists and poets, alongside the Kabuki actors. When actors are represented on *surimono* it is often as a distinct group, separate from the other poets.

Teiga, his friend the Kyoto aristocrat Tomi Doran, and Nitoan (Kabutsu, d. 1800) are all known to have had an interest in Kabuki, and each is represented several times in this catalogue. The earliest *surimono* here dates from 1779 (cat. 104): it was used as a parting gift by Arashi Kichisaburō I (1737–80) when he left Osaka to perform in Kyoto, and Nitoan was the patron.

Haiku (*haikai*) and painting have long been seen as sister arts, and haiku book and *surimono* publications were important stimulants to the development of full-colour woodblock printing, decades before the 1760s when ukiyo-e artists such as Suzuki Harunobu began to design commercial single-sheet colour prints (*nishiki-e*) in quantity. Single-printed sheets with haiku for the New Year (*saitanchō*) survive in considerable numbers from the early eighteenth century onwards. The earliest extant *surimono* (i.e., poems combined with a picture), printed in the two colours of blue and yellow, was issued in Edo in 1717 (Aichi Kyōiku University Collection).[24] Kira Sueo has recently outlined the interconnected development of haiku and colour printing.[25] He points out that several haiku books published between 1725 and 1737 have colour-printed covers. Pre-War lists note as many as thirteen titles, but only three are known to survive today, including *Fuyu no chiri* of 1733 which has four printed colours.

Haiku has long been important to Kabuki in Edo, where the special focus of patronage since the end of the

even to the point of distortion. Female specialists (*onnagata*), in particular, are not usually portrayed as if they are 'real', or even 'ideal' woman; rather, quite clearly as male actors performing female roles. Writings by artists on the techniques of drawing actor prints did not appear in print until Edo artist Utagawa Toyokuni I's book *Yakusha nigao haya-geiko* (*Quick Lessons in Actor Likenesses*, 1817; fig. 30 below). It has been recorded, however, that Ryūkōsai did compile an unpublished sketchbook on the art of designing actor prints. Given the title *Ryūkōsai ikō* (*Testament Manuscript by*

11 This rare printed sheet, dated to the fourth month, 1854, by the Osaka artist Seishū (Sasaki Dōzen, 1802–56), is a lineage of Osaka artists with short biographies. It is the only extant source that specifically states that Ryūkōsai was a pupil of Shitomi Kangetsu (1747–97). The text is transcribed in Haruyama, 1931. Woodblock, 17.9 x 49.0 cm. Ex-coll. Okada Isajirō. (Private Collection, UK)

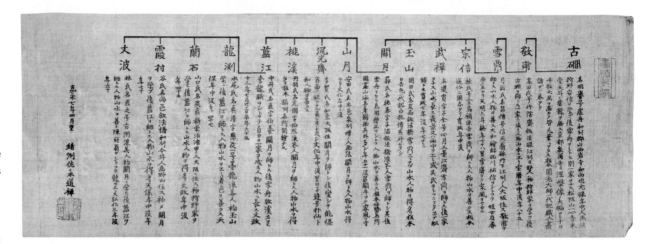

seventeenth century has been the lineage of Ichikawa Danjūrō actors. This patronage produced one of the most important early colour-printed books *Chichi no on* (*To My Father*), a twenty-seventh memorial for Danjūrō I (1660–1704) published in 1730 and edited by his son Danjūrō II (1688–1758).[26] The book has 296 signed verses by poet-fans from Edo, Kyoto and Osaka, which celebrate the careers of Danjūrō I and some seventy other actors who had died between 1704 and 1730. There are several images in black and white by the artist Hanabusa Ippō, and four pages of colour images by the poet and lacquer artist Ogawa Haritsu (Ritsuō, 1663–1747). These were produced using a mixture of printing and hand-painting.[27]

Sono kiku (*That Chrysanthemum*) of 1749 is another important early Edo haiku book with colour printing. It is a memorial to Segawa Kikunojō I (1693–1749), the famous female role specialist (*onnagata*), who had performed in Osaka until he moved to Edo in 1729.[28] His name incorporates the character for 'chrysanthemum' (*kiku*).

Ryūkōsai: visualizing the actor's body

It has been common to describe Osaka actor prints as more 'realistic' than those of Edo because the faces are not idealized and show the physical imperfections of the actors

Ryūkōsai), the original sketchbook was once in the Okada Isajirō collection; unfortunately its present whereabouts are unknown. In about 1930 Haruyama Takematsu surveyed the Okada collection and published an article that quotes an intriguing passage from this sketchbook in the section which Ryūkōsai called 'Drawing preparatory sketches for [actor] likeness portraits' (*kaonise shitagaki no koto*).[29] The comments within parentheses paraphrase those of Haruyama (fig. 12):

> In designing realistic portraits [*kaonise*] the artist should depend on his heart when making the initial sketch [*sōkō*]. As a first principle, if you let your heart guide your first design [*sōan*], then when you prepare the final work, the face [*menbō*] will be well portrayed. Although eyebrows tend to look similar, these will differ depending on each role. The art of depicting faces, too, therefore, should differ depending on the particular performance [*gei*].
> (HARUYAMA: Ryūkōsai gives examples of sketches of the eyes, nose, mouth and facial outline of particular actors in specific roles. He also shows some drawings of actors in full costume.)

The focus on the heart echoes Ki no Tsurayuki's famous preface about the composition of poetry for the *Kokinshū* imperial anthology, compiled in 905; also the literati ideal

12 Sketches of actors' faces by Ryūkōsai. (Haruyama Takematsu, 'Ryūkōsai to Shōkōsai: Naniwa nishiki-e no kenkyū' in *Tōyō bijutsu*, 12 July 1931).

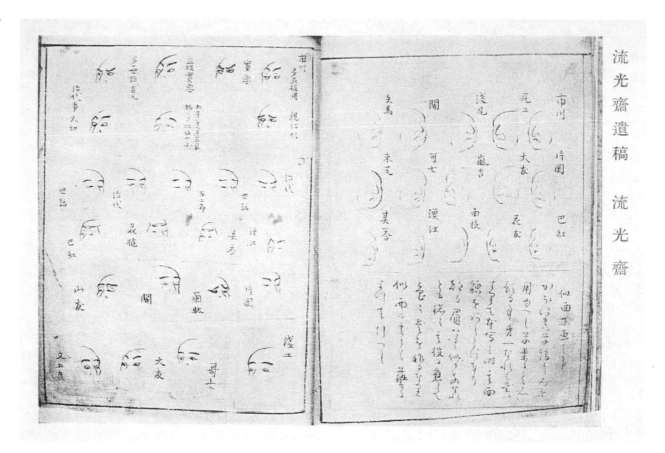

流光齋遺稿

流光齋

of painting from the heart (see p. 23 above). Ryūkōsai's illustration of various facial parts distinguishes between character roles and the faces of individual actors. He continues (see fig. 28 below):

> In general, when one draws a human figure, it is best to imagine them as being naked, then to draw the five extremities of the body at one time, and finally to clothe them with costumes fitting for the role. Especially in the art of creating actor likeness portraits [*yakusha no kaonise*], it is most important to capture the form [*katachi*], and so I will show some examples.

Ryūkōsai includes a sketch of a naked woman standing in a bath, which Haruyama describes as extremely 'modern' (*kindaiteki*).

> When considering drawing an actor in the role of Lord Sugawara [Kanshōjō], it is best first to draw the naked figure and then put on the costume. You must capture his feelings on the face when he looks back and says, 'This is my farewell to this world'.

Ryūkōsai then sketches examples of bodies for different roles. Haruyama remarks jokingly that no one will feel tragedy looking at a naked Sugawara. He also points out that the sketch of Yuranosuke at the ritual suicide (*seppuku*) scene

(from the drama *Chūshingura*) shows him, candidly, with a scar on his back from moxa treatment. There was a raw, down-to-earth dimension to Ryūkōsai's sketches, it seems.

Clearly Ryūkōsai attempted to capture the essence of both the physical body of the actor and the persona of the character portrayed. And it seems that it was this approach that led him to depict female specialists (*onnagata*) not as plausible women but quite clearly as male actors in female roles. This contrasts quite markedly with the Edo tradition as represented by the Katsukawa School, in which the *onnagata* were invariably drawn in the style of 'pictures of beautiful women' (*bijinga*) – idealized and without much expression. The only exception among Edo artists was Sharaku (worked 1794–5), whose portraits of female specialists would seem to have been influenced in some way by Ryūkōsai's example. See fig. 29 below for earlier examples of Maruyama Ōkyo's (1733–95) conception of imagining the naked body as part of the process of painting. Ryūkōsai, who trained as a painter under the Kyoto painter Shitomi Kangetsu (fig. 11), may have been influenced by Ōkyo.[30]

Shōkōsai: passion for the theatre

Ryūkōsai's principal pupil Shōkōsai, in contrast to his teacher, does not appear to have received training in any formal

13 Portrait by
Hokushū (Shunkō)
of Ōtani Tomoemon
II as Inokuma in the
play *Keisei kuruwa
Genji* at the Naka
Theatre; first month,
1802. *Hosoban*,
colour woodblock,
31.2 x 15.0 cm.
(Private Collection,
Japan)

produced paintings (cat. 86) and single-sheet colour actor
prints from about 1795. His early actor portraits follow the
likenesses established by his mentor, and it was only with the
next generation of actors of the early 1800s, such as Arashi
Kichisaburō II (Rikan) and Nakamura Utaemon III (Shikan),
that he produced original portraits. These then in turn
became the models for Hokushū, Ashiyuki and Yoshikuni who
followed in the 1810s. Shōkōsai, like Ryūkōsai, put much of
his effort into book illustration. His *Ehon futaba aoi* of 1798
(cat. 74) is the first full-colour actor book published in
Kyoto–Osaka. Eight illustrated playbooks (*e-iri nehon*) by him
published between 1801 and 1809 established a distinctive
Osaka genre that would last for the next sixty years, yielding
more than eighty titles in total.

Shōkōsai, in turn, drew Hokushū into the world of actor
portraiture. Recently an early portrait has appeared of Ōtani
Tomoemon II, signed Shunkō (Hokushū's art name until
about 1817), which can be dated to the first month, 1802.
This discovery extends back Hokushū's known period of
activity by about seven years. Shōkōsai added a *kyōka* poem
to the portrait by his pupil (virtually invisible in reproduction)
that praises the actor Tomoemon (fig. 13):

> *Ikanareba / katakiyaku sae / kono koro wa /*
> *[kimi] ga kokoro no / hayagawari shite*
> Somehow
> Even in villain roles
> These days
> Your heart
> Does quick-changes

This would also appear to be the earliest surviving example
of a verse on a single-sheet Osaka print. It is also a very early
example of a half-length Osaka actor portrait on a sheet print.

Celebrity rivals: Rikan versus Shikan

Shōkōsai established the first definitive images of the two
stars of Osaka Kabuki culture who dominated the stage for
the first two decades of the nineteenth century: Arashi
Kichisaburō I (Rikan, cat. 92) and Nakamura Utaemon III
(Shikan, cat. 93). Both actors were child prodigies but
otherwise seem to have had very different personalities.
Rikan, nine years senior, became leader of one of the two
top troupes in Kyoto–Osaka in 1805 and after this refused
to perform together with Shikan. Not long after, in 1808,
Shikan's frustration at being unable to achieve the top acting
position in Osaka spurred him to take up an offer to head the
Nakamura Theatre in Edo. He performed to great acclaim and
returned to Osaka triumphantly at the end of 1812.

Shikan was a master at stirring up controversy and during
his first trip to Edo is recorded as having got into a fist fight

painting school. It can be surmised that Shōkōsai was active in
haiku and *kyōka* poetry circles and involved with Kabuki from
at least from the late 1780s, when he was a member of the
Sasase Kabuki fan club. A haiku poem by him is included on a
surimono dated 1790 that marks the twenty-fifth memorial
for a Sasase club leader (cat. 51). This implies that he had
already been an active club member for some time.

Shōkōsai was clearly extremely knowledgeable about
both Kabuki and Bunraku (Jōruri) puppet theatre. His two
guidebooks to Kabuki and Jōruri, *Shibai gakuya zue* (1800,
cat. 70) and the sequel *Gakuya zue shūi* (1802, cat. 71),
are mines of information on the customs of theatre life,
and were kept in print until the early twentieth century.

Shōkōsai became a pupil of Ryūkōsai in the 1790s and

with a fan of Bandō Mitsugorō III, his great Edo rival. One of Shikan's own fans later retaliated against Mitsugorō.[31] Shikan seems to have been greatly disliked by Rikan. A crisis occurred in 1819 after Shikan's return from the last of his three Edo tours, when Rikan presented a formal suit against Shikan and his backer Fushimiya Zenbei (see also cat. 8), claiming that he was ruining Kabuki by playing all types of roles and thereby destroying the specialized role system (*yakugara*) upon which the acting profession was based, and by his fierce competitive nature and the whipping up of his fans to extreme frenzy.[32] Shikan responded by defending his activities, and ultimately the matter seems to have been dropped. But the survival of letters recording the dispute between the two most famous Osaka actors of the day demonstrates the reality of their deep rivalry.

On the other hand, it is clear from an interview with Utaemon III (Shikan) published in 1827 – admittedly some six years after Rikan's death – that Shikan highly respected his rival as a superb actor, the best of his generation.[33] A patron asked Shikan to compare the stage art of Ichikawa Danzō IV and Arashi Hinasuke I (Koroku). Shikan answered that Danzō was tremendously detailed in his portrayal of characters and pleased audiences immensely, but that Hinasuke achieved magnificent effects 'by keeping artifice [*gei*] to a minimum'. Shikan then added that while many could imitate Danzō's style, only Rikan was sufficiently able to follow in Hinasuke's footsteps.[34] This was high praise indeed since Hinasuke was acknowledged as one of the greatest lead role actors of all time.

The core of this catalogue focuses on the rivalry between the two Osaka stars, Rikan and Shikan, and on the activities of the hundreds of their fans and patrons who produced such beautiful tributes – paintings, albums, books, *surimono* and actor prints – all in support of these great heroes of the Kabuki stage.

1 This is Hino Tatsuo's term to describe the art and poetry salons in eighteenth-century Japan; see Hino 1977.
2 Lefebvre 1991.
3 Gunji Masakatsu has argued that actors were conscious of this outsider status and that it was reinforced by periodic government edicts. Actors were not administered by the 'outcast leader' (*hinin-gashira*) but directly by the government (Gunji 1976, pp. 150–68).
4 See Carpenter 2002, pp. 42–9.
5 See Gerstle 1989, pp. 33–50, for more information on Edo *aragoto* style.
6 For an overview of early ukiyo-e see the recent exhibition catalogue Royal Academy 2001.
7 Surviving actor critiques of the late seventeenth and early eighteenth centuries have been collated into modern editions; see *Kabuki hyōbanki shūsei* (first series), 1972–7 and *Kabuki hyōbanki shūsei, daini-ki* (second series), 1987–95.
8 Akama Ryō has produced a thorough survey and analysis of these different genres in Akama 2003.
9 Moriya 1987; Gerstle 1995, pp. 37–57.
10 Morris 1989 quotes several letters of Buson that show his attempts to maintain an anti-commercial stance even when selling paintings (pp. 87–105).
11 Matsudaira 1984 (2002); idem. 1999, pp. 10–36; idem. 1998(a), pp. 173–94. We also have the recent work of Kaguraoka 1998, pp. 121–44, and idem. 2002.
12 Quoted in Matsudaira 1999, p. 21; see also Nishizawa 1906, p. 94.
13 Matsudaira 1999, pp. 21–2; Nishizawa 1906, pp. 94–5.
14 Matsudaira 1999, pp. 24–6; Nakamura 1969, pp. 135–6.
15 Hanyū 2003, pp. 1–11.

16 Kaguraoka quotes from this critique in Kaguraoka 2004, p. 170.
17 *Osaka dachin uma*, 1783 (National Diet Library, Tokyo). This manuscript also notes that Nichōsai had been a famous amateur Jōruri (Bunraku) chanter before he suddenly quit to become an artist, developing his own idiosyncratic style.
18 Nishizawa Ippōken in *Denki Sakusho* uses the term *suijin* to describe the Kyoto–Osaka literati who participated in the arts, without interest in fame or fortune, often keeping their names anonymous. Matsudaira (1999) promoted this *suijin* concept as an essential aspect of Osaka Kabuki culture (pp. 21, 82). Haruko Iwasaki (1984) has written about the world of literati in Edo.
19 I am grateful to Dr Andrew Lo for helping me with the translation from the Chinese.
20 Ogata 1973; Shirane 1998.
21 A print by Yosa Buson which includes a poem each by Takai Kitō (1741–89) and Jūshūtei Koshū can be dated to 1773 and is thought to be one of the earliest full-colour *surimono*; see Itsuō Bijutsukan 2003, no. 91.
22 This research has been presented in several important new publications, including an exhibition catalogue and the special issue of a journal of literary history. These have given a broad overview of the history of *surimono*, with contributions from a variety of specialists. They also include an extensive bibliography of Japanese and Western sources. Chiba-shi Bijutsukan 1999 is the catalogue of an exhibition at the Chiba City Museum of Art, organized by Asano Shūgō; see also the special issue 'Tashoku-zuri no rekishi to haikai ichimai-zuri', *Edo bungaku* 25, 2002, ed. Kira Sueo.
23 This print is no. 526 in a collection of more than 800 *surimono* that was originally compiled

by the poet Narizawa Untai, who lived in Ueda (modern Nagano Prefecture). The collection is published in Gotō 1992.
24 Okamoto 2002, pp. 60–79.
25 Kira 2002, pp. 29–59.
26 Reprinted in Nihon Koten Bungakukai 1986. This edition has essays by Kira Sueo and Suzuki Jūzō on the development of colour printing and *haikai*.
27 Kira 2002, pp. 52–4.
28 *Sono kiku* was reprinted in facsimile edition by Kisho Fukuseikai, 1933.
29 Haruyama 1931, p. 18. It is to be hoped that the staging of this exhibition will serve to draw out the whereabouts of this important sketchbook.
30 Haruyama 1931, p. 4.
31 See *Kabuki nenpyō*, vol. 5, pp. 515–16.
32 See the transcription of the exchange of petition letters in 'Setsuyō kikan', vol. 45, pp. 557–64 (Funakoshi 1926–30, vol. 5).
33 Mori 1980, pp. 89–93, is the record of a conversation between Fujii Takanao, a Shinto priest from Bichū, and Nakamura Utaemon III. A third person, Hashimoto Shingo, recorded the conversation.
34 Ibid., p. 89.

OSAKA KABUKI FAN CLUBS AND THEIR OBSESSIONS

YŌKO KAGURAOKA

The fan clubs set up by Kabuki enthusiasts in Osaka were known as *hiiki renjū*. The earliest club we know of, Ō-renjū, was formed in 1695, but the most important groups were formed during the eighteenth century: Sasase (1720; see cat. 50), Ōte (1735), Fuji-ishi (1770), and Sakura (1775). From then on, the clubs played an important role in supporting the prosperity of the Osaka theatre district. Club members were generally the wealthier Kabuki fans who would form their own cliques to support the theatres, and membership was of itself a mark of status in the city. *Naniwa tamazukushi* (*All the Jewels of Osaka*, 1816), a single printed sheet that was a 'who's who' of the day, lists members of Sasase and Ōte clubs alongside lumber merchants, doctors and actors.

Fan clubs interacted with the theatre world in many ways. Members were of course regular theatregoers, and with their enthusiasm for presenting decorative curtains, banners and lanterns to the theatres, they contributed greatly to the gaudy, festive atmosphere of the theatre neighbourhoods. For example, it was customary in this period for the stage curtains (*hikimaku*) and decorations for the box seat railings to be presented by Sasase club, the lanterns above the stage (*mizuhiki chōchin*) by Ōte, and the red curtains adorning the theatres' external tower (*yagura*), the curtain (*kirimaku*) at the end of the stage-right acting area (*hashigakari*), and large hanging lanterns, and so on by the Zakoba. Clubs would also participate in an annual event known as the 'coming-together to join the troupe' (*zatsuki hiki-awase*; cat. 150). This would take place on stage during the special opening-of-the-season (*kaomise*) performances in the eleventh month, designed to introduce the newly engaged troupe to the audience. With the actors lined up in a row, the fan clubs would dress in matching headgear and costumes, striking together wooden clappers (*hyōshigi*), and delivering praise and gifts to each of the actors in turn. This was known as *te-uchi* ('hand-clapping'), and participation was limited to the four biggest clubs (also known as the *te-uchi renjū*). The hand-clapping clubs also existed in Edo, but there was no custom of them participating in the 'coming-together to join the troupe' (cats 276–8).

Te-uchi gradually became more and more complicated, and by the beginning of the nineteenth century elaborate backdrops started to be used on stage, and musical accompaniment on *koto* and *shamisen* added to the wooden clappers. What began as a homage to the actors by their fans grew into a spectacular performance, talked about in its own right. *Hiiki no hanamichi* (*Fan's Walkway*, 1815) mentions Kyūro and Juraku of Ōte, and Rojū of Sasase (cat. 276) as being particularly skilled at clapping, and even includes a detailed critique of Kyūro and Juraku's performance.

As we have seen, there was a close relationship between fan clubs and theatres, but clubs were equally enthusiastic in their support of individual actors. A good example of this relationship can be seen in the events surrounding Nakamura Utaemon III (Shikan)'s return to Osaka from Edo in 1815. Utaemon arrived back on the fifth day of the eleventh month, and on the sixth visited Dōjima, Zakoba, Sasase and Ōte clubs to pay his respects. On the seventh he travelled ceremoniously by boat to the theatre (*fune norikomi*; cat. 70) in the Osaka version of a tickertape parade, and it is said that Dotonbori canal was filled from bank to bank with his fans' boats. The fans in each boat are even named in the book *Yakusha nazokake-ron* (*Actors' Riddles*, 1817; cat. 192), and the whole event is yet another

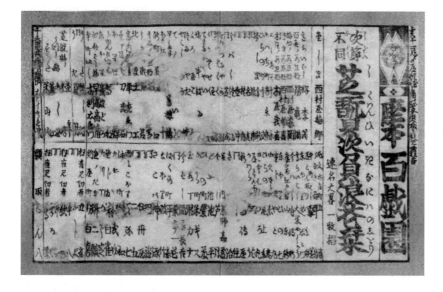

14 'A guide to Shikan fans in Osaka' (*Shikan hiiki naniwa no shiori*), parody flybill, 1815. Woodblock, 19.6 x 31.7 cm. (*Kyota kyakushokujō*, Waseda University Theatre Museum) (see also cat. 2)

example of how fans' activities impacted upon the popular consciousness. After this spectacular arrival, Shikan exchanged cups of sake in his dressing room with fans from the Kita no Ō-renjū in a ceremony called 'the great circle' (*ōbannari*; cat. 70). A similar ceremony was held in a teahouse for all the actors together with Ōte, Sasase and Sakura fan clubs. Such were the events staged by the clubs to welcome Shikan back to Osaka.

Their support was equally fervent for other actors too. For example, according to *Yakusha daigaku* (*Great Learning for Actors*, 1809), when Arashi Kichisaburō II (Rikan, 1769–1821) appeared at the opening-of-the-season performance in Kyoto in 1809, the clubs presented him with thirty long banners dyed with poetry in his honour. Many other examples of the close links between actors and fan clubs could be mentioned.

The clubs also arranged promotional events for theatre audiences. *Kyota kyakushokujō* (Kansai University Library, completed c. 1813; cat. 3) mentions that Hagyoku and four

other members of Sasase club ran a daily competition at the Kado Theatre in 1813 in which members of the audience drew lots to win a crested sake cup. *Surimono* prints of Shikan were the prize in another competition at the Naka Theatre, and prints containing newly composed poems about the actor were given away as gifts to spectators in the expensive box seats (*sajiki*). In these ways, clubs provided a hospitable welcome for theatre audiences.

In summary, the fan clubs served multi-faceted roles, representing Kabuki fans at various ceremonies in the theatre world, and providing passionate support to theatres, actors and audiences. They gave such important support both inside and outside the theatres that it is impossible to conceive of Kyoto–Osaka Kabuki without them. It can be assumed, too, that they were a primary audience for actor prints and printed books about the theatre.

Actor worship: Scrapbooks about Shikan (Utaemon III)

2003 marked the four hundredth anniversary of the birth of Kabuki, an occasion for great celebration. In the theatre world fans flocked to the special commemorative performances.[1] Kabuki's unbroken tradition over this long period points to a close and continuous relationship with its fans, without whom it could not survive. It is they who pack the theatres and who best appreciate the art of the actors. However, the relationship between Kabuki and its fans is not just limited to the hours spent enjoying performances in the theatre. Fans attempt to recreate the world they have enjoyed at live performances by looking at posters, advertising materials and programmes, or by reading reviews in newspapers or specialist magazines. They try to maintain a link to Kabuki by sending letters to fan-club newsletters and theatre magazines, or by publishing their own fan magazines.

This kind of engagement with Kabuki by its fans is by no means a recent development, and is in fact very similar to the situation that existed during the Edo period (1600–1868).[2] Then, too, fans enjoyed looking at various kinds of *banzuke* – promotional materials equivalent in function to today's posters, advertisements and pamphlets.[3] Through perusing and collecting these materials, enthusiasts were able to relive their memories of past performances. By reading the annual actor critique booklets (*yakusha hyōbanki*), similar to today's theatre reviews, fans would become engrossed in reports of actors' performances and backstage gossip. And in the same way as today's fans write reviews of performances and lionize their favourite actors in fan-club newsletters and theatre magazines, Edo fans would compose haiku (*hokku*) or *kyōka* ('crazy verse'), or create

15 *Surimono* by
Ashikuni depicting
Rikan (right),
Bandō Mitsugorō III
(centre) and Shikan
(left), 1813. The Edo
actor Mitsugorō
intervenes to try
to stop their fight.
(*Kyota kyakushokujō*,
Kansai University
Library) (see also
cat. 3)

surimono (privately commissioned, as opposed to commercial, prints) and other texts in praise of their favourites. Just like today's fans, their enjoyment of Kabuki was not limited to performances, and outside the theatres they too had many ways to participate in the Kabuki world.

Scrapbooks (*harikomi-chō*) provide concrete evidence of how Edo-period fans partook in the various forms of Kabuki culture that developed on the periphery of the stage art itself.[4] Through the medium of these scrapbooks I would like to explore the ideals of Kabuki fandom during this period and the interaction between the actors and their fans.

For Kabuki fans of the early nineteenth century the pleasure of collecting Kabuki-related material lay not only in the satisfaction of assembling an impressive, personal

collection: the active exchange of data with other fans, and the channelling of information about Kabuki to the outside world were equally important. Scrapbooks were a physical manifestation of these activities. They contained many different kinds of material relating to performance and handwritten items by actors, alongside prints and texts created by the fans themselves. Scrapbooks were not just a means of putting a collection in order: they were consciously compiled as composite works of art in their own right. In addition to providing enjoyment for their owners, scrapbooks were also circulated more widely among Kabuki fans and were thus appreciated communally.

A good example is the huge, historically invaluable scrapbook of Osaka Kabuki material held at the Waseda University Theatre Museum, Tokyo, and known as *Kyota kyakushokujō* (42 vols, completed *c.* 1827; cat. 2).[5] The core is performance-related materials such as *banzuke*, but there is also a wealth of other miscellaneous items such as actor prints, Kabuki-related single-sheet prints, *surimono*, and so on. The contents were edited and arranged chronologically by Hamamatsu Utakuni (1776–1827) in the 1820s so that the reader could gain an overview of the history of Osaka Kabuki. But the defining characteristic of the *Kyota* scrapbooks is that they were far more than just the arrangement of a personal collection for the pleasure of its owner, Yoshino Goun (d. 1851).[6] Goun's collection was incomplete and when he lacked a particular source, he would leave a blank page for it in the scrapbook and include a note inviting readers who possessed the missing material to add it themselves. Yoshino Goun's collection was used as the foundation, but in his decision to entrust its completion to fellow enthusiasts we can perceive a shared will to create as comprehensive as possible a collection of materials on Osaka Kabuki. In this way fans used their enthusiasm for Kabuki as a communal asset and they exchanged information for mutual benefit. Such exchanges between fans also encouraged the expansion of Kabuki's fan base.

A scrapbook in the collection of Kansai University Library, Osaka, also entitled *Kyota kyakushokujō* (*c.* 1813, cat. 3 and fig. 15), presents a chronology of Osaka Kabuki in a similar fashion to the Waseda scrapbooks. This interest in chronology is significant. In Edo at about the same time, Tatekawa (Utei) Enba (1743–1822) had started to compile his famous chronology of Edo Kabuki history, *Kabuki nendaiki* (published between 1811 and 1815).[7] While there is no comparable printed publication in Osaka, from about the same time we begin to see the appearance of a number of handwritten chronologies. Thus the two sets of *Kyota* scrapbooks can be interpreted as a project to create a chronology of Osaka Kabuki history, but using visual rather than written materials. And, as we have seen, the scrapbooks were not private collections but created with the cooperation of many different individuals. Bearing in mind also their wide circulation, the scrapbooks and *Kabuki nendaiki* represent differing responses to a common desire among many fans to find pleasure and interest in Kabuki history.

Another similarity between the two sets of *Kyota* scrapbooks is that both were created by fans of the Osaka actor Nakamura Utaemon III (Shikan, 1778–1838). Yoshino Goun, the owner of the Waseda scrapbooks, was known as a Shikan fan so it is only natural that his collection should contain many items relating to that actor, although the richness and scope of the materials is truly remarkable. The Kansai University scrapbooks are in seven volumes and the final one seems to have been consciously assembled from a collection of Shikan-related materials. The compiler, Kagaya Kyōjin Onikana, brought together items that included *kyōka*

16 Painting by Nakamura Hōchū of flowers in the shape of cranes, representing Shikan's crest, 1817. (*Minarōte yahari Shikanjō*, 5 vols, Nihon University, Center for Information Networking, Tokyo) (see also cat. 6)

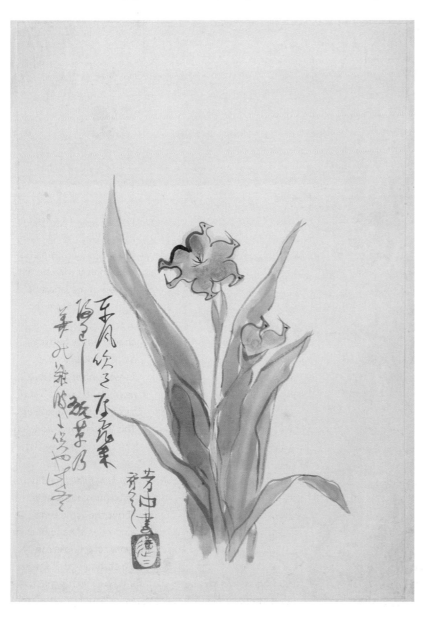

and haiku verses by himself and other Shikan fans in praise of the actor's performances.[8] At this time many Osaka fans participated in cultural salons, and documented their activities through the production of *kyōka*, haiku, Chinese verse (*kanshi*) or humorous prose (*gibun*) in praise of Shikan. Fans would exchange these texts amongst themselves, and some were later assembled into scrapbooks for wider circulation.

A scrapbook given the title *Shikan shōsanjō* (c. 1813, cat. 7) played a crucial role in expanding the ways in which such collections were appreciated by fans of Shikan.[9] Based on the personal collection of the scholar–poet Ozaki Masayoshi (1755–1827), it brought together items by an impressive list of leading Kyoto–Osaka literati (*bunjin*) of the time, including Morikawa Chikusō (1763–1830), Takeuchi Kakusai (1770–1826), Niwa Tōkei (1760–1822) and Okada Beisanjin (1744–1820). The scrapbook was then published in woodblock reproduction with the title *Shikanjō* (cat. 155a, b) in the fifth month, 1814, by the leading Osaka publisher Kawachiya Tasuke, and was advertised as 'the collection of master Ozaki'.[10] It seems that publication of Ozaki Masayoshi's personal scrapbook of materials by literati encouraged other fans to make their own similar collections. In fact, the published *Shikanjō* also includes materials from the seventh volume of the Kansai University *Kyota* scrapbooks. In other words, by the time *Shikanjō* was published, the activities of literati at the centre were already stimulating the activities of other fans on the periphery. Onikana, the owner of the Kansai University scrapbooks, had links with many other well-known fans of Shikan such as Bokuri, Juraku, Rishō and Enraku, and together they created *surimono* in praise of the star. A humorous text by Onikana is included in the Waseda scrapbooks, which also contain materials supplied by Ozaki Masayoshi. Furthermore, one of the editors of the published *Shikanjō*, playwright Hamamatsu Utakuni, is also thought to have been the editor of the Waseda *Kyota* albums. In these ways the activities of various Shikan fans in Osaka overlapped considerably and we can assume that there were close links between them.

Such was the cultural environment in which Shikan fans chose to turn their personal collections into scrapbooks. Each of the fan circles expressed their appreciation of the actor by composing *kyōka* and haiku, sometimes they would collaborate in creating group *surimono*, and on other occasions the scrapbooks themselves became the focus for communal creation that would draw in Shikan fans from other circles. For example, in the second month, 1817, the prominent fan Kodera Enraku created a scrapbook entitled *Minarōte yahari Shikanjō* (cat. 6 and fig. 16) that drew upon contributions from many Shikan supporters. Other examples from around this time include *Yakusha shogajō* (c. 1815,

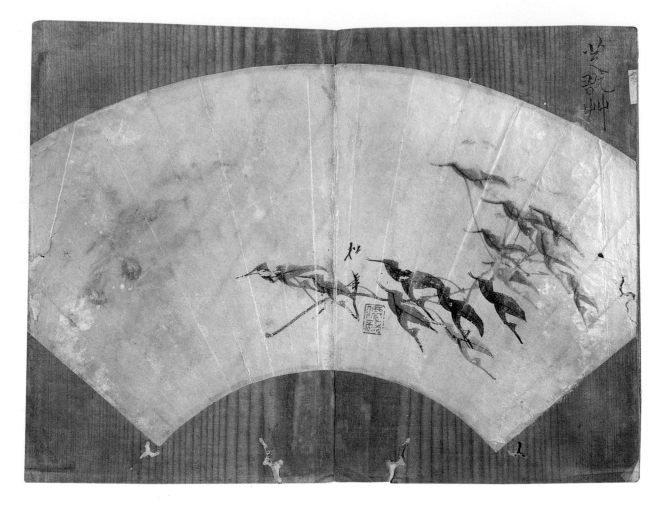

17 Painting by Yamanaka Shōnen of 'Shikan wildflowers' (*shikan-gusa*), 1813. The fan painting has been pasted onto paper of woodgrain design, which is pasted into the album (*Kyota kyakushokujō*, Kansai University Library) (see also cat. 3)

Tokyo National University of Fine Arts and Music) and *Onagori kyōgen issei ichidai* (*c.* 1825, Private Collection).[11]

As we have seen, scrapbooks brought together works created by both literati and ordinary fans, but the literati performed other significant roles. In the case of *Yakusha shogajō*, for example, the title calligraphy 'Elegant Theatreland Collection' (*Gien gashū*) is by Morikawa Chikusō. Morikawa also provided the title calligraphy for *Minarōte yahari Shikanjō* (cat. 6). The Waseda *Kyota* scrapbooks contain prefaces by the poet Kamo no Suetaka (1752–1841) and other noted literati such as the artist Nagayama Kōin (1765–1849; cat. 231) and the *kyōka* poet Kyūjitsuan. The prefaces to the Kansai University scrapbooks are by the *kyōka* poets Ritsutei Fujitake and Takeuchi Kakusai, and the opening page of *Onagori kyōgen issei ichidai* also features calligraphy by Suetaka. Thus the prefaces, endnotes and title calligraphies for many scrapbooks were provided by Kyoto–Osaka literati. Their contributions raised the scrapbooks from mere ordered personal collections to the status of works of art in their own right. In addition to assisting with the editing, literati also became the creative focus and fans were happy to be drawn into their orbit. At this time there was a great deal of general public interest

in the activities of Shikan's fans and in the many texts and *surimono* about him that were officially published, but it was also the most productive period for the compilation of scrapbooks. We find the same fans appearing in both.

The production of scrapbooks did not just involve those who directly participated by contributing materials. Their circulation served to disseminate information about Shikan to a far wider audience, thus expanding the network of fans still further (fig. 17). Wide circulation of the *Kyota* scrapbooks is attested to by numerous pieces of evidence. For example, the Waseda version has hand-painted paulownia wood covers (*kiriban*) that are easily damaged, and so a sheet has been attached explaining how to handle them correctly.[12] In addition, a label has been stuck on requesting information on the whereabouts of two other Shikan-related scrapbooks called *Yōkakujō* and *Shikanjō* that seem to have gone missing during circulation. The preface to *Yakusha shogajō* announces that it is available for public perusal. A single printed sheet with the title *Shikan nendaiki taisei* (*Shikan Year-by-Year, Combined Edition*, 1820) includes the name of Ozaki Masayoshi and eight others, whom it describes as 'owners of rare *Shikanjō* scrapbooks' (*Shikanjō chinzōka*).[13] The sheet summarizes Shikan's career to date and includes lists of comic pictures (giga), surimono, printed books and manuscripts that relate to him, as well as places where fans could buy Shikan memorabilia. Fans who came across this print and learned of the existence of the scrapbooks presumably asked to view them, and we have every reason to believe that their request was granted. Evidence for this can be found, for example, in the actor critique Yakusha kenzumō (1814), where the authors recommend that readers should view some comic pictures of Shikan owned by certain collectors, and that the best way to do so is to make a request through an intermediary. The implication is that it was relatively easy for fans to get to see items of this kind: it was clearly because there was the expectation of such sharing and exchange of information that the names of collectors were made public on the Shikan nendaiki taisei print. We can read the print, too, as an invitation to come and enjoy some personal Shikan collections as fans together. In this way, the world of scrapbooks became increasingly public, and their enjoyment was shared by an ever-wider community.

In the collection of the Chiba City Museum of Art is yet another scrapbook with the title Shikanjō (cat. 5), which was completed in 1854. It was assembled by Kimura Mokurō (1774–1856) and contains many examples of painted portraits of actors, letters written by actors and tanzaku poetry cards. Notwithstanding its title, however, the contents do not have any sustained connection with Utaemon III (Shikan). Rather, the genesis of the title seems to lie in the opening kyōka poem by Kamo no Suetaka which is dedicated to Shikan (see translation p. 64); perhaps it more generally reflects the fact that the scrapbook was compiled in the early nineteenth century when many other examples dedicated to Shikan were being assembled. During this same period,

fans of Shikan's greatest rival Arashi Kichisaburō II (Rikan, 1769–1821) were equally passionate in support of their hero, and the intense rivalry between these two groups of supporters was much commented on.[14] However, Rikan's fans never became as enthusiastic about the creation of scrapbooks. The scrapbooks known as the Nishizawa Ippō harikomi-chō (3 vols; cat. 4), assembled by the playwright Nishizawa Ippōken (1801–52) at the end of his life, were something of an exception.[15] Ippōken was a fan of Rikan, and the scrapbooks include many surimono that commemorate performances by him, quite a few of them illustrated in this catalogue (cats 98, 103, 115, 116, 120, 130, 131, 134, 135, 137, 194). However, the focus is not solely upon Rikan and otherwise much of the content has nothing to do with Kabuki. No other scrapbooks by Rikan fans appear to have survived and so it seems, as a rule, that they were made by fans of Shikan only.

Shikan was by no means the only actor to have surimono commissioned in his name, but the sheer quantity of the creative activities of his fans discussed above was unusual, and seems to have resulted from the support of Kyoto–Osaka literati (bunjin). Kabuki has always been sustained and boosted by the relationships and exchanges between its actors and fans. In the case of Shikan, however, the presence of literati among his fans had an energizing effect that stimulated waves of cultural production. It goes without saying of course that it was the extraordinary personality of Shikan himself that attracted both literati and regular fans, and that without him none of these activities would ever have taken place. Shikan's presence on the Kabuki stage in the first quarter of the nineteenth century left not just a glittering stage legacy, but also inspired a great flowering of Kabuki culture. (Translated by Alan Cummings)

1 Some of these performances are discussed in Tsugane 2004.
2 On Osaka fans see Matsudaira 1984(b), later reprinted in Leiter 2002. See also the essays by Ikeyama, Morinishi, Inumaru and Kaguraoka in Torigoe 1998, vol. 4, pp. 61–144.
3 The different varieties of banzuke – tsuji banzuke ('promotional posters'), yakuwari banzuke ('cast lists') and ehon banzuke ('illustrated programme booklets') – are discussed in detail and illustrated in Akama 2003, pp. 160–80.
4 The author has examined these scrapbooks in detail in Kaguraoka 2002.

5 Reproduced in Geinōshi Kenkyūkai 1975–6.
6 Goun was an Osaka medicine wholesaler, famous for the cure-all ninjin sanzōen. The material is thought to have been collected over at least two generations in the family. The name Goun was passed down from father to son.
7 Republished as Tatekawa 1926.
8 Little is known about Onikana, apart from the fact that he was a mid-ranking fan of Shikan and his family name may have been Ōtsuka. For an analysis of what information does exist, see Kaguraoka 2002, pp. 77–81.
9 Shikan was Utaemon's pen name (haimyō) for

haiku poetry. The scrapbook itself is untitled, but has been ascribed this name by the current owner Hida Kōzō in an essay in Osaka Shiritsu Bijutsukan 1983. See also Kaguraoka 2002, pp. 90–95.
10 Kaguraoka 2002, pp. 106–111.
11 See Kaguroaka 2002, pp. 146–62 for more details on these and other scrapbooks relating to Shikan.
12 This is reproduced in Geinōshi Kenkyūkai 1975 (suppl. vol.), p. 7.
13 Kaguraoka 2002, pp. 163–88.
14 Dunn 1984, reprinted in Leiter 2002. See also Gerstle 2002.
15 See Hida 1997.

READY FOR A CLOSE-UP:

ACTOR 'LIKENESSES' IN

EDO AND OSAKA

TIMOTHY CLARK

It is not just the three main cities where there is a craze for actor likenesses; in every other town and village in the land all enjoy them too.

Notes to the reader in Shōkōsai Hanbei, (*Yakusha*) *Masukagami* (*Actors: A True Mirror*, 1806) (cat. 84)

In the century between the 1760s and the 1860s many thousands of colour woodblock portraits were made of Kabuki actors in Edo (modern Tokyo) and Osaka. Many millions of impressions of the portraits were printed. This phenomenon is unmatched anywhere else in the pre-modern art world. When seeking to explain the essential character and uses of these printed actor portraits, Japanese scholars quite often compare them to something called a *buromaido* ('bromide').[1] The historical usage of this term in Japan warrants further investigation, but the modern dictionary definition is 'portrait photo of an actor, or such'.[2] This appears to be a classic example of a foreign word coined for new uses; and it still retains its validity today. Collectors can now easily net-browse for 'bromide cards' of the stars of both Japanese anime and Japanese baseball. In the West the term 'bromide print' apparently fell into disuse from the 1920s, with the decline of all rival techniques in favour of gelatin silver bromide development paper,[3] but by then *buromaido* had clearly developed a life of its own in Japan.

Figure 18 is a photographic portrait of the twenty-one-year-old Kabuki actor Nakamura Fukusuke IV (Narikomaya) dressed for a *danmari* (silent encounter) role in the play *Hibariyama komatsunagi-matsu*, performed at the Nakamura Theatre, Tokyo, in September 1887. The photo is of a type known as *carte de visite*, since its small size – about 8.5 x 5 cm – was similar to a visiting card. The earliest examples of Kabuki actor portraits of this type seem to date from about 1870 and the genre continued for several decades.[4] Such early photos are (and clearly were) fascinating as a record of the 'actual' appearance of the actors, but the continuing vigour and popularity of the colour woodblock actor portraits, designed by contemporary print artists such as Toyohara Kunichika (1835–1900) right through the 1890s, suggest that there were elements that the photos lacked.[5]

Most immediately apparent, of course, is the lack of colour. After an early period of hand-colouring that lasted about fifty years from the 1690s, woodblock prints in Edo began to use two and then three printed colours in the 1740s and 1750s, finally making the leap to full-colour printing for commercial designs in the late 1760s. After this, colour woodblock was the technology of choice in Edo, only spreading to Osaka quite late, in the 1790s. In Kyoto–Osaka from the middle of the eighteenth century an alternative technique was often used, the application of colours using stencils (*kappa-zuri*), within outlines printed from woodblocks.

18 Photographer unknown. Nakamura Fukusuke IV (Narikomaya). *Carte de visite* photograph, 8.5 x 5.0 cm. September 1887. (The British Museum, London, JA Album 87, 2000.2-15.01, 3)

This method continued in Kyoto–Osaka in parallel with colour woodblock throughout the nineteenth century, stencil-printing generally being used for less expensive commodities, though not exclusively so.[6]

The glory of woodblock actor portraits was in their colour, and the vibrant, essentially non-naturalistic palette added considerably to the *drama* of the image. Increasingly in the nineteenth century this was augmented with ever more elaborate special printing techniques: gradation printing (*bokashi*) by various means, blind-printing/embossing/gauffrage (*karazuri, kimekomi*), surface-lustre (*tsuya-zuri,* or *shōmen-zuri*), cloth-texture printing (*nuno-zuri*), not to mention printing with metallic pigments – brass, copper, tin – as well as occasional applications of gold leaf or flaked mother-of-pearl.[7] These represented a collaborative achievement between the block carvers and printers, operating in quite separate workshops from the artist, the whole process overseen by a publisher who marketed the final products. Special printing techniques became even more refined in the smaller, more privately sponsored world of Osaka printing than in Edo,[8] reaching their apogee in both cities in the art of *surimono* – privately commissioned prints with poems exchanged between fellow enthusiasts at the New Year or to mark other special occasions.

The fine carving and printing of the delicate hairline around the forehead in an actor portrait even came to be appreciated as a *tour de force* in its own right. One block carver, who used the name Koma ('the Colt'), recalled the spectacular work done by fellow carver [Koizumi] Mino ('the Snake'), who was one year his senior, for an actor print by Edo artist Utagawa Kunisada (Toyokuni III, 1786–1864), published in 1852:

> Mino carved the 'Cat Witch of Shirasuga' from the series *Actors and the Fifty-Three Stations of the Tōkaidō Highway* [*Yakusha Tōkaidō gojūsan-tsugi*, by Toyokuni III (Kunisada)] when he was about eighteen. The long strands of the Cat Witch's hair were perfectly arranged, fine at the root and spreading out at the ends. It gave the impression of softness and not a single hair was out of place. It was the most skilfully executed of that whole series of more than one hundred prints and was highly praised at the time.[9]

In addition to the bright, clear colours and elaborate patinas of these beautiful products of art-craftsmanship, colour woodblock portraits of actors also provided a visual stimulation that evoked the excitement of an actual performance. Compared to the stiff poses of the *carte de visite* photographs, which presumably had to be held for several minutes while the exposure was taken, the print artists devised very effective formal methods for suggesting movement, excitement and tension, as the works in this catalogue attest. The Kabuki acting style, with its climactic 'stage poses' (*mie*) struck and held at moments of high drama – memorably described as a sort of 'visual exclamation point'[10] – catered far better to an artist with a brush than to the artist with a tripod. For in a *mie* the actors did not freeze but rather 'quivered' with barely controlled emotion. This surely was what a print-purchaser recalled (or anticipated, as there is some evidence that actor prints were prepared in advance of performances)[11] when they held an actor portrait in their hands, and maybe viewed and discussed it with others.[12]

'Realism' in the arts of eighteenth-century Japan

Growing out of an artistic culture neither grounded in nor committed to mimesis, the schools of actor portraiture in Japan did not have to be either 'realistic' or 'naturalistic'; nor indeed were Kabuki performance styles necessarily like this either. In fact, the earliest acting style to evolve in Edo, the so-called 'rough' (*aragoto*) style associated with the lineage of Ichikawa Danjūrō I (1660–1704), was deliberately declamatory, exaggerated and bombastic, geared to the portrayal of mythic-fantastic superheroes. This was not unrelated to the claim by the Danjūrō actors that they were in fact 'living manifestations' (bunshin) of the fierce esoteric Buddhist deity Fudō Myō-ō, the 'Immovable King of Light'. Appropriately, the artistic style to depict this kind of acting developed by the school of Torii Kiyonobu I (1664–1729) was suitably hyper-charged and dynamic, the faces of heroic characters typically and generically drawn with bulging eyes, ferocious scowls and fixed grimaces.

Nevertheless Kabuki developed and changed, and during the eighteenth century the 'soft' (wagoto) style of acting first established in Kyoto–Osaka by the actor Sakata Tōjūrō I (1647–1709) came to form a counterpoint to the rough Edo

19 William Hogarth (1697–1764) and Charles Grignion (after Hogarth). David Garrick as Richard III. Etching and engraving, 41.3 x 51.0 cm. Published by William Hogarth, 20 June 1746. (The British Museum, London, Ee.3-121 Charles Burney Collection)

style. In the course of the century a succession of great female role specialists (onnagata) brought this soft style to the Shogun's capital of Edo in the east, to tame the drama of that brusque warrior city.

At the same time new currents of empiricism and realism began to ferment elsewhere in the visual arts. Some resulted directly from the first-hand observations made with European scientific instruments imported by Dutch merchants through the port of Nagasaki; others were inspired by the models of European popular prints and book illustrations arriving by the same route. Certain new types of painting imported from China, too, featured at least some elements that were more naturalistic.[13] There were even artists, notably the Edo painter Shiba Kōkan (1747–1818), who advocated the complete abandonment of traditional Far Eastern painting techniques and a switch to European methods; but such artists remained a small minority. There was also considerable influence from Western and Chinese models in the much more mainstream art of the Kyoto

painter Maruyama Ōkyo (1733–95), in terms of a new use of Western-style deep perspective and a renewed interest in sketching from life.[14] Ōkyo's example would have a profound impact on many other contemporary schools of art, including, as we shall see, Osaka actor imagery.

Traditions of portraiture were extremely different in Japan from those in Europe. The idea of sketching someone from life was quite unusual; before the Edo Period (1600–1868) 'portraits' were quite often made after the individual's death, and primarily used for memorializing purposes. The settings and poses in both court and samurai portraits were generally hieratic and stereotypical, and although there were exquisitely subtle attempts to create a likeness (nise-e), particularly within the sophisticated court painting circles of the Kamakura Period (1185–1333), this was generally done within a very narrow stylistic range. Half-length or bust portraits were virtually unknown. Before the nineteenth century, naturalistic modelling of the features was only found in the memorial portraits created of (and by) monks of the Ōbaku Zen sect, which arrived in Japan from China in the middle of the seventeenth century. One simple, telling difference between conventions of portraiture in Europe and Japan in the pre-modern period is that in the case of Japan the subject is invariably shown in three-quarter profile and almost never engages his/her gaze with the viewer. This fact surely stems from profoundly different cultural notions of self and self-projection, and is not simply a matter of artistic convention.

This meant that when artists came to develop schools of actor portraiture in Edo and Osaka, they were creating something that was essentially quite new; unlike their contemporaries in Europe, who were building on traditions of mimetic portraiture that were perhaps two thousand years old. Figure 19 is a splendid example of actor portraiture from the English tradition, Hogarth's 1746 etching of David Garrick in the role of Shakespeare's Richard III. Hogarth brilliantly captures the actor's expression and gesture of terror and alarm as he awakes from a nightmare before the final battle. The composition was based on a history painting from the previous century by Charles Le Brun (1619–90) and Hogarth also used as a model, like other artists of his day, Le Brun's treatise on the expressions of the passions, Methode pour apprendre à dessiner les passions (published posthumously, 1698).[15] It was not until the end of the eighteenth century in Japan that Ōkyo carried out a project somewhat similar to Le Brun's in painted studies such as the set of three handscrolls Correct Depictions of Human Figures (Jinbutsu seisha sōhon, 1770, Tenri University Library, Nara), which showed the characteristic appearances of men, women and children, some of them drawn naked, of different ages and social types; also in the

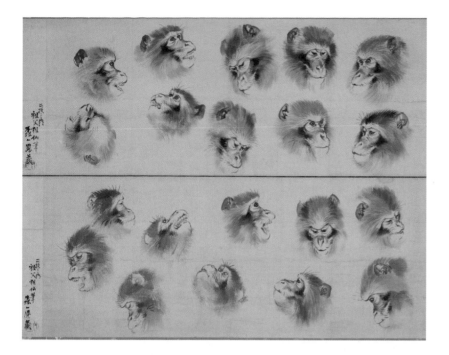

20 Attr. Mori Sosen (1747–1821). *Twenty Studies of the Facial Expressions of Macaques*. Two sections of a handscroll, mounted as a hanging scroll, ink on paper, 53.7 x 68.0 cm. (The British Museum, London, Japanese Painting ADD1264)

set of three handscrolls *Seven Disasters and Seven Felicities* (*Shichinan shichifuku*, 1768, Manno Art Museum, Osaka). The 'disasters' scrolls in particular explored the full range of human poses and expressions provoked by life-threatening situations such as earthquake, fire and flood – surely what Le Brun would have recognized as 'passions'. Two important limits to Ōkyo's experiments should be emphasized, however: firstly, he did categorize his human figures in terms of 'types', often adding descriptive notes which reveal a belief in the archaic pseudo-science of physiognomy (*ninsōgaku*) derived from China; actual portraits of known individuals of his day are very rare within his *oeuvre*. As Sasaki Jōhei has pointed out, Ōkyo's study of physiognomy is not necessarily the same thing as the pursuit of realism.[16] Secondly, none of Ōkyo's followers seem to have been inclined to take these experiments further; rather, it was pupils of the Edo artist Tani Bunchō – Watanabe Kazan (1793–1841) and Tsubaki Chinzan (1801–54) – working two generations later who first achieved truly naturalistic portraits of their living contemporaries, painted during the second quarter of the nineteenth century.

Where some artists of the late eighteenth and early nineteenth centuries did take a remarkable interest in capturing plausible poses and expressions was in the painting of animals, drawing on a great Asian tradition that went back at least to the Song dynasty in China, but now much stimulated by direct, empirical curiosity. A certain projection – maybe even a displaced depiction – of human passions can surely be detected in perceptive animal studies attributed to the Osaka painter Mori Sosen (1747–1821), *Twenty Studies of the Facial Expressions of Macaques*

(fig. 20). After a visiting Chinese commented that Sosen's sketches of the monkeys he kept chained in his garden betrayed the fact that they were held captive, the artist is supposed to have spent several years observing wild monkeys in the mountains.[17]

It will become clear in what follows that during the second half the eighteenth century the main preoccupation of those drawing actor portraits in both Edo and Osaka was to capture a recognizable 'likeness' (*nigao*, *nizura*, *kaonise*, *tsuranise*). Given the outline-based style of the woodblock print in Japan, it was probably inevitable that such a likeness would be highly schematic, invariably presented in three-quarter profile, and with the features assembled around the single prominent line of the nose. There is no way that they could be convincingly naturalistic, capturing the modelling of the face and the fall of light on it in the way that an etching or photograph makes possible. The commercial imperative was to come up with a formula that the public would recognize *again and again*, encouraging the serial purchase of many different images of their favourite actor(s). This is perhaps the most fundamental way in which colour prints abetted the promotion of stardom. In the light of the discussion above, however, one concern of this essay will be to assess actor prints not just as recognizable likenesses but also as portraits that capture the human passions.

'Likenesses' (*nigao*)

Nigao-e means, literally, a 'picture that resembles the face'. The term will be translated here as plain 'likeness', and the reader is asked to bear in mind the caveats about realism and naturalism broached above: the defining characteristic of a 'likeness' is that it must be recognizable, but the extent to which it is 'realistic' is quite another matter. There are several issues to be explored here. Knowing what a *nigao-e* became by the end of the eighteenth century, where are its origins to be sought earlier in the century? When did *nigao-e* come to be recognized as a distinct genre, and what is the history and meaning of the term? Most importantly in the context of this catalogue, how did *nigao-e* develop and influence one another in Edo and Osaka, and what do any differences tell us about the nature of Kabuki culture and its arts in these two distinctive cities?

To explore the second question first, use of the term *nigao-e* seems to have been secure in Edo by the end of the eighteenth century and was applied almost exclusively to actor portraits; indeed this was the main context in which it developed and was used.[18] For the opening of the new theatrical season in the eleventh month, 1791, for example – and presumably just before he fell victim to a paralysis of the right hand that curtailed his career as a print artist –

generation Torii School artist who she convincingly demonstrates was a key figure in the development of *nigao-e* and a vital precursor to the achievements of Shunshō and Bunchō.[24] During the 1750s and early 1760s Kiyoshige designed full-length portraits of actors in the somewhat larger than normal *ō-hosoban* (large *hosoban*, otherwise called *ō-tanzaku*, large *tanzaku*) format that, particularly in the cases of male lead and villain roles, have faces that capture a distinct likeness. The novel addition of a haiku poem, often by the actor himself, as a printed inscription above the figure in this tall format is reminiscent of a hanging scroll painting, argues Mutō, and indeed she thinks that the impetus to design likeness prints of actors in the first place partly came from imitating paintings.[25] In the collection of the British Museum is a painting by Kiyoshige of Ichikawa Ebizō II and Nakamura Tomijūrō I in 'Momiji-gari' (fig. 24), which shows the veteran Edo actor coupled with the leading female role specialist from Osaka, as the warrior Taira no Koremochi and the mysterious beautiful woman of Mt Togakushi who turns into a she-devil. Ebizō II (formerly Danjūrō II) is immediately recognizable by his 'trademark' features of large, wide-open eyes – here with the pupils crossed for a ferocious stage 'glare' (*nirami*) – prominent nose with large nostrils, and large down-turned mouth; his face is completely covered in vermillion striped *suji-guma* makeup.

There were already many different theories in texts of the early nineteenth century as to who was the originator of *nigao-e*. Mutō conveniently lists and comments on the sources that argue for each of the five main contenders: Furuyama Moromasa, Toriyama Sekien, Ōba Hōsui, Katsukawa Shunshō and Yanagi Bunchō (a different artist from Ippitsusai Bunchō). Concerning the second candidate, the memoir *Chirizuka monogatari* (*Tales of the Dust Heap*, 1814) by Ogawa Kendō describes the very public setting for the display of a novel *nigao-e* painting by Sekien:

> About the beginning of the Hōreki era [1751–64] the artist Toriyama Sekien painted a likeness of the female role specialist Nakamura Kiyosaburō in performance, on a framed panel of rough, unfinished wood 2 *shaku*, 4 or 5 *sun* [42.4–45.5 cm] high and 8 or 9 *sun* [24.2–27.3 cm] wide. It was hung on a pillar to the side of the incense burner in the Asakusa Kannon Hall and everyone was talking about how unusual it was. This should be regarded as the origins of the *nigao-e* in Edo.[26]

The work does not appear to have survived among the extensive collection of votive panel paintings (*ema*) still preserved at Asakusa Kannon Temple, Tokyo,[27] and no Kabuki actor paintings by Sekien have yet been discovered. Recently, however, a hanging scroll painting of Ichikawa Ebizō II in the

24 Torii Kiyoshige. Ichikawa Ebizō II and Nakamura Tomijūrō I in 'Momiji-gari'. Hanging scroll; ink, colour and gold on paper, 87.0 x 27.5 cm. Before 1758. (The British Museum, Japanese Painting ADD141)

role of Nitta Shitennō by Yanagi Bunchō (worked about 1751–1801), and another of Ebizō II in the 'Shibaraku' role, attributed to Furuyama Moromasa (worked about 1741–8), have come to light which both show the actor in similar *nigao-e* fashion and appear to date from the Hōreki era (1751–64).[28] Quite a few actor paintings of this type from the middle of the eighteenth century are scattered in museum collections waiting to be carefully dated and otherwise studied in detail, and their existence lends a good deal of weight to the theory that *nigao-e* started out as paintings before being imitated in colour woodblock.

The connections between *nigao-e* and actor paintings specifically on fans – of the two common types, folding (*ōgi*) and round, non-folding (*uchiwa*) – warrant closer examination. Shunshō and Bunchō's *Ehon butai ōgi* (*Picture Books: Actor Fans*; cat. 9) of 1770, as we have seen, made a particular feature of presenting half-length actor portraits inside the distinctive shape of a paper for a folding fan, aligned vertically. Also, there were rare precursors for this earlier in the century (fig. 23). A fair amount of evidence survives that both printed and painted fans of this type were actually used. This is surprising in as much as fans are perhaps the most ephemeral painting format imaginable; cheerfully discarded both because they get tattered so quickly, also because, as fashion accessories, their designs and patterns so soon become passé.

From 1775 Shunshō began a series of large colour prints entitled 'Fans of the East [i.e., Edo]' (*Azuma ōgi*, 1775–82; fig. 25). Each featured a half-length portrait of an actor in role and had printed instructions from the publisher, Iwatoya Genpachi, on how to cut it out and stick it onto ribs recycled from an old fan.[29] It was also suggested that you might like to stick the portraits onto a folding screen or sliding door panel. Ōta Nanpo mentioned the vogue for this series in a diary entry of the fifth month, 1776, where he used the word *nigao* to described the actor portraits.[30] Among the crop of comic illustrated novelettes (*kibyōshi*) issued at the New Year, 1776, was one by the author–artist Koikawa Harumachi in which both he and Shunshō appeared as the main characters. The realistic power of the new actor portraits painted by Shunshō on large non-folding fans (*uchiwa*) is mustered to alter the outcome of a long-running battle between spooks and foxes (the spooks win, fig. 26).[31] The title of the book is (*Kokon meihitsu*) *Sono henpō bakemono-banashi* (*All-time Masterpiece: Tale of the Spooks' Revenge*) and the text praises Shunshō's realism: 'when it comes to [his] drawings of actors, it really is as if they are alive'.[32] The term used to describe the actor

25 Katsukawa Shunshō (d. 1792). Ōtani Hiroji III as Satsuma Gengobei (?), from the series 'Fans of the East' (*Azuma ōgi*). Double *aiban*, colour woodblock, 42.0 x 31.0 cm. Second month (?), 1775. (Art Institute of Chicago, The Clarence Buckingham Collection, 1928.987)

26 Koikawa
Harumachi
(author–artist,
1744–89). *(Kokon
meihitsu) Sono
henpō bakemono-
banashi. Kibyōshi*
book, woodblock,
2 vols. Published by
Urokogataya, 1776.
Spooks hiding
behind fans of
Ichikawa Danjūrō V
(right) and Segawa
Kikunojō III (left)
[8*u*/9*o*]. (Tokyo
Metropolitan
Central Library,
913/WK)

portraits, incidentally, is not 'likeness' (*nigao*) but 'mug-shot' (*nizura*),[33] definitely a bit more slangy. In the Weber Collection, New York, is an actual (used) fan painting of Ichikawa Danjūrō V in the 'Shibaraku' role by Shunshō (fig. 27), datable on the form of the artist's signature to about 1787–8. Carefully removed from its ribs and flattened out at a later date, the fan painting is also inscribed with a 'crazy verse' (*kyōka*) by none other than the courtesan Hanaōgi IV,[34] arguably the most sought-after woman of the whole Yoshiwara pleasure quarter. What better strategy could there be to flaunt the original owner's floating world credentials than to couple the greatest actor with the grandest courtesan?

27 Katsukawa
Shunshō. Folding-
fan painting of
Ichikawa Danjūrō V
in 'Shibaraku' role,
inscription by the
courtesan Hanaōgi
IV. Ink and colour
on paper,
15.9 x 45.4 cm.
c. 1787–8. (John C.
Weber Collection,
New York)

Early actor portraits in Osaka

The account will now be shifted to Osaka, the main focus of this catalogue. It has been demonstrated above that actor portraits had been popular in Edo almost a century before they really took off in Osaka in the 1780s; also that the conventions of likeness portraiture in Edo had already been well established for several decades by that time. In Kabuki itself, there would continue to be vital influence – and the movement of actors and playwrights – in both directions between Edo and Kyoto–Osaka. From the late eighteenth century onwards, the position was somewhat similar with actor portraiture; although, given the long head start and relatively much bigger size of the phenomenon in Edo, much of the influence would be from Edo to Osaka, as will be demonstrated below.

Although there were sporadic attempts at actor portraits in Kyoto–Osaka earlier in the century,[35] it was not until the 1780s that the sustained activities of a 'school' can be tracked. As discussed elsewhere in this catalogue (pp. 23–4 above) the first two books of actor portraits – *Ehon mizu ya sora* (*Picture Book: Neither Water nor Sky*, 1780; cat. 13, fig. 8) by Nichōsai, and *Suifutei gigafu* (*Album of Actor Caricatures by Suifutei*, 1782; cat. 14, fig. 9) – were studiedly amateur, quite self-consciously so, in comparison to the slickness and suave professionalism of the Katsukawa style of Edo. In their different ways, Nichōsai and Suifutei went out of their way *not* to idealize the depiction of the actors, an artistic stance which can surely be linked to the un-flashy and realistic 'soft' style of the Kyoto–Osaka acting tradition. Aptly characterizing Suifutei's portraits, Matsudaira Susumu praises their combination of deep 'humour and sobriety' (*kokkei to shibumi*).[36] As we have seen (pp. 16–19), there was a strong tradition in Osaka of passionate amateurism on the part of merchant patrons who participated keenly as 'men of taste' (*suijin*) in the coterie arts, epitomized by the example of the otherwise unknown 'Suifutei'. This was quite unlike the commercialism that already dominated the colour printing industry in Edo, with its professional ukiyo-e artists and substantially larger markets.

Ryūkōsai Jokei

In the case of the first major theatrical artist of the Osaka school, Ryūkōsai Jokei (Taga Jihei, worked about 1777–1809), the question of his professional or amateur status is not clear-cut. As Kishi Fumikazu has pointed out, his earliest work, an illustration in the poetry anthology *Kyōka narabi no oka* (1777), appears alongside others by the professional artists Ōkyo, Yosa Buson (1716–83) and Ryūkōsai's teacher Shitomi Kangetsu (1747–97). Kangetsu was known for his study of

the ink landscape style of the great medieval master Sesshū (1420–1506). More significantly perhaps for Ryūkōsai, Kangetsu was also a pupil of Tsukioka Settei (1710–86), whose very accomplished paintings of beautiful women were the Osaka equivalent of the many beauty paintings being done by the ukiyo-e artists of Edo at that time. Settei is not known to have painted any pictures of actors, however. Although producing in all the main genres of paintings, single-sheet prints and book illustrations, Ryūkōsai's small total oeuvre for his thirty years of artistic activity make it unlikely that being an artist was his only trade. To be exact, the most recent tally for his colour woodblock single-sheet prints, for example, which cluster mainly between the eleventh month, 1791, and the fourth month, 1794, is sixteen signed works and twenty-two unsigned works; also cut-outs from five attributed prints pasted into the Waseda *Kyota* albums.[37] Apart from one *ōban*-sized print (cat. 33), these are all in the small, narrow *hosoban* format. In comparison with Edo print artists of the Katsukawa school who specialized in theatrical subjects, this puts him way behind even Shunjō (worked about 1778–87), a minor but talented pupil of Shunshō who is known by about seventy designs from the decade when he was active.[38] Not that quantity is everything, and Ryūkōsai's best works (for example, cats 26–8) have an unvarnished sincerity unique among actor portraits. The attrition rate of Ryūkōsai's works has quite likely been extremely high, since some of the print designs which must originally have been published in hundreds of impressions now only survive in a unique specimen. In the case of autograph brush paintings the losses seem to be even worse. Fan paintings with actor likenesses by Ryūkōsai were mentioned in the manuscript *Ōsaka dachin uma* (preface, 1783; National Diet Library, Tokyo) as being all the rage in the city:

> Since the spring of last year [1782?], there has been a vogue for folding fans with actor likenesses. The artist uses the name Ryūkōsai and I hear that he lives at Kameibashi in Kita-horie. There is nothing to compare with the wonderful way he captures a likeness of the actors. He drew the poses of the actors on request, just how each person wanted them.[39]

At present, just two fan paintings of actors by Ryūkōsai are known to have survived: one trimmed example showing the full-length figure of Arashi Hinasuke I (Ikeda Bunko Library),[40] and the other pasted into the Chiba *Shikanjō* album (cat. 5).

Ryūkōsai's most sustained performance is in the illustrated book *Yakusha mono-iwai* (*A Celebration of Actors*; cat. 18) of 1784, which contains fifty full-length portraits of actors from all three cities, printed in monochrome one to a page otherwise blank, save for a haiku verse and the actor's pen name. Once again the treatment is consistently bald and unflattering, presenting to the public simple, strong and 'floating-world artist' (*ukiyo-eshi*) was much more likely to be used and which connoted many other subjects such as courtesans, warriors and landscapes. This same source and other related evidence has been used to suggest that in Osaka, unlike Edo, the print artists were first and foremost Kabuki fans, who happened to design a few portraits in support of their idols. Statistics certainly seem to support this. In 1812–13 in Osaka there was a general and quite sudden shift from the small narrow *hosoban* format to the large *ōban*-sized sheet. This remained the most common format for actor prints until 1842, when the Tenpō Reforms banned them altogether (see p. 51). (In comparison, the *ōban* sheet steadily came to predominate in Edo in the last quarter of the eighteenth century and was completely dominant by the beginning of the nineteenth.) During the thirty-year so-called 'ōban period' from 1812 to 1842, Matsudaira Susumu has calculated that although there were 176 artists in Osaka who did works in this format, about four-fifths of these are now known by less than ten designs apiece. Even in the case of the more prolific artists, among those primarily active to about 1830 only Shunkōsai Hokushū, Gigadō Ashiyuki, Shunkōdō Yoshikuni and Ganjōsai Kunihiro are known by more than one hundred designs each. Among those primarily active from 1830 to 1842, this is also true of Shunbaisai Hokuei, Ryūsai Shigeharu, Hasegawa Sadanobu and Gochōtei Sadamasu. Overall Hokuei is the most prolific Osaka print artist in the period before 1842, currently known by some 260 works (totalling over 400 sheets) from a nine-year period.

These numbers are very modest when compared to the much more prolific Edo artists. Although catalogues raisonnés do not yet exist, already in the eighteenth century Suzuki Harunobu (d. 1770) is credited with about 1,000 single-sheet designs and Kitagawa Utamaro (d. 1806) with about 2,000.[49] (Neither of these artists primarily designed theatrical subjects, of course, but so far comprehensive statistics are lacking for the Katsukawa and Utagawa School artists who did specialize in actor prints.) In the nineteenth century the output of Edo artists become even more industrial in scale: Utagawa Kunisada, probably the most prolific graphic artist who has ever lived, and the major designer of theatrical prints of the day, is credited with as many as 40,000 prints during a career of more than half a century.[50] And it was recorded in a late nineteenth-century account that popular designs from a series of half-length portraits of actors by Kunisada combined with background views of the Tōkaidō Highway by Utagawa Hiroshige regularly sold 3,000 to 4,000 impressions each. In the course of the year 1852, when the vogue for these 'Actors at the Fifty-Three Stations of the Tōkaidō Highway' prints really took off, Kunisada prepared almost 300 different designs of this kind alone.[51]

Clearly the respective industries for publishing sheet prints in the two cities were of a totally different order of magnitude. However, before the balance comes to appear too weighted in favour of Edo, it should be pointed out that there were at least two genres in which Osaka was strong. One of these was in fact unique to Osaka, the illustrated playbook (*e-iri nehon*) genre, that took the actual plots of plays and presented them as illustrated stories, populated by the leading actors (who may or may not actually have played the roles). The second was the large *surimono* print, many examples of which are presented in this catalogue. These were often issued to commemorate anniversaries of the death of a particular actor, generally sponsored by poetry groups who were also theatre fans, or by other wealthy patrons. *Surimono* were certainly produced in quantity in Edo too, but the grand, large-format examples seem to have been a speciality of Kyoto–Osaka, often illustrated by artists of the Maruyama-Shijō school. In Edo, the feudal authorities generally kept a much more watchful eye on what were deemed 'overly-extravagant' techniques in popular printing.[52]

One leading *surimono* artist in Kyoto–Osaka was Niwa Tōkei (Daikokuya Kihei II, 1760–1822), whose career provides a good example of the not uncommon pattern of an Osaka businessman who was also a passionate practitioner of the arts, in a manner that was semi-professional or semi-amateur, depending on your perspective. Tōkei's main business was as the second-generation proprietor of the Daikokuya firm that sold patent medicines. So his extensive outputs as book illustrator (mainly of illustrated gazetteers) and *surimono* artist seem to have been a secondary occupation.[53] Tōkei was also active as a *kyōka* poet in the Maruha group, using the pen names Niwamaru and Chidō.[54] His artistic teacher was said to be Shitomi Kangetsu, making him a fellow pupil of Ryūkōsai. A similar pattern is also seen in the case of the artist Ganjōsai Kunihiro, who occasionally signed himself Tenmaya Kunihiro, and is for this and other reasons thought to have been first and foremost the print publisher Tenmaya Kihei, also an influential Kabuki patron by the name of Ganjō.[55] The artist Asayama Ashikuni (Kyōkakudō, worked about 1801–20) was also active as a writer and seems to have been the same individual as the publisher Nunoya Chūsaburō, who specialized in *yomihon* (illustrated adventure stories) and *e-iri nehon* (illustrated playbooks).[56] Shunkōsai Hokushū (worked 1802–32) was the most important artistic pupil of Shōkōsai, with more than 200 works to his name. Although his primary career is not specifically known, he is thought to have been a wealthy merchant, perhaps a lumber merchant, in the Funaba district of the city.[57] He used the name Shunkō until 1818, when a visit to Osaka by the famous Edo master Katsushika Hokusai led him to affiliate as a pupil and change his name to Hokushū. Hokuyō and Hokkei also seem to have become pupils of Hokusai at this time. Hokusai was not inclined to draw actor prints, of course, but nevertheless he seems to have granted to Hokushū use of his 'Yoshinoyama' art name, which appears on quite a few Hokushū works in the form of a seal that closely imitates one used by Hokusai himself.[58] In the present catalogue is a painting by Hokushū of Nakamura Utaemon III (Shikan) in the role of a courtesan on which this seal is found (cat. 186); here, rather than the sheet prints of actors that were Hokushū's staple, is a painting of a 'beautiful woman' that stands comparison with – and shows the influence of – the great hanging scroll paintings of beauties done by Hokusai in his 'litsu' period (about 1820–34).[59]

Actor likenesses in Osaka in the early nineteenth century

Ryūkōsai's principal pupil was Shōkōsai Hanbei (active about 1795–1809). The recent rediscovery of a group of twenty-six painted half-length actor likenesses datable to the period 1795–8 (cat. 86), seventeen of which are by Shōkōsai, has transformed our understanding of this key artist. The likenesses are quickly and deftly captured, with just the same humane candour as seen in works by Ryūkōsai; the inclusion in the group of two almost identical portraits of Nakayama Bunshichi II even implies a certain mass production. When combined with other similar works now scattered in different sources, it becomes clear that, as in the case of Ryūkōsai, the artist began by doing quite a substantial number of small painted actor portraits, before publishers decided to issue sheet prints. And yet only fifteen actor prints in the hosoban format by Shōkōsai have survived from the period 1795–1809. More substantial at this time were Shōkōsai's activities as an illustrator of theatre-related books. In fact, there is evidence that the publication of single-sheet prints was deliberately suppressed, in order that they did not compete with illustrated books. Matsudaira Susumu gives an account of the legal suit lodged with city officials in the eighth month, 1793, by the publisher Shioya Chōbei against the 'single-sheet off-prints [nukezuri] of actor likenesses' issued by Ōsakaya Sashichi and Moritaya Uhachi, which were competing with his books Ehon niwatazumi (cat. 21) and Ehon butai ōgi (cat. 9). The suit seems to have been successful because Shioya was able to maintain a virtual monopoly over the publication of theatre-related books and prints in Osaka until this was first challenged in 1814 and later broken at the end of 1817 by other publishers keen

to join the trade; principally the four firms of Wataya Kihei, Tokuraya Shinbei, Hon'ya Seishichi and Tenmaya Kihei.[60]

The collection of forty-two half-length likenesses of actors in Shōkōsai's illustrated book (Yakusha) Masukagami (Actors: A True Mirror, 1806; cat. 84) is in many ways a colour printed version of the group of small-format paintings discussed above.[61] With a preface and some of the kyōka poems by the artist, as well as three by his pupil Shunkō (the future Hokushū), this was clearly a work produced very much under Shōkōsai's control. The preface says that by having kyōka poems on actor portraits Shōkōsai is following the Edo fashion, but his craving of the indulgence of the great Edo kyōka poet Ōta Nanpo smacks somewhat of an inferiority complex. Notes to the reader at the beginning of the book record a nationwide fad: 'It is not just the three main cities [Osaka, Kyoto, Edo] where there is a craze for actor likenesses; in every other town and village [literally 'every inlet and bay'] in the land all enjoy them too'. Surely Shōkōsai and publisher Shioya would have been well aware of the succession of successful colour picture books of actor portraits with kyōka poems published in Edo in recent years, notably Yakusha gakuya tsū (Connoisseur's Guide to the Actors' Green Room, 1799; cat. 76) by Toyokuni and his pupil Kunimasa, and Yakusha awase-kagami (Actors in Paired Mirrors, 1804; cat. 82) by Toyokuni alone. The direction of influence was reversed, however, in the case of the much-reprinted encyclopaedia of theatre matters both authored and illustrated by Shōkōsai, Shibai gakuya zue (Backstage at the Theatre: An Illustrated Guide, 1801; cat. 70) and its sequel Gakuya zue shūi (1802; cat. 71). These served as the model for the Edo equivalent, Shibai kinmō zui (Illustrated Encyclopaedia of Theatre, 1803; cat. 72), written by Shikitei Sanba and illustrated with actor portraits by Toyokuni.[62]

When were half-length likenesses of actors first issued as single-sheet prints in Osaka? It will be recalled that sporadic examples were already published in Edo by about the late 1730s (fig. 23). Ehon futaba aoi (Picture Book: Double-leafed Hollyhock, 1798; cat. 74), the first colour-printed book of (full-length) actor pictures in Osaka, by Shōkōsai, includes an advert for 'a selection of single-sheet colour prints with half-length likenesses of actors' by him, but none appear to have survived from quite such an early date.[63] A half-length portrait of Segawa Rokō in dated to about 1801;[64] another early example shows Rikan as Tsukushi Gonroku (cat. 92) in a performance of the first month, 1804, a handsome and virile portrait of the rising young star soon to be promoted to head of his troupe. Just to remind ourselves of the latest actor likenesses in Edo at this time, fig. 31 shows Onoe Matsusuke I as the villain Kudō Suketsune in a performance at the Ichimura Theatre, Edo in the first month, 1799, one of the most forceful works by Toyokuni. The actor's fiercely

31 Utagawa
Toyokuni. Onoe
Matsusuke I as
Kudō Suketsune.
Colour woodblock,
37.1 x 24.3 cm.
Published by
Tsuruya Kinsuke,
first month, 1799.
(Victoria & Albert
Museum, London,
E.994-1914)

during the period from 1812 to about 1840, Kunisada alone designed more than 200,[66] and after this very many more, as we have seen (p. 48) – the quantities produced in Osaka during the so-called 'period of the ōban size' from about 1812 to 1842 were much more modest.[67] The actor most frequently portrayed in half-length likenesses was, undoubtedly, Nakamura Utaemon III (Shikan), whose large bulging eyes and prominent aquiline nose are immediately recognizable in many of the prints reproduced in this volume. Half-length portraits of his rival Arashi Kichisaburō II (Rikan) were comparatively few in number and almost all were designed during the last year of the actor's life from his assumption of the specially coined name Kitsusaburō I at the New Year, 1821, until his death on the twenty-seventh day of the ninth month. Immediately after Rikan's death some of the earlier half-length portraits were reissued as memorials – so-called 'death pictures' (shini-e) – with appropriate annotations.

It may just be coincidence, but the period of publication of the half-length portraits of Rikan seems to have corresponded with the visit to Osaka of the leading Edo master of actor prints, Kunisada. Exactly when Kunisada arrived and how long he stayed in Osaka is not known. However, his triptych print 'Picture of backstage at a theatre in Dōtonbori, Osaka' (Ōsaka Dōtonbori shibai gakuya no zu; cat. 216), in addition to featuring the Edo actors then touring in Osaka – Bandō Mitsugorō III, Matsumoto Kōshirō V and Iwai Hanshirō V – also includes Rikan, named as 'Arashi Kitsusaburō', and therefore it shows a scene set during the first nine months of 1821 (even though the print was published back in Edo, maybe at the New Year, 1822).[68] Evidence of Kunisada's continuing influence even after his return to Edo is provided by Yoshikuni's untitled 1824–5 series of half-length likenesses of Osaka actors (cats 252 and 259), drawn as if they were a padded cloth picture (oshi-e) mounted on a large battledore (hago-ita). These copy exactly the idea of Kunisada's series Tōsei oshi-e hago-ita (Modern Cloth-Picture Battledores) published in Edo around 1823.

During the period 1820–25 some of the most magnificent half-length portraits of the whole Osaka school were designed by Hokushū to champion the achievements of Shikan, of whom the artist is known to have been a strong fan. Shikan as Katō Masakiyo (cat. 187) is one of the most striking, placing the actor's furious cross-eyed expression central to the composition, as he strikes an Edo-style 'rough' stage pose (mie) – dressed in voluminous black robes that recall similar persimmon-coloured ones used for Danjūrō's 'Shibaraku!', the most famous scene in all of Edo Kabuki. But, lest his fans should doubt Shikan's loyalty to his native city,

glaring face is presented as a vortex of jutting angles and, as in the past, Edo bombast can once again be contrasted with Osaka candour. Some of Toyokuni's contemporaries had no taste for this kind of depiction. The great Edo artist of female beauties, Utamaro, famously did not deign to design actor prints. On one of the very few occasions when he made an exception, for the retirement performance of Ichikawa Yaozō III in 1803, Utamaro added this inscription above his picture of Iwai Kumesaburō I and Yaozō as the fleeing lovers Ohan and Chōemon:

> My design of Ohan and Chōemon is not a likeness [nizura-e] that sets out to reproduce their faults. Chūsha [pen name of Yaozō] is a handsome fellow. Kumesaburō is the [leading] actor of young woman roles today. In drawing their attractive faces made up for the stage and their charming demeanour, I simply want the true beauty of Edo actors to be known in all corners of the land.[65]

For Utamaro, who excelled in passionate idealization of the human form, actor likenesses simply reproduced the faults (warukuse o nisetaru) of their subjects.

Compared to the large numbers of half-length actor likenesses that would be produced in Edo – for example, the role here is in fact the quintessential Osaka warrior Katō Masakiyo (in history Katō Kiyomasa, 1562–1611), who defied Tokugawa Ieyasu of Edo.

For Shikan's 'retirement' performances in Osaka in 1825 (he actually went on to perform right up to his death in 1838), Hokushū pulled out all the stops (cats 232–6). Placing the actor's head and shoulders tight within the framing device of a non-folding fan (uchiwa), the artist orchestrated a series of dynamic poses for the star that make him threaten to burst out of the picture. The medley of varied warrior, villain and female characters is promoted as the 'Last retirement performance of his hit roles' (Issei ichidai atari kyōgen). Impressions survive with extensive use of metallic pigments and surface burnishing, suggesting that they were perhaps prepared for Shikan to distribute among his special patrons and fans.

It will be recalled that in 1815 a sumo-style parody flybill (mitate banzuke) was published which ranked Osaka Kabuki patrons and included a list of forty-four 'Osaka likeness artists' (Naniwa nigao eshi; see p. 47 above, also cat. 183b). Another example which ranked just the artists themselves has the title 'Collection of Osaka likeness artists' (Naniwa nigao gakōshū), and has been dated to 1828 or early 1829.[69] Now sixty-one artists (and eight publishers) are listed, pride of place being given to Hokushū. Also prominent are Yoshikuni, Kunihiro, Shigeharu, Ashiyuki, Hikokuni and Hokuyō, as well as the Kyoto artist Urakusai Nagahide and the writer Akatsuki Kanenari. Hokuei (listed by his early name Shunkō), who would soon rise to prominence in the 1830s, is still awarded a relatively minor position. It is from the Tenpō era (1830–44) that several contemporary sources mention Ryūsai Shigeharu (1803–53) as the first in Osaka to earn his main livelihood as an artist of actor likenesses.[70] In one of these texts, Machi no uwasa (Street Gossip, 1835), which consists of fictionalized conversations between the Edo author Hata Ginkei and local Osaka residents, the observation is made by one of the characters that colour prints in Osaka have improved in recent years and that there are quite a lot that are 'not especially different from Edo now' (Edo to kakubetsu ima de wa chigawanu).[71]

The perspective from Edo was different. In the collection of the Tokyo National Museum is an important group of eight letters from the artist Kunisada (Toyokuni III) to his patron Mitani, a wealthy wholesaler of metal goods, written at the time that the two were collaborating with the Edo publisher Ebisuya Shōshichi on a luxurious (untitled) series of actor likeness prints. Sixty such designs by Kunisada were published between 1860 and 1865. In one of the letters Kunisada recalled two examples of Osaka actors who toured to Edo during the Bunka era (1804–18) and how struck he was by the different way in which Osaka artists drew these actors' likenesses after their return to their native city. Kunisada's opinion of Osaka actor likenesses done in a style very different from his own was not flattering, and perhaps we can detect here not a little local partisan pride: 'The faces are strange and, in contrast to Edo likenesses, they do not look like the actors and are boring'.[72]

Epilogue: After the Tenpō Reforms

Although falling chronologically beyond the scope of the present exhibition, brief mention should be made of new developments in actor likenesses after the severe restrictions imposed during the period of the government's so-called 'Tenpō Reforms'. As part of an attempt to crack down on popular culture and so restore, it was hoped, ailing Shogunal finances, during the five-year period from 1842 to 1847 the following draconian restrictions were in force in Osaka: a number of theatres were closed; the production and sale of actor prints and any related actor imagery in books was completely forbidden; the leading actor Ichikawa Danjūrō VII (1791–1859) was banished from Edo and moved to Osaka, virtually for the rest of his life; female role specialist Nakamura Tomijurō II (1784–1855) was exiled from Osaka and never permitted to return.[73]

From the beginning of 1840, not long before the Reforms were imposed, Osaka print artist and wealthy publishing patron Sadamasu began to experiment with close-up likenesses of actors in the smaller half-block or chūban format, which were issued in modest editions with expensive technical refinements. Sadamasu encouraged fellow print artist Hirosada to design prints of a similar type (the two had both been pupils of Kunisada in Edo in the early 1830s).[74] After the sudden, unexpected five-year interruption to print production during the Reform period, it was Hirosada who led a spectacular revival of actor likenesses in chūban format from the spring of 1847, again encouraged and probably financed by Sadamasu (now using the name Kunimasu). In the period up to 1852 Hirosada designed approximately 800 single-sheet prints, making him the most prolific of the Osaka print artists by far and unquestionably a 'professional'. Figure 32, a likeness by Kunimasu (the former Sadamasu) of the actor Arashi Rikan III in the role of courtier–calligrapher Ono no Tōfū from a performance of the seventh month, 1848, is typical of the prints of the immediate post-Reform years. (Ono no Tōfū had become a signature role of Rikan I after he first performed it to acclaim in 1813 [cats 116–18]).

What immediately catches the attention is how the background is now completely filled with rich, saturated colours, with the effect of making the white, powdered face of the courtier seem to project vividly out of the

THE CATALOGUE

NAKA THEATRE   KADO THEATRE

Map of Osaka, dated 1847, with north at the top and the castle at top right. A network of rivers and canals leads to the port at bottom left. Colour woodblock on paper, in two parts, 85.1 x 91.2 cm and 40.9 x 36.1 cm. (British Library, no. 16084 c12)

Detail: The Dōtonbori entertainment district with the two main Kabuki theatres marked.

1

PASSION FOR KABUKI: COLOUR PRINTING AND ACTOR PORTRAITS 1770–1805

Introduction: Kabuki culture

Technological progress towards full-colour woodblock printing during the eighteenth century brought great changes to popular art in Japan. This lead to a golden age of so-called 'floating world' (ukiyo-e) colour print production that would eventually burst upon the Western art world from the 1850s and be an important catalyst for the Impressionist movement. Colour woodblock printing, first nurtured by the private patronage of samurai lords, aristocrats or wealthy merchants in the early to mid-eighteenth century, was adopted by commercial publishers in the city of Edo (modern Tokyo) from the late 1760s and in Osaka from the 1790s.

Section One chronicles the development of 'likeness pictures' (kao-nise, nigao-e) of Kabuki actors from 1770 to the early years of the nineteenth century, first in Edo and then in Osaka. The narrative begins with the seminal illustrated book *Ehon butai ōgi* (*Picture Book: Actor Fans*; cat. 9) by Edo artists Ippitsusai Bunchō and Katsukawa Shunshō, published in 1770, which established a recognizable but schematic 'likeness' of all the famous actors performing in Edo at the time. The focus of this exhibition is Osaka, however, and we show how from a decade later Osaka artists reacted to Edo examples and were determined to create a distinctive style of actor portraiture based more on the realistic acting traditions of that city. See pp. 36–53 above for the development of actor likenesses in both Edo and Osaka.

After an initial group of scrapbook compilations particular to Osaka (cats 2–7), works are organized more or less in chronological order, clustered into discrete genres or themes. Particularly featured are works by the first two founding artists of the school of Osaka actor imagery, Ryūkōsai Jokei and his successor Shōkōsai Hanbei.

Illustrated books (cats 9–21 and 68–85) played an important role in the development of actor likenesses, particularly in the Osaka school. Books conveniently brought together an encyclopedia of recognizably distinctive likenesses of the famous actors of the day. Once fixed, an actor's likeness tended to remain fairly constant even in the designs of different artists. Also highlighted is the essential role played by poetry circles – in both popular genres of haiku and *kyōka* ('crazy verse') – as a forum for interactions between actors, poets, artists and fans. A considerable number of the poems and texts that appear in the books, single-sheet prints and *surimono* (special edition prints) have been translated here in order to convey the voices of actors and fans. The overall aim is to explore what is referred to as 'Kabuki culture' – creativity within and around Kabuki theatre, stimulated by performance.

The Osaka cultural setting, scrapbook albums (cats 1–8)

A six-panel folding screen shows a large panoramic landscape of the northern outskirts of Osaka (cat. 1), a rare survival in comparison to the many views of Kyoto that are known. The scene is relatively pastoral and reminds us that Osaka was a city criss-crossed by rivers and canals. Also depicted, almost exactly in the centre, is the Kita-Shinchi (Sonezaki) Theatre, part of a thriving entertainment district north of the city centre. The other Kabuki theatres were located in the Dōtonbori district in the southern part of Osaka proper (see map, pp. 54–5).

Osaka fans were extraordinarily devoted to their Kabuki actor heroes, and cherished memories of their performances. A craze developed among individuals, groups of friends and families in the early years of the nineteenth century for keeping scrapbooks, a passion particular to Osaka. Cats 2–7 bring together the largest group of this genre ever assembled. The scrapbooks contain a vast array of theatrical materials dating from the early eighteenth to the mid-nineteenth centuries, including playbills of performances (*banzuke*), ephemeral parody flybills (*mitate banzuke*), actor prints, *surimono*, small paintings and pages from illustrated books. See pp. 30–5 for the characteristics and significance of the scrapbook phenomenon.

The informal scrapbook albums were used at the time by literati as important sources to create formally published books on actors and the theatre. They have also continued to serve as an invaluable record of the lives and careers of actors, particularly of the Osaka star Nakamura Utaemon III (Shikan). Two collections with the same title *Kyota kyakushokujō*, one now in Waseda University Theatre Museum, Tokyo (42 vols, cat. 2) and the other in Kansai University Library, Osaka (7 vols, cat. 3) are unparalleled source materials on theatrical matters, and preserve many items otherwise unrecorded. They were compiled by fans of Shikan, as were the three different scrapbook albums with the title *Shikanjō* (cats 5–7). *Nishizawa Ippō harikomi-chō* (cat. 4), compiled by the scholar–playwright Nishizawa Ippōken, on the other hand, contains a large number of *surimono* celebrating the actor Arashi Kichisaburō II (Rikan), Shikan's arch rival (see Section Two).

Early illustrated books (cats 9–21)

A comprehensive selection is presented of early illustrated books of actors from among those published in both Edo and Kyoto–Osaka. Rare paintings by Osaka artists Ryūkōsai and Nichōsai are contrasted with works by the much larger Katsukawa school of Edo from the same period. The album entitled *Rien shoga* (preface 1788; cat. 19) is shown for the

first time and contains paintings by Ryūkōsai and Nichōsai. Ryūkōsai's masterpiece book *Ehon niwa-tazumi* (*Picture Book: Flowing Rainwater*, 1790; cat. 21) completes this first book section. It was published in Osaka, Kyoto and Edo, and although only in monochrome, its magnificent depiction of stage scenes across double-page spreads proved to be influential in the development of actor prints in both Osaka and Edo. Importantly, it established alternative Osaka-style likenesses for most of the famous actors of the day from all three cities that were more candid and less flattering. This style seems to have influenced the great Sharaku, who designed highly idiosyncratic portraits of actors in Edo for a brief period from 1794–5 (cats 43–6).

Nakamura Tomijūrō I (Keishi), a superstar female-role specialist (*onnagata*), is featured to show how different artists constructed their own recognizable likeness. Comparison of portraits of Tomijūrō by the Edo artist Bunchō and by the Osaka artists Nichōsai and Ryūkōsai shows just how strikingly different these 'likenesses' could be. Tomijūrō is representative of actors who were active in wider cultural circles as poets and artists. Using the pen name Keishi, he was a keen amateur artist and cats 15–17 are examples of a painting, book illustration and *surimono* by him.

Ryūkōsai and his Edo contemporaries (cats 22–48)

The books are followed by a representative array of single-sheet colour prints by Ryūkōsai (cats 22–35). The first (cat. 22) dates from the twelfth month, 1791 – the second oldest print by the artist currently known – and is a magnificent specimen in pristine condition. Ryūkōsai designed the first full-colour actor prints in Osaka, and many in this catalogue are illustrated in colour for the first time. The prints are followed by three other Ryūkōsai works: the illustrated book *Ehon hana ayame* (1794, cat. 36), and two paintings, the first a hanging scroll (cat. 37) and the second a handscroll (cat. 38). Ryūkōsai's burst of creative activity in 1784–94 established an alternative style to the dominant Katsukawa school of Edo. Finally, Ryūkōsai's works are presented in contrast to those of his Edo contemporaries: Katsukawa Shunkō, Katsukawa Shun'ei, Tōshūsai Sharaku and Utagawa Toyokuni.

Surimono: actors and poetry groups (cats 49–52)

Theatre-related *surimono* (specially commissioned prints with poems) were a key genre within Kabuki culture. Poetry groups produced *surimono* to commemorate gatherings, often hosted by Kabuki fans who were literati, and actors actively took part. These salons were vital for the actors, who needed to cultivate contacts with wealthy and cultured patrons. Actors would then distribute the *surimono* to their patrons and fans. Quite a few early examples from the 1780s to 1800s are introduced and four of these (cats 49–52) commemorate important theatrical occasions. An actor's lineage was an important asset for claiming fame and celebrity. One unusual *surimono* commemorates the twenty-fifth anniversary of the death of Setomonoya Denbei (cat. 51), a merchant of chinaware who was head of the Sasase Kabuki fan club. It is clear that for many, both businessmen and others, Kabuki culture was a singularly important part of their lives.

Ephemeral publications: parody flybills and erotica (cats 53–63)

Kabuki culture extended into all aspects of daily life. Two *sugoroku* board games even feature Kyoto–Osaka actor likenesses. Other parody flybills (*mitate banzuke*) show how the celebrity of actors was brought down to the neighbourhood level. The range of these flybills is fascinating, and examples here include: 'Osaka locals – men and women – who look like actors', 'Actors' salaries', 'Actors as emperors', and 'Actors' wives'. Yet another presents actors as the feudal rulers of all the provinces of Japan.

Star actors took part in high society and art or poetry salons as sophisticated literati in their own right, but they were also erotic idols, much like film stars of today. Two rare examples of Osaka actor erotica suggest how fans also fantasized about actors' sexual prowess and allure.

Actor memorial books (cats 64–7)

Osaka Kabuki culture produced the unique genre of actor memorial books (*yakusha ichidaiki*). These chronicle the theatrical careers of individual stars, and contain many poems by other actors and by their fans. Four titles are featured as representative of this genre that flourished in the 1780–90s. They memorialize three actors: Onoe Kikugorō I (Baikō), Arashi Hinasuke I (Minshi) and Arashi Sangorō II (Raishi).

Actor guidebooks and picture books: Edo and Osaka (cats 68–85)

The late 1790s saw a burst of publications about Kabuki in both Edo and Osaka, and this was a period of outright competition between publishers of the two cities. Two sub-genres developed. The first was guidebooks about actors and all other aspects of theatrical life. For example, Shōkōsai's *Shibai gakuya zue* (1800, cat. 70) and the sequel *Gakuya zue shūi* (1802, cat. 71) are treasure houses of detailed information about Osaka's Kabuki and Bunraku theatres. In Edo, Shikitei Sanba and Utagawa Toyokuni produced a similar book, *Shibai kinmō zui* (cat. 72), in imitation only a year later. The existence of a pocket guide by Shōkōsai, *Ryōmen kagami* (1803, cat. 73), provides evidence of the fans' passionate wish to keep constantly up to date with all the facts and customs surrounding their Kabuki heroes.

The second sub-genre was portrait books. The first Osaka colour-printed book of actor likenesses was Shōkōsai's *Ehon futaba aoi* (1798, cat. 74), the style of which follows Ryūkōsai in showing actors in performance across a double-page opening. A rare wooden portrait mask of the actor Onoe Shinshichi (cat. 75) offers us a three-dimensional counterpart to the actor likenesses in books and prints. The years between 1798 and 1806 witnessed an intense burst of actor book publication in Osaka and Edo. After this time relatively expensive actor books gave way to large *ōban*-sized single-sheet actor prints, which became the standard size that replaced the smaller *hosoban*. Production levels increased dramatically first in Edo and then in Osaka.

Shōkōsai: paintings and prints (cats 86–94)

The final part of this first section presents a series of paintings and prints by Shōkōsai Hanbei. This important Osaka artist inherited the likenesses for many established stars from Ryūkōsai, but was able to create distinctive likenesses for two rising young stars – Arashi Kichisaburō II (Rikan, cat. 92) and Nakamura Utaemon III (Shikan, cat. 93), who feature as arch rivals in Section Two.

CHRONOLOGY

1603 Okuni performs dances at the Kamo River, Kyoto, beginning of all-female Kabuki

1629 Women's Kabuki banned

1652 *Wakashu* (young men's) Kabuki banned

1653 *Yarō* (adult male) Kabuki begins

1680–1720 Establishment of Kyoto–Osaka *wagoto* ('soft', realistic) Kabuki and Edo *aragoto* ('rough', flamboyant) Kabuki

1690s–1760s Torii School of Kabuki imagery (Edo)

1695 Founding of Ō-renjū Kabuki fan club (Osaka)

1700–1780s Heyday of Bunraku (Jōruri) play production (Osaka)

1720 Founding of Sasase Kabuki fan club (Osaka)

1735 Founding of Ōte Kabuki fan club (Osaka)

Late 1760s Commercial colour printing begins (Edo)

1760s–90s Katsukawa school of Kabuki imagery (Shunshō, Shunkō, Shun'ei) (Edo)

1770 Founding of Fuji-ishi Kabuki fan club (Osaka)

1770 Shunshō and Bunchō: *Ehon butai ōgi* (*Picture Book: Actor Fans*), first colour actor book (Edo)

1773 Full-colour *surimono* (privately commissioned prints) by artist Yosa Buson (Kyoto–Osaka)

1775 Founding of Sakura Kabuki fan club (Osaka)

1777–1809 Period of activity of artist Ryūkōsai Jokei (Taga Jihei) (Osaka)

1779 Colour-printed Kabuki *surimono*, featuring Arashi Kichisaburō I (Osaka)

1780 Nichōsai: *Ehon mizu ya sora* (*Picture Book: Neither Water nor Sky*) (Osaka)

1782 *Suifutei gigafu* (*Album of Actor Caricatures by Suifutei*); Ryūkōsai fan paintings of actors popular in Osaka

1784 Ryūkōsai: *Yakusha mono iwai* (*A Celebration of Actors*) (Osaka)

1786 Death of actor Nakamura Tomijūrō I (1719–86)

1790 Ryūkōsai: *Ehon niwatazumi* (*Picture Book: Flowing Rainwater*) (Osaka)

1791 First colour actor prints by Ryūkōsai (Osaka)

1796 Death of actor Arashi Hinasuke I (1741–96)

1790s–1809 Shōkōsai Hanbei period of activity (Osaka)

1790s–1825 Period of activity of artist Utagawa Toyokuni I (Edo)

1794–5 Period of activity of artist Tōshūsai Sharaku (Edo)

1798 Shōkōsai: *Ehon futaba aoi* (*Picture Book: Double-leafed Hollyhock*), first colour actor book in Osaka

1799 Toyokuni: *Shibai gakuya tsū* (*Connoisseur's Guide to the Actors' Green Room*) (Edo)

1800 Shōkōsai: *Shibai gakuya zue* (*Backstage at the Theatre: An Illustrated Guide*) (Osaka)

1801–1809 Shōkōsai: Production of illustrated playbooks (*e-iri nehon*) (Osaka)

1803 Shikitei Sanba and Toyokuni: *Shibai kinmō zui* (*Illustrated Encyclopaedia of Theatre*) (Edo)

1805 Arashi Rikan I (1769–1821) becomes troupe leader in Osaka

1806 Shōkōsai: *(Yakusha) Masukagami* (*Actors: A True Mirror*) (Osaka)

1

1 Panorama of Osaka

c. 1770

Artist: Yoshimura Shūzan

Signature: Hōgen Shūzan Tansensō hitsu ('From the brush of Shūzan Tansensō, of *Hōgen* rank')

Seals: Tankōsai Shūzan, Tansensō

Six-fold screen, ink, colour, gold and gold-leaf on paper, 159.4 x 363.2 cm

The British Museum, London (Japanese Painting ADD 1177)

Few cityscape screen paintings of Osaka have survived. This panoramic view, punctuated by conventional gold clouds, shows the area along the Yodo River, north of the city (in the mid-eighteenth century this area was not part of Osaka proper, whose population was then about 400,000). First and foremost we are struck by the contrast between the deep blue of the water – Osaka was a city of rivers and canals – and the golden clouds. The impression is very different from the more commonly encountered genre paintings of Kyoto that focus on human activity in that city. It is possible that the screen was originally paired with another showing the south and east part of Osaka, which included the thriving merchant city with its grand castle.

Particular prominence is given to local shrines and temples. Sonezaki (Ohatsu) Tenjin Shrine is featured in the middle of the composition on the third panel from the right, and nearby is a

red-and-white curtained tower (*yagura*) with family crest, indicating a theatre in the area of Sonezaki Shinchi. Osaka's four permanent Kabuki theatres were at Dōtonbori on the southern edge of the city. In addition, shrines and newly developed land (*shinchi*) were regularly the locations for temporary theatres for Kabuki and puppet performances. This is most likely the Kita-Shinchi (Sonezaki Shinchi) Theatre, which had been granted a government licence to pre-

sent theatrical performances since 1708. Very few records about this theatre survive, but a rare playbill in the Ikeda Bunko Library collection advertises a performance in the seventh month, 1759. Arashi Kichisaburō I is listed as the theatre manager (*zamoto*), performing alongside Ichikawa Danzō III. In 1763 there were two theatres at this site (*Kabuki nenpyō*, vol. 3, p. 509), while in 1765 only one is listed (ibid., p. 564). Puppet theatre performances were also regularly

held there almost every year during the 1760s and 1770s (*Gidayū nenpyō*, vol. 1).

Yoshimura Shūzan (1700–73) was a leading Osaka painter trained in the academic Kano style, and both his son (Shūkei, 1736–95, cat. 16) and grandson (Shūnan, 1763–1812, cat. 95) were also artists.

The screen depicts the upper-middle area of the Osaka map on p. 54.

2 *Kyota kyakushokujō* (Waseda)
Album of Osaka Theatre Sources

c. 1827

Folding albums, 42 vols, 27.0 x 20.0 cm (covers)

Waseda University Theatre Museum, Tokyo
(6288-001/002)

The passion for collecting Kabuki memorabilia reaches a level of obsession in this set of forty-two volumes containing 3,088 items, compiled and edited in Osaka in the 1810s and 1820s. Two sets of scrapbook albums in the collections of Waseda University Theatre Museum, Tokyo ('Waseda'), and Kansai University Library, Osaka ('Kansai', cat. 3), have the same title, which confusingly can be pronounced in three different ways: *Kyota kyakushokujō*, *Amata kyakushokujō* and *Amata shikumi-chō*. This literally means 'scrapbook of various sources of the theatre'.

The Waseda *Kyota* was collected by the family of Yoshino Goun, a successful pharmacist in Osaka. Playwright–scholar–literatus Hamamatsu Utakuni was commissioned in the mid-1820s to edit the vast array of Kabuki materials that had been collected over at least two generations. The compilation is most complete up to 1827, the year that Utakuni died. The aim was to compile a full record of Osaka Kabuki performances at the two main theatres, the Kado and the Naka. Three further volumes were later added. The Yoshino were particular patrons of Nakamura Utaemon III (Shikan), and consequently the material about him is thorough, including playbills for all his performances in Edo during three different tours. The bulk of the material is theatre playbills, but there are many actor prints, *surimono* prints, paintings, pages cut out

of books and an array of ephemeral parody flybills (*mitate banzuke*) on various aspects of actors and the theatre. One particular feature is that figures have often been cut out of larger compositions, or large prints divided into pictures and sections of text, in order to fit them into the album format. This collection of source material on Osaka theatre is unparalleled in its scope and a vital tool for Kabuki research.

More than thirty items from the albums have been reproduced in this book, including actor prints, parody flybills, *surimono* and a painting.

For complete reproductions of the set of albums in black and white photographs see Geinōshi Kenkyūkai 1975–6.

3a

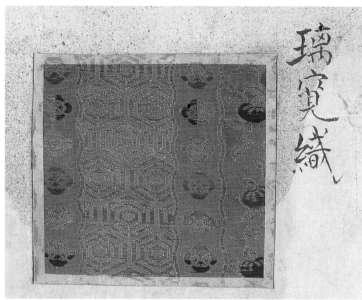

3b

3 *Kyota kyakushokujō* (Kansai)
Album of Osaka Theatre Sources
1813
Album, 7 vols, 27.0 x 18.0 cm (covers)
Kansai University Library, Osaka (C.774.4.AI)

This is an important set of seven albums of sources relating to Osaka Kabuki, mostly various kinds of playbills, but also *surimono*, actor prints and other materials. It covers the years from 1781 to 1813. The title literally means 'scrap-book of various sources of the theatre'. Volume 7 contains material from 1813, much relating to Nakamura Utaemon III (Shikan) and his rival Arashi Kichisaburō II (Rikan). This is an early demonstration of the dedication of theatre fans, who collected such materials as a hobby. Many of those involved were literati, also active as poets, artists, writers and as participants in Kabuki fan clubs. Since most of volume 7 relates to Shikan and since it was compiled by one of his fans, the *kyōka* poet Kagaya Kyōjin Onikana (Shichimonjiya), the album was most likely pre-pared to celebrate the return of Shikan to Osaka in the tenth month, 1812, after five years away performing in Edo. This makes it similar, there-fore, to *Shikan shōsanjō* (cat. 7), an album also

compiled by literati fans in support of Shikan to assist in his rivalry with Rikan. And like this other album, some of the material in volume 7 is also reproduced in the printed book *Shikanjō*, pub-lished in the fifth month, 1814 (cat. 155a and b). The large number of individuals involved in the production of these albums and books empha-sizes how Kabuki functioned as a hub for cultural interchange.

Illustrated are two fabric patterns with motifs based on the crests of the actors Rikan ('Rikan-ori', right) and Shikan ('Shikan-ori', left). It was common for the names of famous actors to be used on products and fashion items. Rikan complained in a formal letter to his rival Shikan that the flooding of the market with 'Shikan' brands was hurting his own 'Rikan' brand (see Introduction to Section Two of this catalogue, pp. 132–3).

An album of the same name in the collection of Waseda University Theatre Museum, Tokyo (42 vols, cat. 2) was compiled separately from this one now in Kansai University Library; however, certain individuals such as the poet–artist–scholar Hamamatsu Utakuni were involved in both projects.   YK

4 *Nishizawa Ippō harikomi-chō*
Scrapbook Album of Nishizawa Ippō
c. 1852
Album, 3 vols, 38.0 x 28.5 cm, 42.7 x 30.5 cm,
43.7 x 30.5 cm (covers)
Waseda University Theatre Museum, Tokyo (3804)

This album was most probably compiled by Nishizawa Ippōken (1801–52) and contains materials he and his father Nishizawa Ippō (d. 1812) assembled. Both were Kabuki play-wrights and had wide contact with the literati of the day in Kyoto–Osaka and Edo. Ippōken is also known for his *Denki sakusho*, a massive collec-tion of his comments on contemporary theatre and culture. The albums contain an array of poems, *surimono*, letters, documents and other miscellaneous materials. For a summary descrip-tion of the entire contents see Hida 1997. The largest group of *surimono* is in the third volume and focuses on the actor Arashi Kichisaburō II (Rikan). Many of these are otherwise unknown. There are ten large-format *surimono* celebrating Rikan's performances and several other smaller ones. Eleven *surimono* are illustrated in the pre-sent catalogue (cats 98, 103, 115, 116, 120, 130, 131, 134, 135, 137 and 194).

5

5 *Shikanjō*
Shikan Album

1854

Folding album containing 174 works, 3 vols,
48.0 x 35.4 cm (covers)

Chiba City Museum of Art (2941006)

The album was compiled by Kimura Mokurō
(1774–1856), a senior samurai official (*karō*) of
the Takamatsu domain, and friend of the popular
writer Takizawa (Kyokutei) Bakin (1767–1848). It
is a magnificent collection of actor portraits and
other art and poetry relating to Kabuki. The
album contains 174 works: paintings, poems,
letters and a few prints, mostly of Osaka Kabuki
actors, all in pristine condition. The artists
include Ryūkōsai Jokei, Shōkōsai Hanbei and
others from Osaka, as well as Katsukawa
Shunshō and Utagawa Kunisada from Edo. The
album was completed in 1854. Some works date
from the 1780s, but most are from the first
thirty years of the nineteenth century. The
album also includes many poems by actors.

The preface by Mokurō reads as follows:

From a young age I have enjoyed watching Kabuki.
Even after I grew up and became busy with duties
serving my lord, I went out secretly to enjoy Kabuki
in Osaka or Edo at any chance I could get. However,
in the 1820s the Shogunate carried out a stern
crackdown on any extravagance among the samurai.
Every domain in the land followed suit and
individuals were reprimanded. I was cautious and
decided to stop secretly going to Kabuki. Yet as I
grew older I had few other pleasures, and so I got
artists to paint actor portraits and collected them
into an album, intending to call it *Shikanjō* with
characters that mean 'an album of actors no longer
seen'. [In Tendai Buddhism *shikan* can also mean the
opposite: total concentration on something to

achieve enlightenment, see below.] This title
Shikanjō, of course, has the same pronunciation
as the name of the actor Shikan [Nakamura
Utaemon III and Utaemon IV both used this name].
I remembered a *kyōka* poem by the Kyoto poet
Kamo no Suetaka, which is about the actor Shikan.
I decided to call the album *Shikanjō* after that actor
and put the Suetaka poem at the beginning.

The poem, which in fact precedes the preface, is
by Kamo no Suetaka (1752–1841):

*Tendai no / shikan wa shimei / tōdai no / shikan wa
shibai / kagayakashikeri*
Priest Shimei's was the Tendai 'shikan'
Our times have the theatre 'Shikan'
Who shines so brightly
UNKIN JINNIN (Kamo no Suetaka)

Illustrated is a fan painting by Ryūkōsai of the
actor Nakamura Tomijūrō I (signature: Ryūkōsai
Jokei; seals: Ji, Hei). The seal is the same as the one
used in *Rien shoga* (cat. 19) and would suggest
that this painting dates from the mid-1780s.

See Chiba-shi Bijutsukan 2001, no. 42; *Nikuhitsu ukiyo-
e taikan*, vol. 10, 1995, no. 58, pp. 240–5
(essay by Matsudaira Susumu).

6 *(Minarōte yahari) Shikanjō*
(The well-known, of course) Shikan Album

Second month, 1817

Album, 5 vols, 38.0 x 27.0 cm (covers)

Nihon University Center for Information Networking,
Tokyo

This extraordinary collection of art and poetry in
praise of Nakamura Utaemon III (Shikan) totals
five volumes, kept in a specially crafted wooden
storage box. The final volume states that the

collection was completed in the second month,
1817. Shikan had returned from his second Edo
tour at the end of 1815, and the albums therefore
celebrate his successes during 1816. The owner
was the Shikan fan Kodera Enraku (also known as
Kanka no Hitonari, 'Member of the Shikan Clan').
No compiler's name is recorded, but the core of
the artists and poets included is the same as
those involved in *Kyota kyakushokujō* (Kansai University Library, cat. 3) and *Shikan shosanjō* (cat. 7).
The preface is by Hakujakuen and the postscript
by Agōsai. There is a total of some 350 items:
about a hundred *tanzaku* poem cards, fifty fan
paintings, forty *surimono*, and 140 other poems,
paintings, and miscellaneous ephemera. Most of
these works are in praise of particular Shikan performances, but also included are letters and
poems by the actor himself.

Illustrated is a painting from vol. 3 by Ashikuni
of Shikan as Sano Genzaemon in the play *Yayoi
ni hiraku ando no funahashi* at the Kado Theatre
in the third month, 1816. See cats 161 and 162
for other representations of this performance.

Tsuki to hana / yuki ni ya / Sano no ō-atari
With the moon and cherry blossoms,
In snow as well
A great success as Sano
SUMIREYA

Snow, moon and flowers (cherry blossoms)
(*setsu getsu ka*) are three important poetry
themes and represent elegant aesthetic experience across the four seasons. Shikan is a success
in any season. YK

The full contents of the albums have recently been
published as part of a DVD of theatre-related material
held at Nihon University; see Kasuya 2004.

6

7

7 *Shikan shōsanjō*
Album in Celebration of Shikan

c. 1813

Album of paintings, ink and colour on paper,
and one *surimono*, 34.3 x 22.5 cm (covers)

Private Collection (Japan)

Nakamura Utaemon III (Shikan) was a magnet for the patronage of the literati of Osaka. This album of paintings, poems and one *surimono* was compiled upon his return to the city in the tenth month, 1812, after five years away performing in Edo. Shikan had garnered rave reviews during his tour and was an equal success upon his return, especially in the dance play *Minarōte chotto nana-bake* (*Seven Well-known Quick Changes Given a New Twist*), in which he performed seven quick-change roles. The paintings and prints pasted in this album subsequently formed the basis for the printed book *Shikanjō* (cat. 155a and b), published in the fifth month, 1814, and it therefore served as an important catalyst for further publications in support of the star.

Illustrated is a painting by Niwa Tōkei. On the left is the outline of the first character of Utaemon's name *uta* ('song'), held up by his fans and being painted in with black ink. To the right various Kabuki characters look on. The figures are in a comic, caricature-like style, similar to a genre known as *haiga* (haiku-style painting), which was unusual for the artist. Most other Tōkei *surimono* are in the elegant Maruyama–Shijō style and tend to show nature scenes or still-life flowers.

The original owner of the album, and most likely Its compiler, was Shikan's fan Ozaki Gaka, a noted literatus. It was Gaka's circle, which included Morikawa Chikusō, Takeuchi Kakusai, Niwa Tōkei, Nakamura Hōchū and Okada Beisanjin, who contributed to the album. These same artists had also been active in the influential literati group of the wealthy Osaka sake-brewer, scholar and patron Kimura Kenkadō (1736–1802). YK

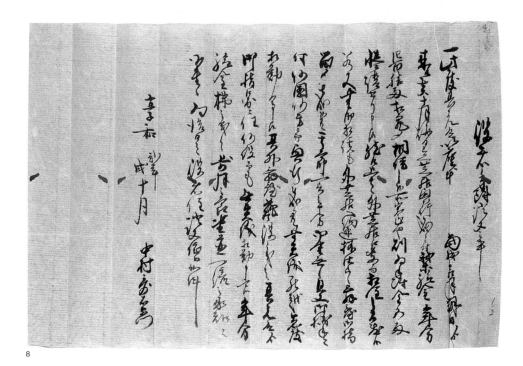

8

8 'Fushimiya Zenbei archive'
Fushimiya Zenbei monjo

ILLUSTRATED 'Nakamura Utaemon III (Shikan) agreement
for a deposit to an actor, tenth month, 1802'
(described below)

Ink on paper, 1 vol., 28.0 x 40.9 cm (Illustrated)
Osaka City University

'Osaka north group: census of persons in Moto-Fushimizakamachi'
Osaka kita-gumi Moto-Fushimizakamachi ninbetsuchō

Ink on paper, 12 vols, 27.8 x 21.1 cm (covers)
Osaka City University

Fushimiya Zenbei was the business name of a teahouse with prostitutes (legally, 'tea-serving employees', *chatate hōkōnin*) located in Moto-Fushimizakamachi in Osaka. It was the largest teahouse in the Sakamachi prostitute quarter, owning several buildings for rental, and was also involved in financial services. Fushimiya is listed in the Moto-Fushimizakamachi local census from 1811 onwards, but it is not clear when the business moved to this location. Before this it was operating a teahouse in Dōtonbori. With considerable financial resources at its disposal, Fushimiya was active as a patron of Dōtonbori theatre productions. There are many documents that relate to the theatre in the *Fushimiya Zenbei Archive* (*Fushimiya monjo*), which have already been studied by scholars from various perspectives.

The Fushimiya documents that relate to the theatre range over a period of some sixty-three years, from 1796 to 1858, and are of many dif-

ferent types: agreements for deposits for actors' lodgings; agreements for advances; agreements for loans; agreements for the rental of theatres; vouchers for the use of theatre boxes; receipts for wages. The archive provides very concrete information about the Dōtonbori entertainment world, including the activities and financial circumstances of Kyoto–Osaka Kabuki stars of the early nineteenth century such as Nakamura Utaemon III (Shikan), Kataoka Nizaemon VII, Bandō Mitsugorō III, Asao Kuzaemon I, Nakamura Tomijūrō II, Ichikawa Yonejūrō (Kodanji IV) and others.

Brief introductions follow to several documents relating to the Dōtonbori entertainment industry in the years 1803 and 1816.

Fujikawa Hachizō, agreement for a deposit to an actor, eleventh month, 1802

The is an actor's employment agreement (memorandum) for the year 1803 with respect to Fujikawa Hachizō, who had worked as a theatre manager (*zamoto*) for the Kado Theatre's first production of *Ise ondo koi no netaba* in 1796. The survival of this contract agreement suggests that his employment as theatre manager in 1796 in some way reflected the wishes of Fushimiya.

Nakamura Utaemon III (Shikan), agreement for a deposit to an actor, tenth month, 1802
Kataoka Nizaemon VII, agreement for a deposit to an actor, intercalary first month, 1803

At the end of 1802 Segawa Kikunojō III (Rokō) came to Osaka from Edo and acted in *Azuma-giku Naniwa no kisewata*, the opening-of-the-

season production at the Naka Theatre. Utaemon III (Shikan) and Hachizō were in the same troupe. The first of the two agreements here, and the previous one for Hachizō, relate to this production. However there are no seals on either agreement, so it seems that Fushimiya was unable to enter into a contract with the two actors and they were enticed away by the Naka. Shikan then left that theatre and took the whole troupe to perform at the Ichinokawa Theatre. In the first month, 1803, he returned to the Naka and was joined by Nizaemon.

Meanwhile, there was no opening-of-the-season production at the Kado Theatre. It was only when Rokō's troup transferred from the Naka on the twelfth day of the second month that they were able to begin performances. Hachizō left the troupe for good; Nizaemon performed together with Rokō in *Ōtō no miya asahi no yoroi* and *Atsurae orishiyusu no obiya* from the thirteenth day of the fifth month, and then went to Kyoto. The second of the two agreements here relates to this Nizaemon/Rokō performance and seals have been added. The period of employment specified in the contract and the actual period Nizaemon worked at the Kado Theatre correspond, so it can be inferred that Fushimiya was acting as financial backer of the Kado Theatre for that year.

Agreement for a deposit on the rental of a theatre, seventh month, 1815

This is the agreement for a deposit on the rental of the Kado Theatre for the forthcoming season of 1816. Utaemon III (Shikan) had been employed by Fushimiya, who at the time was the backer of the Naka Theatre, from the eleventh month, 1812, until his departure from Osaka in the fourth month, 1814. During this period the actor had made quite a lot of money for Fushimiya with his series of 'seven quick-change' (*nana henge*) performances that were a great hit. Now the dream was to get the Dōtonbori theatre district moving again by bringing the actor back to Osaka. In the eleventh month, 1815, Shikan duly returned to Osaka and installed himself at the Kado. He was joined there by Nizaemon from the first month, 1816. However, Ōkubo Imasuke, who was financial backer of the Nakamura Theatre in Edo, later sued Shikan for breaking his Edo contract. There was also a dispute with the Naka Theatre about their contract with Nizaemon. Clearly Fushimiya was very good at getting Shikan to make money, and this agreement for rental of the Kado Theatre is made in anticipation of the actor's return to Osaka. The person renting out the theatre, one Yamatoya, was perhaps the owner of a Dōtonbori teahouse.

Kataoka Nizaemon VII, promissary agreement, twelfth month, 1816

Kataoka Nizaemon VII borrowed money from Fushimiya on many occasions. In the twelfth month, 1816, he indentured a young woman, perhaps his daughter Yana, to Fushimiya for 200 gold *ryō*. According to other surviving documents at Fushimiya the most ever paid to contract a prostitute was 60 *ryō*, so this was a large amount in comparison. In addition, the phrase 'there are some other small loans to Yana' suggests that even before this there had been some kind of relationship between Yana and Fushimiya. In *Census of Persons in Moto-Fushimizakamachi* (*Moto-Fushimizakamachi nin-betsuchō*, Osaka City University; see below) the entry 'young woman Yana' appears with Fushimi Zenbei after 1811, but it is not certain that this was the same person. At any rate, it is clear that the connections between Zenbei and the actor also related to Fushimiya's main business as a teahouse and involved young women such as this person.

'Osaka North Group: Census of Persons in Moto-Fushimizakamachi'

Osaka North Group: Census of Persons in Moto-Fushimizakamachi (*Osaka kita-gumi Moto-Fushimizakamachi ninbetsuchō*) is a census by religious affiliation of persons living in Moto-Fushimizakamachi (present-day Sakamachi, Chūō-ku, Osaka City), located south of Dōton-bori and east of Hōzen-ji Temple, made annually between 1818 and 1830. Fushimizakamachi had developed as a pleasure quarter with teahouses since the Genroku era (1688–1704) and is still famous as a bustling part of modern Osaka. Because of the nature of the neighbourhood, there was obviously a great deal of coming and going by outsiders. The census, however, represents a basic resource for understanding changes in the resident population, down to the individual level. This is a unique census among surviving examples, bearing in mind the character of the neighbourhood and the concentrated period during which it was undertaken.

This is the original document preserved from the neighbourhood. It consists of twelve bound volumes, one for each year. Each volume has more than one hundred pages (*chō*) and the overall total is 1,403 pages. Many of the individuals included also appear in the *Fushimiya Zenbei Archive* (also owned by Osaka City University; see above), and the two documents complement one another considerably. HS

9 *Ehon butai ōgi*
Picture Book: Actor Fans

ILLUSTRATED Nakamura Shichisaburō II by Shunshō (right) and Nakamura Tomijūrō I by Bunchō (left)

1770

Artists: Ippitsusai Bunchō and Katsukawa Shunshō (Edo)

Publisher: Kariganeya Ihei (Edo)

Hanshibon book, colour woodblock, 3 vols, 28.5 x 18.9 cm (covers)

Gerhard Pulverer Collection (Germany)

The book contains one hundred and six dynamic half-length portraits of actors who performed in Edo, inside fan-shaped borders. Fifty-seven are by Bunchō and forty-nine by Shunshō, both Edo artists, and each picture has a printed seal. This is the first full-colour actor portrait book and was extremely influential on later publications in both Edo and Kyoto–Osaka (see the pirate edition, cat. 10). It confirmed the standard 'likeness picture' (*nigao-e*) devised for each actor by Bunchō and Shunshō, based on their innovative single-sheet prints of the previous five-year period, after the introduction of full-colour printing in about 1764–5. This

example is considered the best-preserved first edition of the book to have survived, with the most complete listing of actors; various corrections were subsequently made as the circumstances of the actors changed.

The book begins with a preface in Chinese by 'Tōkaku, grandson of Saikaku of Osaka' and one in Japanese by haiku judges 'Hoku Zaiten' and 'Chū Gitoku' (dated sixth month, 1770), and ends with a total of thirty-seven haiku by famous historical poets such as Bashō, Kikaku, and Saikaku (many of them deceased), and by the artists Shunshō and Bunchō; finally there is a postscript by 'Rekisen Sanjin Futsūkan Kikudō' of Osaka. Each actor is shown in role with his acting name and pen name (*haimyō*) carved in white reserve from block that printed the light blue background (invariably faded to a sand colour, as here). The preface suggests that the publication was created for Tōkaku when he returned to Osaka, so that he could take back a souvenir of all the famous Edo actors. TC

Fully reproduced with detailed commentary in *Hizō ukiyo-e taikan* (Pulverer Coll.), 1990, pp. 258–61, nos 158–216; see also Hattori 1993, pp. 103–120.

9

10

script of the first edition, by Rekisen Sanjin, has here become the preface. There is much wear evident in the printing blocks; but its publication is proof of the book's continuing popularity in the Kyoto–Osaka area. TC

11 *Yakusha natsu no Fuji*
Actors Without Makeup, Like Mt Fuji in Summer
1780 (Preface)

Artist: Katsukawa Shunshō (Edo)

Author: Ichiba Tsūshō

Publishers: Okumura Genroku and Matsumura Yahei (Edo)

Hanshibon book, woodblock, 1 vol., 21.5 x 15.0 cm (covers)

The British Museum, London (JH138)

A book showing thirteen scenes of actors in daily life, the first to present them as cultivated celebrities off-stage. For example, Ichikawa Danjūrō V is shown writing a verse on an elegant folding fan in the presence of three other actors (illustrated). Arashi Hinasuke I is shown in a similar setting, with arms crossed as a sage-like figure, in front of three others. These two actors represented the competing worlds of Edo and

10 *Ehon zoku butai ōgi*
Picture Book: Actor Fans, Sequel
ILLUSTRATED Nakamura Utaemon I (Kashichi, right) and Ichikawa Dai'emon (Kiju, left)

First month, 1778

Artists: Ippitsusai Bunchō and Katsukawa Shunshō (Edo)

Publisher: Kikuya Yasubei (Kyoto)

Hanshibon book, woodblock, 2 vols, 28.6 x 18.5 cm (covers)

Gerhard Pulverer Collection (Germany)

A black-and-white, much-abridged version of the original *Ehon butai ōgi* (cat. 9, published eight years earlier in Edo), with various radical changes, including removal of the actors' names. The printing blocks were first purchased by the Kyoto publisher Kikuya, and then, before 1790, by Shioya Chōbei of Osaka. This particular edition has a much smaller number of actors, only 41 compared to 106 in the original, and is only a shadow of the first, colour printing. The post-

11

Osaka Kabuki, respectively. Another scene early in the book shows a group of women gathered around a new season playbill (*kaomise banzuke*), pointing to their favourite actors' names and images (fig. 4 above). In his preface, artist Shunshō modestly professes:

> I am fond of the theatre and it is my habit to see plays performed, but as I am not personally acquainted with the actors, I know nothing of their private lives … but finally I acceded to Tsūshō [the author]'s earnest request, hoping that things which are not accurately portrayed may yet be entertaining.
>
> (Trans. Gookin 1931, p. 194)

12 Nakamura Nakazō I at the New Year in formal attire

c. First month, 1779
Artist: Katsukawa Shunshō (Edo)
Signature: Shunshō ga
Hosoban, colour woodblock, 32.5 x 14.9 cm
Bristol's City Museum & Art Gallery (Mb4775)

Prominent Edo actor Nakamura Nakazō I (1736–90) stands in a garden dressed in formal attire (*kamishimo*). This is likely a New Year scene, with a plum tree blossoming behind. Nakazō was famous for his arch-villain (*jitsu aku*) roles and for his skill at Kabuki dance. He spent just one season performing in Osaka, from the end of 1786. Print artist Katsukawa Shunshō frequently depicted Nakazō, more than he did any other actor.

The verse is signed with Nakazō's pen name Shūkaku, but could be by a patron since it openly praises the actor:

Seiyō no / sora ni hiideshi / ika no tsuru
The sky in spring
Is clear, pierced by
The splendid crane-shaped kite
SHŪKAKU

The crane is an auspicious symbol and the second character (*kaku*) of Nakazō's pen name; it is also the design on the small lacquer *inrō* (container for personal accessories) hanging at his waist. In fact, the poem weaves in both characters that make up the name Shūkaku (read here as *hiide* and *tsuru*, respectively).

This is most likely the middle sheet of a triptych. For an impression paired with the left sheet of Ichikawa Danjūrō V see Sotheby's 1993, no. 78. Another impression of the Danjūrō print in the collection of the Art Institute of Chicago is reproduced in Clark and Ueda 1994, no. 423, and bears the false signature of Sharaku. Danjūrō and Nakazō performed together from the eleventh month of 1778, when Nakazō was head of the troupe at the Morita Theatre in Edo.

See also the painting of Nakazō I attributed to Shunkō (cat. 20).   HI

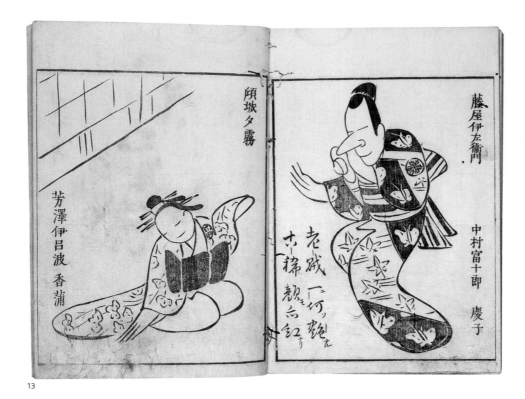

顧城夕霧

芳澤伊呂波香蒲

藤屋伊左衛門

中村富十郎　慶子

老賊一何ッ艶を　杢稀顔点糺す

13

13 Ehon mizu ya sora
Picture Book: Neither Water nor Sky

ILLUSTRATED Nakamura Tomijūrō I as Fujiya Izaemon (right)
and Yoshizawa Iroha I as the courtesan Yūgiri (left)

1780

Artist: Nichōsai

Publisher: Hachimonjiya Hachizaemon

Chūbon book, woodblock, vols 1 and 2 (of 3),
22.2 x 16.0 cm (covers)

Ashmolean Museum, University of Oxford
(X5771/X5772)

The first three Osaka actor-portrait books were
produced by independent artists (*bunjin*, *suijin*)
rather than by professional ukiyo-e artists, as
was the case in Edo. Prefaces and afterwords in
Ehon mizu ya sora (1780), *Suifutei gigafu* (1782,
cat. 14) and *Yakusha mono iwai* (1784, cat. 18)
all insist that the artists are amateurs who love
the theatre.

Ehon mizu ya sora is the first Osaka book of
portraits of actors from the three cities of Osaka,
Kyoto and Edo, one volume given to each city. Its
comic manner was sometimes referred to as
'Toba pictures' (*Toba-e*), after the late Heian
period monk-painter Toba Sōjō (Kakuyū,

1053–1140), who was thought to have originated
the style. The full-length images are not realistic
portraits (*nigao-e*), but more like caricatures,
drawn with considerable warmth and charm (see
also fig. 8 above). Each actor's name, pen name
(*haimyō*) and role is listed, often with a poem or
phrase in Chinese. Little is known about Nichōsai
(d. 1803), a painter-literatus who produced several other illustrated books, including a volume on
the actor Arashi Hinasuke I, *Arashi Koroku: kako
monogatari* (1797). He was active from the late
1770s until his death in 1803. Several of his non-
theatre-related paintings and books are featured
in Kansai Daigaku 1997. He was also known to
have been a talented Jōruri (Bunraku) chanter and
to have painted actor images on fans.

The preface opens modestly, stating 'of course
with drawings a professional is better than an
amateur', but then goes on to insist that the
portraits do indeed capture the essence of the
actors performing on stage. A postscript by
Dōmyaku Sensei (Hatakenaka Kansai, 1752–
1801) – who was considered the equal of the
famous Edo writer and poet Ōta Nanpo in the
composition of comic Chinese poetry (*kyōshi*) –

praises Nichōsai's style as unique and not slave
to any tradition. It is between traditions, neither
'water nor sky' (*mizu ya sora* – the title of the
book). Nichōsai can thus be seen as an important literati figure in an Osaka tradition that
emphasized individuality. Although the Edo
prints and books of professional artist Katsukawa
Shunshō (d. 1792, cats 9–12) would have been
well known to him, he nevertheless chose to
portray actors in his own idiosyncratic style.

A highly significant album of actor paintings,
Rien shoga, by Nichōsai and Ryūkōsai, dated
1788, has recently been rediscovered (Osaka
Museum of History; cat. 19), which includes full-
length, colour portraits comparable in style to
the printed illustrations in this book.

14 Suifutei gigafu
Album of Actor Caricatures by Suifutei

ILLUSTRATED Arashi Hinasuke I

1782

Artist: Suifutei

Privately published

Hanshibon book, woodblock, 1 vol., 26.0 x 16.0 cm
(covers)

The British Museum, London (JH139)

A privately published single volume of idiosyncratic actor portraits, *Suifutei gigafu* is considered to be the first example of 'likeness picture'
(*nigao-e*) portraits in Osaka. Thirty-six actors are
featured, one to a page, each with their acting
name and pen name (*haimyō*) supplied. The
Chinese-style preface criticizes the styles of *Ehon
butai ōgi* (Edo, 1770; cat. 9) and *Ehon mizu ya
sora* (Osaka, 1780; cat. 13), saying that the first
has too much lustre but does not leave a pure,
pleasant resonance, while the second is objec-
tive and cool, but too shallow. Although basically
printed in black and white, there is subtle use of
additional light grey tones to give gradated
effects to the portraits. This book would have
been an important influence on Ryūkōsai, who is
thought already to have been producing fan
paintings of actors around this time.

It is not known who the author of the preface
was, nor is there any idea who Suifutei himself
was. This book is an ultimate expression of the
Osaka *suijin* (literati) sensibility; writers and
artists are modest and remain anonymous to
the public, their real identity known only to
close associates.

14

The preface may be translated as follows:

My friend Suifutei is fond of painting and drama to the same excessive degree as I, but the ingenuity of his hand is marvellous and unfathomable, and I truly am not up to his achievement. In his leisure he drew thirty-six pages of famous actors, which he then showed to me. As I turned the pages, I could not help but burst out with cries. It seemed that I was in the arena of a grand vision. I enjoyed them the whole day, and could not stop admiring them.

Up until now, there has been no shortage of people drawing portraits of actors, and illustrated manuals and albums are very popular. I have often regretted that while [Ehon] Butai ōgi is sensually beautiful [jōen], it does not have enough pure resonance [seiin]. As for [Ehon] Mizu ya sora,

although it is fine – plain and aloof – it is also too light and frivolous. The current book appeared later, and is rich, beautiful, elegant and plain. It has combined what is appropriate in every aspect, and can be called theatre drawings in the proper style. He has not deigned to apply colour, but shows off the marvels of his methods of plain outlining. This is the brushwork of a cultivated gentleman [bunshi] roaming in the realm of art, and there are few in this world who can equal him. Even if we were to bring Zhao Songxue [Zhao Mengfu, 1254–1322] back to life today, or rely on Li Boshi [Li Gonglin, 1049–1106] of past times, I am afraid they would not be able to surpass this. It is regrettable that Suifutei, with his marvellous skill, gave up on [the better things in life] and placed himself in this

situation, and, with all his fine qualities, grew old in the world of the theatre. Could it be because he could not help it? I cannot be free of regrets. Here, because I have the same excessive fondness, I simply write down what I feel. Readers should not laugh at my pedantry.
Alert Immortal from the Realm of Drama (Giiki Kassen)
(Adapted from a trans. by Andrew Lo)

Matsudaira Susumu has written on this book in Matsudaira 1999, and in the introduction to a facsimile edition, *Kinsei Nihon fūzoku ehonshū*, 1979–81.

15

15 Hen and two chicks

Before 1786

Artist: Nakamura Tomijūrō I (Keishi)

Signature: Keishi ga

Fan painting, ink and colour on paper, 48.0 x 35.4 cm (album covers)

Chiba City Museum of Art (*Shikanjō* 2941006)

Keishi (the actor Tomijūrō I, 1719–86) was well known for his skill at painting (see cats 16 and 17). The folding fan here was perhaps painted for a patron and certainly seems to have been used: it is decorated with a simple, spontaneous rendering of a brooding hen and two chicks.

16 *Uta keizu*
Anthology of Song Titles

ILLUSTRATED Mandarin ducks by Keishi (Nakamura Tomijūrō I)

1782

Author: Ryūseki-an Hazumi

Publishers: Yamamoto Heizaemon (Kyoto), Suhara Mohei (Edo), Usuki Saichi and Ōnoki Ichibei (Osaka)

Yoko kohon book, woodblock, 12.5 x 18.4 cm (covers)

Waseda University Theatre Museum, Tokyo (*to*-11-7)

A collection of almost 500 popular song titles with the names of the lyricists and composers listed, but not the lyrics. We know very little about the author, Ryūseki Hazumi, but his name also appears in the miscellany *Kyojitsu satona-*

mari (1794) as a 'patron' (*daijin-kabu*) and 'man of taste' (*sui-kabu*).

In addition there are twelve pictures, including some by leading Osaka artists of the day (in order of appearance): Yoshimura Shūkei (1736–95), Mori Shūhō (1738–1823), Tetteki Dōjin, Ryūkōsai Jokei, Katsura Sōshin (1735–90), Shūrinsai, Shitomi Kangetsu (1747–97), Ōoka Shōsen, Ōoka Shunzan, Nichōsai, Keishi (Tomijūrō) and Fukuhara Gogaku (1730–99).

Yoshimura Shūkei was the son of Yoshimura Shūzan, who painted the screen 'Panorama of Osaka' (cat. 1), and the father of Yoshimura Shūnan, artist of the votive panel 'Rikan as the monkey-trainer Yojirō' (cat. 95). Mori Shūhō was one of the pupils of Yoshimura Shūzan, and his picture of cranes and pine trees reflects his traditional Kano-school training. Katsura Sōshin and Shitomi Kangetsu were both pupils of Tsukioka Settei (1710–86), and Ryūkōsai is said to have been a pupil of Kangetsu. Both Ōoka Shōsen and Shunzan were followers of Ōoka Shunboku (1680–1763), who did commissions for various temples, particularly Daigakuji. Keishi is a pen name of the Kabuki actor Nakamura Tomijūrō I. His inclusion suggests that his painting skill was regarded as comparable to professional artists. Fukuhara Gogaku studied with Ike no Taiga (1723–76) and was an early Osaka literati (*bunjin*) painter. AY

The text and illustrations of this book are fully reproduced in Funakoshi 1930, with a brief introduction.

17 Flowers in a hanging basket

Before 1786

Artist: Nakamura Tomijūrō I (Keishi)

Signature: Keishi ga

Surimono, colour woodblock, 35.4 x 47.8 cm

Private Collection (Japan)

The actor Nakamura Tomijūrō I (d. 1786) was also an accomplished amateur artist, using his pen name Keishi. The illustration shows a gorgeous bouquet of white-and-red peonies, irises, pinks and other flowers arranged in a hanging bamboo basket. The *surimono* features verses by the *haikai* poet Nitoan (Kabutsu), also known as Shii-no-moto IV (d. 1800), and by the actor Ichiyama Shien. Nitoan's anthology of poetry *Tenmei shichinen chōmi saitan* (1787) included verses by a large number of Kabuki actors. He regularly welcomed actors to his poetry group; and he contributed to several Kabuki-related *surimono* (cats 49 and 104), and a preface to *Uta keizu* (cat. 16). He was also active in storytelling clubs (*hanashi-kai*) during the 1770s and 1780s. The *surimono* appears to celebrate the return of Shien after a period of illness.

Kōhone yo / ukigusa no bu o / noite sake
Water lily
Free from the floating weeds
May you bloom
NITOAN

Kakimori Bunko 1991, no. 127.

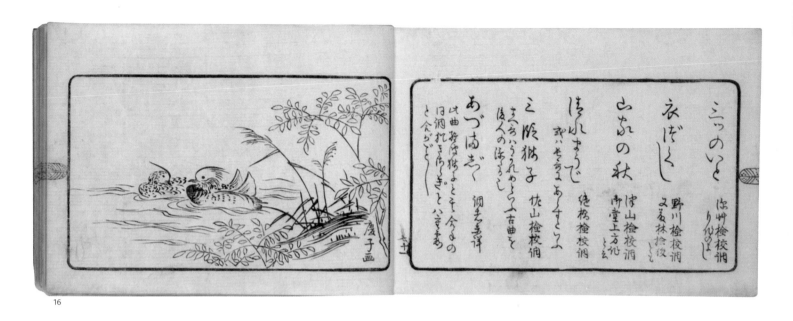

16

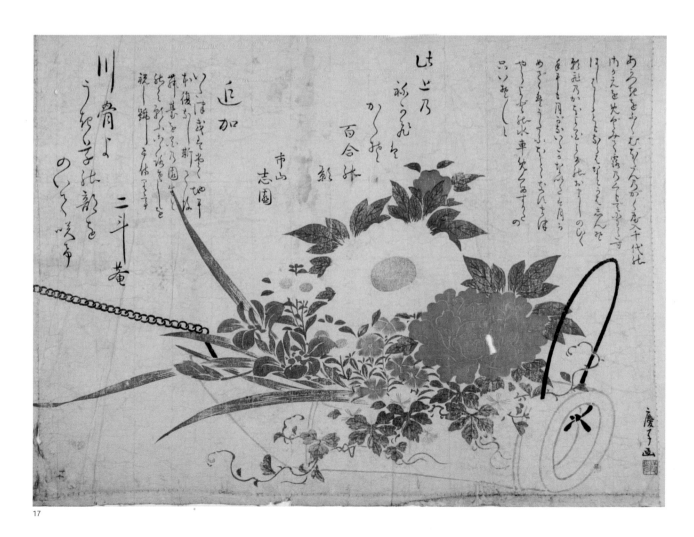

17

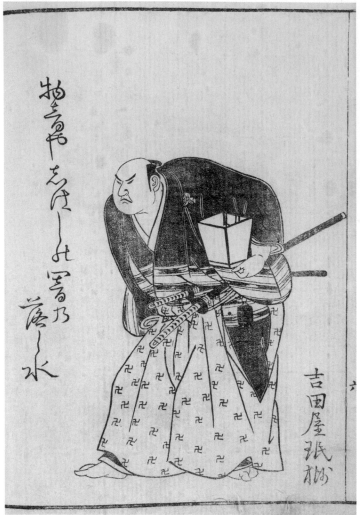

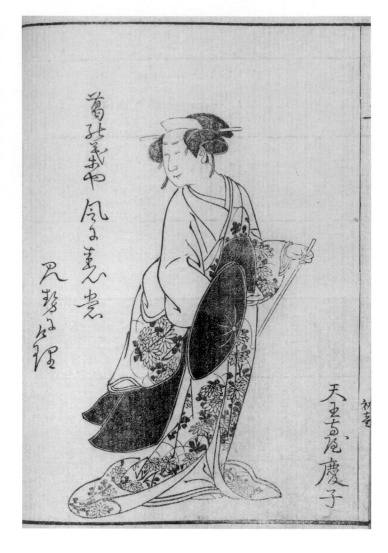

18

18 *Yakusha mono iwai*
A Celebration of Actors

1784

Artist: Ryūkōsai Jokei

Publishers: Inaba Shin'emon and Murakami Kuhei

Hanshibon book, woodblock, 2 vols, 23.6 x 16.8 cm

Freis Collection (USA)

Ryūkōsai's first actor book illustrates forty-nine individuals from the three major cities, each with a poem. The portraits are inscribed only with their stage clan name (*yago*) and haiku pen name (*haimyō*), not with the normal actor name. Like other actor portrait books, *Yakusha mono iwai* presents them as being a part of the larger cultural network of artists and poets. The last page of each volume has a useful table of the actors depicted, listing their *yago*, actor name and *haimyō*.

The preface takes up the theme of amateurs, taking its lead from the two other recent Osaka actor books (cats 13 and 14). An allusion to a passage in the *Analects* of Confucius reappears: 'In painting, one begins with the white [*shiro*] background and after that applies the colour. In all the arts, the heart of the amateur [*shirōto*] comes first; being an amateur, he takes his time to observe and to express the image better.' Ryūkōsai is consciously placed within a tradition of independent artistic expression, free from commercial demands.

Illustrated are two stars of the age: Nakamura Tomijūrō I (Keishi, 1719–86, right) and Arashi Hinasuke I (Minshi, 1741–96, left), each accompanied by a haiku verse. Ryūkōsai was the first artist in either Edo or Osaka consistently to illustrate the female-role actors (*onnagata*) not in the traditional, stylized manner of 'pictures of beautiful women' (*bijinga*), but as individual males with distinctive features.

Tomijūrō appears in the role of Kuzunoha (literally, 'arrowroot leaf'), the 'fox-woman'. The poem, presented as his, reads:

Kuzunoha ya / kaze ni omote mo / misenikeri
The leaf of the arrowroot
Blowing in the wind, shows its regret
Even from the front

This refers to a verse crucial to the plot of the play, and hinges on the notion of *urami* (regret, anger; also divining the future), punned with the back (*ura*) of the arrowroot leaf. The character Kuzunoha is a fox that has taken human form and married. The actor plays quick changes between the two roles, like two sides of a leaf, and the climax is when the fox-woman must reluctantly abandon her husband and son so that the son can grow up in normal human society. He becomes the court soothsayer and diviner Abe no Seimei (921–1005). Tomijūrō, famous for this role, tried to distinguish the feelings for her son of both fox and mother, even while keeping those feelings partially hidden below the surface (for a translation of the play see Brandon and Leiter 2002, vol. 1, pp. 140–62).

19

Hinasuke, of portly stature, appears in a samurai role, holding a square lantern. The poem may be translated as follows:

Mono oto ya / shibashi no yami no / otoshi-mizu
Sharp sounds
A moment of the darkness
Falling drops

For two more contrasting portraits of Hinasuke, see figs 7 and 8.

19 *Rien shoga*
Pleasure Garden of Calligraphy and Paintings
ILLUSTRATED Nakamura Tomijūrō (Keishi) by Nichōsai (right), Minshi (Hinasuke I), Keishi (Tomijūrō I) and Okuyama (Tamejūrō I) by Ryūkōsai (left)

1788 (Preface)

Artists: Ryūkōsai Jokei and Nichōsai

Signatures: Ryūkōsai Jokei, Nichōsai sha

Artist's seals: Ji, Hei (Ryūkōsai)

Album, ink and colour on paper, 3 vols, 26.4 x 19.6 cm (covers)

Osaka Museum of History (Reki 14685)

The album consists of three volumes and contains both half-length and full-length painted portraits of famous actors of the 1780s, together with poems by them and others. The first and second volumes (*jō* and *chū*) contain actor portraits mainly by Ryūkōsai, and the third volume (*ge*) contains ones mainly by Nichōsai. The portraits are on one half of the page-openings facing poems (haiku or *kyōka*) or ink drawings by the actors themselves. There are 132 items altogether.

A certain 'Hōjidō' (his identity in otherwise unknown) compiled the album and wrote the preface. According to the preface and postscript, he had collected hundreds of paintings and calligraphies by famous artists before he started collecting arts relating to Kabuki actors to complete his collection. It is likely that Hōjidō first asked Ryūkōsai and Nichōsai – who were already famous at that time for their Kabuki-related pictures and books – to paint portraits of actors. He then composed the preface and also asked Kabuki actors to add their contributions. The paper is lavishly decorated with a printed cloud-pattern frame and the name 'Hōjidō', which shows his pride as a connoisseur.

The preface is dated 1788 and it is probable that the works were gathered around that time. The individuals depicted include famous actors such as Nakamura Tomijūrō I and Nakamura Utaemon I, and the puppeteer Yoshida Bunzaburō II. There is also a Chinese poem by playwright Namiki Gohei I.   KS

20 Portraits of Edo actors in round windows

c. 1789–90

Artist: Katsukawa Shunkō (attributed, Edo)

Eleven sections from a handscroll (?), ink and colour on paper, various sizes

The British Museum, London (JP ADD 882-4, JP ADD 1084-91)

Painted likeness portraits of leading Edo actors appear inside round windows. From the dates of activity of the actors, these were probably made *c.* 1789–90. Illustrated is a portrait of Nakamura Nakazō I (pen name Shūkaku, 1736–90), who specialized in roles of the evil lover (*iro aku*) and arch villain (*jitsu aku*), and excelled in Kabuki dance. Nakazō was frequently depicted in prints by Edo artist Katsukawa Shunshō (cat. 12) and toured to Osaka just once for a year from late 1786.

It was Shunkō who consolidated the 'bust portrait' or 'big-head' (*ōkubi-e*) actor likenesses of the Katsukawa school in Edo, in a series of seventeen printed portraits he designed between the eighth month, 1788, and the first month, 1790 (p. 41, fig. 22). Shortly after this he fell victim to paralysis of his right hand and ceased to design prints, concentrating instead on paintings done with his left hand.   TC

21 *Ehon niwatazumi*
Picture Book: Flowing Rainwater

1794 (originally 1790)

Artist: Ryūkōsai Jokei

Publishers: Shioya Chūbei, Shioya Kisuke (Osaka), Kikuya Yasubei (Kyoto) and Maekawa Rokuzaemon (Edo)

Hanshibon book, woodblock, 3 vols, 21.5 x 15.4 cm (covers)

Hendrick Lühl Collection (Germany)

A total of seventy actors are portrayed in role, facing one another on opposite pages, as if on stage with background scenery. The style is very close to later single-sheet prints and must have influenced the development of actor prints in both Osaka and Edo; the book was published in all three main cities – Osaka , Kyoto and Edo. The colophon of this copy is that of *Ehon hana ayame*, published in 1794 (cat. 37). *Niwatazumi* was rebound together with a few pages from *Hana ayame* and its preface. The original preface for *Niwatazumi* is by Nishimura Teiga (Suisenshi, 1744–1826) (see also cat. 67). The advertisement for *Niwatazumi* makes its selling point clear: the artist 'captures the actors' poses [*miburi*] and details of the stage props'.

Ryūkōsai may have been influenced by a much earlier book by the Edo artist Katsukawa Shunshō, with the attributed title *Yakusha kuni no hana* (*Actors: Flowers of the Realm*, about

20

1772; only a few pages are known in the collection of the Art Institute of Chicago). These colour illustrations show actors in plays with full background scenery, and continue across the page opening. However, Shunshō's book seems to have had very limited circulation; the blocks may have been destroyed in the major Edo fire of 1772 (see Clark and Ueda 1994, pp. 164–71).

Nakamura Tomijūrō I (d. 1786) is shown in the dance-play *Musume Dōjōji*, a role for which he was famous. *Kyota* (Waseda) 10: 28 has a painting attributed to Ryūkōsai of the actor in the same pose, possibly from *Kyoganoko musume Dōjōji* at the Kita Theatre, Kyoto, in the third month, 1783. The seal, lower left on the illustrated page, is of the Nanki Bunko collection.

21

22 Yoshizawa Iroha I as Ariwara no Narihira

PLAY *Hana kurabe Ise monogatari* at the Kado Theatre; twelfth month, 1791

Artist: Ryūkōsai Jokei

Signature: Ryūkōsai ga

Publisher's seal: Ki

Hosoban, colour woodblock with embossing, 31.6 x 14.8 cm

The British Museum, London (2004.7-1.01)

Yoshizawa Iroha I (Ayame V, 1755–1810) was a female role specialist (*onnagata*) but here he plays Ariwara no Narihira (825–80), the famous male poet–lover of the courtly Heian period. Gallant yet effeminate in appearance, in the scene depicted Narihira is either coming from a tryst or perhaps setting off for another. It was common for *onnagata* to play male lover roles, especially courtiers or men with delicate features. Iroha was the grandson of the great Yoshizawa Ayame I and the son of Ayame III.

The play, written by a team led by Nagawa Kamesuke and Tatsuoka Mansaku, was first performed in the fourth month, 1775, at the Naka Theatre, Osaka, and was revived regularly in Kyoto–Osaka until the 1860s. Later published versions included an illustrated Kabuki playbook (*e-iri nehon*), entitled *Date kurabe Ise monogatari* (1828).

One of Narihira's affairs in *Tales of Ise* is with a woman known as Izutsu, daughter of the aristocrat Ki no Aritsune. Izutsu means 'well-curb' and evokes the later famous Noh play in which the spirit of Narihira's lover, obsessed with his memory, gazes into the well water and imagines she sees him in her own reflection, in a moment of passionate madness. This story is alluded to in a print attributed to Ryūkōsai of Hinasuke I as Odai (cat. 24).

At the time of his affair with Izutsu, Narihira was also visiting another woman in Takayasu (called Ikoma in this play). Both women pursue Narihira's love and all three become involved in an imperial succession dispute between two brothers: Prince Koretaka, the older of the two, characterized as a reckless, cruel usurper; and the younger, Prince Korehito, who is forced to defer to him. Narihira is portrayed as an elegant if effete courtier, who is nonetheless loyal and eventually helps to overthrow Koretaka's evil forces and ensure the accession of the admirable Korehito.

22

This is a magnificent example of the elaborate and carefully balanced compositions found in Ryūkōsai's earliest prints. Pastel pinks and reds evoke a delicate mood, appropriate to the elegant poet–lover. The supple outer robe has a pattern of pink plum blossom on a faint pink background, with wisteria on the green lower robe. Blind-printing is used to pick out a pattern on the inner white robe, and slight gradation on the rain hat skilfully creates volume. The light grey background may represent evening. Ryūkōsai is at pains to create a sense of space around the actor, joining the fence and gate at an angle that projects deep into the composition.

Chronologically, this is the second colour actor print by Ryūkōsai currently known, and the only recorded impression. His first was for a performance only one month earlier: Nakayama Raisuke as Momonoi Wakasanosuke in *Chūshingura* at the Naka Theatre in the eleventh month, 1791 (ex-coll. Huguette Beres, Paris). Very few Ryūkōsai prints of his earliest group from 1791–4 have survived, implying perhaps that the print runs were very small and that they were sponsored by patrons.　　AY

23

23 Sawamura Tosshi (Sōjūrō III) as Nankata Yohei

PLAY *Miyako Kiyomizu yo-gaichō* at the Naka Theatre; intercalary second month, 1792

Artist: Ryūkōsai Jokei (attributed)

Hosoban, colour woodblock, 30.3 x 13.4 cm

Mukogawa Women's University, Nishinomiya

Sawamura Sōjūrō III (Tosshi, 1753–1801) was one of the great Edo actors of his time, very popular as a handsome male lead. He regularly performed in Kyoto and Osaka as well, and is prominent in both Edo and Osaka prints. He is usually portrayed in Edo with a relatively slight build and a thin face, but Ryūkōsai depicts him as a more robust figure. Although the performance depicted dates from the second month, 1792, the more simple style would possibly suggest a later date. Actor prints were in general produced around the time of the performance, but Ryūkōsai may also have designed retrospective prints on request from patrons. Sōjūrō came to Osaka in the eleventh month of 1791, performed for a year, then returned to Edo in the first month of 1793. He came again to Osaka in the eleventh month, 1793, and then left for Edo in the first month of 1794, not to return for another five years.

Ex-coll. Okada Isajirō.

24 Arashi (Kanō) Hinasuke I as Higaki no Odai

PLAY *Shōbukawa yakko Dōjōji* at the Kado Theatre; first month, 1793

Artist: Ryūkōsai Jokei (attributed)

Publisher: Shioya Rinbei (mark trimmed)

Hosoban, colour woodblock, 30.3 x 13.4 cm

The British Museum, London (2004.3-27.02)

The playwright Nishizawa Ippō noted that the play was a flop and ran for only a week (*Denki*

25

sakusho, quoted in *Kabuki nenpyō*, vol. 5, p. 149). Hinasuke played two roles, the male lead Watanabe Tōru and the old woman Odai. Ippō added, however, 'How striking it was when Odai came to the well dressed in a courtier's hat [*kanmuri*] and gazed at her reflection in the water below'. The scene alludes to the poet Narihira's lover in the Noh play *Izutsu* (*The Well Curb*), who dons his courtier cap and looks into the well, seeing in a moment of supernatural madness not herself but his reflection. Hinasuke had played female roles in his youth but generally switched to male lead roles from midcareer.

Although this print does not have an artist's signature, it can be securely attributed to Ryūkōsai because of the date of the performance and the style of representation. In his sketchbook *Ryūkōsai ikō* (*Testament Manuscript by Ryūkōsai*) the artist wrote that it was necessary to imagine the unclothed body of the actor when preparing an actor print (quoted in Haruyama 1931, p. 18). This design achieves a successful and relatively realistic representation of Hinasuke's massive body. Many of Ryūkōsai's signed prints show that he was also concerned to create a geometrically stable composition. The large well at the bottom left corner supports and balances the mass of Hinasuke's body in the middle of the picture, and the cherry tree stretching toward the top right corner systematically connects the well and figure, completing the diagonal composition. The delicate depiction of flowers, courtier's hat, folds of the robe and the old woman's grey hair also achieves a remarkable effect of complementing and softening Hinasuke's large body.

This impression was formerly in the Okada Isajirō collection (Haruyama 1931). Another impression, formerly in the Berès Collection, Paris, includes part of the mark of the publisher Shioya Rinbei (*Hizō ukiyo-e taikan*, Berès Collection, 1991, no. 104). A third impression is in the Museum of Fine Arts, Boston (Bigelow Collection).　　AY

25 Ichikawa Danzō IV as Oguri Buzen

PLAY *Shōbukawa yakko Dōjōji* at the Kado Theatre; first month, 1793

Artist: Ryūkōsai Jokei (attributed)

Publisher: Daisa (Osakaya Sashichi)

Hosoban, colour woodblock, 32.0 x 14.3 cm

Waseda University Theatre Museum, Tokyo (016-0758)

This is from the same production as cat. 24. Danzō was known for his rough look and masculine power. Here he is shown with sword drawn, the top half of his outer *kosode* robe shrugged off and striking a defiant pose.

26 Onoe Shinshichi (Fujaku) as Isshiki Yūki no Kami

PLAY *Keisei yanagi-zakura* at the Naka Theatre;
first month, 1793

Artist: Ryūkōsai Jokei (attributed)

Publisher: Shioya Chōbei

Hosoban, colour woodblock, 32.7 x 14.3 cm

Mukogawa Women's University, Nishinomiya

'Courtesan' (*keisei*) plays were regularly produced for New Year productions in Osaka. This
was the first production of this play by Tatsuoka
Mansaku and Chikamatsu Tokuzō. The story was
based on the Yanagizawa uprising in the seventeenth century as well as the Christian
Shimabara uprising in 1639, but transposed further back, into the fifteenth century. Shinshichi
played one of the dashing heroes of this tale of
a plot to overthrow the Ashikaga shogunate.

Ryūkōsai produced several prints for this performance: cat. 27; a print of Arashi Sangorō II
(Matsudaira [Waseda] 1995(c), vol. 4, no. 3);
Yoshizawa Iroha I (Schwaab 1989, no. 3);
Yamashita Kinsaku II (*Ukiyoe taikei*, vol. 7, no.
171); and further scenes are depicted in his
illustrated book *Ehon hana ayame* (1794, cat. 36).

Compare with the carved wooden portrait
mask of Shinshichi I (cat. 76).

Ex-coll. Okada Isajirō.

27 Yamamura Giemon II as Sakae Hida no Kami

PLAY *Keisei yanagi-zakura* at the Naka Theatre; first month, 1793

Artist: Ryūkōsai Jokei

Signature: Ryūkōsai, with handwritten seal (*kaō*)

Publisher: Shioya Rinbei

Hosoban, colour woodblock, 30.9 x 14.1 cm

Chiba City Museum of Art (2933155)

Yamamura Giemon II (1736–1803) is shown in the villainous role of Sakae Hida no Kami, disguised as a mountain bandit. He plans an insurrection against his own lord, the Ashikaga shogunate. Interesting comparisons can be made with the painted portrait of the actor in *Kyota* (Waseda) 13: 43 and the printed portrait in *Ehon niwatazumi* (cat. 21). Giemon was a villain-role specialist, particularly skilled at the portrayal of crafty older characters. This is a magnificent early print by Ryūkōsai, carefully composed and powerfully executed.

See cat. 26 for a list of other prints that relate to this performance.

Ex-coll. Helmut Kühne; Chiba-shi Bijutsukan 2001, no. 190.

27

28 Arashi (Kanō) Hinasuke I as Akizuka Tatewaki

PLAY *Keisei mutsu no tamagawa* at the Kado Theatre; second month, 1793

Artist: Ryūkōsai Jokei

Signature: Ryūkōsai, with handwritten seal (*kaō*)

Publisher: Shioya Rinbei

Hosoban, colour woodblock, 31.5 x 14.1 cm

The British Museum, London (2004.3-27.01)

The play, by Namiki Jūsuke (worked 1748–1801), was first performed in the first month, 1767. It transplants the famous story of factional fighting within the Date fief of Sendai (*Date sōdō*) to a location yet further north in the country. Tatewaki is one of the heroes, who saves the clan from the evil machinations of the villain Kageyu. This is one of Ryūkōsai's finest single-sheet prints: imposing and serious, with a monumentality that transcends the modest format.

An alternate (presumed later) printing is known, with the name of the role removed (Schwaab 1989, no. 1).

Ex-coll. Okada Isajirō; Kuroda 1929, no. 52.

29 Hanagiri Shisei (Toyomatsu III) as Ohaya

PLAY *Hirai Gonpachi Yoshiwara-gayoi* at the Kado Theatre; third month, 1793

Artist: Ryūkōsai Jokei (attributed)

Hosoban, colour woodblock, 30.9 x 13.5 cm

Mukogawa Women's University, Nishinomiya

Hanagiri Toyomatsu III (1743–96) made his debut as a child performer (*iroko*) in Osaka in 1756, and performed regularly in Osaka and Kyoto. He was known for his realistic acting rather than for his dance skills, and was not considered a beautiful female role specialist (*onnagata*). Toyomatsu is also portrayed in a similar pose in Ryūkōsai's *Ehon niwatazumi* (1790, cat. 21).

Ex-coll. Okada Isajirō.

30 Hanagiri Toyomatsu ?IV (Sanchō)

c. Mid- to late 1790s

Artist: Ryūkōsai Jokei (attributed)

Publisher: Shioya Chōbei

Hosoban, colour woodblock, 30.3 x 13.3 cm

Mukogawa Women's University, Nishinomiya

The identification and dating of this print are not straightforward. The names of the actor, clearly visible on the print, would suggest that this is Toyomatsu III (1743–96), whose pen name is also listed as Sanchō in Ryūkōsai's book *Ehon hana ayame* (1794, cat. 37). Indeed, it has been suggested that this print depicts Toyomatsu III in the role of Akishino in the play *Taiheiki kikusui no maki* at the Kado Theatre in the ninth month, 1793. However, Toyomatsu III is also recorded as using the pen name Shisei (cats 18, 21 and 29).

29

The actor Hanagiri Tomimatsu is portrayed in the Ryūkōsai books *Ehon niwatazumi* and *Ehon hana ayame* under the pen name Sanchō. Tomimatsu was Toyomatsu III's son and they are recorded as living in the same house. Comparing the two prints cats 29 and 30 would suggest that these are two different actors and that the actor in cat. 29 is much older. The portrait in cat. 30 is similar to the Tomimatsu figure in *Ehon hana ayame*. However, we have no definite record that Tomimatsu succeeded to the name Toyomatsu, and he disappeared from the playbills of the top theatres later the same year that Toyomatsu III died, 1796. Very little is known of Tomimatsu's later career, other than that after the death of his father he came under the tutelage of Yoshizawa Iroha I (Ayame V, 1755–1810) and is thought to have died young (Ihara 1913, p. 243). It is suggested on the basis of this print that he may have briefly taken the name Toyomatsu IV. Another impression (Private Collection, Japan) shows the round shapes in the background to be flowers.

Ex-coll. Okada Isajirō.

30

31 Asao Tamejūrō I as Ishidō Kageyu

PLAY *Taiheiki kikusui no maki* at the Kado Theatre; ninth month, 1793

Artist: Ryūkōsai Jokei (attributed)

Publisher: Shioya Chōbei

Hosoban, colour woodblock, 31.5 x 14.1 cm

Mukogawa Women's University, Nishinomiya

Tamejūrō was famous for his villain-role characters. However, Kageyu is not a true villain, but simply a character caught up in the civil war between the Northern and Southern Courts. Tamejūrō performed this role several times. The text to the right was handwritten with a brush and says 'on arrival at Osaka in the New Year, 1802' (the significance is unclear).

Ex-coll. Okada Isajirō.

32a, b Anegawa Shinshirō III (Ikkō) as Ishidome Busuke

PLAY *Igagoe norikake gappa* at the Kado Theatre; eleventh month, 1793

Artist: Ryūkōsai Jokei (attributed)

Publisher: Shioya Chōbei

Hosoban, colour woodblock, left sheet of a triptych, 31.6 x 14.2 cm (a), 31.5 x 14.2 cm (b)

Mukogawa Women's University, Nishinomiya (a, illustrated)

Waseda University Theatre Museum, Tokyo (016-0773) (b)

The play, written by Nagawa Kamesuke, was first performed in the twelfth month, 1776, at the Naka Theatre in Osaka. It was based on two incidents in the castle town of Iga Ueno in the early seventeenth century: one a vendetta carried out by a samurai who avenged the murder of his younger brother; and the other a power struggle and scandal in the same Ikeda fief. The vendetta and power struggle incidents were put together and transformed into an elaborate tale that was retold time and again in the puppet theatre (Jōruri), popular storytelling (*kōdan*) and Kabuki.

Roger Keyes has argued that this print is the left sheet of a triptych, showing a scene in which Karaki Masaemon (Arashi Hinasuke I) (centre) and Ishodome Busuke (Shinshirō) (left) confront the villain Kawai Matagorō (Asao Tamejūrō I) (right). The left and centre sheets from the original triptych were reissued by the publisher almost twelve years later for a performance of the same play in the eighth month, 1805. The signature of an otherwise unknown artist, Rankōsai, was added. The blocks were plugged and re-carved in the areas of the heads to depict the new actors; in the case of this left sheet Arashi Isaburō I replaced Shinshirō III. Plugging small areas of old printing blocks with new wood

31

32a

and re-carving the heads was a not uncommon practice used by publishers to save money.

For a full account of the vicissitudes of this design see Keyes and Mizushima 1973, pp. 50–51, no. 5.

Ex-coll. Okada Isajirō (cat. 32a).

33 Asao Tamejūrō I (right, front) as Yamaguchi Kurojirō, Ichikawa Danzō IV (left, front) as Konoshita Tōkichi, Seki Sanjūrō I (left, rear) as Oda Harunaga, and two other actors

PLAY *Meisho zue hana no konoshita* at the Kado Theatre; second month, 1792

Artist: Ryūkōsai Jokei

Signature: Ryūkōsai ga

Publisher's seal: Ki

Ōban, colour woodblock with embossing, 35.2 x 24.3 cm

Private Collection (Japan)

This is the only known *ōban*-sized print by Ryūkōsai. There is the clear sense that the artist is challenging his medium by depicting five figures in different positions within a single composition. The scene is a contest between two warriors, Kurojirō and Tōkichi (the historical Toyotomi Hideyoshi), in the presence of Lord Harunaga (the historical Oda Nobunaga) and two other vassals. Ryūkōsai pioneered the style of representing actors as if on stage with background props in his book *Ehon niwatazumi* (1790; cat. 21). Here he applies the same technique in the vertical *ōban* format. The overlap of figures is logically composed and the group inhabits a single consistent space. This impression is in a very fine state of preservation. The general colour scheme and the embossing technique on the robes are similar to Ryūkōsai's design of Yoshizawa Iroha (cat. 22), published only two months earlier, which also has the same publisher's seal. AY

Nihon Keizai Shimbun 1975, no. 13; Matsudaira 1999, p. 115, no. 79.

34

34 Nakamura Noshio II (Rankō) as Yūgiri (right) and Izumikawa Tatezō I (Karyō) as Izaemon (left)

PLAY *Keisei Awa no Naruto* at the Kado Theatre; eleventh month, 1793

Artist: Ryūkōsai Jokei (attributed)

Publisher: Shioya Chōbei

Hosoban, colour woodblock, diptych, 32.0 x 14.3 cm (right), 30.8 x 13.5 cm (left)

Victoria & Albert Museum, London (right, E52-1969); Private Collection (Japan, left)

Yūgiri (1654–78) was a famous courtesan in Osaka's Shinmachi pleasure quarter and her suitor Fujiya Izaemon was from a rich Osaka family. Their love story was a popular theme for both puppet and Kabuki theatres from the 1690s onwards, and is still regularly performed today as the play *Kuruwa bunshō*, originally written by Chikamatsu Monzaemon (1653–1725).

This is a rare example of a diptych by Ryūkōsai in the *hosoban* format, here reunited from different collections for the first time.

Matsudaira in *Hizō ukiyo-e taikan*, vol. 5, 1989, pp. 260–61, no. 139.

35 Yoshizawa Hakō (Iroha I) as Umegae (right) and Arashi Raishi (Sangorō II) as Kajiwara Genta (left)

PLAY *Hiragana seisuiki* at the Tenma Theatre; third month, 1798

Artist: Ryūkōsai Jokei (attributed)

Hosoban, colour woodblock, diptych, 30.3 x 13.3 cm (right), 32.2 x 14.7 cm (left)

Mukogawa Women's University, Nishinomiya

35

This records the final farewell performance (*issei ichidai*) of the Kyoto actor Arashi Sangorō II at the Tenma Tenjin Shrine, Osaka. He performed a medley of roles and the proceeds went to the shrine. Just a few months earlier Ryūkōsai had portrayed the actor in his twenty-two favourite roles in the book *Kiri no shimadai* (eleventh month, 1797; cat. 67) to mark the occasion when Sangorō changed his stage name to Raishi and

his son succeeded him to become Sangorō III. Yoshizawa Iroha (Ayame V, 1755–1810) was one of the stars of his day, a grandson of the great Ayame I. Iroha performed regularly with Sangorō.

For a Shōkōsai print of Sangorō in another role from the same performance see cat. 89. For another fine Ryūkōsai design of Iroha see Schwaab 1989, no. 3.

Ex-coll. Okada Isajirō.

36 *Ehon hana ayame*
Picture Book: Iris Flowers

First month, 1794

Artist: Ryūkōsai Jokei

Publisher: Shioya Chōbei

Hanshibon book, woodblock, 2 vols, 21.5 x 15.8 cm
(covers)

Waseda University Theatre Museum, Tokyo
(*i*-11-815-1/2)

The iris is often associated with actors in Japan, where there is a long tradition of describing an actor's performance as a blossom. Thirty-nine pairs of actors are shown in role facing one another across the page-openings. The style is very close to later single-sheet prints of actors interacting in dramatic poses in front of stage props. Ryūkōsai was at his most active in the period 1790–94, with the issue of two major actor books and nearly all of his single-sheet colour prints in the *hosoban* format. His books and prints would have been available to Edo artists, such as Utagawa Toyokuni and Sharaku, who flourished in the mid-1790s.

Illustrated is Azuma Tōzō III (1756–98) as Fuji no Kata (right) and Onoe Shinshichi I as Kumagai no Jirō Naozane (left) in *Ichinotani futaba gunki* at the Naka Theatre, Osaka, in the fifth month, 1793.

37 Nakamura Noshio II as Okaru (top), Arashi Hinasuke I as Ōboshi Yuranosuke (middle) and Asao Tamejūrō I as Ono Kudayū (bottom)

PLAY *Kanadehon Chūshingura*

c. 1790s

Artist: Ryūkōsai Jokei

Signature: Ryūkōsai Jokei

Artist's seal: Ryūkōsai

Hanging scroll, ink and colour on paper,
117.3 x 15.5 cm

The British Museum, London (Japanese Painting
ADD 1261)

This vertical composition shows the famous scene from Act Seven of *Chūshingura*, set in the Ichiriki brothel in Kyoto. Yuranosuke, leader of a group of loyal samurai secretly plotting to avenge the death of their lord, feigns that he has lost all interest in the revenge by wallowing in dissipation. One night he receives a letter from his former master's wife about the plot. He tries to read it discretely out on a veranda, under the light of a lantern. At that moment Okaru, who has sold herself into prostitution to help her husband (another member of the vendetta group), happens to be on a balcony on the upstairs floor. She reads the letter surreptitiously in her pocket mirror, suspecting it to be from another of Yuranosuke's sweethearts. Simultaneously, the villain Kudayū, who is hiding under the floorboards of the veranda, reads the letter from below. Suddenly

Okaru's ornamental hairpin accidentally drops down with a clatter, and Yuranosuke realizes that she has read the secret letter.

Yuranosuke is shown holding Okaru's hairpin and speaking to her. Realizing she now knows the plan, he suggests that he buy out her contract to make her his wife, intending to kill her to keep the contents of the letter secret. He hides the letter but has not yet noticed Kudayū beneath the veranda.

Ryūkōsai, a pupil of Osaka painter Shitomi Kangetsu (1747–97), is considered to be the founder of the Kamigata (Kyoto–Osaka) region tradition of actor portraiture. Here the faces of the actors are drawn with considerable sophistication. The technique was first to draw some slight strokes to fix the proportion of the eyes, nose and mouth, and then to depict each facial feature with very thin lines in dark ink. In contrast, the outlines of the costumes were drawn in quick and bold lines. For Hinasuke and Tamejūrō, white or skin-colour pigment was applied before the ink lines and other colours. For the face of the female character played by Noshio, in contrast, no white paint is apparent. Instead, a very slight red was applied to both sides of the eyes and neck.

The actors represented are Nakamura Noshio II (1759–1800), Arashi Hinasuke I (1741–96) and Asao Tamejūrō I (1735–1804). Noshio looks somewhat similar to his adoptive father Nakamura Tomijūrō I (cats 18 and 21), who was always drawn with a distinctive mouth that has an accent at the edge, and small eyes. However, Tomijūrō was never drawn with the single-fold eyelids seen here. Hinasuke is one of the main

actors featured in Ryūkōsai's prints (cats 24 and 28) and always represented as sturdily built. Tamejūrō is often represented as quite ugly (cats 31 and 33), with bulging eyes, and he usually played villain roles (*jitsuaku*). Although each actor played these roles at some point in their career, it seems that they never performed them together in the same production. The painting therefore represents an ideal, imaginary line-up (*mitate*), performed by the most popular actors of the time. Perhaps this was a special commission from one of Ryūkōsai's patrons.

Since it does not refer to a particular performance, the painting is difficult to date exactly. Noshio left for Edo in the eleventh month, 1794, and stayed there until the end of 1799. Hinasuke 'retired' for the first time at the end of 1789, although he continued to perform until his death in 1796. At the New Year of 1794, Hinasuke acceded to the name Arashi Koroku III. Hinasuke, Noshio and Tamejūrō all performed together regularly from the ninth month, 1793, until the third month, 1794. The painting could, therefore, be a memorial for Hinasuke's 'retirement', or a farewell for Noshio. The only dated Ryūkōsai paintings are in the album *Rien shoga* (1788, cat. 19). The four years from 1790 to 1794 were his busiest period for actor publications.

The tall rectangular format is reminiscent of a 'pillar print' (*hashira-e*). Several examples parodying this scene were created by late eighteenth-century Edo ukiyo-e artists such as Isoda Koryūsai and Torii Kiyonaga in the 1770s and 80s. These were the likely model for Ryūkōsai's composition.   AY

Ex-coll. Okada Isajirō.

36

37

37 detail

38

38 Illustrated handscroll of actors in plays (*Kyōgen-zukushi zukan*)

Mid- to late 1790s

Artist: Ryūkōsai Jokei

Title: Kyōgen-zukushi Naniwa Ryūkōsai hitsu ('Actors in plays by Ryūkōsai of Osaka')

Handscroll, ink and colour on paper, 26.7 x 857.5 cm

Chiba City Museum of Art (2911009)

This rare painted handscroll of thirty-four Osaka Kabuki actors would have been commissioned by a Kabuki patron, and shows the stars of the Osaka stage in the 1790s.

Illustrated is a scene most likely from a performance of *Yoso-oi rokkasen* at the Naka Theatre in the eleventh month, 1789. This was a dance piece, presented as part of the retirement performance of Arashi Hinasuke I (see also cat. 65). The actors portrayed are (from the right): Ogawa Kichitarō II (1760–94); the Edo actor Azuma Tōzō III (1756–98), who performed in Osaka at Hinasuke's retirement production; Sawamura Kunitarō I in the role of Komachi – the most famous female poet and a contemporary of Ariwara no Narihira; Hinasuke I; Anegawa Minato; and Arashi Sangorō II (Matsudaira considered this last to be Arashi Bungorō). Hinasuke performs the role of the famous ninth-century poet–courtier–lover Narihira. The poetry of Narihira and Komachi is celebrated for its striking imagery and passion, which the Kabuki dance reflects. Hinasuke played five poets in this production to great acclaim, and Hinasuke and Kunitarō repeated these roles in Kyoto in the third month, 1790, and again at the Kita Shinchi Theatre, Osaka, in 1791. Finally Hinasuke performed the role one more time, opposite Yoshizawa Iroha I as Komachi, at the Kado

Theatre in the first month, 1796. The play then formed the basis for later revivals in Osaka and Edo (see cats 265 and 273–4).

This is one of the most sustained performances by Ryūkōsai in painting to have survived. A comparison with the recently rediscovered album of portrait paintings by Ryūkōsai and Nichōsai, *Rien shoga* (cat. 19), shows how here he has developed a very different style of depicting actors interacting with others in performance on stage. This style is also evident in two of Ryūkōsai's actor books, *Ehon niwatazumi* (1790, cat. 21) and *Ehon hana ayame* (1794, cat. 36).

For reproductions of the complete scroll see Chiba-shi Bijutsukan 2001, no. 43, and *Nikuhitsu ukiyo-e taikan*, vol. 10, 1995, no. 59, which has a commentary by Matsudaira Susumu.

39 Sawamura Kunitarō I as Ran no Kata

PLAY *Kana-utsushi Azuchi mondō* at the Naka Theatre; eleventh month, 1794

Artist: Shunko

Signature: Shunko ga

Hosoban, woodblock with stencil-printed colours (*kappa-zuri*), 32.0 x 15.0 cm

Waseda University Theatre Museum, Tokyo (016-0397)

This is a rare print by the otherwise unknown Shunko (not to be confused with Shunkō, the early name used by Hokushū). It is perhaps an early example of a Kabuki fan designing a print of his favourite actor.

The design is modelled on the portrait of Kunitarō I in Ryūkōsai's *Ehon niwatazumi* (1790, cat. 21).

39

40 Album of Edo actor prints by Katsukawa school artists

c. 1770s–1790

Artists: Shunshō, Shunkō and Shun'ei (Edo)

Album of *hosoban* prints, colour woodblock, 30.7 x 42.8 cm (covers)

SOAS, University of London (Japanese Prints 44/1-100)

The album contains eighty-four Edo actor prints by artists of the Katsukawa school, all in the small, narrow *hosoban* format – many forming diptychs and triptychs, and one pentaptych. Most (sixty-three) are by Katsukawa Shunshō, seventeen are by Shun'ei and three are by Shunkō. The three prints illustrated do not form a triptych.

(right)

Ichikawa Ebizō (Danjūrō V) as Banzui Chōbei

PLAY *Gozen-gakari sumō Soga* at the Kawarazaki Theatre (Edo); second month, 1793

Artist: Katsukawa Shun'ei (Edo)

Signature: Shun'ei ga

Publisher: Nishimuraya Yohachi (Edo)

The scene takes place in Suzugamori forest. The chivalrous commoner Banzui Chōbei swears blood-brotherhood with the samurai Shirai Gonpachi (played by Iwai Hanshirō IV, not shown), who has become the leader of some bandits in order to search for a missing heirloom sword. This was the performance at which the great Edo actor Ichikawa Danjūrō V changed his acting name to Ebizō.

(centre)

Sawamura Sōjūrō III as Teraoka Hei'emon

PLAY *Kanadehon Chūshingura* at the Nakamura Theatre (Edo); fifth month, 1787

Artist: Katsukawa Shunkō (Edo)

Signature: Shunkō ga

This is from Act Seven of the play, when Hei'e-mon comes to the Ichirikiya brothel, Kyoto, to see his sister Okaru, and Yuranosuke. Okaru (played by Arashi Murajirō, not shown) has sold herself into prostitution to assist the cause of the loyal samurai. However, she has inadvertently seen the contents of a secret letter sent to Yuranosuke, their leader, and her brother Hei'emon now draws his sword to kill her, thereby ensuring her silence and demonstrating his commitment to the cause. An early scene in this act is depicted in the hanging scroll painting by Ryūkōsai (cat. 37).

(left)

Osagawa Tsuneyo II as a female character

c. 1786–9

Artist: Katsukawa Shunkō (Edo)

Signature: Shunkō ga

For another impression ex-coll. Henri Vever, see Sotheby's 1974, no. 131.   HI

41 Ichikawa Komazō III (Kōrai-ya, Kinshō)

c. 1791–3

Artist: Katsukawa Shun'ei (Edo)

Signature: Shun'ei ga

Publisher: Iseya Jisuke (Edo)

Censorship seal: *kiwame*

Hosoban, colour woodblock, 31.1 x 13.3 cm

The British Museum, London (1906.12-20.0170)

Although the precise role has not been identified, with unkempt wig and a touch of sinister blue makeup around the eyes, the Edo actor Ichikawa Komazō III (1764–1838) is shown drawing his sword in one of the villainous roles that would become his speciality for many decades to come (after 1801 using the name Matsumoto Kōshirō V). He was nicknamed 'big nose' (*hanadaka*) Komazō, as apparent in this likeness. At least four more designs are known with the same blue background, each giving an actors' stage clan sobriquet (*yagō*) and poetry name (*haimyō*). Their periods of activity suggest a date for the series of *c.* 1791–3.

After fellow pupil Shunkō fell victim to paralysis of his right hand in about the spring of 1790, and the death of their teacher Shunshō in 1792, Shun'ei was left as the leading artist of the Katsukawa school in Edo that specialized in actor portraiture. Within a few years he would be challenged in this by the new Utagawa school, led by the young Toyokuni (1769–1825). In contrast to the balance and poise that had characterized Shunshō's actor prints of the 1770s and 1780s, Edo actor portraits of the 1790s have a nervous, excited quality that seems to reflect in some way the tenor of the age.   TC

Hizō ukiyo-e taikan, vol. 2, 1987, pp. 255–6, no. 111.

42 Sawamura Sōjūrō III as Ōgishi Kurando

PLAY *Hana-ayame Bunroku Soga* at the Miyako Theatre
(Edo); fifth month, 1794
Artist: Katsukawa Shun'ei (Edo)
Signature: Shun'ei ga
Publisher: Tsuruya Kiemon (Edo)
Censorship seal: *kiwame*
Ōban, colour woodblock, 36.5 x 24.0 cm
The British Museum, London (2004.5-5.02)

Sōjūrō III was a very popular actor of male
leads in both Edo and Kyoto–Osaka. The play
transposes historical events of the so-called
'Soga Brothers' revenge of the Genroku era
(1688–1704)' – a vendetta by samurai of the
Kameyama domain against their father's
enemy – to the distant Bunroku era (1592–6).
Ōgishi Kurando is an honourable character who
finally assists the brothers Ishii Gennojō and
Ishii Hanjirō in the revenge.

After the partial paralysis suffered by Shunkō in
early 1790 and the death of their teacher
Shunshō in 1792, Shun'ei was left as the mainstay
of the Katsukawa school of Kabuki print designers
in Edo. From the New Year, 1794, he was challenged first by Utagawa Toyokuni (cats 47 and
48) and then, from the fifth month of that year
(the date of this print), by Sharaku (cats 43–6).
However, Shun'ei seems to have been the first
artist to use a shiny, printed mica background for
his half-length portraits of actors from the New
Year, 1794, in the medium (*aiban*) size.

This larger, *ōban*-sized portrait originally had a
pale blue background, now almost completely
faded. It depicts the same actor, role and performance as the much better-known portrait by
Sharaku (cat. 43), and the two versions by the
rival artists present a fascinating comparison.
Shun'ei's portrait is profoundly gentle and
humane, but lacks the dramatic, wide-eyed stare
and erect posture of Sharaku's version, in which
the character of Kurando really does seem to
weigh the serious choices with which he is
confronted.

Formerly in the Adolphe Stoclet Collection,
this is one of only two impressions recorded
(the other is in the Freis Collection, USA). TC

Asano 1992, pp. 327, 329.

42

43 Sawamura Sōjūrō III as Ōgishi Kurando

PLAY *Hana-ayame Bunroku Soga* at the Miyako Theatre (Edo); fifth month, 1794

Artist: Tōshūsai Sharaku (Edo)

Signature: Tōshūsai Sharaku ga

Publisher: Tsutaya Jūzaburō (Edo)

Censorship seal: *kiwame*

Ōban, colour woodblock with dark grey mica background, 36.1 x 24.5 cm

The British Museum, London (1909.6-18.043)

The dignity of the character Ōgishi Kurando is well conveyed in this portrait in which he seems to weigh the rights and wrongs of the cause (compare cat. 42). His fan is decorated with a pattern of stylized flowing water (*kanze mizu*) that was personal to the actor Sōjūrō.

Sharaku designed more than 150 prints for the Edo publisher Tsutaya Jūzaburō in just ten months, from the fifth month, 1794. Twenty-eight of these were half-length actor portraits with dark grey mica backgrounds, which all record performances at the three rival Edo theatres in the fifth month, 1794. Sharaku's idiosyncratic approach, giving startling autonomy to each facial feature, creates a highly nuanced psychological dimension within his portraiture. Perhaps for this reason – that his actor portraits are so unlike those of his Edo contemporaries Shun'ei and Toyokuni – Sharaku has occasionally been linked to the Osaka master Ryūkōsai (see pp. 46–7 above). It seems most likely, however, that he was one Saitō Jūrōbei (died before about 1818), a Noh actor in the service of the Lord of Awa, and thus not a professional print artist at all. Contemporaries thought that he strove 'too hard to draw the truth' (*amari ni shin o egakan tote*: Ōta Nanpo in *Ukiyo-e kōshō*, before the fifth month, 1800) and this may account for the short duration of his activities.   TC

Nakano in Hamada 1988, vol. 18, pp. 446, 688–91; Matsudaira in *Hizō ukiyo-e taikan*, vol. 2, 1987, pp. 284–5, no. 207.

44 Segawa Tomisaburō II as Yadorigi, wife of Ōgishi Kurando

PLAY *Hana-ayame Bunroku Soga* at the Miyako Theatre (Edo); fifth month, 1794

Artist: Tōshūsai Sharaku (Edo)

Signature: Tōshūsai Sharaku ga

Publisher: Tsutaya Jūzaburō (Edo)

Censorship seal: *kiwame*

Ōban, colour woodblock with dark grey mica background, 36.1 x 23.8 cm

The British Museum, London (1909.6-18.039)

Tomisaburō II plays the role of Yadorigi, wife of Ōgishi Kurando, in the same play as the previous two entries (cats 42 and 43). In fact, it may be

43

that Sharaku meant the two designs to be viewed as a complimentary pair. Sharaku's complete refusal to idealize his actor portraits means that we are very aware of the bony chin and strong jaw of the male actor beneath the white makeup. Matsudaira Susumu challenged the mistaken interpretation that the actor's nickname Niku-Tomi meant 'Ugly Tomi[saburō]' – quite the reverse – and encouraged us to find an ethereal beauty in the portrait. The small, radically angled eyes pierce us with the strength of their unwavering gaze; a faint smile plays around the lips; and an elegant movement is suggested at the periphery, as the sensitively rendered hand draws the black surcoat (*uchikake*) with chrysanthemum pattern around the shoulder of this proud samurai woman.   TC

Matsudaira in *Hizō ukiyo-e taikan*, vol. 2, 1987, p. 285, no. 208.

45

45 Segawa Kikunojō III as the courtesan Katsuragi (right) and Sawamura Sōjūrō III as Nagoya Sanza (left)

PLAY *Keisei sanbon karakasa* at the Miyako Theatre (Edo); seventh month, 1794

Artist: Tōshūsai Sharaku (Edo)

Signature: Tōshūsai Sharaku ga

Publisher: Tsutaya Jūzaburō (Edo)

Censorship seal: *kiwame*

Ōban, colour woodblock with pink mica background, 35.9 x 23.6 cm

The British Museum, London (1909.6-18.057)

Segawa Kikunojō III (1751–1810) was arguably the greatest specialist in female roles (*onnagata*) of his age. Like so many female specialists, he was born and trained in the Kyoto–Osaka region before conquering the Edo stage from soon after his arrival in that city in 1773. Here he plays opposite Sōjūrō III, the equally popular male lead (see also cats 42 and 43).

The story of the love between the courtesan Katsuragi and the playboy Nagoya Sanza is one of the oldest in Kabuki, based on the real-life affairs of Okuni, the 'founder' of Kabuki, in the first years of the seventeenth century. Toying with the stem of her pipe, the courtesan leans back against the lover who stands protectively over her. Sharaku does not disguise the lumpy features or large hands of the female impersonator; nevertheless the stable triangular grouping of the two figures and their tender expressions evoke sentiments appropriate to such an intimate love scene.   TC

46 Ichikawa Yaozō III as Fuwa no Banzaemon (right) and Sakata Hangorō III as Kosodate no Kannonbō (left)

PLAY *Keisei sanbon karakasa* at the Miyako Theatre (Edo); seventh month, 1794

Artist: Tōshūsai Sharaku (Edo)

Signature: Tōshūsai Sharaku ga

Publisher: Tsutaya Jūzaburō (Edo)

Censorship seal: *kiwame*

Ōban, colour woodblock with pink mica background, 35.9 x 23.6 cm

The British Museum, London (1909.6-18.058)

The seated Fuwa no Banzaemon, who leans forward powerfully and stares defiantly out at us, braced by the sheathed sword he holds upright, is the unsuccessful rival of Nagoya Sanza for the affections of the courtesan Katsuragi (see cat. 45). Towering over him, leaning menacingly and drawing back his sleeve for a fight, is the evil monk Kannonbō. The extraordinary tension and agitation of Sharaku's composition, typified by the monk's cross-eyed glare, suggest that the actors are striking a dramatic 'stage pose' (*mie*),

46

likely to be rewarded with thunderous approval from the audience. An illustration in the published programme for the play records that Banzaemon went on to overcome and tie up his adversary.   TC

Matsudaira in *Hizō ukiyo-e taikan*, vol. 2, 1987, p. 286, no. 213.

47 Kataoka Nizaemon VII as Iyo no Tarō

PLAY *Seiwa nidai ōyose Genji* at the Miyako Theatre
(Edo); eleventh month, 1796

Artist: Utagawa Toyokuni (Edo)

Signature: Toyokuni ga

Publisher: Izumiya Ichibei (Edo)

Ōban, colour woodblock, 36.8 x 24.5 cm

Chiba City Museum of Art (2903015)

Nizaemon VII performed regularly in Edo, as well
as in his native Kyoto–Osaka region. He was
known for his portrayal of rough or villainous
characters, and in this play he had disguised
himself in order to steal a secret document.
Here his true evil character is revealed and he
fights with enemies in the dark. Toyokuni had
recently become established as the leading
artist of actor portraits in Edo, and his dynamic
style would become dominant in that city in the
first half of the nineteenth century.

Ex-coll. Werner Schindler; Chiba-shi Bijutsukan 2001,
no. 127.

48

47

48 Interior of the Nakamura Theatre, Edo

PLAY *Shunkan futatsu omokage* at the Nakamura
Theatre (Edo); third month, 1800

Artist: Utagawa Toyokuni (Edo)

Signature: Toyokuni ga

Publisher: Nishimuraya Yohachi (Edo)

Ōban, colour woodblock, triptych, 37.7 x 25.0 cm
(right), 37.7 x 25.1 cm (centre), 37.8 x 24.8 cm (left)

The British Museum, London (1907.5-31.0490)

An unusually large and detailed 'perspective
view' (*uki-e*) of the interior of the Nakamura
Theatre in Edo, during a performance of the play
Shunkan futatsu omokage in the third month,
1800. Appearing in the title role of priest
Shunkan (the bearded figure, standing, centre) is

Ichikawa Danzō IV, mainly active in Osaka, but here on an extended tour in Edo (1798–1801). Among other actors identifiable by their likeness and crests is 'big nose' Ichikawa Komazō III (centre-left, red under-robe, sword drawn; see also cat. 41).

This is an accurate representation of the main features of a Kabuki theatre of the time. Performances were staged in daylight hours to lessen the risk of fire from lanterns. Illumination flooded in through large skylights, top left and top right. The gabled stage was inherited from the medieval Noh theatre. Although originally open-air, in the eighteenth century Kabuki stages had become covered by large, more permanent wood and tile buildings. Actors often made their bravado entrances and exits along the 'flower path' (hanamichi) walkway, passing among the heads of the audience (left sheet). Musicians and percussionists are discretely hidden behind the black screen (right sheet). The cheapest entry was for those willing to stand in the so-called rakan-dai ('arhat gallery'), back left of the stage where a fight has apparently broken out between rival fans. Most expensive were the first level boxes (sajiki), here occupied on the left side by ladies-in-waiting from a feudal mansion. Drinks and food were served to the seats from local theatre teahouses (shibai-jaya) and the audience was anything but respectfully attentive. Entrances and exits of the stars were accompanied by ritualized calls from the audience.

No Kabuki theatre building has survived from the Edo period in the major cities of Japan; however, the Kanemaru Theatre at Mt Kompira on the island of Shikoku, completed in 1835 and now designated an Important Cultural Property, is closely modelled on metropolitan theatres of that time. Kabuki performances have been revived and staged there regularly since 1985. TC

Matsudaira in *Hizō ukiyo-e taikan*, vol. 2, 1987, p. 290, no. 219.

49

49 Seventh memorial for Nakayama Itchō

Ninth month, 1782

Surimono, colour woodblock, 38.6 x 50.1 cm

Private Collection (Japan)

This early Kabuki-related *surimono*, with a colourful picture of an arrangement of cut flowers and tree branches, was produced to commemorate the seventh anniversary of the death of the Kyoto–Osaka actor Nakayama Itchō (Shinkurō I, 1702–1775). The image reflects the metaphors of the poems. It was presented by the actors Nakayama Shinkurō II (Nakayama Raisuke I, Sharyū, Itchō, 1738–83) and Nakayama Bunshichi I (Yoshio, Jōkō, 1732–1813; retired ninth month, 1782), together with the *haikai* poet Nitoan (Kabutsu, d. 1800), who contributed to several Kabuki-related *surimono*.

Nakayama Raisuke I assumed the name Nakayama Shinkurō II in the ninth month, 1782. The *surimono* is therefore both a memorial to Shinkurō I and a celebration of Raisuke's accession to the name of his mentor. Shinkurō I's adopted son Bunshichi I retired at the same time. He accepts Raisuke as his new 'younger brother' and the inheritor of his father's name.

> We now approach the seventh-year memorial of our teacher and father, Nakayama Itchō. I accept his name, and promise never to besmirch it. Just thinking of him again makes me miss him all the more, and now I feel the solemnity of this auspicious occasion. With greatest respect and warmth, I fold my hands in prayer.

Omokage ya / tsumoreba hitotsu / mutsu no hana
His visage so clear
With the passing of the years
Snow piles up, like flower petals
SHARYŪ (Shinkurō II)

Tsumoreba can mean both the piling up of snow and of years. *Mutsu no hana*, literally 'six flowers', is a poetic name for snow.

> At this moment when 'younger brother' grass is replanted in a new field, although you feel sad, almost seven years have passed this winter. Now as Sharyū offer your prayers and when you perform let it strengthen you, even though the memory of him causes you pain.

Kangiku ya / mitsuba yotsuba wa / somenagara
Winter chrysanthemum
Three or four leaves
Tinge with colour
YOSHIO (Bunshichi I)

Kakimori Bunko 1991, no. 129.

50 Celebrating accession to the name Kataoka Nizaemon VII

1788

Surimono, colour woodblock, 34.0 x 46.2 cm

Private Collection (Japan)

This grand, anonymous *surimono* celebrates Kyoto–Osaka actor Asao Kunigorō II's change of name to become Kataoka Nizaemon VII (1755–1837). The image of a mountain scene with pine trees and plum blossoms is in the classical Kano School style. A lion is falling down the cliff, which is a reference to the *Shakkyō* story, originally from China and often depicted in theatre and art. A father lion tosses his son over the cliff to test his skill and endurance so that he can prove himself as a mature lion, king of the beasts. In the story the young lion climbs up the ravine and is reunited with his father and they perform an auspicious dance. Here the new 'Nizaemon' is being tossed out into the stage world and the group of senior actors expect him to live up to the Nizaemon heritage. To carry on an illustrious acting name was (and is) an effective way of creating celebrity and fame.

The Nizaemon name has a long and somewhat complicated history, with several generations (III, V and VI) carrying forward the name but not actually using it onstage. Nizaemon I and Nizaemon IV (Fujikawa Hangorō II, d. 1758) both used the pen name Sakoku. Fujikawa Hangorō III was an adopted son of Nizaemon IV and is counted as Nizaemon V. The 'Sakoku' who introduces Nizaemon VII in this print is most likely Fujikawa Hangorō III, who disappeared from the stage world in the 1770s. Mihogi Giemon II (1731–89) is counted as Nizaemon VI, but never actually performed using that name and did not contribute to this *surimono*. Kataoka Nizaemon is one of the few names in Kyoto–Osaka Kabuki to have been kept alive to the present day: the current incumbent is Nizaemon XV.

The 'Kunigorō' mentioned in the text on the print is the former name of Nizaemon VII himself. Poems are offered to him by many of the leading stars: Minshi (Arashi Hinasuke I), Koyū (Nakamura Jūzō II, 1740–88), Ikkō (Anegawa Shinshichirō III, 1748–1805), Fujaku (Onoe Shinshichi I, 1745–1809), Hakō (Yoshizawa Iroha I, 1755–1810), Kitō (Sawamura Kunitarō I) and Raishi (Arashi Sangorō II). The final poem is from a patron.

I am delighted that on this occasion Kunigorō has agreed to my wishes to accept the Kataoka name. I am sure that he will flourish and bring new blossoms to this old tree.

Tensha / yorozu yoshi to iwareyo / ume-goyomi
On this heaven-blessed day
All is well and good
Like the plum blossoms that herald spring
FUJIKAWA SAKOKU (Hangorō III)

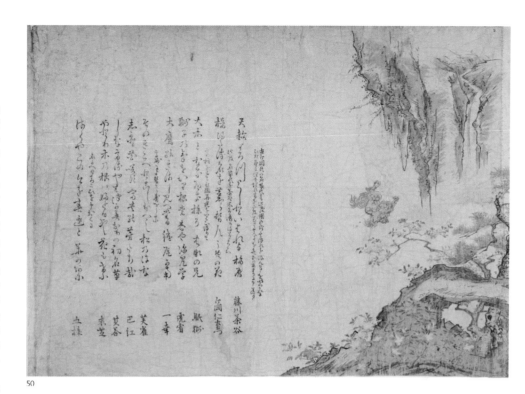

50

I thank Sakoku for his kindness in passing on the Kataoka name to me.

Tsugietaru / na o kaorasen / ume no hana
This august name
May I bring new fragrance
To the plum blossom
KATAOKA NIZAEMON

These poems are offered in celebration that the Kataoka name will flourish again from such a fine seed.

Taiboku to / narubeki kabu zo / hana no ani
Growing into a great trunk
From a fallen tree
First plum of the season
MINSHI (Arashi Hinasuke I)

The imagery is of a great tree (*daiboku*), a fallen tree (*kabu*, which also means a role or position), and the plum (*hana no ani*; literally, 'elder brother of flowers' because it blossoms first in the season). Kataoka was a famous name in Osaka Kabuki and the hope is that it will again stand tall, first among the many.

Shishi no ki o / kari ne mo haru ya / fukami-gusa
Taking on the spirit of the lion
In spring
Play among the peonies
KOYŪ (Nakamura Jūzō II)

With Takasago as our inspiration, we offer songs in celebration.

Sono kikoe / tokoshinae nari / matsu no hana
May his fame
Last forever
Flower of the pine
FUJAKU (Onoe Shinshichi I)

Shika to hana / sakeru fūki no / medachi ka na
May he blossom proudly
This bud
And prosper
HAKŌ (Yoshizawa Iroha I)

Shinateru ya / hatsu kaminari no / hatsu nagusa
On the hillside [Kataoka]
A first clap of thunder
Winter plum
KITŌ (Sawamura Kunitarō I)

Shinateru ya is a conventional poetic epithet (*makura kotoba*, literally 'pillow word') often placed before *Kata*; here it replaces the name Kataoka altogether. Repetition of the sound *hatsu* (first) suggests the launch of the new star under his new name.

Yadoriki no / ne wa futoru nari / hana mo kyō
A sheltered tree
Its roots grow broad
And it flowers today
RAISHI (Arashi Sangorō II)

Offered on this occasion of taking a new name.

Saku ya kono / ima o harube to / hana no ani
May it blossom now
At the cusp of spring
This old plum
GOSHU

Kakimori Bunko 1991, no. 131.

51 Twenty-fifth memorial for Setomonoya Denbei

1790

Surimono, colour woodblock, 35.1 x 46.5 cm

Private Collection (Japan)

This *surimono* commemorates the twenty-fifth memorial of the death of Setomonoya Denbei, a former leader of the Sasase Kabuki fan club and owner of a chinaware business. It presents no less than twenty-nine haiku poems by fan-club members and six actors: Arashi Hinasuke I (Minshi), Seki Sanjūrō I (Kota), Sawamura Kunitarō I (Kitō), Arashi Sangorō II (Raishi), Yamashita Kinsaku II (Rikō) and Bandō Iwagorō (Ganshi). The artist Shōkōsai (Shōkō) also contributed a poem, suggesting that he was already an active Kabuki fan by the late 1780s. A verse signed Bantō ('peach tree banner') could be by the noted Osaka philosopher Yamagata Bantō (1748–1821), although the first *ban* character is slightly different from the pen name ('peach tree wood louse') he used in later career. Bantō was the successful manager (*bantō*) of a business in Osaka, who went on to became a scholar–philosopher later in life. His pen name was thus a homophone for his job title.

> Though we all eventually become moss on the ground, the Sasase club's roots were well established by Denbei, and it flourishes like the bamboo grass [*sasa*] of its name. Here we offer poems in honour of the twenty-fifth anniversary of his death.

> *Tomurai no / te mo uchiawase / hotoke no za*
> Even in prayer
> I clap my hands
> In front of the Buddha
> SHŌKŌ (Shōkōsai)

The fan clubs had elaborate hand-clapping rituals. *Hotoke* means Buddha, but here also refers to the deceased.

> *Sono ato o / taezu tōtari / neri-kuyō*
> Hereafter
> May we always
> Parade together in prayer
> BANTŌ

The fan club held ritual processions at certain Kabuki performances during the year.

> *Awasu te mo / tamuke to narite / hana-gumori*
> Folded hands too
> Become a farewell
> Hazy spring sky
> MINSHI (Arashi Hinasuke I)

> *Itadaita / te sae tsumetashi / hana shikimi*
> Even his hand
> Now cold
> An offering of flowers
> KITŌ (Sawamura Kunitarō I)

Kakimori Bunko 1991, no. 126.

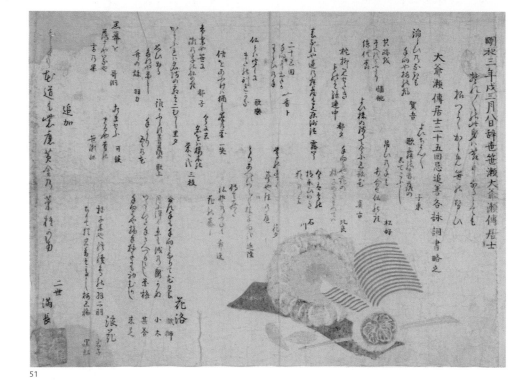

51

52

52 Third memorial for Asao Tamejūrō I

1806

Artist: Niwa Tōkei

Signature: Tōkei sha

Surimono, colour woodblock with metallic pigment and embossing, 27.5 x 38.7 cm (picture)

Waseda University Theatre Museum, Tokyo
(*Kyota* 19: 28–9)

Tamejūrō died on the first day of the fourth month, 1804. The image from a *surimono* of a painted folding screen of flowers and grasses has been cut out and pasted into a Kyota album (see also cat. 2). Before the screen sits an open letter and other letters still in a pouch. The text (not shown) includes poems by Kitō (Sawamura Kunitarō I), Tomi and Doran. Tomi, Tamejūrō's wife, also contributed to two later memorial *surimono*: the first by Tōkei in 1812, *Kyota* (Waseda) 22: 17–19, and the second by Yamanaka Shōnen (cat. 139) in 1819.

Niwa Tōkei (Daikokuya Kihei II, 1760–1822) was the second-generation owner of the Daikokuya, an Osaka business selling patent medicines. His extensive activities as a book illustrator and artist of *surimono* prints, many examples of which are included in this catalogue, seems to have been a secondary career (Takasugi 2004). Tōkei was also active as a *kyōka* poet in the Maruha group, using the pen names Niwamaru and Chidō (Hanyū 2004). His artistic teacher was said to be Shitomi Kangetsu (1747–97), making him a fellow-pupil of the actor print artist Ryūkōsai Jokei. Tōkei's subjects for his *surimono* illustrations were mainly elegant still-lives.

53 'Newly published: game board of actors in hit plays, like the thirty-six immortal poets'
Shinpan yakusha atari-kyōgen sanjū-rokkassen tobi-sugoroku

c. New Year, 1794

Artist: Unknown

Publisher: Sumiya Kichibei (Kyoto)

'Parody' *sugoroku* board game, woodblock with slight hand-colouring, 32.2 x 45.7 cm

The British Museum, London (1916.7-17.04), given by W. Bateson

This is an early example of an actor *sugoroku* board game, featuring twenty-three actors; it also serves as a 'spoof' actor listing (*mitate banzuke*).

The actors' names are listed but the faces are not realistic portraits, as is the case in the following example (cat. 54). Players rolled dice to determine their moves and the aim was to progress to the top of the board first. The name changes of particular actors suggest a date of the first month, 1794, since this kind of board game was usually issued at the New Year. Also the prominence of the tiger implies the year of the tiger, 1794. Arashi Kichisaburō II (Rikan) is given a leading position, centre bottom, in the role of Watōnai, who overcomes a tiger in the play *Battle of Coxinga*. He had not yet performed this role in the top theatres, so he is being presented as a rising star with potential.

HK

53

54

54 'Actor likenesses: a Chūshingura board game' *Yakusha kao-nise Chūshingura sugoroku*

c. New Year, 1799

Artist: Nagahide (attributed) (Kyoto)

Publisher: Kashiwaya Sōshichi (Kyoto)

Parody *sugoroku* board game, woodblock with slight hand-colouring, 32.5 x 45.6 cm

The British Museum, London (1916.7-17.05), given by W. Bateson

The actor portraits follow the style established by Ryūkōsai and Shōkōsai Hanbei. *Sugoroku* was a board game popular in the Edo period, which used dice to determine a player's progress or retreat, somewhat like snakes and ladders. The group of actors does not represent an actual performance, but is rather an ideal casting of stars of the late 1790s that might perform the classic play *Chūshingura*. So although this could have been used as an actual game-board, it also serves as a 'spoof' actor listing (*mitate banzuke*). There are several clues to the dating of the print. Twenty-three actors are depicted and most of these were performing together in the year 1798; Sawamura

Sōjūrō III returned from Edo to perform in the eleventh month of 1798. Furthermore, Arashi Sangorō II had held his final show at the Tenma Tenjin Shrine in the third month, 1798. Such novelty publications were usually issued at New Year. Given the publisher and date, Nagahide (of Kyoto) is the most likely artist.   HK

55 'One hundred poems by one hundred actors' *Yakusha hyakunin isshu*

c. 1798–9

Parody flybill (*mitate banzuke*), woodblock, 35.0 x 24.8 cm

Waseda University Theatre Museum, Tokyo (*Kyota* 16: 38)

Arashi Hinasuke II (Minshi) and Sawamura Kunitarō I (Kitō) are presented as emperors. There is a poem for each of the other actors, who are also named as either emperor, courtier or poet. The illustration is of 'Emperor Minshi'. Hinasuke II was still young but he is presented as the top actor, in the image of his famous father Hinasuke I. This is a good example of the Kabuki world trying to promote the celebrity of a rising star – the

emperor (Hinasuke I) is dead; long live the emperor (Hinasuke II).

56 'Newly updated: rankings of actors' salaries' *(Shinpan kaisei) Yakusha mitate kane-zukushi*

1804

Parody flybill (*mitate banzuke*), woodblock, 33.0 x 22.8 cm (left), 33.0 x 21.9 cm (right, illustrated)

Waseda University Theatre Museum, Tokyo (*Kyota* 17: 38–9)

A parody flybill (*mitate banzuke*) that ranks actors' salaries. Amounts cannot necessarily be taken as literal, although we do know that the top actors commanded very high figures. The document certainly gives a good indication of the actors' relative audience-pulling power. It is an audacious display of stars' wealth, similar to the way film or sports stars' incomes are trumpeted in the media today. The top salary listed is for Ichikawa Danzō IV, at 1,100 gold *ryō*, an enormous sum for the time. Next come Kataoka Nizaemon VII, Onoe Koisaburō I, Sawamura Kunitarō II, Segawa Rokō III,

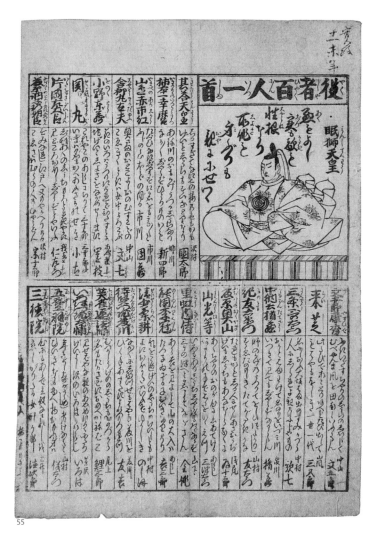

55

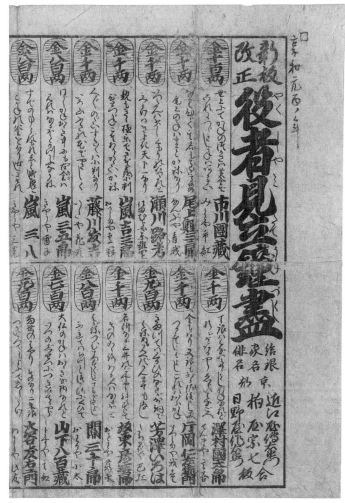

56

Fujikawa Tomokichi I and Arashi Kichisaburō II, at 1,000 *ryō* each.

In the eighth month, 1842, during the Tenpō Reforms, the government required the theatres to report actors' salaries. The top two were Onoe Kikugorō III and Nakamura Utaemon IV, at 500 gold *ryō* each – still a huge sum. Since the reforms were a crackdown on all kinds of extravagance, these reported salaries were most likely kept to the minimum (*Kabuki nenpyō*, vol. 6, pp. 459–61). Star actors commanded wealth far above their lowly social position.

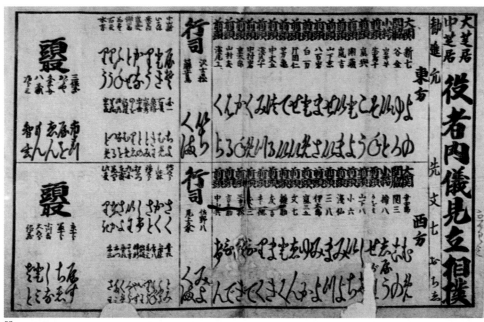

57

57 'Top and middle theatres: actors' wives ranked like sumo wrestlers'
(Ōshibai, chūshibai) Yakusha naigi mitate sumō
c. First month, 1796
Parody flybill (*mitate banzuke*), woodblock, 26.5 x 38.4 cm
Waseda University Theatre Museum, Tokyo (*Kyota* 17: 112)

This parody flybill lists the top actors in small print, with their wives' names given in large print, all ranked like sumo wrestlers.

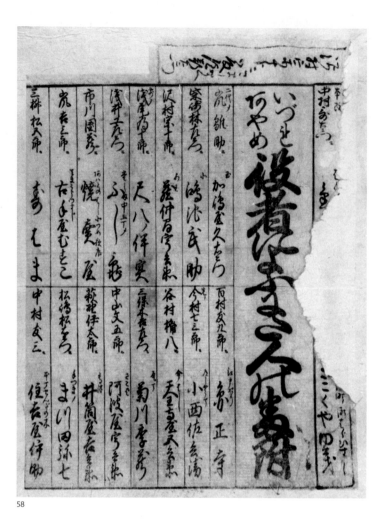

58

58 'Every one a star: flybill of people who really look like actors'
(Izure ayame) Yakusha ni you nita hito no banzuke

c. 1805

Parody flybill (*mitate banzuke*), woodblock, 32.3 x 23.7 cm (right. illustrated), 29.5 x 25.4 cm (left)

Waseda University Theatre Museum, Tokyo
(*Kyota* 18: 71–2)

A list of names of neighbourhood men who look most like actors: an excellent early example of 'fifteen minutes of fame' for Osaka fans. Cat. 59 is the complementary list of young women.

59 'Every one a star: flybill of young women who really look like actors'
(Izure Ayame) Yakusha ni you nita musume no banzuke

c. Eighth month, 1807

Parody flybill (*mitate banzuke*), woodblock, 27.4 x 38.9 cm

Waseda University Theatre Museum, Tokyo
(*Kyota* 19: 27)

A parody flybill (*mitate banzuke*) that lists young Osaka women who look like actors. Only an address and shop name are given, however, adding to the fun of trying to work out their real identities. This offered a moment of fame by association for the young women concerned.

59

60

61 Illustrated pamphlet for the play
Chūshin hata-soroi yamabushi settai

Tenth month, 1789

Ezukushi (ehon) banzuke, woodblock with stencil-
printed colour (*kappazuri*), 20.2 x 14.4 cm (covers)

The British Museum, London (1916.4-3.045),
given by W. Bateson

This is an illustrated pamphlet (*ezukushi
banzuke*, or *ehon banzuke*) for the retirement
performance of Arashi Hinasuke I at the Kado
Theatre. Such pamphlets typically have five or
so pages and include the names and roles of
actors, and simple illustrations of most scenes in
the day's performance. The cover is generally
illustrated in colour, using the stencil (*kappazuri*) technique characteristic of Kyoto–Osaka.

**60 'Parody map of Great Japan listing the
actors as lords'**
Dai-Nippon kuni-zukushi mitate yakusha-shū

c. 1809

Parody flybill (*mitate banzuke*), woodblock,
27.8 x 38.2 cm (size of page-opening)

Waseda University Theatre Museum, Tokyo
(*Kyota* 20: 92–4)

Each actor is indicated as controlling an actual
province, just like a feudal lord (*daimyō*), and a
critique is included of his performance style.
Settsu, home province of Osaka, for instance, is
ruled by Arashi Kichisaburō II (Rikan). Nakamura
Utaemon III (Shikan) rules Nagoya. This originally would have looked much more obviously
like a map of Japan, but has been cut into pieces
to fit the album.   MK

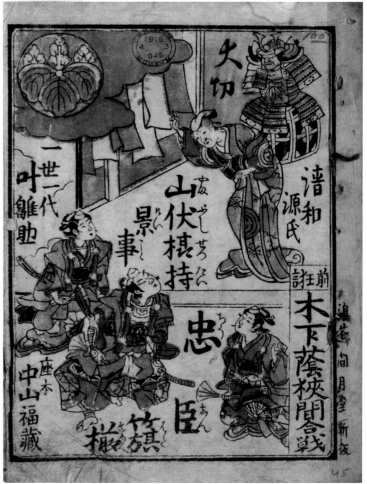

61

73 'Guide to theatre: double-sided mirror'
Shibai annai ryōmen kagami

Late 1803
Artist: Shōkōsai Hanbei
Publishers: Shioya Chōbei and Harimaya Gohei
Woodblock, 58.9 x 80.5 cm
Osaka Museum of History (Gei 2089)

This unusual print is a large encyclopaedia-like broadsheet packed with information about the two main Osaka theatres, Kado and Naka, offering aspiring connoisseurs a wealth of knowledge to prepare them to enjoy the magic of the theatre. It was most likely folded to be easily portable: several folds are still apparent in both vertical and horizontal directions. *Ryōmen kagami* implies that the sheet has been printed on both sides of the paper, but this impression was printed on one side only.

As many as thirty-eight topics are squeezed into the one sheet. The range is impressive and includes 'Origins of Kabuki', 'Chronicle of play titles at the Kado and Naka Theatres', 'Chronicle of Osaka theatre', 'Prices of seats', 'Theatre picture-playbill suppliers', 'Dealers in old playbills and illustrated books', 'Signboard painters', 'Costumes for hire', 'Theatre builders', 'Actor likeness painters', 'Names of stage devices', 'Theatre staff', 'Sponsors and patrons', 'Guardian deities of actors', 'Actors who are fond of the tea ceremony, haiku and comic verse', 'A guide to the code of off-stage clappers that signal scene changes', 'Fan club song', 'Types of costumes', 'Annual rituals of the theatre', 'Fan clubs and their favourite teahouses', 'Etiquette in the theatre' and 'Crests of actors'.

Ogita Kiyoshi has published a detailed account of this kind of printed theatrical ephemera (*ichimai-zuri*) (Ogita 1999). He notes that the layout is similar to the genre of *Banreki ryōmen kagami*, an almanac for daily life published regularly from about 1747 until the late nineteenth century. The title was clearly based on this. Hōseidō Kisanji wrote a theatre parody of the encyclopaedia format in 1791, entitled *Ukan sandai zue* (cat. 68), which in turn was based on the popular illustrated encyclopaedia *Wakan sansai zue*. Shōkōsai had already published two extensively illustrated theatrical encyclopaedias: *Shibai gakuya zue* (1800, cat. 70) and *Gakuya zue shūi* (1802, cat. 71). Unlike these two books, however, this broadsheet has only one picture and is densely covered with text, much closer to the model *Banreki ryōmen kagami*.

The single illustration is titled 'scene in a backstage room' (*heya no zu*) and shows an actor, identifiable from the likeness as Arashi Kichisaburō II, facing a mirror. A similar image of Kichisaburō facing a mirror, with the title 'Fashions backstage today' (*Tōryū gakuya fūzoku*, cat. 107), is dated the eleventh month 1800. Clearly this image-type was popular at the time.   AY

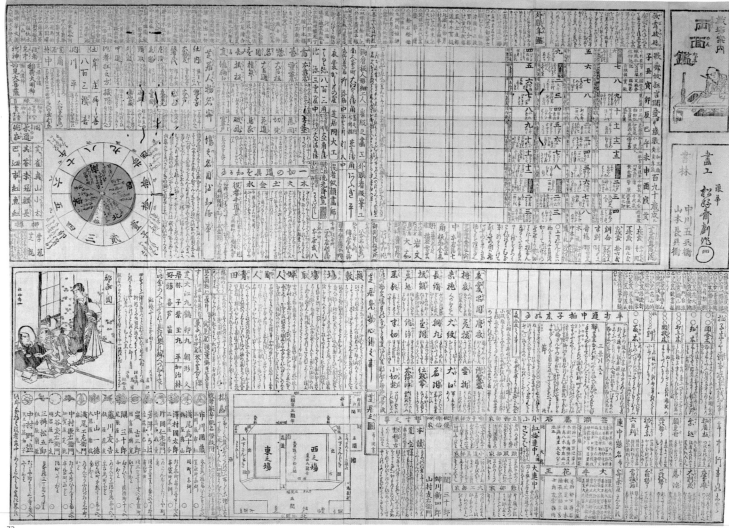

73

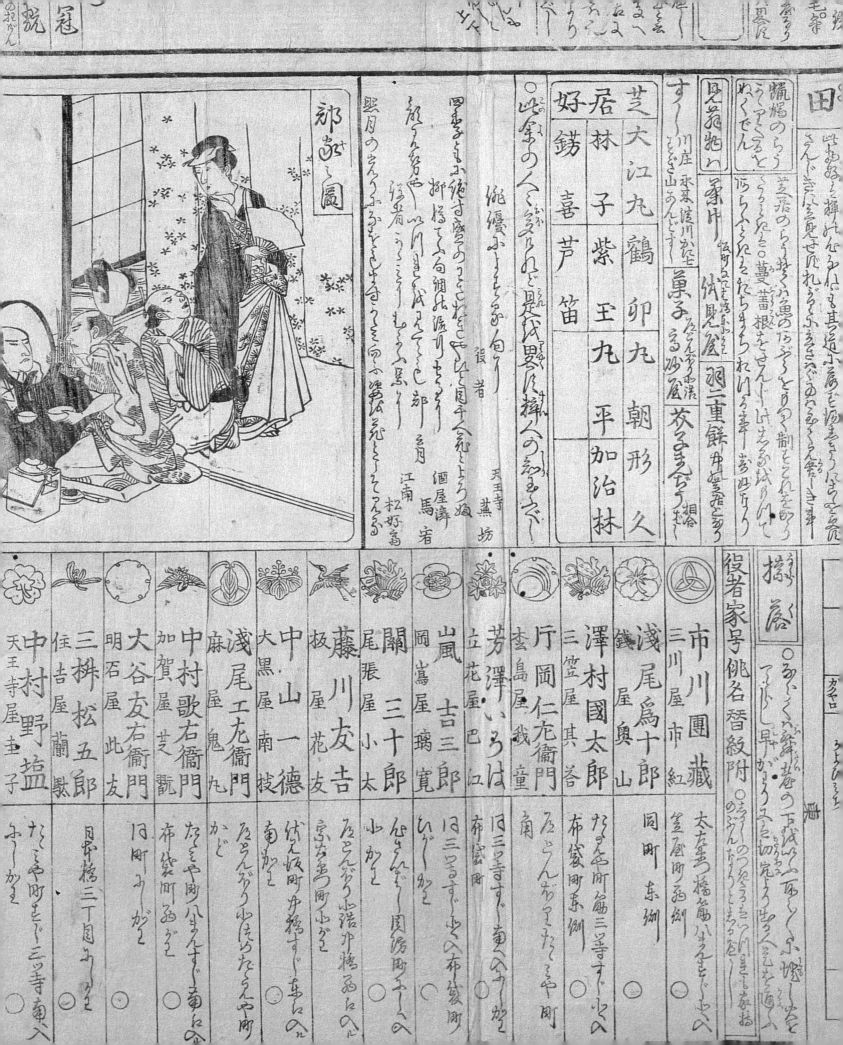

役者家号俳名替紋附

郎家の図

上段（囲み内）

芝	大江	九鶴	卯九	朝形	久
居	林	子	紫	玉九	平	加治	林
好	錺	喜	芦	笛			

下段 役者名（右より）

市川團藏	浅尾為十郎	澤村國太郎	庁岡仁左衛門	芳澤いろは	嵐吉三郎	關三十郎	藤川友吉	中山一徳	中村歌右衛門	浅尾工左衛門	大谷友右衛門	三桝松五郎	中村野塩
三川屋市紅	三川屋奥山	三笠屋其蓉	三島屋栽童	立花屋巴江	岡嶌屋璃寛	張屋小太友	坂屋花友	大黒屋南枝	加賀屋芝翫	麻屋鬼九	明石屋此友	住吉屋蘭獣	天王寺屋圭子

74

74 *Ehon futaba aoi*
Picture Book: Double-leafed Hollyhock
1798
Artist: Shōkōsai Hanbei
Publisher: Shioya Chōbei
Hanshibon book, colour woodblock, 2 vols
(bound as one), 25.8 x 18.2 cm (covers)
Gerhard Pulverer Collection (Germany)

This is the first colour-printed book of actor portraits (*yakusha ehon*) published in Osaka, and depicts scenes from plays performed between 1793 and 1798. Volume 1 features sixteen actors; volume 2 shows twenty-four, including two from Edo.

Illustrated is a scene from the play *Keisei yanagi-zakura* (*Courtesans and Willowing Cherry Trees*), performed at the Naka Theatre in the first month, 1793, with Onoe Koisaburō I (Shinshichi I) in the role of Isshiki Yuki no Kami (right), and Arashi Sangorō II as Yodoya Tatsugorō (left). (See also cat. 26).

75 Carved portrait mask of Onoe Shinshichi I
Seventh month, 1788
Carver: Shōgetsudō Yūshō (Yoshinao)
Signature: Shōgetsudō Yūshō (Yoshinao)
Wood, 20.0 x 14.4 x 10.0 cm
The British Museum, London (1998.12-19.80),
given by Nobutaka Oka

Onoe Shinshichi I (Fujaku, Koisaburō, 1742–1809) was an established star, at the peak of his career in 1788 when this carved wooden mask was made. The carver, who is otherwise unknown, notes in an inscription that it is 'copied from life' (*iki-utsushi*, or *shō-utsushi*). No similar examples seem to have survived elsewhere and the exact use in not known; the wooden bar across the back implies that it was held rather than worn. There is a striking similarity to painted and printed 'likeness pictures' (*nigao-e*) of the actor by Ryūkōsai and Shōkōsai (cats 26, 36 and 74).

Setsuyō kikan (*Interesting Aspects of Life in Osaka*), a chronicle of the late Edo period, has an intriguing entry in volume 39 regarding actor likeness carvings. Under the year 1786, two years before the date on the Shinshichi mask, it says: 'a famous maker of false teeth called Kusaka Taizan, who lived in Shinsaibashi-suji, made carved masks (*men*) of actors around that time, including likenesses of [Arashi] Hinasuke, [Ichikawa] Danzō, [Nakayama] Bunshichi, [Asao] Tamejūrō and [Yamashita] Kinsaku. Years later he died in prison for some reason.' The relation between the carver of this Shinshichi mask and Kusaka Taizan has not been confirmed; however, Taizan most likely knew Ryūkōsai. Taizan often visited Kimura Kenkadō, the great literati figure of late eighteenth-century Osaka, and an entry in Kenkadō's diary notes that Taizan visited him on the same day as Ryūkōsai, the twelfth day of the third month, 1788, only four months before the date of this likeness. AY

Funakoshi 1926–30, vol. 4, p. 471; Noma 1972, p. 221.

75

78

78 *Yakusha sangaikyō*
Actors: Their Activities on the Third Floor Backstage

ILLUSTRATED Ichikawa Danjūrō V (left) and Arashi Hinasuke II (right)

First month, 1801

Artist: Utagawa Toyokuni (Edo)

Author: Shikitei Sanba (Edo)

Publishers: Nishinomiya Shinroku and Yorozuya Tajiemon (Edo)

Hanshibon book, colour woodblock, 2 vols, 21.8 x 15.6 cm (covers)

The British Museum, London (JH196)

'Third [top] floor backstage' was where many dressing rooms were located. The first half of each volume contains illustrations by Edo artist Toyokuni that depict Edo actors in everyday dress and settings. The preface, written by popular author Shikitei Sanba, tells how publisher Nishinomiya Shinroku brought Toyokuni's draft pictures to him to request an accompanying text. Sanba laughed as the pictures were much like those of Shunshō's *Yakusha natsu no Fuji* (1780, cat. 11). Particularly similar are the open-

ing New Year scene and the last illustration, which depicts Hakuen (Ichikawa Danjūrō V) bestowing the house name Naritaya upon Arashi Hinasuke II. (In *Yakusha natsu no fuji* the father, Hinasuke I, also appears.)

The illustrations are followed by a text by Sanba, which bears little relation to them. It begins by recounting the stage achievements of Ichikawa Danjūrō VI and his premature death some eighteen months earlier. This leads into a story of how after death Sanjō (Danjūrō VI's pen name) enters the 'Kabuki Kingdom', where everyday life is acted out as if on stage. There he meets the king, the famous deceased Osaka playwright Chikamatsu Monzaemon, who asks Sanjō to take over his throne. Sanjō becomes King Chikamatsu II and rides around the kingdom on a crane, similar to Wasōbei, protagonist of a comic novel of the same name (first published in 1774).

Danjūrō VI had died unexpectedly early at the age of twenty-two, in the fifth month, 1799, and Sanba's text serves as an unofficial memorial piece (*tsuizen*). The official memorial, *Azuma*

sodachi na satsuki no ochigiwa, was written shortly after the death by Sanba's rival, fiction writer Takizawa Bakin. Two Edo publishing houses collaborated to produce *Yakusha sangaikyō*: Nishinomiya Shinroku, publisher of most of Sanba's fiction; and Yorozuya Tajiemon, the family into which the author had been adopted. So Sanba, using his business name Yorozuya Tajiemon, was essentially working alongside Nishinomiya Shinroku in the production of his own book. This arrangement continued for another theatrical work, *Shibai kinmō zui* (cat. 72), and a guide to *kyōka* poetry, *Kyōkakei*, both published in 1803.

Hinasuke II performed in Edo in 1800. His father and grandfather had close connections with the Danjūrō family. Here the young Hinasuke meets the grand old man of Edo, Danjūrō V, who writes his clan sobriquet 'Naritaya' on a lantern for him. This refers back to the book *Yakusha natsu no fuji* (1780) by Shunshō (cat. 11), which has Danjūrō V as the last image of volume 1 and Hinasuke I as the final actor represented in volume 2.

BC

79 *Ehon konote-gashiwa*
Picture Book: Garden Oaks

ILLUSTRATED Asao Tamejūrō I as Araki Murashige (right) and Rikan I as Kosobe Mondo (left) in *Keisei hana yamazaki* at the Kado Theatre; first month, 1800

1802

Artist–Author: Shōkōsai Hanbei

Publisher: Shioya Chōbei

Chūbon book, woodblock, 2 vols (bound as one), 22.0 x 15.5 cm (covers)

The British Museum, London (XBL113)

An alternate title is *Yakusha konote-gashiwa* (*Actors among the Garden Oaks*). The book has twenty-one scenes from plays performed during the several years around 1800, each printed in black and white across the page-opening. The title alludes to the image of actors as part of a garden world (*rien*); here the metaphor is that they are ornamental oak trees.

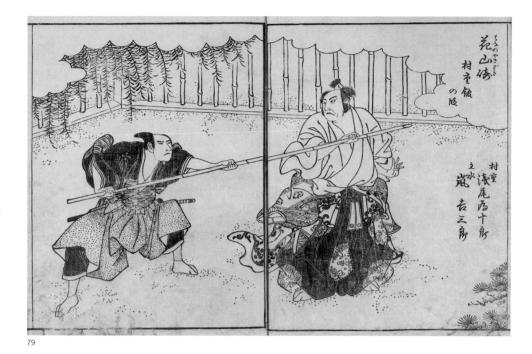

79

80 *Gekijo gashi (Shibai gashi)*
Pictorial History of Theatre Scenes

1803

Artist–Author: Ryūkōsai Jokei

Publisher: Eikōsha

Hanshibon book, woodblock, 2 vols, 25.7 x 18.2 cm (covers)

The British Museum, London (JH 439)

The book depicts famous landscapes that feature in plays. The style is very different from other theatre books, more in the elegant and naturalistic Maruyama-Shijō style prevalent at the time. Also included are examples of actors' poems in their own hand by Arashi Sangorō II and Nakayama Bunshichi I. Two other volumes planned for the series were never published.

Illustrated is a scene from the famous play *Chūshingura*, in which the Ichiriki brothel-keeper comes to fetch Okaru from her home in the country to take her to Kyoto.

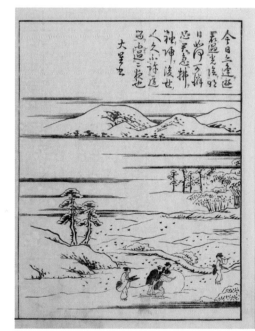

80

81 *Yakusha konote-gashiwa*
Actors among the Garden Oaks

ILLUSTRATED Ichikawa Danjūrō VI (deceased)

1803

Artist: Utagawa Toyokuni (Edo)

Author: Utei Enba (Edo)

Publisher: Enjudō (Edo)

Hanshibon book, colour woodblock, 2 vols,
20.5 x 14.8 cm (covers)

The British Library, London (16104- a39)

Each double-page opening has two bust portraits of the same actor, in colour: a portrait in
costume facing one in everyday dress. The
actors' names are not given. The title copies
Shōkōsai's book of the previous year (cat. 79)
and alludes to the image of actors as part of a
garden world (*rien*).

82 *Yakusha awase-kagami*
Actors in Paired Mirrors

ILLUSTRATED Iwai Kumesaburō (Hanshirō V, right)
and Bandō Mitsugorō III (left)

1804

Artist: Utagawa Toyokuni (Edo)

Author: Asakusa no Ichihito (Edo)

Publisher: Yamadaya Sanshirō (Manshundō, Edo)

Hanshibon book, colour woodblock, 2 vols,
26.1 x 18.0 cm (covers)

The British Museum, London (JH200)

The *awase-kagami* of the title is a pair of hand-
mirrors used by actors (and others) to view the
front and back of the head at the same time. The
book contains thirty-two half-length actor portraits in full colour, most with signed *kyōka*
poems. No acting names or *haimyō* pen names
are listed to assist identification. The pairings are
more considered than in earlier Edo actor books,
and each opening can be viewed as one image
with two halves. The author Asakusa no Ichihito
(1755–1820) was best known as a *kyōka* poet.

83 *(Kokkei ehon) Yakusha hama no masago*
(Comic Picture Book) Myriad Actors, Like Sand
on a Beach

1805 (originally 1803)

Artist: Shōkōsai Hanbei

Publisher: Obiya Ihei (Wakayama)

Hanshibon book, woodblock, 8 vols, 22.3 x 15.6 cm
(covers)

The British Library, London (16104-a38)

The preface is by Edo writer Takizawa (Kyokutei)
Bakin and the illustrations by Shōkōsai Hanbei;
an earlier, first edition was published in Osaka in
1803. Actors are not given their acting name but
presented instead in role, as if on stage, and by
their pen name (*haimyō*). Accompanying *kyōka*

81

82

verses are signed by poet-fans. This is an illustrated version of a play text (*e-iri nehon*), a
genre particular to Osaka. As many as eighty
plays were published in this manner from about
1800 to the 1860s.

The original play, *Sanmon gosan no kiri* (*The
Temple Gate and the Paulownia Crest*) by Namiki
Gohei, was first performed in the fourth month
of 1778 at the Kado Theatre. Ishikawa Goemon
tries to avenge the death of his father, a Chinese
official, by killing Mashiba Hisayoshi (Toyotomi

Hideyoshi). Parts of the play are still performed
today; a translation of a scene is in Brandon
2002, vol. 2.

Included among the poets is the artist
Shōkōsai himself and the playwright–scholar
Hamamatsu Utakuni. Information is known
about a few of the others, mainly local business-
men and doctors, but most are unrecorded
(Kawai 2003).

Rikan is included in the role of Junkikan
(Yatahei) and Arashi Sangorō II as Hisaaki (not

illustrated). Hamamatsu Utakuni (1776–1827, editor of the Waseda album *Kyota*) offers a poem in praise of Rikan:

Yatahei de / atta yoru yo na / omoi-ne no /
yume ni mo mitaki / kono otoko-buri
In the role of Yatahei
Night after night
Thinking of him
Want him in my dreams as well
This man among men
YAEGAKI UTAKUNI

Yatahei was a role Rikan played in disguise in the play.

The illustration shows Ichikawa Danzō IV (Shikō, right) and Arashi Hinasuke I (Koshichi, left). Danzō played the role of Mashiba Hisayoshi, the name used in theatre for the late sixteenth-century military leader Toyotomi Hideyoshi, whose seat of government was in Osaka. The poem that celebrates his performance is:

Omoi-ne no / makura kotoba ya / nubatama no /
yume ni koishiki / sugata mikawaya
Thinking of him
Head on my pillow
The dark jewel of the night
Delightful to see his visage
In my dreams
SETSUGETSUAN HANA NO SAKUNARI

'Hana no Sakunari' was Takezō Jūbei, leader in Osaka of an 'Edo-style' *kyōka* poetry group called Hana no Sakunari. He and his group also contributed poems to Shōkōsai's book *Masu-kagami* (1806, cat. 84).

Arashi Hinasuke I created the role of the famous thief Ishikawa Goemon at the first performance of this play in 1778, making it one of his favourites, and performed Goemon in other plays as well. Hinasuke II (1774–1801) had also performed this role in Osaka and in Edo in the second month of 1800 at the Ichimura Theatre. A fan celebrates the memory of Hinasuke:

Koiji ni wa / shinobi no jutsu ya / oya no me o /
nusumu shōne no / tama de koso are
In the ways of love
One needs the skill of stealth
Stealing the eye of your father
Such spirit
Truly the jewel among all.
SHŌYU SANJIN ('Soy sauce brewer')

The poem celebrating Yoshizawa Hakō (Iroha I and later Ayame V, 1755–1810) in the role of the courtesan Hana Tachibana is by Shōkōsai himself (see fig. 3 above):

Koyoi koso / shubi yoshizawa to / hatsukoi no / kao ni
momiji no / iroha somekeri
Tonight especially
Things will go well
First love with Yoshizawa
Cheeks glowing, colour deep
As autumn leaves swirling about Iroha
SHŌKŌSAI

The poem expresses excitement and fascination with the sexual allure of the female role specialists (*onnagata*) on stage. It turns on double meanings for the sounds within his name Yoshizawa Iroha: *yoshi* for 'good' and *iroha* meaning 'colour'.

The two copies of *Yakusha hama no masago* in UK collections (The British Library, Cambridge University Library) are both from the edition published in Wakayama in 1805.

83

86 Twenty-six bust portraits of Osaka Kabuki actors

ILLUSTRATED Nakayama Bunshichi II (right) and Yoshizawa Iroha I (left)

c. 1795–8

Artists: Shōkōsai Hanbei (17), Yasutaka (3), Kijōsai (1), Shungyoku (1), Tōkōsai (1) and Jūbai (1)

Ink and colour on paper, *tanzaku* formats, various sizes

The British Museum, London (Japanese Paintings ADD 1220-1245)

Shōkōsai was involved with Kabuki theatre from at least the late 1780s; he contributed a poem to a memorial *surimono* for a former head of the Sasase fan club, which is dated to 1790 (cat. 51). His earliest actor print dates from 1795. This is the largest group currently known from the 1790s of half-length painted portraits of Osaka actors, done principally by Shōkōsai, working with a group of five probably amateur pupils. We can surmise that Shōkōsai regularly took commissions from patrons wanting images of their favourite stars. The fact that two portraits of Nakayama Bunshichi II (see also cats 10 and 11) are almost identical implies a certain level of mass production, even.

Recently the identifications of the actor portrayed have been substantially revised by Kitagawa Hiroko. Birth and death dates of the individual actors have been added where known. If Arashi Hinasuke I were still alive when the portrait of him was done then this would date it to before the third month, 1796; certainly given the prominence of Nakayama Bunshichi II it seems safe to assume that his three portraits were done before his death in the second month, 1798. Bringing this information together, it can be suggested tentatively that the group was done about 1795–8.

1. Yasutaka. Yamamura Giemon II (1736–1803). 23.9 x 8.4 cm

2. Yasutaka. Yoshizawa Kamezō (Mimasu Daigorō III, 1782–1824). 25.5 x 8.3 cm

3. Yasutaka. Nakayama (Izumikawa) Tatezō I (dates unknown). 23.6 x 8.1 cm

4. Yasutaka. Onoe Koisaburō I (Shinshichi I, 1745–1809). 23.6 x 8.1 cm

5. Kijōsai. Yoshizawa Iroha I (1755–1810).
   28.2 x 7.7 cm

6. Shungyoku. Nakayama (Hyakumura) Tomokurō I
   (d. 1815). 24.3 x 7.8 cm

7. Jūbai. Asao Tamejūrō I (1735–1804, acted to 1803).
   20.9 x 7.5 cm

8. Tōkōsai. Anekawa Shinshirō III (1748–1805).
   26.1 x 8.0 cm

9. [Unsigned]. Yoshizawa Iroha I. 21.9 x 7.2 cm

10. Shōkōsai. Nakayama Bunshichi II (1755–98).
    27.7 x 8.2 cm

11. Shōkōsai. Nakayama Bunshichi II. 28.1 x 8.0 cm

12. Shōkōsai. Asao Tamejūrō I (right) and Nakayama
    Bunshichi II (left). 27.9 x 15.8 cm

13. Shōkōsai. Nakayama Bunshichi II (right) and
    Yoshizawa Iroha I (left). 28.3 x 14.9 cm
    (Illustrated)

14. Shōkōsai. Arashi Sangorō II (1732–1803).
    28.4 x 8.0 cm

15. Shōkōsai. Fujikawa Tomokichi I (1759–1808).
    28.4 x 8.0 cm

16. Shōkōsai. Mimasu Tokujirō I (1750–1812).
    28.4 x 8.1 cm

17. Shōkōsai. Arashi Hinasuke II (right, 1774–1801)
    and Yamashita Kinsaku II (left, 1733–99).
    28.2 x 14.0 cm

18. Shōkōsai. Seki Sanjūrō (San'emon) I (1747–1808).
    28.2 x 8.1 cm

19. [Unsigned]. Ichikawa Danzō IV (1745–1808).
    27.2 x 7.9 cm

20. Shōkōsai. Arashi Hinasuke II. 27.8 x 8.2 cm

21. Shōkōsai. Yoshizawa Iroha I and Sawamura Kunitarō
    I (left, 1739–1818; retired 1805). 24.7 x 16.0 cm

22. Shōkōsai. Otowa Jirosa (dates unknown).
    28.0 x 8.1 cm

23. Shōkōsai. Yamamura Giemon II. 29.1 x 8.4 cm

24. Shōkōsai. Yoshizawa Enjirō I (above, 1783–1819)
    and Onoe Koisaburō I (below). 28.0 x 16.0 cm

25. Shōkōsai. Arashi Hinasuke I (1741–96).
    27.7 x 8.0 cm

26. Shōkōsai. Asao Tamejūrō I. 27.2 x 8.1 cm

The paintings are listed in Haruyama 1931, pp. 22–3,
with the following, sometimes different actor
identifications: 1. Bandō Iwagorō; 2. Arashi Bungorō;
3. Nakayama Bungorō; 4. Onoe Shinshichi; 5. Fujikawa

87

Tomokichi; 6. Nakayama Tomokurō; 7. Ichikawa Danzō
IV; 8. Fujikawa Hachizō III; 9. [Unidentified];
10. Nakayama Bunshichi II; 11. Nakayama Bunshichi II;
12. Ichikawa Danzō (right) and Nakayama Bunshichi II
(left); 13. Nakayama Bunshichi II (right) and Yamashita
Yaozō I (left); 14. Arashi Sangorō II; 15. Fujikawa
Tomokichi I; 16. Mimasu Tokujirō; 17. Arashi Hinasuke II
(right) and Yamashita Kinsaku (left); 18. Seki Sanjūrō;
19. Ichikawa Danzō IV; 20. Arashi Hinasuke II;

21. Yoshizawa Iroha (right) and Sawamura Kunitarō
(left); 22. Mihogi Giemon; 23. Yamamura Giemon;
24. Yamamura Kumetarō (above) and Onoe Shinshichi I
(below); 25. Arashi Hinasuke I; 26. Asao Tamejūrō I. Similar
identifications were written on small accompanying slips
of paper, possibly by the former owner Okada Isajirō or
the scholar Haruyama Takematsu.

For six similar works, three by Kijōsai, see Nihon
Keizai Shimbun 1975, painting nos 9 and 10 (Kitō
Bunko Collection). Several similar fragments are
preserved in the album *Kyota kyakushokujō* (Waseda
University Theatre Museum, Tokyo), illustrated in
Matsudaira (Waseda) vol. 5, 1995(d), nos 26, 39, 40, 50
and 65, etc.; also Geinōshi Kenkyūkai 1775–6. Nine
similar works by Shōkōsai are included in the album
Shikanjō (Chiba City Museum of Art; cat. 5); see
Chiba-shi Bijutsukan 2001, no. 42.

Ex-coll. Okada Isajirō.

87 Nakayama Bunshichi II as Ogurusu Jūbei

PLAY *Kataki-uchi an'eiroku* at the Kado Theatre;
ninth month, 1796
Artist: Shōkōsai Hanbei
Signature: Shōkō ga
Publisher: Shioya Chōbei
Hosoban, colour woodblock, 31.0 x 13.5 cm
Mukogawa Women's University, Nishinomiya

The play title suggests the vendetta (*kataki-uchi*)
genre, but details of the plot are not known. The
depiction may be compared with a painted half-
length portrait of the same actor, also by
Shōkōsai (cat. 86), of about the same period.

Shōkōsai's earliest *hosoban* print is thought to
date from mid-1795. The collection of half-
length paintings (cat. 86) is thought to have
been produced at the request of Kabuki patrons
around 1795–8. It can be surmised that these
(or similar) paintings may have prompted Shioya
Chōbei to begin publishing single-sheet colour
prints that followed the style of Shōkōsai's predecessor Ryūkōsai.

Ex-coll. Okada Isajirō.

See Keyes and Mizushima 1973, no. 4; Matsudaira
(Waseda) vol. 5, 1995(d), no. 5-45.

88

88 Arashi Hinasuke II as Hanarekoma Chōkichi

PLAY *Futatsu chōchō kuruwa nikki* at the Kado Theatre; first month, 1797

Artist: Shōkōsai Hanbei

Signature: Shōkō ga

Publisher: Shioya Chōbei

Hosoban, colour woodblock, 32.0 x 14.1 cm

Chiba City Museum of Art (2963001)

Hinasuke appears in the role of the noble sumo wrestler Chōkichi.

Chiba-shi Bijutsukan 2001, no. 191.

89 Arashi Sangorō II in a retirement performance, as Yamanaka Saemon

PLAY *Hanagoromo iroha engi* at Tenma Tenjin Shrine; third month, 1798

Artist: Shōkōsai Hanbei

Signature: Shōkō

Publisher: Shioya Chōbei

Hosoban, colour woodblock, 31.0 x 13.6 cm

The British Museum, London (2004.3-27.04)

Arashi Sangorō II retired in the final month of 1797, taking the name Mitsugan. In the third month of 1798, however, he did a special final performance (*issei ichidai*) of six of his trademark roles in a medley from different plays, as a subscription (*kishin*) for the Tenma Tenjin Shrine, Osaka. Sangorō, a Kyoto actor, was popular for his handsome good looks and for his brilliant 'soft' (*wagoto*) interpretation of the roles of young lovers and aristocrats.

Ex-coll. Okada Isajirō.

89

90 Arashi Hinasuke II as Kudō Saemon Suketsune

PLAY *Ume wa kaoru homare Soga* at the Ichimura Theatre (Edo); first month, 1800

Artist: Shōkōsai Hanbei

Signature: Naniwa Shōkō ga ('by Shōkō of Osaka')

Hosoban, colour woodblock, 30.3 x 13.4 cm

Mukogawa Womens University, Nishinomiya

Plays about the Soga brothers Jūrō and Gorō, who carried out a vendetta to avenge their father's murder in 1193, always featured in New Year productions at Edo theatres. Kudō Suketsune is the villain who has killed their father. Hinasuke was a rising Osaka star and went to Edo to boost his career; but he fell ill and died there in the second month, 1801, at the young age of twenty-seven.

The publisher's seal is not one known among Osaka actor print publishers and this may be from an Edo publisher. It is also seen on cat. 91.

Ex-coll. Okada Isajirō.

91 Segawa Rokō as Urakata Ohyaku

PLAY *Azuma-giku Naniwa no kisewata* at the Naka Theatre; eleventh month, 1802

Artist: Shōkōsai Hanbei

Signature: Shōkō

Hosoban, colour woodblock, 30.9 x 13.3 cm

Mukogawa Women's University, Nishinomiya

The actor Rokō (Kikunojō III, 1751–1810) was one of the great specialists in female parts (*onnagata*). He was born in Osaka and started his career early as a child actor. His elder brother also began as an actor, but then became a playwright with the name Segawa Jokō. Rokō performed in Osaka until 1774 when he made his first trip to Edo, where he was to spend most of the rest of his career. He returned to Osaka only once, and stayed for two years from 1802 to 1804. Shōkōsai's poem welcomes him home:

Azuma-giku / iro mo hitoshio / oshiteru ya / Naniwa ni ima wa / kaeri-zaki shite
The eastern [Edo] chrysanthemum
Its precious colour
Shining brightly
Now returns to
Naniwa [Osaka] to bloom

Oshiteru (shining brightly) is a conventional poetic epithet for Naniwa, the historic name for Osaka: the Edo actor Rokō blooms again in Osaka.

The publisher's seal on this print is the same as on cat. 90, and may have been an Edo publisher.

Ex-coll. Okada Isajirō.

90

91

筑紫權六　嵐吉三郎

92 Arashi Kichisaburō II as Tsukushi Gonroku

PLAY *Keisei hako denju* at the Kado Theatre;
first month, 1804

Artist: Shōkōsai Hanbei

Signature: Kōnan Shōkōsai ga

Publisher: Shioya Chōbei

Hosoban, colour woodblock, 31.8 x 14.9 cm

The British Museum, London (2004.3-27.03)

Kichisaburō II (Rikan) was a star lead-actor at
this time and the head of his troupe. The print
celebrates his image as a handsome and virile
hero. Shōkōsai inherited depictions of the older
actors, public portraits that had been established by his teacher Ryūkōsai. In the case of
younger actors like Kichisaburō, however, he was
able to establish his own style, creating a 'likeness picture' (*nigao-e*) that would serve as the
basis for Hokushū and other later artists. An
illustrated playbook (*e-iri nehon*) of this play by
Shōkōsai was published in 1807 with Rikan in
the star role.

Ex-coll. Okada Isajirō; Kuroda 1929, no. 54.

**93 Nakamura Utaemon III (Shikan)
as Hanazono Michitsune**

PLAY *Keisei nazuna no sekku* at the Naka Theatre;
first month, 1806

Artist: Shōkōsai Hanbei

Signature: Kōnan Shōkōsai ga

Publisher: Shioya Chōbei

Hosoban, colour woodblock, 30.6 x 14.9 cm

Waseda University Theatre Museum, Tokyo
(016-0762)

Utaemon III (Shikan) is here depicted as the rival
of Rikan. Shōkōsai uses the same composition as
in cat. 92 to contrast the two actors' styles. The
text, in an elegant running style (*chirashi-gaki*),
appears at first glance to be a *kyōka* poem, but is
in fact a straightforward description of his performance.

   This early portrait of Shikan at the age of
twenty-eight shows him as older and rough-
looking, in the mould of his father who played
villain (*jitsuaku*) roles. Shikan was not considered
to be good-looking but as he became more
famous the depiction of his face softened.

93

94 Ichikawa Danzō IV (top), Arashi Isaburō I (middle) and Asao Tamejūrō I (bottom)

PLAY *Chūshingura*

c. 1800

Artist: Unknown

Publisher: Sudō

Hosoban, woodblock with stencil-printed colours (*kappazuri*), 33.7 x 15.5 cm

Hendrick Lühl Collection (Germany)

A scene from the final revenge attack in the drama *Chūshingura*, the vendetta of the forty-seven loyal samurai of the Akō fief (based on a sensational historical incident of 1702). No record has survived of the three actors performing together in these roles, so it is likely a 'dream' or 'imagined' ensemble (*mitate*). It would also seem to be a promotional print in support of Isaburō, Rikan's older brother. The other two other actors depicted were senior figures at the time and Isaburō had only just begun performing minor roles in the top level theatres.

94

2

THE GREAT RIVALRY:

RIKAN VERSUS SHIKAN

1805–25

Introduction

Section Two is the core of the catalogue, and focuses closely on two superstar actors whose lives are magnificently documented in both literary and visual sources. Arashi Kichisaburō II (Rikan, 1769–1821) and Nakamura Utaemon III (Shikan, 1778–1838) were both precocious and dynamic men, born of successful actor fathers, who together in rivalry dominated Osaka Kabuki from about 1805 until Rikan's death in 1821. The two had performed together in their youth, but once Rikan became a troupe leader in 1805 he refused to perform with the more junior Shikan, whom he seems to have despised. They had very different – and seemingly conflicting – personalities, which comes through visually in the prints and verbally in their poems.

In Kabuki history today, Shikan is the more famous of the two, primarily because of his three long and successful tours to Edo (Tokyo), and because his career spanned a golden age of Osaka actor print production, seventeen years longer than Rikan's. He was also a master at cultivating audiences and sophisticated patrons, both on the stage and in cultural salons. Shikan played the complete range of roles, and often performed dazzling quick-change pieces. He gives the impression of having been a tremendously energetic and strategic performer – on and off stage. The timing of his death, just a few years before the shadow cast by the Tenpō Reforms of 1842, which imposed a general crackdown on social and cultural extravagance that also affected Kabuki, guaranteed him a place as a legendary figure in Kabuki history.

Rikan (known after his death as 'Great Rikan'), on the other hand, is relatively less well remembered. He never performed in Edo, only ever travelling as far as Nagoya, and primarily appeared in Osaka and Kyoto; he died in 1821 at the peak of his career, less than a decade into the golden age of Osaka actor-print production that had blossomed from 1813. Rikan was a prolific poet and seems to have been a perfectionist in realistic character portrayal, rather than a showman like Shikan. He limited his repertoire to lead roles only, refusing to play female roles or extravagant dance pieces. He was critical of Shikan's tendency to be a showman who played all role-types (*yakugara*), and even took the decisive step of complaining formally in a letter to Shikan and his producer.

This fascinating exchange of letters between Rikan, Shikan and Shikan's financial backer (*ginshu*) Fushimiya Zenbei (see cat. 8) survives in the book *Setsuyō kikan* (*Interesting Aspects of Life in Osaka*).[1] The correspondence dates from the end of 1819, after Shikan had returned to Osaka to extravagant fanfare following his final tour to Edo. Rikan makes the case that Shikan is harming the success of Rikan's performances and hurting Kyoto–Osaka Kabuki in general by his outlandish showmanship and fierce competitiveness. Rikan argues that Shikan is an outsider to Osaka Kabuki, learning his trade in low-level Osaka theatres and then in Edo before returning to Osaka. He also attacks Shikan's producer, Zenbei, for being obsessed with profit to the detriment of Kabuki tradition. Rikan as the senior Osaka actor makes a case that Shikan is trying to ruin him and thereby topple Kabuki. He complains about all the things that Shikan does to whip up a frenzy among his fans, including the massive flotilla of boats that greeted Shikan's return from Edo. Rikan claims that these actions are ruining other Kabuki performances and disrupting business in general. Rikan also chides him for flooding the market with Shikan-brand products such as fabric designs, to overwhelm Rikan's own brand (cat. 3). Rikan is most vehement in his attack on Shikan's crass showmanship in performing seven quick-change roles and upbraids him for wrecking the inheritance from earlier great actors such as Tomijūrō and Hinasuke, who had first established the dance pieces. The impression is that Rikan, a relatively conservative Osaka actor at the peak of his career, is disgusted with Shikan, who had gone back and forth three times to Edo over an eleven-year period, spending more than seven years away. In Rikan's eyes Shikan is obsessed with promoting his own career to the detriment of Rikan and Osaka Kabuki.

Shikan and Zenbei both responded, pleading that they had no intention of harming the success of Great Rikan. They astutely apologize, professing their innocence and pleading that it has been the fans themselves who have whipped up the frenzy of activity. Shikan is clever. He deflects Rikan's criticisms, taking up most of the points one by one, defending himself, and at the same time seeming to challenge Rikan. The letters give us a taste of the very different personalities of these two giants of the stage. The rivalry between them may at times have been acrimonious, but for their fans and patrons it served as a magnificent catalyst for creativity – witness the flood of actor prints, illustrated books, surimono, paintings, scrapbook albums and parody flybills that ensued.

Frustrated at not being able to lead his own troupe in Osaka, Shikan accepted an invitation to become the head of a troupe at the Nakamura Theatre, Edo, in 1808. This five-year tour proved a great success and Shikan returned to Osaka triumphantly at the end of 1812 to take his place as Rikan's rival. Section Two presents first a sequence of works that relate to Rikan (cats 95–144) and then one which relates to Shikan (cats 145–67), in order to establish the styles and troupes of the two stars. Next comes their rivalry (cats 168–93). Rikan's taking of a new name (cats 194–9) and death (cats 200–14)

are followed by Shikan left as the unrivalled king of Kabuki (cats 215–30). The section ends with Shikan's 'retirement' in 1825 (cats 231–41). Theirs is the history of Kyoto–Osaka Kabuki in the first quarter of the nineteenth century.

Rikan (cats 95–144)

The first group (cats 95–103) brings together representative images of Rikan, each supporting his persona as a rising star. His first great hit role was in the late 1790s as Yojirō the monkey-trainer. The character of a poor but handsome, filial, loyal and compassionate fellow seems to have captured the hearts of his audience, particularly the women fans, for whom he remained the supreme idol until his death. Various media show the range of representation: a painting on a votive panel (ema) presented to a shrine, an illustrated playbook (e-iri-nehon), an actor print, a surimono, a painting in an album and, finally, two scroll paintings.

Thereafter, the Rikan sequence is mostly chronological, starting with a rare early surimono (cat. 104) that marks Rikan's father Kichisaburō I's departure from Osaka to perform in Kyoto in 1779; this is followed by a surimono (cat. 105) that celebrates the promotion of Rikan to become a troupe leader in 1805. Rikan, like his father before him, was deeply involved in literati circles, and surimono were vehicles for confirming an actor's links with a wider culture beyond the stage. The patron of the 1805 surimono was Tomi Doran, a Kyoto courtier and important literati figure who became a major patron of Rikan. The early prints are in the narrow hosoban format, common in Osaka until about 1812. Prints with stencil-applied colour (kappazuri), mostly produced in Kyoto, are also prominent among the representations of Rikan's early career.

The first larger ōban-sized actor prints of 1813 by Hokkei (Shun'yō) and Hokushū (Shunkō) depict the two sides of Rikan that appealed to his audience: Rikan as the muscular hero (the character Yoshizane, cat. 114) and Rikan as the cultured aristocratic gentleman (Ono no Tōfū, cats 117 and 118). The Hokkei print is a rare example from the period that retains its colours almost unfaded, close to their original pristine brilliance. Ono no Tōfū became a Rikan signature role and the surimono by Ashifune (cat. 116) is a good example of a new type of actor-centred surimono that portrayed the person of the actor himself, rather than a still life or nature scene. Rikan was most often paired with the female role specialist Kanō Minshi, son of the great Arashi Hinasuke I. The Minshi–Rikan duo is featured in many diptych and surimono prints (cats 108–9, 111, 121–4, 126 and 130).

One of the most fascinating representations is of Rikan as 'emperor' (cat. 119), the final portrait in the book *Rikanjō*, an adulatory work compiled by patrons and literati that even includes fan letters from women. There is also the rare survival of a painting by Rikan (cat. 136). A group of *surimono* (cats 128, 130–1, 133–5, 137–9) includes magnificent examples of rare works, many introduced here in colour for the first time. The memorial *surimono* made to mark the death of Tomi Doran (cat. 138), a diptych of two large sheets, includes poems by most of the famous Osaka actors (excepting Shikan and some of his troupe) and is one of the largest and most extravagant prints of the age.

A group of five books (cats 140–4) introduces the important genre, unique to Osaka, of illustrated playbooks (*e-iri nehon*), complete Kabuki texts presented as play texts (*daihon*, *daichō*) with roles, actors and stage directions included. Shōkōsai, Ashikuni and Shunkō (Hokushū) all designed books of this type and most feature Rikan in a heroic role. Later illustrated playbooks bring Rikan and Shikan together for an imagined performance.

Shikan (cats 145–67)

For Shikan as well, *surimono* were an essential proof of his links with poetry circles, and added sophisticated lustre to his celebrity. The first two (cats 145–6) are memorials to his father Utaemon I. Lineage was of fundamental importance to actors and memorial *surimono* were the means to establish contemporary links with a legendary past. Prints by Toyokuni (Edo) and Hokkei (Osaka, cat. 147) of Shikan in the same role as Yojirō the monkey-trainer (first made famous by Rikan, see above) show how very different actor likenesses by different artists could be.

Many items relating to Shikan show him travelling between Osaka and Edo, and the enthusiastic farewells and receptions that he received on each of his three tours. Shikan and his backers were masters at creating popular excitement and anticipation. A distinctive Shikan-related genre was to show him in multiple roles in a sequence of Kabuki dances. These were often great hits with the public and attracted new audiences. Cats 157, 159, 160 and 185 show Shikan at his most magnificent, as the show-stopping performer.

Shikan was also good at spotting and fostering talented younger actors and supporting them to stardom. His network among non-Kabuki performers was also wide. Two *surimono* (cats 165 and 167) present him as the patron rather than as the focus. The first is a memorial for the great Bunraku puppeteer Yoshida Bunzaburō and the other is for the promotion of a shamisen-player Suzuki Banri. Shikan

also is often encountered in *surimono* in the guise of patron celebrating the promotion of geisha. His network throughout society was extensive and impressive.

The great rivalry (cats 168–93)

This group includes many works that were created in support either of Rikan or Shikan, the one pitted against the other. Often a work would be produced, for example, by Shikan's fans and then this would be quickly followed by a retort from Rikan's side (cats 170–1). A magnificent *surimono* printed in 1817 (cat. 173), supporting Rikan against Shikan, for instance, consciously aims to better a similar work made one year earlier in support of Shikan (cat. 172), the artist Kunihiro creating an almost mirror-image of the earlier Ashikuni work. One of the very rare images of Rikan looking directly out of the picture (cat. 176) was most likely created by Kunihiro in response to a print of a few months earlier showing Shikan's acting partner Ichikawa Ebijūrō I (cat. 175) in similar pose. Ebijūrō had just returned with Shikan from an Edo tour. Other works show the rivals in competition as sumo wrestlers (cat. 183) or in tug-of-war neck-pulling battles (cats 178 and 181). Parody flybills describing which actor had outdone the other in competing Kabuki performances were also popular at the time (cat. 179).

As described above, Rikan refused to perform with Shikan after 1805, when Rikan became a troupe leader. After Shikan's return from Edo in 1819, however, there was a rash of 'dream team' (*mitate*) prints (cats 188–90) and books (cat. 193) imagining the pair performing together as rivals.

Rikan's change of name and death (cats 194–214)

In the first month, 1821, Rikan created a completely new stage name, Kitsusaburō I, a rare occurrence in Kabuki history. It was a moment of pride at the peak of his career. 'Kitsu' was another reading for the Chinese character for *tachibana* ('mandarin orange'), his personal crest. It was a clever strategy to promote himself and his troupe. Rikan passed on the name Kichisaburō to his young nephew, thereby keeping it within the family, while at the same time establishing the second, new name so that someone else would be able to inherit Rikan's acting mantle on their own merits. It was common to issue celebratory *surimono* prints upon the accession to a new name (cats 194–5). These were aimed specifically at patrons.

At the behest of their fans, Rikan and Shikan finally agreed in the summer of 1821 to perform together later that same year (cat. 199), but Rikan died in the ninth month before this dream could be realized. Memorial prints or 'death pictures' (*shini-e*) were commonly issued when an actor died and usually contain information that gives the exact day of death, his posthumous Buddhist name and final testament poems (cats 200–7). The first year anniversary was another key moment to issue memorial *surimono* (cats 208–11). These served to honour the dead but were also crucial for their successor in demonstrating continuity within the tradition: the king is dead; long live the king.

Shikan unrivalled (cats 215–41)

With Great Rikan no longer his rival, Shikan was left at the pinnacle of the acting world. Another long-standing rivalry, with the great Edo actor Bandō Mitsugorō III was temporarily revived by Mitsugorō's tour to Osaka (cats 215 and 217–18), but it is clear that fundamentally Shikan had no other rivals in Osaka. Kitsusaburō II (Rikan II) would rise to challenge him in later years, but from 1822 to 1825 at least Shikan reigned supreme. A partnership between Shikan and the artist Hokushū resulted in a magnificent series of bust portraits (*okubi-e*, cats 229–30 and 233–6) centred around Shikan's first so-called 'retirement' in 1825. A pair of Kōin *surimono* (cat. 231) also marked this grand occasion, which took place at the very peak of his career. Shikan did not in fact retire, but toured to Kyoto and other cities before returning to Osaka the following year to even greater acclaim. Ever the showman, Shikan continued to perform until his death in 1838 at the age of sixty (cat. 241).

1 Funakoshi 1926–30, vol. 5, pp. 557–64.

CHRONOLOGY

1798 Arashi Rikan I (Kichisaburō II) finds success in the role of Yojirō, the monkey-trainer

1790s Large format (*ōban*) becomes standard in Edo for actor prints

1801–1860s Illustrated playbook (*e-iri nehon*) production in Osaka

1802–1830s Period of activity of the artist Hokushū (Shunkō) (Osaka)

1805 Retirement of the actor Sawamura Kunitarō I; Arashi Rikan I becomes troupe leader

1808–12 Nakamura Utaemon III (Shikan)'s first tour of Edo

1812–21 Rivalry between Arashi Rikan I and Nakamura Shikan (Utaemon III)

1813 Large-format (*ōban*) becomes standard in Osaka for actor prints

1814–15 Nakamura Utaemon III (Shikan)'s second Edo tour

1815 Ichikawa Ichizō I receives the name Ebijūrō from Ichikawa Danjūrō VII in Edo

1817–19 Nakamura Utaemon III's final tour of Edo

1818 Edo artist Katsushika Hokusai visits Osaka

1819 Death of courtier–literatus Tomi Doran

1820–1 Bandō Mitsugorō III and other Edo actors visit Osaka

c. 1821 Edo artist Utagawa Kunisada visits Osaka

1821 (New Year) Rikan takes new stage name Arashi Kitsusaburō I

1821 (summer) Reconciliation of Rikan and Shikan, and agreement to perform together

1821 (ninth month) Death of Rikan

1822 Arashi Tokusaburō II succeeds to the name Arashi Kitsusaburō II (later, in 1828, to Rikan II)

1825 'Retirement' of Nakamura Utaemon III (Shikan)

1820–5 Hokushū produces large head (*okubi-e*) prints of Utaemon III (Shikan)

1825 Nakamura Tsurusuke I takes Shikan as his stage name and becomes Utaemon III's artistic heir

95 Arashi Kichisaburō II (Rikan) as Yojirō the monkey-trainer

1802

Artist: Yoshimura Shūnan

Signature: Hokkyō (Hōkyō) Shūnan
(Shūnan of *hokkyō* rank)

Votive panel (*ema*), ink and colour on wood,
151.1 x 90.7 cm

Dōmyōji Tenmangū Shrine, Osaka Pref.

A votive panel (*ema*) painted by the Osaka artist Shūnan (1763–1812), grandson of Yoshimura Shūzan (1700–73, cat. 1). It was common for actors to make offerings at shrines with which they had particular connections. The Tenmangū Shrine affiliated with Dōmyōji Temple venerates the deified Sugawara Michizane, a high official of the Heian government who was exiled from Kyoto to Daizaifu in Kyushu in 901. Osaka actors often prayed and made offerings at this temple and at Osaka's Tenma Tenjin Shrine when they performed in plays that featured Michizane, such as *Sugawara and the Secrets of Calligraphy* (*Sugawara denju tenarai kagami*).

The image here is of Kichisaburō II (Rikan) in the role of Yojirō the monkey-trainer. He became famous for this role from his first success in 1798 in a seventh-month performance at the Kado Theatre, and performed it again several times in Kyoto and Osaka over the next year, and one time at the Zama Shrine to help raise funds (*kishin*). Hokkei (Shun'yō) did a print of Rikan in the role in a much later performance of the eighth month, 1814 (cat. 97).

Rikan also performed as Terukuni, Michizane's loyal escort in *Sugawara and the Secrets of Calligraphy* at the Kado Theatre in the fifth month, 1799. It is from around this time, 1798–1802, that the actor came to be recognized as a superstar. This framed painting has hung for more than two hundred years in the 'votive panel hall' (*emadō*) in the precincts of Dōmyōji Tenmangū Shrine.

96 *Sarumawashi kadode no hitofushi* *Life of an Itinerant Monkey-trainer*

1811 (reprinted 1835)

Artist: Hokushū

Publishers: Kawachiya Tasuke and others

Hanshibon book, colour woodblock, 3 vols
(bound together as one), 22.2 x 15.0 cm (covers)

Waseda University Theatre Museum, Tokyo (*ro* 5-116)

An example of the illustrated playbook (*e-iri nehon*) genre. The character of Yojirō, the monkey-trainer, was one of Kichisaburō II (Rikan)'s hit roles, first performed in 1798. Here the play is published with Rikan as the lead. For more detail on the play see cat. 97, a print from 1814 of Rikan in this role, and 95 for a votive painting (*ema*) of Rikan as Yojirō.

Illustrated is the double-page colour illustration of Rikan in the role of Yojirō with the monkey Toku on his back. He signs the poem Rikan *sho* ('written by Rikan'), with the seal 'Okajimaya', his clan stage sobriquet (*yago*).

> *Mada samuki / haru ni ta ga bebe / karite kiyo*
> Still cold this spring
> Whose coat
> Shall I borrow for you?
> RIKAN

Rikan shows his warmth toward Toku the monkey, who is like his child.

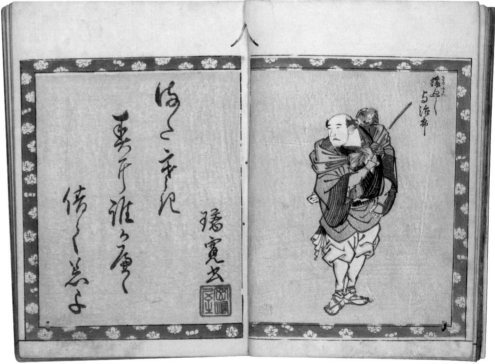

96

97

old mother as a street entertainer, performing with a monkey named Toku, which he treats almost as his own child. Toku has a baby monkey as well. Rikan was successful in presenting the warmth and loyalty of Yojirō toward his mother and younger sister Oshun. Oshun is an indentured prostitute who is in love with Denbei. Denbei in a fight kills a man and flees with Oshun to Yojirō's house. Yojirō at first tells Oshun to keep clear of Denbei, but in the end agrees to help them escape. The play ends happily when it is revealed that the man Denbei killed was in fact in the wrong. Rikan's simple but good-hearted Yojirō, warm and loyal to his family and to the monkey, seems to have been a hit with women fans and launched him as a heart-throb star actor from the first performance in 1798.

98 *Surimono* celebrating Arashi Kichisaburō II (Rikan) and Kanō Minshi I

c. Eleventh month, 1814

Artist: Mitani Goun (attributed)

Signature: Goun

Artist's seals: Unread

Surimono, colour woodblock, 39.2 x 51.9 cm

Waseda University Theatre Museum, Tokyo
(*Nishizawa Ippō harikomichō*, vol. 3)

The two figures seen here are not depicted as likenesses of real actors. The blue robe worn by the aristocratic-looking person to the rear, however, has a design that includes a mandarin orange, which was Rikan's crest. The picture is executed in the suave Maruyama–Shijō style of Kyoto and may be the work of Mitani Goun (worked c. 1790–1822), a pupil of the great Maruyama Ōkyo. There are eighteen verses in total, including two featured next to the picture by the actors Rikan and Minshi. Many of the other poets list their home towns, such as Naniwa (Osaka), Ikeda, Nara, Iga and Aizu, and it is likely that this was produced after a poetry gathering in Kyoto. Kikutarō Kisei, the final, most significant poet who contributed (bottom left), was the Kyoto publisher Kikusha Tahei, also active in haiku circles.

Fuyu ki suru / eda ni mo yuki no / megumi ka na
Even the bare branches
Of a winter tree
Are blessed with snow
RIKAN

Rikan is being modest, saying that he is like an old tree. This poem also appears on a *surimono* dating from the ninth month, 1816 (cat. 134a).

Mimizuku ya / yoru yori hiru no / mono omoi
The horned owl
Worries more in the daytime
Than at night
MINSHI

97 Arashi Kichisaburō II (Rikan) as Yojirō the monkey-trainer

PLAY *Sarumawashi kadode no hitofushi* at the Kado Theatre; eighth month, 1814

Artist: Hokkei (Shun'yō)

Signature: Shun'yō sha

Artist's seal: Unread

Publisher: Shioya Chōbei

Ōban, colour woodblock, 36.6 x 24.8 cm

Victoria & Albert Museum, London (E14737-86-28)

This was one of Rikan's trademark roles from the late 1790s onwards, and is the same image as seen in the votive painting from Dōmyōji Tenman Shrine (1802, cat. 95). Yojirō is initially an unsympathetic character, but later proves to be loyal and heroic. Hokkei made a print of Nakamura Utaemon III (Shikan) in same role in the third month, 1817 (cat. 147). An illustrated playbook (*e-iri nehon*) with the same title as the play, featuring Rikan, was also published in 1811 (cat. 96).

Yojirō is a poor, simple fellow who supports his

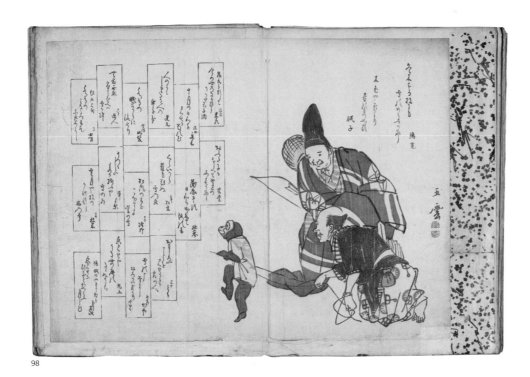

98

scenes were painted across the page-opening suggests they were done around the Bunka era (1804–18).

The second volume (*hen*) contains actor portraits matched with poems (haiku and *kyōka*). The artists involved were Ryūkōsai, Utagawa Toyokuni I (of Edo), Shunkō (Hokushū), Shōraku-sai, Ashikuni and Ashiyuki. In the latter half of the album are bust portraits (*ōkubi-e*) of Arashi Kichisaburō II (Rikan) and Nakamura Utaemon III (Shikan).   KS

Composed about Rikan and Minshi:

Kaomise ni / hiki zo wazurau / tsuki to hana
Seeing both in performance at the beginning
of the season
So hard to choose
Between moon and blossoms
KIKUTARŌ KISEI

Kaomise literally means 'showing one's face', but is also the term for the opening-of-the-season performances usually held in the eleventh month. Rikan and Minshi had performed in *Sarumawashi kadode no hitofushi* in the eighth month of 1814 (see cat. 97). They also performed together in the eleventh month *kaomise* performance at the Kita Theatre in Kyoto. So it seems likely that this *surimono* dates from around that time.

99 *Kaoyobana*
Collection of Iris

ILLUSTRATED Arashi Kichisaburō II (Rikan) as Yojirō
the monkey-trainer

c. 1813–18

Album, ink and colour on paper, 2 vols, 26.5 x 18.3 cm
(covers, *ru*), 28.6 x 21.2 cm (covers, *hen*)

Osaka Museum of History

The album consists of two volumes, entitled *ru* and *hen*. The first volume (*ru*) is dedicated to portraits of Nakamura Utaemon III (Shikan). After two bust portraits (*ōkubi-e*) by Shun'yōsai Hokkei, there are a number of paintings with light colour by Ashikuni. The fact that these

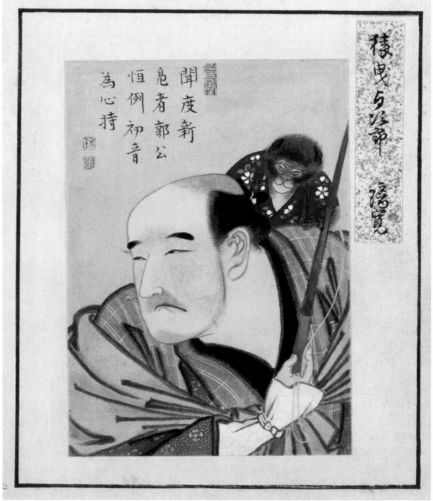

99

100 Arashi Kichisaburō II (Rikan) as Chūbei

c. 1818

Artist: Hokushū

Signature: Shunkō

Artist's seals: Shun, Kō

Hanging scroll, ink and slight colour on paper,
30.4 x 20.7 cm

Chiba City Museum of Art (2941008)

Kameya Chūbei is the lead role in Chikamatsu's famous play *Courier for Hell* (*Meido no hikyaku*). He is a typical handsome Osaka fellow, a better lover and talker than fighter. Chūbei falls desperately in love with a courtesan, Umegawa, but does not have the huge sums needed to ransom her contract. He steals the money, but the pair are caught and executed. Here he is shown in half-length close-up, leaning over the top of a painted folding screen; he is in the courtesan's apartments in the pleasure quarters where he is about to reveal to Umegawa that he has stolen the money to ransom her and is doomed. Rikan was the idol of women fans and here he is presented in a role that he had performed only once, in the third month of 1809 in a new version of the play entitled *Iro-kawase kuruwa ōrai*, paired with Kanō Minshi as Umegawa.

Only a handful of paintings by Hokushū are presently known. This and the next of Rikan (cat. 101), also the one of Nakamura Utaemon III (Shikan, cat. 186), were most likely commissioned by special patrons of the actors.

Nikuhitsu ukiyo-e taikan, vol. 10, 1995, BW no. 16.

101

101 Arashi Kichisaburō II (Rikan) as Torii Matasuke

c. 1818

Artist: Hokushū

Signature: Shunkō

Artist's seals: Shun, Kō

Hanging scroll, ink and slight colour on paper,
28.4 x 19.9 cm

Chiba City Museum of Art (2941009)

Rikan performed the heroic lead of Matasuke in the play *Kagamiyama kuruwa no kikigaki* at the Naka Theatre in the first month, 1818. In this painted close-up portrait in dramatic profile, he pulls a straw rain cape about his head to shelter from torrential rain. For a depiction of the same performance in a print by Kunihiro see cat. 129, where more detail is given of the plot. Rikan had first played this role in the first month of 1801 to great acclaim.

Shunkō began using the name Hokushū from early in 1818.

Nikuhitsu ukiyo-e taikan, vol. 10, 1995, BW no. 17.

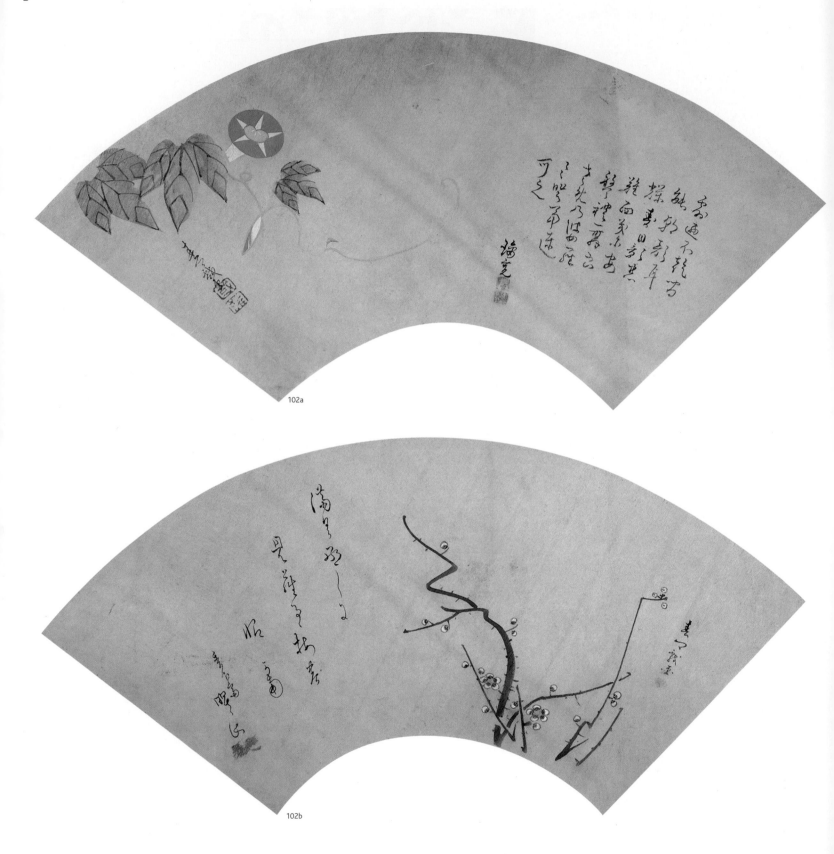

102a

102b

102 Morning Glory Blossoms (a), Plum (b)

Artist: Shunkyō

Signature: Shunkyō giga

Two fan paintings, ink and colour on paper,
48.0 x 35.4 cm (album covers)

Chiba City Museum of Art (*Shikanjō* 2941006)

These two fan paintings by Shunkyō, who was active for only a few years around 1814–15, have poems by Sawamura Tanosuke II (Shōzan) and Arashi Kichisaburō II (Rikan), respectively. They seem to be the models for similar printed images by Shunkyō that appear in the book *Rikanjō* published in the first month, 1815 (cat. 119), and for two *surimono* that celebrate performances by these two actors (see cat. 103 for more details on the performance).

See Chiba-shi Bijutsukan 2001, no. 42; *Nikuhitsu ukiyo-e taikan*, vol. 10, 1995, pp. 237–47, no. 58 (essay by Matsudaira Susumu).

103 Two *surimono* with poems by Arashi Kichisaburō II (Rikan, upper) and Sawamura Tanosuke II (Shōzan, lower)

PLAY *Keisei Tsukushi no tsumagoto* at the Kado Theatre; first month, 1814

Artist: Shunkyō

Signatures: Shunkyō giga, Shunkyō ga

Artist's seals: Unread

Surimono, colour woodblock (2 sheets), 21.4 x 56.8 cm (top), 21.4 x 57.0 cm (bottom)

Waseda University Theatre Museum, Tokyo
(*Nishizawa Ippō harikomi-chō*, vol. 3)

Two long *surimono*, featuring different actors, have been pasted one above the other into the *Nishizawa Ippō* albums (cat. 4). The top print of a morning glory blossom celebrates Rikan and the lower one, of white plum blossoms, Sawamura Tanosuke II (1788–1817). Each has ten poems, with several individuals contributing verses to both. The poets include the artists Shunkyō and Ashifune, as well as the two actors. Nunoya could be the artist Ashikuni, who is known to have used this name.

Tanosuke was the son of Sawamura Sōjūrō III. He first came from Edo to Kyoto–Osaka in 1807 and performed with Rikan. He came again from 1813 to 1815, and in the first month, 1814, the two actors performed together in *Keisei Tsukushi no tsumagoto*. Shunkyō also designed actor prints for this production (Ikeda Bunko 1997, vol. 1, no. 191).

Shunkyō's images of the morning glory and plum blossoms are found in various other contexts. Morning glory appears in the book *Rikanjō* (cat. 119) and in a painting, 'Morning glory', in the *Shikanjō* album (cat. 102) at Chiba City Museum of Art; 'Plum blossoms' is also in the same album. Both paintings incorporate poems by the two actors. The morning glory is also in the book *Shikanjō* (cat. 155a, b).

> *Arigata no / yo ya hana sakanu / kusa mo naki*
> How blessed we are –
> Not a plant in this world
> That does not bloom
> RIKAN

> *Yuki maite / sakura sakura to / arawaruru*
> Snow dances
> Cherry blossom, cherry blossom
> Appears
> ASHIFUNE

Cherry blossom is an image associated with Rikan.

> *E ni wa kakedo / fude ni todokazu / hana-zakari*
> I try to draw him
> But my brush falls short
> This flower at its peak
> SHUNKYŌ

> *Ume ni kite / hatsune hazukashi / hina sodachi*
> Coming to the plum [Osaka]
> Ashamed at my debut
> Raised in the country
> SHOZAN

Tanosuke is modest about having spent most of his time in Edo, away from Kyoto and Osaka where he was born.

> *Narabu mono / hoka ni araji na / ume yanagi*
> There is no other
> To compare to
> Plum and willow
> NIBYŌ

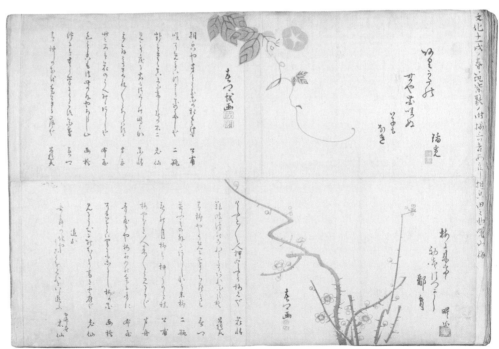

103

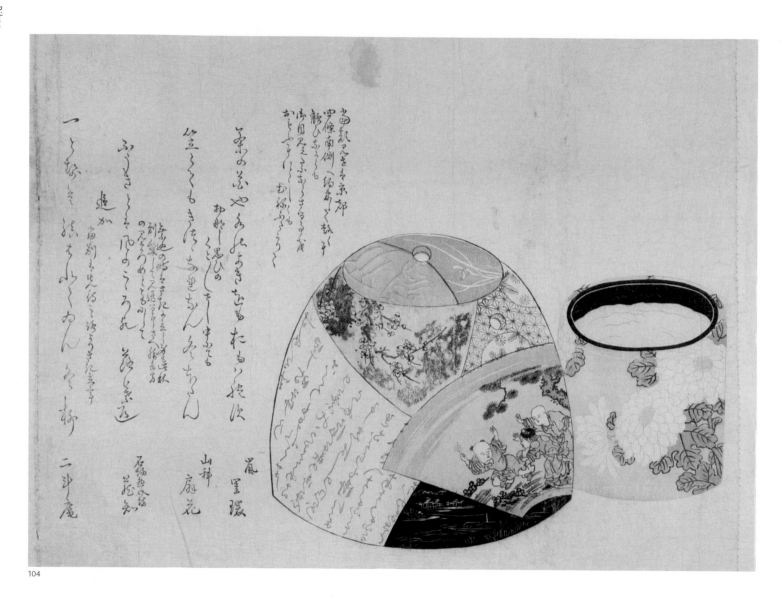

104

104 Arashi Kichisaburō I's farewell to Osaka

Eleventh month, 1779

Surimono, colour woodblock,
34.9 x 46.5 cm

Private Collection (Japan)

Kichisaburō I (1737–80) was Rikan (Kichisaburō II)'s father, and they shared the same pen name (although written with different Chinese characters that have the same pronunciation). This is a very early example of a colour printed *surimono* that relates to Kabuki. It commemorates Kichisaburō I's departure from Osaka to perform in Kyoto for the first time in three years, at the opening-of-the-season (*kaomise*) performance in the eleventh month, 1779, at the Minami Theatre there. The image is of an elegant hand-brazier (*te-aburi* or *hibachi*), the brazier itself painted with chrysanthemums and the domed cover apparently pasted with a fan painting of

Chinese boys and a collage of other, perhaps printed, texts and pictures.

Yamashina Senka, included among the poets, is the actor Yamashina Tsuchigorō. He was in Osaka performing with Kichisaburō I and then went with him to Kyoto. Nitoan (Kabutsu) was well known as a haiku poet and appears in many *surimono* of this time, including several that have actors' poems in them (see, for example, the Keishi *surimono*, cat. 17). His father's obvious connections with literati would have been important for the young Rikan, who was then only ten years old. Kichisaburō I died in Kyoto on the eighth day of the twelfth month, 1780.

The actor critique, *Yakusha shiro-nezumi: kyō*, published in the first month, 1780 (Waseda University Theatre Museum, Tokyo), notes that Kichisaburō I came to Kyoto with Yamashina Senka and that 'he distributed a *surimono* print

with a brazier motif' as his farewell to Osaka. The important role of poetry and *surimono* in actor–patron relations is already evident in this early example.

> Although I am happy to have a contract to perform at Kyoto's Minami Theatre, I am sad to say farewell to good friends.

> *Cha no hana ya / mizu no yoki o mo / omowarezu*
> The flower on the tea bush
> Thinks not
> Of the quality of the water
> ARASHI RIKAN (Kichisaburō I)

Kichisaburō I is saddened to depart for Kyoto and leave his friends behind.

> *Kasa totemo / kitsutsu narenan / fuyu botan*
> Practised though I am
> At wearing a travelling hat
> A peony [brazier] in winter
> YAMASHINA SENKA

A traveller's hat is likened to the straw cover used to protect a peony bloom from the snow in winter. 'Winter peony' is also a nickname for a brazier which, too, has a domed cover like a hat.

> Usually the first one to greet you on arrival, this autumn I shaved my head and retired. So now I join the others to see you off.

> *Fūki to wa / kaze no kokoro ka / ochiba michi*
> Does the wind
> Reflect the season's heart
> A path of fallen leaves
> ISHIBA SŌSUKEBŌ, ZŌCHI

> Finally, the hearts of those left behind, rather than waiting for your return, go first before you.

> *Hito tose wa / musubarete in / fuyu yanagi*
> A year away
> Bound to another
> Weeping winter willow
> NITOAN

Kichisaburō I entered a year's contract to perform in Kyoto. He died there just over a year later.

Kakimori Bunko 1991, no. 133.

105 Retirement of Sawamura Kunitarō I and congratulations to Arashi Kichisaburō II (Rikan)

Fourth month, 1803

Surimono, colour woodblock, 25.6 x 37.5 cm (picture)

Waseda University Theatre Museum, Tokyo
(*Kyota* 18: 59–61)

Text (not illustrated) and picture are now cut up into fragments and pasted into one of the *Kyota* albums. The *surimono* commemorates the retirement of Sawamura Kunitarō I and the promotion of Arashi Kichisaburō II (Rikan) to head of the troupe (*za-gashira*). A branch of mandarin orange (Rikan's emblem) lies across a tasselled cypress-wood court fan (*hiōgi*), decorated with a flying crane above stylized clouds and reeds; Niwa Tōkei is the likely artist. Several other Tōkei *surimono* exist from around this time with Kunitarō, Rikan and Tomi Doran as poets. There are eight actors, one playwright (Chikamatsu Tokuzō), and two others represented among the poets here.

> *Tachibana mo / mukashiya koishi / sode kaoru*
> Fragrance of a mandarin blossom
> Ah, what lovely memories
> Still scent my sleeve
> KITŌ (Sawamura Kunitarō I)

The fragrance of the mandarin flower (*tachibana*), Rikan's crest, is a common metaphor in poetry for evoking memories of lovers long ago. On the surface this certainly refers to the magnificence of handsome Rikan, in his prime and a favourite with women. Kunitarō played woman's roles and

he therefore speaks of Rikan as a sexy man; also, he would have witnessed with pleasure the younger man grow into a first-rate actor. In another way it might also refer to Kunitarō's memory of performing with Rikan's father Kichisaburō I (1737–80), who was only two years older than Kunitarō. Kunitarō retired from the theatre at the time this *surimono* was issued.

> *Osamarite / chiyo no michisuji / suzushikare*
> All well and done
> May the long road ahead
> Be pleasant and smooth
> RIKAN (Arashi Kichisaburō II)

Rikan defers to the elder Kunitarō, wishing him well in retirement, and at the same time modestly hopes that his own tenure as a Kabuki star and troupe leader will be smooth.

> *Mirubusa ni / sake no wakayagu / yoake ka na*
> Long strands of hair
> Lively and young, the saké flowing
> Is it dawn already?
> DORAN

Doran cleverly shifts the imagery back to the poetry gathering and the party atmosphere. The image of young flowing hair (*mirubusa*, literally 'strands of seaweed') evokes Rikan's vibrancy. A new dawn is rising that will lead to a bright future for Rikan, the young and lively actor, and for Osaka Kabuki.

105

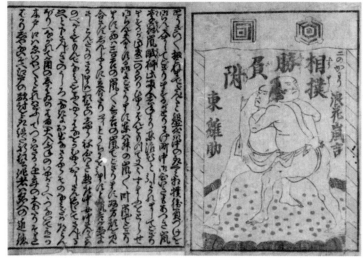

106

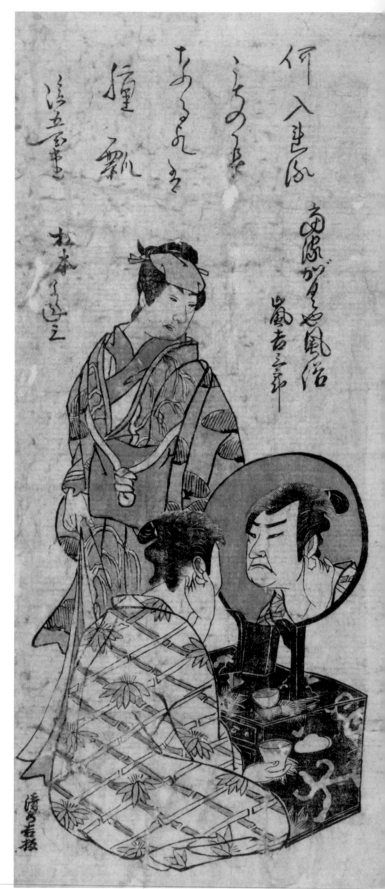

106 'Sumo competition (between two actors)
at the New Year performance'
Ni no kawari sumō shōbu-zuke

c. First month, 1800

Parody flybill (*mitate banzuke*), colour woodblock,
19.4 x 12.8 cm (picture)

Waseda University Theatre Museum, Tokyo
(*Kyota* 16: 83)

With Arashi Hinasuke I deceased and Arashi
Sangorō II retired, Osaka Kabuki needed new
rival stars. This ephemeral comic print promotes
the two young hopefuls Arashi Kichisaburō II
(Rikan, right) and Arashi Hinasuke II (left), as if
they are sumo wrestling opponents. Each actor
grapples to win the bout: who will inherit the
mantle of the great Hinasuke I? In the first
month, 1800, the actors were performing, respectively, at Osaka's Kado Theatre (Rikan) and Edo's
Ichimura Theatre (Hinasuke). The conclusion for
the time being is that neither is better than the
other. However, Hinasuke II died in the second
month, 1801, at the young age of twenty-seven,
before ever becoming a superstar.   MK

107 'Fashions backstage today'
(*Tōryū gakuya fūzoku*), Arashi Kichisaburō II
(Rikan) and Matsumoto Yonesa I

Eleventh month, 1800

Publisher: Shimizu Kichi (Kyoto)

Hosoban, woodblock with stencil-printed colours
(*kappazuri*), 34.5 x 15.0 cm

Hendrick Lühl Collection (Germany)

Rikan is seated in front of the mirror, making up
in his dressing room. The poem is by one Rakugo
Kadō, probably a fan.

For a more detailed discussion of this print see
Matsudaira 1999, p. 149.

107

108 Kanō Minshi I as Ōboshi Rikiya (right) and Arashi Kichisaburō II (Rikan) as Suwa Katsuemon (left)

PLAY *Ehon Chūshingura* at the Kita Theatre (Kyoto); fourth month, 1801

Artist: Shōkōsai Hanbei (attributed)

Publishers: Shioya Chōbei and Futoku

Hosoban, colour woodblock, 31.7 x 14.2 cm

Waseda University Theatre Museum, Tokyo (016-0759)

The play was a theatrical adaptation of an illustrated novel (*yomihon*) of the same title published a year earlier in 1800 in Osaka by the author–illustrator Hayami Shungyōsai (1767–1823). It was one of the many stories that portrayed aspects of the vendetta of the forty-seven loyal samurai, commonly known as *Chūshingura*. Rikiya is the young son of Ōboshi Yuranosuke, the leader of the vendetta group, and is usually played by a female role specialist (*onnagata*). Here Rikiya is played by the actor Minshi, and his costume has elements of the garb of an itinerant mendicant monk. Rikan plays the upstanding samurai Katsuemon, who grasps a pole-arm. This is one of the earliest surviving prints to feature Rikan as a star actor.

109 Kanō Minshi I as Tamanoi Gonpachi (right) and Arashi Kichisaburō II (Rikan) as Hirai Gonpachi (left)

PLAY *Futatsumon kuruwa no nishiki-e* at the Minami Theatre (Kyoto); eleventh month, 1806

Artist: Nagahide (Kyoto)

Signature: Nagahide ga

Octagonal fan print, woodblock with stencil-printed colour (*kappazuri*), 27.1 x 26.1 cm (maximum)

Ikeda Bunko Library (St. N2-2)

Minshi (Arashi Koroku IV, 1783–1829), a star female role specialist (*onnagata*), was the son of Arashi Hinasuke I and often partnered Rikan in performances. Female role stars often also took roles as youths, as here. This unusual octagonal-shaped 'stencil print' (*kappazuri-e*) by Nagahide is one of several he made around 1806–8. The artist was active in Kyoto over a long period from the late 1790s to about 1830, working in the media of both stencil- and woodblock-printing.

Hirai Gonpachi was a samurai who killed another man in a fight and fled to Edo, and was finally executed in 1679. His prostitute lover Komurasaki followed him to Edo and committed suicide at his grave. There are many versions of the tale performed in Kabuki, in all of which Gonpachi is a rough and wild character.

08

110 Sawamura Tanosuke II as the courtesan Azuma (right) and Nakayama Raisuke IV as Yamazaki Yojibei (left)

PLAY *Futatsu chōchō kuruwa nikki* at the Kita Theatre (Kyoto); third month, 1807

Artist: Nagahide (Kyoto)

Signature: Nagahide ga

Octagonal fan print, woodblock with stencil-printed colour (*kappazuri*), 27.0 x 26.3 cm (maximum)

Hendrick Lühl Collection (Germany)

Yojibei is a wealthy merchant whose son Yogorō falls in love with the high-ranked courtesan Azuma, even though he is married. The father sets out to get his son to mend his ways, but in the end is won over and helps him to be with Azuma. This was originally a puppet play, first performed in 1749, which was quickly adapted for Kabuki and is still performed regularly today.

111 Kanō Minshi I as Kagetsuin (right) and Arashi Kichisaburō II (Rikan) as Aoyagi Danjō (left)

PLAY *Keisei itako-bushi* at the Naka Theatre; first month, 1809

Artist: Hokushū (Shunkō)

Signature: Shunkō

Publisher: Shioya Chōbei

Hosoban, colour woodblock, 32.1 x 14.8 cm

The British Museum, London (1906.12-20.0154)

Itako-bushi was a boatman's song from the Tone River that became popular from the 1760s and then again in the early 1800s. A novel *Chūkō itako-bushi* by the Edo author Utei Enba, illustrated by Katsushika Hokusai, was published in 1809, and this play is thought to be a stage version. A lord's retainer pawns a family treasure, throwing the estate into chaos. Loyal followers win out only after long travails, including the selling of a woman into prostitution, and restore order by recovering the treasure and ousting the villains.

The earliest known print by Hokushū (signed with the name Shunkō) dates from the first month, 1802 (fig. 13 above), and his first print in the larger *ōban* format is from the fifth month, 1812 (Ikeda Bunko 1997, vol. 1, no. 34). Only from 1813 did the *ōban* become the standard format for Osaka actor prints, until they were curtailed by the Tenpō Reforms of the 1840s.

111

110

112 Nakayama Hyakka III as Takamaru Kamejirō (right) and Arashi Kichisaburō II (Rikan) as Tadotsu Ikkaku (left)

PLAY *Keisei sato no funauta* at the Kado Theatre; first month, 1810

Artist: Hokushū (Shunkō)

Signature: Shunkō, with handwritten seal (printed, red)

Publisher: Shioya Chōbei

Hosoban, colour woodblock, 32.1 x 14.8 cm

The British Museum, London (2004.3-27.05)

Kamejirō is the heir to a samurai fief, but as a dissolute figure he spends all his time with the Yoshiwara courtesan Higaki. Ikkaku is the senior minister of the fief and tries to get Kamejirō to mend his ways, but with little success. Here Kamejirō, wearing a colourful feminine kimono, gets angry at his retainer, perhaps for scolding him for wasting his time in the pleasure quarter. The play was a revision of *Kuwanoya Tokuzō iri-fune monogatari*, written by Namiki Shōzō I and first performed in 1770. The actor Nakayama Hyakka III (1764–1853) also used the name Nakayama Bunshichi III.

Ex-coll. Okada Isajirō; Kuroda 1929, no. 57.

112

Not used.

113 Arashi Kichisaburō II (Rikan, above) as Kowari Dennai and Arashi Kanjūrō I as Kanzan (below)

PLAY *Kataki-uchi ura no asa-giri*, Naka Theatre; ninth month, 1815

Artist: Nagahide (Kyoto)

Signature: Nagahide ga

Publisher: Kashiwaya Sōshichi (Kyoto)

Hosoban, woodblock with stencil-printed colour (*kappazuri*), 34.0 x 15.0 cm

Hendrick Lühl Collection (Germany)

This play was based on an incident involving the lord of Akashi and a hunter, here called Dennai, who shoots a stranger by accident with a rifle. Dennai is dressed in the guise of an itinerant pilgrim, with stout wooden staff and brass gong hanging at the waist that he beats to accompany his chanting.

114 Arashi Kichisaburō II (Rikan) as Yoshizane

PLAY *Ono no Tōfū aoyagi suzuri* at the Kado Theatre; fourth month, 1813

Artist: Hokkei (Shun'yō)

Signature: Shun'yōsai

Artist's seal: Unread

Publisher: Shioya Chōbei

Ōban, colour woodblock, 38.3 x 25.5 cm

Private Collection (UK)

Rikan appears in the role of Yoshizane, a muscular and sexy rough-edged character, who is nonetheless loyal and even willing to sacrifice his own son for the cause of an imperial prince. In the same performance Rikan also played another role as the famous aristocrat–calligrapher Ono no Tōfū (cats 116–18), a contrasting portrayal of an elegant and refined gentleman scholar which was received with great acclaim. The play was originally a puppet drama, first performed in Osaka in 1754.

115 Thirty-third memorial for Arashi Kichisaburō I (1737–80)

Twelfth month, 1812

Artist: Satō Masuyuki

Signature: Masayuki

Surimono, colour woodblock with metallic pigment, 42.6 x 56.2 cm

Waseda University Theatre Museum, Tokyo (*Nishizawa Ippō harikomichō*, vol. 3)

The picture – a thundering waterfall in a snowy landscape – is by Satō Masuyuki (Suiseki, active *c.* 1805–37), an Osaka pupil of the famous Kyoto artist Go Shun (1752–1811). There is an impressive collection of thirty-one poems by actors, puppet-theatre performers and patrons; the last two poems are by Jōkō (Nakayama Bunshichi I, 1732–1813) and Tomi Doran.

This was a grand occasion, marking the anniversary of the passing of the actor Kichisaburō I, who had died on the eighth day of the twelfth month, 1780. The timing of this memorial suited Kichisaburō II (Rikan) and the Arashi stage clan. In 1812 Rikan was at the peak of his popularity, but had to face the return from Edo of Nakamura Utaemon III (Shikan) after a five-year absence. Shikan returned in the eleventh month for the opening of the season, bringing with him the famous Edo actor Bandō Hikosaburō III to compete against Rikan. It was in this year that the rivalry between Rikan and Shikan, which was to last until Rikan's death in 1821, began in earnest.

The text is formal and the immediate family take precedence: Arashi Isaburō I, the first born; then Takemoto Nakadayū (a puppet-theatre chanter); Rikan; Rikan's son Yoshisaburō; and Isaburō's son Daisaburō (who later became Kichisaburō III). The actor Sawamura Kunitarō (Ebimaru, retired) is also listed among 'the family'. Jōkō (Nakayama Bunshichi I, 1732–1813), as the most senior, is the last actor to offer a verse. Poet and patron Tomi Doran then concludes on an auspicious note. The *surimono* is a memorial for the patriarch, but also a celebration of the success of Rikan's clan and was most likely distributed at the New Year, 1813.

> How delighted I am that we have been able to get all the family together to commemorate this thirty-third anniversary. Nothing could please me more.
>
> *Oi-zuri ni / yuki no mashiro ya / tamuke-gusa*
> To the pilgrim with his load
> The snow was pure white
> I offer these flowers
> KANSHI (Isaburō)
>
> *Sanjū mitose / iza ya tsukuran / yukibotoke*
> Thirty-three years
> Time to make
> A 'snow Buddha'
> NAKATAYŪ

Hotoke means both the 'Buddha' and the 'deceased'.

> *Waga kage no / utsuru ya aka no / mizu kōru*
> My reflection
> In the holy water
> Frozen
> RIKAN
>
> *Yuki no take / horieshi gotoki / tamuke ka na*
> Like the faithful son who
> Found bamboo shoots in the snow
> I make my offering
> EBIMARU (Kunitarō)

Even at the twenty-fifth memorial there were few who came to make their offerings. Now even more so after thirty-three years have passed, only a rare few are left from that time. The floating world is like a dream, they say. But now looking back, to survive to see this day, though I say it myself, how terrifying, how overwhelming.

> *Mata kotoshi / tomurau ya kamiko no / sode nururu*
> Again this year I mourn
> The sleeves of my paper robe
> Are wet
> JŌKŌ (Bunshichi I)

Kamiko is a cheap 'paper' kimono. It is associated with certain characters in Kabuki who have fallen on hard times.

> With each passing month and day the Arashi family grows more famous. Today it commemorates the thirty-third anniversary of his death. His spirit must surely rejoice to see this occasion. And for those who conduct this service, doesn't this reflect their success in this life.

> *Nigiyakasu / samusa wa shiranu / butsuma ka na*
> With all this activity
> The memorial altar room
> Never knows the cold
> DORAN

Doran turns the focus back to the living and celebrates their liveliness and success.

Another impression, with text, is included in *Kyota* (Waseda) 23: 71–3.

116 Arashi Kichisaburō II (Rikan) as Ono no Tōfū

PLAY *Ono no Tōfū aoyagi suzuri* at the Kado Theatre; fourth month, 1813

Artist: Ashifune

Signature: Ashifune sha

Artist's seal: Ashifune (hand-impressed)

Surimono, colour woodblock with metallic pigment, 41.7 x 57.1 cm

Waseda University Theatre Museum, Tokyo (*Nishizawa Ippō harikomichō*, vol. 3)

The play was a great success for Rikan, in the two roles of the aristocrat–calligrapher Ono no Tōfū, seen here, and as Yoshizane (see also cats 117 and 118). The actor was competing against his younger arch-rival Nakamura Utaemon III (Shikan), who had returned with great fanfare to perform in Osaka in the eleventh month, 1812, after five years away touring in Edo. Shikan was successful with his dance medley *Minarōte yahari shichi henge* performed at the nearby

116

Naka Theatre in the same month, but his appearance as the warrior Kumagai in *Ichinotani futaba gunki* was a flop.

This *surimono* designed by Ashifune is offered in support of Rikan against Shikan. There are seven poems, one by Rikan, one by the aristocrat–literatus Tomi Doran, and five by unknown individuals including two women – probably amateur poet-fans. Rikan is known to have been a particular favourite with women. A fascinating letter survives from Doran to one of his female students, Fujie, in which he discusses the performances during this period of Rikan and Shikan at the rival neighbouring Kado and Naka theatres. He praises Rikan and says how Shikan's performance paled in comparison. Doran also says that a group of Rikan's Kyoto fans had sent ten large banners to celebrate Rikan's Osaka successes, and that Doran and Rikan had prepared a *surimono* as a gift of thanks to them. He then says that he is sending a copy of the *surimono* with the letter. Doran refers to Rikan as

'Teruhiro', praises him as a magnificent haiku student, and adds that there is no other actor who compares (*Kabuki nenpyō* vol. 5, pp. 515–17).

Hototogisu / matsu ni arashi no / ataru koe
Cuckoo cry in summer
Like a storm [Arashi]
Striking the pine
SAKUJO (Woman)

The Japanese cuckoo has a striking cry, which is here likened to a storm (*arashi*) striking a pine (*matsu*). 'Arashi' refers to Arashi Rikan and 'matsu' to Shikan (Shikan's crest was a crane which is associated with pine). Rikan's performance is magnificently popular (*ataru*), showing up that of Shikan.

Urigoe ni / senryō wa ari / hatsu-gatsuo
The vendor's cry
Worth a thousand gold pieces
First bonito of the year
KIKUJO (Woman)

Like rising auction bids to buy the first bonito of

the season, the audience cries out for Rikan's performance, worth a thousand gold pieces. A top actor's annual salary was indeed said to be a thousand gold pieces.

Sono fude ni / shōbu no ka ari / sumi no tsuya
On his brush
Fragrance of the iris
Lustrous ink
DORAN

Rikan is presented as the most elegant of artists, fittingly able to perform the role of aristocrat–calligrapher Ono no Tōfū.

The right half of the *surimono*, comprising most of the image, was reprinted as a sheet print when Rikan took the new name Kitsusaburō I in the first month, 1821 (cat. 117). Ashifune, who was only active as an artist for a few years *c*. 1814–16, may have been the actor Yamashita Mangiku II (also Mansaku, *c*. 1792–1811): one of the actor's four pen names (*haimyō*) was Roshū, also read Ashifune.

118

117 Arashi Kitsusaburō I (Rikan) as Ono no Tōfū

PLAY *Ono no Tōfū aoyagi suzuri*; first month, 1821

Artist: Ashifune (after)

Ōban, colour woodblock with metallic pigment, 34.7 x 23.6 cm

Private Collection (UK)

Rikan first performed the role of the aristocrat–calligrapher Ono no Tōfū in the play *Ono no Tōfū aoyagi suzuri*, staged to great acclaim at the Kado Theatre in the fourth month, 1813. This performance was celebrated in an Ashifune *surimono* (cat. 116), the right half of which has here been reused, in the first month, 1821, when Kichisaburō took the new name Kitsusaburō I. The original poems have been omitted and a different text added, with a note that the calligraphy is in Rikan's own hand. In the play Ono no Tōfū is portrayed not only as a calligrapher but also as a strong and loyal character who restores the fortunes of the imperial house after an insurrection.

> *Tomomashite / sanshi ni egao ya / yuki no tori*
> How lucky to have patrons
> I perch smiling three branches down
> A bird in the snow
> RIKAN

Rikan refers to a Chinese saying: 'A dove sits three branches below its parents in gratitude; a crow brings food to the mouths of its parents to serve them.' Rikan is thanking his patrons and the older actors for supporting him in taking a new stage name.

The large Chinese characters at the top left are a playful, game-like riddle playing around with the characters of his name, praising him as a true gem of the theatre.

118 Arashi Kichisaburō II (Rikan) as Ono no Tōfū (right) and Asao Kuzaemon I as Tokko no Daroku (left)

PLAY *Ono no Tōfū aoyagi suzuri* at the Kado Theatre; fourth month, 1813

Artist: Shunkō (Hokushū)

Signature: Shunkōsai ga

Publisher: Shioya Chōbei

Ōban, colour woodblock, diptych, 37.5 x 25.6 cm (right), 37.4 x 25.5 cm (left)

The British Museum, London (2004.6-19.01,1-2)

The performance as the aristocrat–calligrapher of the classical period, Ono no Tōfū, was a great success for Rikan. This became a trademark role in his later career when he and his patrons promoted his image as a poet and calligrapher. See cat. 116 for a *surimono* celebrating this performance; also cat. 114 for another print depicting the same production.

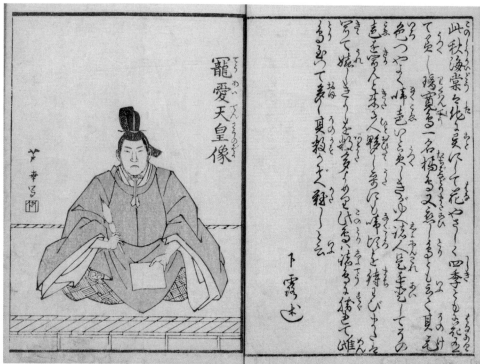

龍愛天皇像

119

119 (Shōsan gagen) Rikanjō
Elegant Words of Praise: Rikan Album

First month, 1815

Author: Akatsuki Kanenari

Publishers: Kawachiya Tasuke, Ishikawaya Wasuke and Matsuya Zenbei (Nagoya)

Chūbon book, woodblock, 2 vols, 18.0 x 12.4 cm

Private Collection (UK)

The book is in praise of Arashi Kichisaburō II (Rikan) and was composed to rival *Shikanjō* published less than a year before (cat. 155a, b). Shikan was away performing in Edo by the time this book was issued. One extraordinary image (illustrated) is a 'parody picture' (*mitate-e*) by Ashiyuki of Rikan as 'Our Beloved Emperor' (Chōai Tennō); another shows Rikan as the scholar Kumazawa Banzan, a theatrical role he had played the year before. There are also several verses by *kyōka* poets and one haiku poem by Rikan himself. The book even records a love letter from a female fan. The drawings in the book are by artists who also designed prints and *surimono* around this time: Ashikuni, Ashiyuki, Ashifune, Yoshikuni and Shunkyō.

The Shunkyō image of a morning glory vine is similar to a *surimono* he designed (cat. 103), and also to a painting by him in *Shikanjō* (cat. 102).

For a full transcription and commentary see Ogita 2002.

120 Arashi Kichisaburō II (Rikan) travels in Bizen

Eleventh month, 1813

Surimono, colour woodblock, 2 sheets (of 4), 19.1 x 50.9 cm (top), 19.0 x 50.8 cm (bottom)

Waseda University Theatre Museum, Tokyo (*Nishizawa Ippō harikomichō*, vol. 3)

In this travelogue *surimono*, which has a very long text, Rikan elegantly recounts his journey of about three weeks through Bizen Province

west of Kyoto–Osaka in the ninth month, 1813. The narrative, interspersed with more than thirty haiku and *kyōka* poems by Rikan about the places visited, ends with his return to the residence of Tomi Doran at Higashiyama, Kyoto, where he joins Doran's poetry circle. Rikan signs himself 'Kinkitsurō Rikan', using his art-name (*gō*). Here we have an image of Rikan as an elegant and refined gentleman scholar, not as a Kabuki actor. Twelve fans, including two priests, offer eight haiku and four *kyōka* verses. Doran contributes a *kyōka*. Rikan performed at Kyoto's Minami Theatre from the fifteenth of the eleventh month, 1813. Included was the role of the Kyoto courtier Ono no Tōfū, as depicted in cats 116 and 118.

On leaving Osaka behind;

Furusato o / idete nagame ya / no no susuki
Departing my home town
The view ahead
Pampas grasses in the fields
RIKAN

Two patrons offer particular support:

Yuki ni kite / arashi ni tsuru no / yukue ka na
Arriving in snow
The crane is lost
In the storm
ROYŪ

'Crane' refers to Rikan's rival Utaemon III (Shikan) who is lost in the 'storm' (*arashi*) of Rikan. The next verse is even more explicit:

Tsuru o kete / modoru ya taka no / hito-arashi
Kick out the crane
The hawk has returned
Like a storm
SOKYŌ

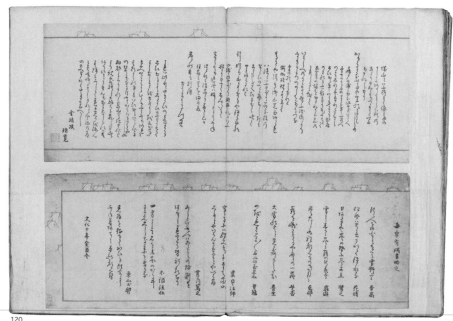

120

121

Kenbutsu o / matasete oini / tsugō you / fune tsuki-ateshi / kyō no kaomise
Keeping his
Audience waiting
Arriving just in time
The boat lands
Kyoto's season-opening
HIGASHIYAMA DORAN

Actors arrived in boats at the opening-of-the-season (*kaomise*) performance in the eleventh month of the year, which was mid-winter by the lunar calendar.

121 Kanō Minshi I as the young woman Okiyo (right) and Arashi Kichisaburō II (Rikan) as Kowari Dennai (left)

PLAY *Kataki-uchi ura no asa-giri* at the Naka Theatre; ninth month, 1815

Artists: Hokushū (Shunkō, right) and Shunchō (left)

Signatures: Shunkō ga, Shunchō ga

Publisher: Shioya Chōbei

Ōban, colour woodblock with metallic pigment, diptych, 37.5 x 51.2 cm (right), 38.5 x 52.0 cm (left)

Hendrick Lühl Collection (Germany)

Dennai was one of Rikan's most popular roles. He is a hunter who gets mixed up in a murder.

The original story was based on a real incident of 1804, which involved the lord of Akashi and a hunter named Gennai. Nagawa Harusuke wrote this play specifically for Rikan to take the lead role.

The diptych print is an example of a 'joint production' (*gassaku*) between two or more artists. Such collaborations in multi-sheet prints were quite common in Osaka; in contrast to Edo, where they were rare. Compare the Ashikuni *surimono* (cat. 131) which features the same performance.

122a

122b

122a Arashi Kichisaburō II (Rikan) as Kajiwara Heizō

PLAY *Yoshitsune senbon-zakura* at the Naka Theatre; second month, 1816

Artist: Shungetsu

Signature: Shungetsu sha

Publisher: Jū (mark)

Koban, colour woodblock, 17.3 x 11.5 cm

Hendrick Lühl Collection (Germany)

This is one of a group of small-format (*koban*) prints, many by otherwise unknown minor artists, most likely Kabuki fans, all published in 1816. The Lühl Collection includes as many as fifty such *koban* prints from around 1816–17. Once again it is fascinating to observe the participation of fans in Kabuki culture. Most of the series feature Nakamura Utaemon III (Shikan), who had returned from his second trip to Edo in the tenth month, 1815. The album *Kyota kyakushokujō* (Waseda 26: 55–6) includes three slightly larger, *chūban*-sized prints dating

from the fifth month, 1816 – two by Shunkō (Hokushū) and one by Shunsen – as well as one related anonymous *chūban*-sized painting. All are in a similar style to these *koban* prints.

Kajiwara Heizō is a stern samurai who represents the power of Shogun Yoritomo, in pursuit of the routed Taira (Heike) clan warriors who flee from Yoritomo's triumphant armies.

122b Kanō Minshi I as Fujiya Azuma

PLAY *Abura-uri kuruwa monogatari* at the Naka Theatre; eighth month, 1816

Artist: Shunki

Signature: Shunki sha

Publisher: Tsuji (mark)

Koban, colour woodblock, 17.7 x 11.8 cm

Hendrick Lühl Collection (Germany)

Azuma is an alluring courtesan. Compare this print with the Hokushū print of the same actor in the same role (cat. 123).

122c Nakamura Utaemon III (Shikan) as Mohei (not illustrated)

PLAY *Yado nashi Danshichi shigure no karakasa* at the Ichinokawa (Horie) Theatre; eighth month, 1816

Artist: Shunri

Signature: Shunri sha

Publisher: Tsuji (mark)

Koban, colour woodblock, 17.7 x 11.6 cm

Hendrick Lühl Collection (Germany)

122d Ichikawa Ebijūrō I as Yamaguchi Kurojirō (not illustrated)

PLAY *Gion sairei shinkōki* at the Kado Theatre; fifth month, 1816

Artist: Shōkō

Signature: Shōkō ga

Publisher: Tsuji (mark)

Koban, colour woodblock, 17.0 x 11.8 cm

Hendrick Lühl Collection (Germany)

Lühl n.d., nos 25–38.

123

123 Kanō Minshi I as Azuma (right) and Arashi Kichisaburō II (Rikan) as Yohei, the oil-seller (left)

PLAY *Abura-uri kuruwa monogatari* at the Naka Theatre; eighth month, 1816

Artist: Shunkō (Hokushū)

Signature: Shunkō ga

Publisher: Shioya Chōbei

Ōban, colour woodblock, diptych, 38.2 x 26.6 cm (right), 37.8 x 26.6 cm (left)

Fitzwilliam Museum, Cambridge (P.381-1996)

Rikan plays the dandyish character of Yohei, an oil-seller. Here he drops his pipe and tobacco case in sudden amazement when the beautiful courtesan Azuma looks back seductively at him.

This play was first performed in the fifth month, 1803, at the Kita Theatre, Kyoto, with Rikan in the lead role of Yohei. The print shows the scene when Yohei is smitten by the charms of Azuma, a high-class courtesan, and he subsequently struggles to get the money to engage her. His trip into the world of the pleasure quarter with its complex etiquette was considered a highlight of the play – a perfect role for Rikan who was considered a matinée idol by his women fans. Although Azuma likes Yohei, she refuses to sleep with him because she is committed to another man due to her father's money problems. After persevering, the pair are united in the end. With this revival of the play in 1816 at the height of his popularity, Rikan established it as one of his trademark roles.

Another impression in the collection of Ikeda Bunko Library is a reissue at the time of Rikan's death in 1821 (Ikeda 2001, vol. 3, no. 531). It includes one of the actor's poems.

124 Arashi Kichisaburō II (Rikan) as Sasahara Hayato (right) and Kanō Minshi I as Chigusa-hime (left)

PLAY *Koi momiji ogura no shikishi* at the Naka Theatre; ninth month, 1816
Artists: Shunkō (Hokushū, right) and Ashikuni (left)
Signatures: Shunkō ga, Ashikuni ga
Publishers: Hon'ya Seishichi and Sōshiya
Ōban, colour woodblock, diptych, 39.5 x 26.0 cm (right), 39.3 x 26.5 cm (left)
Hendrick Lühl Collection (Germany)

Nagawa Harusuke and a team of other writers composed this play for Rikan and his troupe, with Rikan performing the lead roles of Hayato, the fox Sankichi and the boat captain Koheiji. Hayato is a loyal minister to his lord, but is slandered by evil plotters and fired from his position.

He becomes a master-less samurai (*rōnin*) but still remains faithful to the lord and the fief. See the Ashikuni two-sheet *surimono* (cat. 134a, b) for another representation of this performance.

The scene shown here is from towards the end of the play. Hayato holds up the precious 'Ogura no shikishi' (part of the title of the play), an inscribed poem card that is the most important treasure of the fief, which had been stolen. The recovery of the heirloom allows for the resolution of the crisis. In the play the fox Sankichi gives Hayato supernatural powers, here represented by the hovering flames, which can also represent dead spirits. Lady Chigusa, daughter of Hyōgo, leader of the insurrection plot, is unaware of her father's evil deeds and loves Hayato.

125 Arashi Kichisaburō II (Rikan) as Benkei

PLAY *Gosho-zakura Horikawa yo-uchi* at the Naka Theatre; eleventh month, 1816
Artist: Ashikuni
Signature: Ashikuni
Publisher: Sōshiya
Ōban, colour woodblock, 37.5 x 25.6 cm
Hendrick Lühl Collection (Germany)

Musashibō Benkei is one of the best-loved figures in Japanese history. He was sent to Enryakuji Temple to become a monk but spent his time instead in martial training, later becoming the loyal right-hand man of warrior general Minamoto no Yoshitsune. Benkei appears in many plays, always as a brash, strong and loyal soldier. This particular drama was originally a puppet play, first performed in Osaka in the first

125

126 Arashi Kichisaburō II (Rikan) as Kaiya Zenkichi (right) and Kanō Minshi I as Oroku (left)

PLAY *Kamikakete chikai no tsuma-gushi* at the Kado Theatre; eighth month, 1814

Artist: Ashikuni

Signature: Ashikuni sha

Artist's seal: Ashikuni (?)

Surimono, colour woodblock, 17.7 x 25.0 cm

Hendrick Lühl Collection (Germany)

Rikan is in the role of Kaiya Zenkichi and Minshi plays his lover Oroku. The play was written by Nagawa Harusuke for Rikan and his troupe, and was based on the final 'Nibugawa' section of Takizawa Bakin's novel *Aoto fuji tsuna mori yōan* (1812). Zenkichi is framed by his wife and her lover, and faces the death penalty, but in the end his lover of long ago, Oroku, saves him by revealing the truth.

> *Furusato o / omou tabine ya / sayo kinuta*
> Dreaming of home
> Asleep on a journey
> Sound of a fulling-block in the night
> RIKAN

> *Murasame ni / furikomerarete / mado no chō*
> In the autumn shower
> Trapped at the window
> A butterfly
> MINSHI

> *Ogi hagi ya / onaji soyogi no / chikamasari*
> Reeds and bush clover
> Bending in the wind
> Look better closer
> KOTOSHA

There is an illustrated playbook (*e-iri nehon*) of this drama, with illustrations by Ashikuni (cat. 193b). The two figures also appear cut out and pasted into *Kyota* (Waseda) 24: 44.

month, 1737. Benkei meets young Yoshitsune (then known by his adolescent name Ushiwakamaru) for the first time at Gojō Bridge in Kyoto, where they fight. To Benkei's surprise, he is defeated by the younger warrior. (The story is reminiscent of the first encounter between Robin Hood and Little John.)

The scene depicted is immediately after Benkei has had to kill his own illegitimate daughter Shinobu, to protect her mistress Kyō no Kimi, who is Yoshitsune's wife. Shinobu is willing to die for her mistress's sake. Benkei here reveals the red kimono to show Shinobu's mother that he knows that he is, in fact, the father of Shinobu. The actor must show both his loyalty and the pain at having to kill his daughter.

126

127a

127b

127a, b Arashi Kichisaburō II (Rikan) as Sutewakamaru

PLAY *Chigo ga fuchi hana no shiranami* at the Naka Theatre; first month, 1817

Artist: Ashihiro

Signature: Ashihiro ga

Publisher: Shioya Chōbei

Ōban, colour woodblock, 38.1 x 25.8 cm

Hendrick Lühl Collection (Germany)

The play was a version of *Keisei chigo ga fuchi*, first performed in Kyoto in the first month, 1782. Based on historical events, it told the story of the defeat of the warrior general Akechi Mitsuhide (1528–82), who had assassinated supreme warlord Oda Nobunaga and then himself been killed. Akechi's followers attempt to attack Hideyoshi, Nobunaga's successor. Sutewakamaru, Akechi's heir, becomes an acolyte (*chigo*) at Kiyomizu Temple, Kyoto. He dives into

Chigo-ga-fuchi Pond, ostensibly to atone for his father's crime, but secretly to recover a famous heirloom sword from under a rock. He then escapes with Okaji.

This is the left sheet of a diptych and shows Rikan as the acolyte Sutewakamaru, from the same performance as the two *surimono*, cats 128 (by Ashikuni) and 173 (by Kunihiro). He struggles out of the pond amid torrential rain and lightning, a stone statue of the Bodhisattva Jizō still roped to his back. The right sheet shows Kanō Minshi as Okaji (Ikeda Bunko Library; see Ikeda 1997, no. 406). Cat. 127b (Private Collection, UK) illustrates a print by Shunkō (Hokushū) showing Rikan in the same role.

Rikan and Shikan both played the role of Sutewakamaru at this same time, in competition at the Naka and Kado Theatres respectively. A parody playbill (*mitate banzuke*), which com-

pares the two performances, gives Rikan the decision over Shikan on this role (*Kyota* [Waseda] 27: 18).

128 Arashi Kichisaburō II (Rikan) as Sutewakamaru

PLAY *Chigo ga fuchi hana no shiranami* at the Naka Theatre; first month, 1817

Artist: Ashikuni

Signature: Ashikuni sha

Artist's seal: Ashikuni (hand-impressed)

Surimono, colour woodblock with metallic pigment, 38.9 x 52.1 cm

Private Collection (Japan)

Sutewakamaru, young son of the assassin Akechi Mitsuhide, has been sent to become a monk to atone for his father's sins. He carries a branch of blossom in a flower-bucket. In the background,

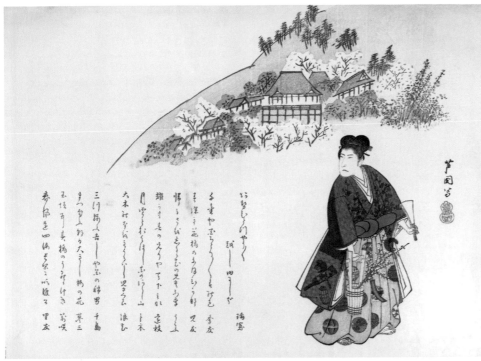

128

129

Tsuki yuki mo / oyobaji hana no / Arashi-yama
Neither moon nor snow
Can compare to blossoms
On Mt Arashiyama
BOKUBOKU

Comparisons between 'Snow, moon and flowers' (*setsugekka*) were standard fare from classical poets.

Harukaze o / shikai chōkan ni / fukiwataru
A spring wind
Blows across the four seas
All is calm
RIYŪ

129 Arashi Kichisaburō II (Rikan) as Torii Matasuke

PLAY *Kagamiyama kuruwa no kikigaki* at the Naka Theatre; first month, 1818
Artist: Kunihiro
Signature: Kunihiro ga
Publishers: Sōshiya and Hirooka
Ōban, colour woodblock, 39.1 x 25.3 cm
Private Collection (UK)

This print represents the epitome of the strong hero as depicted by Rikan: sword at the ready, he poses on a rock amid torrential rain and racing floodwaters. It is the right sheet of a diptych, the other half of which shows Ichikawa Ebijūrō I as Mochizuki Chōgen (see Matsudaira [Kōnan] 1997[c], no. 46). A Hokushū painting (cat. 101) shows Rikan in the same role. Rikan performed three heroic roles in this production opposite Ebijūrō's villains; the latter had stayed in Osaka when Shikan went off again to Edo for another tour late in 1817.

The play was first performed in Kyoto in the ninth month, 1780. The story follows the so-called 'Kaga Disturbance' of 1745, which occurred in the large Kaga fief ruled by the Maeda clan. After the death of the lord an internal struggle for succession resulted for a period in murder and chaos. Because of censorship rules, Kabuki and Jōruri puppet plays could not portray this story directly, so the setting was put back to the Ashikaga period in the sixteenth century. Here Rikan, as Matasuke, is tricked into drowning his own lord. He later realizes this and sacrifices himself to thwart the enemy. In the culminating scene his spirit returns finally to overthrow the villains.

in painterly Maruyama-Shijō style, is a distant view of Kiyomizu Temple in Kyoto, still a popular spot for admiring the blossoming cherry. The *surimono* was issued by a group of Rikan fans to support him against Shikan, who was performing in competition in similar roles at the Naka Theatre. The names of the poets seem to have been made up for the occasion. One of them reads Riyū, which could mean 'friend of Rikan'. Another reads Koyū which could mean 'friend of the young acolyte [*chigo*]' – the role shown in the print. An interesting comparison can be made with the Ashihiro print of Rikan in the same role (cat. 127).

Aze hitotsu / you you koeshi / tanishi ka na
Crossing just one path
Finally finishing
Like a mud snail
RIKAN

Rikan is being modest.

Senkin ya / momo chidori tori / haru no iro
A thousand gold coins
Myriad birds flutter around
Harbingers of spring
KIYŪ

Rikan's performance is worth a thousand gold coins (said to be the year's salary of a superstar actor).

135

135 Arashi Kichisaburō II (Rikan) as Jinbei, a peddler of Arima baskets

PLAY *Iro kurabe chō no monbi* at the Minami Theatre (Kyoto); third month, 1817

Artist: Kunihiro

Signature: Kunihiro sha

Artist's seal: Kunihiro (hand-impressed)

Surimono, colour woodblock, 42.3 x 57.1 cm

Waseda University Theatre Museum, Tokyo (*Nishizawa Ippō harikomi-chō*, vol. 3)

Rikan played two roles. The first was Nanbō Yohei, a samurai from Yawata, who falls in love with an Osaka courtesan Miyako, is tricked by villains into being accused of murder, but is able to prove himself a noble samurai. The other was Jinbei, a farmer who peddles Arima baskets in the off season. He gets into a fight in a country theatre, faints, and ends up making friends with his assailants and receiving an expensive coat as a parting gift from Chōkichi, the young master of a business. He stops a young girl from drowning herself, then discovers a drowned man, and sells everything he is carrying to a trickster who is planning to extort money, claiming that Jinbei died because of the earlier fight. In the end, Jinbei saves Chōkichi from the murder charge by visiting to repay his kindness and thereby proving himself still alive. Thus both Rikan's roles were noble characters from the country that prove themselves honest, loyal and upright.

Ase kaite / kaze o ninau ya / uchiwa-uri
Sweating in the heat
Looking for a fan-peddler
Riding on a breeze
RIKAN

136

136 Blossoms and court cap

c. 1819

Author–artist: Rikan

Signature: Rikan

Artist's seal: Arashi (?)

Fan painting, ink and colour on paper,
17.4 x 43.8 cm (fan)

Waseda University Theatre Museum, Tokyo
(*Kyota* 28: 8)

The mandarin is Rikan's crest. The poem is a
thank you to his patrons. With their favour he
flourished on the first day of the performance:

> *Mederarete / mi mo tachibana ya / hatsu hi-kage*
> Loved by others
> The mandarin blossoms
> In the first sunlight
> RIKAN

137

137 Memorial for Sawamura Kunitarō I (Ebimaru)

Autumn 1818

Artist: Niwa Tōkei

Signature: Tōkei sha

Artist's seals: Tō, Kei

Surimono, colour woodblock, metallic pigment
and embossing, 26.5 x 32.0 cm

Waseda University Theatre Museum, Tokyo
(*Nishizawa Ippō harikomi-chō*, vol. 3)

Kunitarō (b. 1739) retired in 1805 and died on
the second day of the seventh month, 1818. This
surimono, with appropriate picture of lotus
plants, the symbol of Buddhist rebirth, commemorates his death. The white blooms are
delicately embossed into the paper. Included is a
final farewell poem from the actor, signed
Hyakuryūkyaku Ebimaru, composed 'the day
before he died'. The other verses are by Tomi
Doran, Koroku (Minshi, Arashi Koroku IV) and
Rikan. Kunitarō had been mentor to both Koroku
and Rikan. He is remembered in the *surimono* as
a gentle and cultivated man.

> *Mada chiranu / yanagi ya tsuyu no / mi-burui su*
> My body trembles
> Like dew still clinging
> To the willow
> HYAKURYŪKYAKU EBIMARU (Kunitarō)

138 Memorial to Tomi Doran: Autumn at Tōfukuji Temple, Kyoto

Ninth month, 1819

Artist: Niwa Tōkei

Signature: Tōkei

Seal: Tōkei

Printer's mark: Bokusendō Kataoka shi (bottom left)

Surimono, colour woodblock with cut gold-leaf, diptych, 40.0 x 52.2 cm (right), 40.0 x 52.0 cm (left)

Chiba City Museum of Art (2973004)

The image is a magnificent autumn scene in south Kyoto at Tōfukuji Temple, showing a bench laid with a picnic set for a gathering to admire the brilliant maple foliage there. Tomi Doran ('Rōbaikutsu Shujin', 1759–1819) was a lively Kyoto aristocrat of court fifth rank, who resided in the nearby Higashiyama district. His forays into the world of popular culture were broad and significant: he is known to have written actor critiques and comic fiction, and was very active in haiku and *kyōka* poetry circles. He was, in addition, a haiku teacher and patron of many Kabuki actors. This *surimono* was a memorial from the actors after he died on the seventh day of the ninth month, 1819. It is one of the largest and grandest *surimono* from this period. For more on Doran see Nakano 1993.

The actors are listed by their pen names (*haimyō*) and many also list their art-name (*gō*). Doran played an important role in bringing these actors into a broad cultural network of artists, writers and patrons, which was useful both for practical patronage and for poetic and artistic stimulation. The actors took care with their verses and the final arrangement has been carefully crafted to preserve a sense of linkage between poems.

The actors represented are: Arashi Koroku IV (Koroku), Nakayama Shinkurō III (Kiraku, 1761–1827), Ichikawa Ebijūrō I (Shinshō), Arashi Kanjūrō I (Keisha, 1774–1846), Bandō Jūtarō I (Ganshi, b. 1769), Sawamura Kunitarō II (Kinshi, d. 1838), Asao Kuzaemon I (Kigan, 1758–1824), Kataoka Nizaemon (Gadō), Arashi Koroku V (Sanchō), Arashi Danpachi (Danpū), Arashi Isaburō I (Kanshi), Fujikawa Tomokichi II (Kayū, d. 1834), Nakayama Shinkurō IV (Itchō), Arashi Kichisaburō II (Rikan), Arashi Rikō I (1784–1839), Nakayama Bunshichi III (Hyakka, 1764–1853), Arashi Sangorō III (Raishi, d. 1838). Two playwrights are named as the organizers (*hokki*): Kanazawa Issen (Nagawa Tokusuke, 1764–1842)

138

and Nagawa Harusuke (1768–1829). The identities of Kitoku and Sogyō are not known.

> Our teacher's final testament was a haiku composed when he was ill. We present it here.
>
> *Asagao ya / yo wa nanibun ni / tsuyu no naka*
> Morning Glory
> Our world is quite
> Within a dewdrop
> RŌBAIKUTSU SHUJIN (Doran)
>
> *Shimenaki ni / koe no karuru yo / tō chidori*
> Though it stifles cries
> Its voice is broken
> Distant plover
> UNKINTEI KOROKU
>
> *Bundai ni / kyō wa imasazu / tsuyu no ato*
> At the writing desk
> No longer today
> Only a trace of dew
> TENJUSAI KIRAKU (Shinkurō III)

The desk was used during the judging of verses at a poetic gathering.

> *Moetsukanu / hota no kemuri yo / tomo namida*
> The kindling smokes
> And does not catch
> It weeps as well
> SENKINTEI SHINSHŌ (Ebijūrō I)
>
> *Nishi e fuku / kaze no nikusa yo / yare bashō*
> The west-blowing wind
> Is hateful
> Rending the banana tree
> KEISHA (Kanjūrō)
>
> *Itodo sae / aki no aware o / tamuke to wa*
> How sad
> Even a normal autumn
> How more so this farewell
> MEIYŪEN GANSHI (Jūtarō)
>
> *Aki no aware / hoi nasa masaru / namida ka na*
> Sadness at the end of autumn
> Losing self more and more
> Into tears
> KINSHI (Kunitarō II)

He often attended to offer his condolences on other sad occasions. Now that is all in the past.

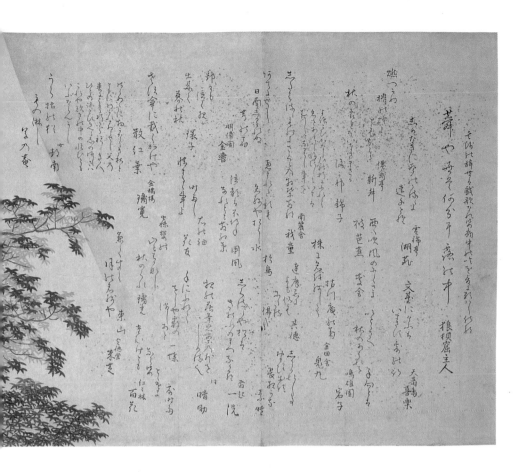

As evident from several works in this catalogue, Doran had deep relationships with many actors over many years.

Shitawaruru / mono yo sakura no / momiji chiru
How precious
Those times long ago
Cherry and maple leaves scatter
NANREISHA GADŌ (Nizaemon)

Daruma-ki ni / yo mo ni mo nitaru / hotoke ka na
Daruma memorial
How very much
He resembled him
KITOKU

'Daruma-ki', a memorial for Bodhidharma, patriarch of Zen Buddhism, was held on the fifth day of the tenth month. Here the sense is that Doran looked like the round-headed, round-bodied Daruma figure depicted in sculpture and painting.

Shikarareshi / koto omoidasu / nagayo ka na
Remembering
All the scoldings
Long nights now
SOGYŌ

Ate ni seshi / nichinan shigurenu / tsuta no yado
I hoped for southern sun
But autumn rain falls
On my ivy hut
MEIHOKAKU KINPI (Tomoemon)

Megumareta / kage mo nagori ya / otoshi-mizu
How blessed I was
Now even his shadow must part
Fields drained in autumn
SANCHŌ (Koroku V)

Naki-gao wa / fuete naredomo / chiru momiji
Not usually
One to cry
Autumn leaves have fallen
DANPŪ (Danpachi)

Shigururu ya / matsu wa kinō no / matsu nagara
The rain falls and falls
Yet yesterday's pine
Is the same today
(HOKKI) ISSEN

Yo no ochiba / shian no hoka o / shimeru nari
Leaves fallen in the night
Can think
Of nothing else
(HOKKI) HARUSUKE

Miyako ni mo / naku yo ga dekite / kure no aki
In the capital too
A night only for weeping
Autumn eve
KANSHI (Isaburō)

Oshimaruru / koto yo shigure shi / migi no sode
Such a loss
Autumn showers
On my right sleeve
KAYŪ (Tomokichi)

Te ni furete / oshiya arare no / kieshi ato
In my hand
How sad
Only melted hailstones remain
ITCHŌ (Shinkurō IV)

Sasu kasa ni / itadaku kage ya / chiru momiji
My umbrella is blessed with
The shadow
Of fallen autumn leaves
KINKITSURŌ RIKAN

Ne-sugata no / yama mo hakanashi / aki no kure
The mountains too
Lying down seem fragile
End of autumn
RIKŌ

Doran often signed himself Higashiyama, the 'Eastern Mountains' of Kyoto.

Tamuke tomo / naraba todoke yo / tsuyu shigure
Making this offering
May it reach you
Dew-like rain
KŌGŌRIN HYAKKA (Bunshichi)

Kanete kiku / tsuki no nagori ya / Higashiyama
Heard so much of him
Now farewell to the moon
Over Higashiyama
REITOKUDŌ RAISHI (Sangorō)

Even if someone has not departed, autumn is so sad – but to lose my father. Hidden away in mourning, how marvellous to talk of him with so many of his friends; to find such joy amid my grieving.

Ura-gare no / nao mono sabishi / kusa no an
Withered before
Even lonelier now
This grass hut
TONAN (Daughter)

139 Seventeenth memorial for Asao Tamejūrō I and thirteenth memorial for Asao Tamejūrō II

1819

Artist: Yamanaka Shōnen

Signature: Shōnen

Artist's seals: Shō, Nen

Surimono, colour woodblock, 40.0 x 54.5 cm

Victoria & Albert Museum, London (E.3973-1916)

This *surimono* with its bunch of summer flowers done in Shōnen's spiky, idiosyncratic style, is the third example known of a memorial print for Tamejūrō I. The two earlier examples are cat. 52, and another by Tōkei in *Kyota* (Waseda) 22: 17–19, from 1812. Tamejūrō II was the son of Tamejūrō I but he died only two years after his father. Verses are offered by eleven individuals, including Tamejūrō I's wife Tomi, Ebimaru (Kunitarō I), Rikan, Kigan (Kuzaemon I), and Okuyama (Tamejūrō III). Furyū, who also appears in the 1812 *surimono*, may be Tamejūrō II's wife. The final poem is by Gosei, a samurai from Saga in Hizen Province, Kyūshū.

> Words offered in prayer before the souls of these two.
>
> *Omoidasu / sora ya satsuki no / usugumori*
> Remembering them now in the sky
> The mid-summer moon
> Hidden by a thin veil of clouds
> TOMI

140 *Ehon shibai shiori*
Picture Book: Guide to the Theatre

1802

Artist: Shōkōsai Hanbei

Publishers: Kawachiya Tasuke and three others from Osaka, Kyoto and Nagoya

Hanshibon book, woodblock, 3 vols, 22.0 x 15.5 cm (covers)

Waseda University Theatre Museum, Tokyo (*ro*-5-94-1/2/3)

Illustrated playbooks (*e-iri nehon*) were a genre unique to Osaka, the first, *Omowaku kuruwa katagi*, dating from 1784 and the last from 1873. In total about eighty titles are known.

This is the earliest illustrated playbook (*e-iri nehon*) by Shōkōsai. The original Kabuki play by Namiki Shōzō (1730–73) was *Yado-nashi Danshichi shigure no karakasa*, first performed in 1767. Publishers did not have the rights to publish the plays as official Kabuki texts, it seems, and *nehon* usually have a different title from the stage version. (It was common in any case in the Kabuki world to rewrite plays under a variant title.) The character Namiki Shōzō in the play was only introduced after Shōzō's death. The book has a list of the actors and their roles, but there is no record of a performance of this group in these particular roles. So Shōkōsai created a new performance text by *imagining* a troupe of actors

he considered ideal for the various roles. This concept of an imagined (*mitate*) line up would become a common feature of the *nehon* genre.

This genre of Kabuki playbooks was unique to Osaka. Over the next sixty or so years more than eighty titles were published. Shōkōsai himself published eight, first establishing the genre. Osaka had been the centre for Jōruri (Bunraku) puppet-play publication (in the *maruhon* or *shōhon* genres) from the late seventeenth cen-

tury. As many as 1,500 titles were published during the eighteenth century, generating the predominant narrative genre that would remain popular throughout the country until the twentieth century because of the widespread hobby of learning *gidayū*, the term for Bunraku puppet theatre chanting. The plays were 'read' primarily by those who had taken lessons, and therefore it was expected that readers could understand the musical code of notation in the texts and

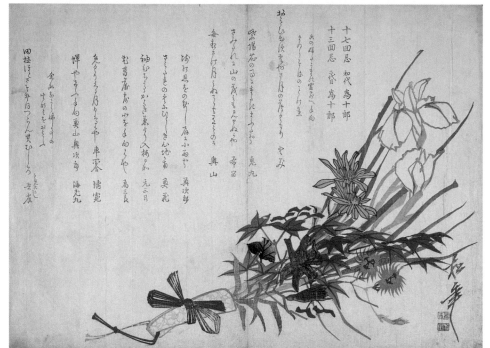

139

140

141

perform them either by voicing the parts or by imagining the performance. These puppet plays were an essential source for both Kabuki playwrights and fiction writers.

After 1800 few new Bunraku plays were written, and it would seem that Osaka publishers (particularly Kawachiya Tasuke) suspected that there would be a market for Kabuki playbooks. Shōkōsai was the natural figure to produce such illustrated texts, having produced several books on actors and the theatre in general. Kabuki plays had never been published in the manner of puppet plays. Manuscripts had circulated and illustrated summary editions were common, but *e-iri nehon* were the first complete texts. The form is that of a Kabuki libretto (*daihon*) or playscript (*nehon*). The format varies somewhat, but it is clear that readers expected to read the plays as performance, and to picture their favourite players voicing and acting the roles.

We can imagine that readers, often practised in Bunraku chanting, also acted out the famous soliloquies and dialogues.

Illustrated is a scene from vol. 3, p. 18, in which Nakayama Bunshichichi II plays Mohei, Asao Tamejūrō I plays the playwright Namiki Shōzō, Bandō Jūtarō plays the actor Arashi Sangorō II, and Nakamura Kumetarō II plays the actor Sawamura Kunitarō I.

This is a fascinating scene in which actors play other actors. The playwright and actors are discussing the plot of a play and ask the hairdresser Mohei for his opinion. Mohei is a former samurai, fallen on hard times. The play being discussed is about a man betrayed by his lover. The actors, in describing the scene, say how the man is not a real man unless he kills the woman. Mohei later murders a man and kills himself. Thus the play toys with the worlds of fiction and reality.

141 *Chūshin renri no hachiue*
Loyal Retainers and Entwined Potted Trees
1803

Artist: Shōkōsai Hanbei

Publisher: Kawachiya Tasuke

Hanshibon book, colour woodblock, 2 vols, 22.6 x 15.8 cm (covers)

Kansai University Library, Osaka (912.5/c, 2/1)

An example of the illustrated playbook (*e-iri nehon*) genre. The original Kabuki play was entitled *Gishinden yomikiri kōshaku*, written by Namiki Gohei (1747–1808), and first performed in Osaka in 1788 in eight acts. It was then rewritten, and Acts Three and Four became a separate play performed in 1794. This book follows the rewritten performance text of 1794. The opening double-page colour illustration shows the main actors who appear in the book, an imagined dream cast (*mitate*).

142

142 *Ehon hana-momiji akiba-banashi*
Picture Book: A Tale of Autumn Leaves

1807

Author: Shōkōsai Hanbei

Signature: Shōkōsai Hanbei

Alternate title: *Ehon kakehashi monogatari*

Publishers: Kawachiya Tasuke and others

Hanshibon book, woodblock, 6 vols, 22.2 x 16.0 cm
(covers)

Cambridge University Library (FJ.722.1)

An example of the illustrated playbook (*e-iri
nehon*) genre. The original 'Akiba' play (*Akiba
gongen kaisen-banashi*) was first performed in
the twelfth month of 1761 at the Naka Theatre.
It was a hit and thereafter regularly performed
and rewritten for new sets of actors. *Ehon
hana-momiji akiba-banashi* is based on a version entitled *Kara nishiki akiba-banashi* (*A Tale of
Chinese Brocade and Autumn Leaves*), performed
in the ninth month, 1799, at the Kado Theatre.

The play by Chikamatsu Tokusō was a great success and launched the career of Arashi Kichisaburō II (Rikan) as a superstar after his success
the year before in the role of Yojirō, the monkey-
trainer (see cat. 95). Rikan has top billing in two
lead roles, Tsukimoto Hajimenosuke and
Tokushima Gohei. The other main roles in the
playbook are also from the 1799 production and
include figures such as Asao Tamejūrō I, who was
dead at the time of publication, or Sawamura
Kunitarō I, who had retired two years earlier. The
timing of the publication was clearly to promote
Rikan, but target readers were also expected to
recall the performances of favourite actors no
longer on the stage.

Illustrated is Rikan in the role of Hajimenosuke, the strong, brave and loyal heir to the fief,
a good contrast to the role of Yojirō, a poor but
warm-hearted monkey-trainer.

143 *Shibai itsumade gusa*
Theatre Forever among the Ivy

Alternate title: *Godairiki koi no fūjime*

ILLUSTRATED Arashi Kichisaburō II (Rikan) as
Wakatō Hachizaemon

1808

Artist: Shōkōsai Hanbei

Signature: Shōkōsai Hanbei

Publishers: Kawachiya Tasuke and others

Hanshibon book, colour woodblock, 4 vols,
21.0 x 15.6 cm (covers)

Waseda University Theatre Museum, Tokyo
(ro-5-483-1/2/3/4)

An illustrated playbook (*e-iri nehon*) of famous
actors of the time. Arashi Kichisaburō II (Rikan)
is listed as a star, along with Asao Tamejūrō I
and Sawamura Kunitarō I, neither of whom
were active by 1808. Actor's names are used in
dialogue instead of role names, indicating that
readers were expected to remember the par-

143

144

ticular actors and imagine them in performance.

The original play, *Godairiki koi no fūjime*, was written by Namiki Gohei and first performed in Kyoto in the fifth month, 1794. Later that same year Gohei took up an offer to move to Edo to write plays there. The story is based on an incident of 1734 in Sonezaki Shinchi, north Osaka, when a Satsuma samurai murdered five people in a jealous rage. Onoe Koisaburō (Shinshichi I) plays the murderer Gengobei.

On the left page is the signature of the artist: '*Ukiyo eshi*' ('Artist of the Floating World') Shōkōsai Hanbei *ga*, with his seal, 'Shōkō'.

144 *Fumizuki urami no kiriko*
Revenge at the Stone Lantern in the
Seventh Month
1810
Artist: Shunkōsai (Hokushū)
Signature: Shunkōsai
Publishers: Kawachiya Tasuke and others
Hanshibon book, woodblock, 4 vols, 21.8 x 15.3 cm
(covers)
Waseda University Theatre Museum, Tokyo
(*ro*-5-96, 1-4)

An example of the illustrated playbook (*e-iri nehon*) genre. Versions of this play were performed in both the puppet and Kabuki theatres during the eighteenth century in both Edo and Osaka. This version was first performed in Osaka at the Naka Theatre in the eighth month, 1764, soon after a notorious murder of a woman in that city. In the play, Furuteya Hachirōbei kills his wife and mother who plan to reveal his attempt to steal money that has been set aside to save a princess. Hachirōbei eventually confesses and commits suicide to atone for his crime. In 1810 Utaemon III (Shikan) was away performing in Edo and Rikan was the top star of Osaka Kabuki.

Illustrated is the scene showing Rikan as Hachirōbei about to commit suicide; the ghost of his wife Otsuma looks away.

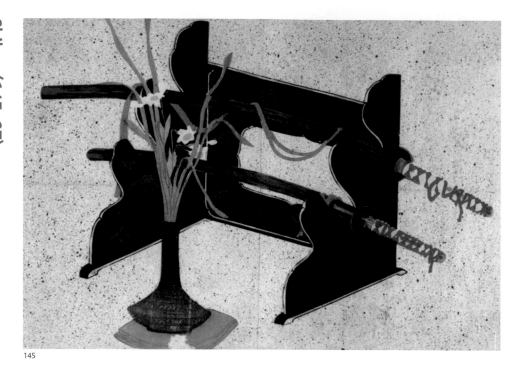

145

145 Seventeenth memorial for Nakamura Utaemon I

1807

Surimono, colour woodblock with metallic pigment, 27.7 x 36.5 cm (picture)

Waseda University Theatre Museum, Tokyo (*Kyota* 19: 65–6)

Text (not illustrated) and image are now cut up into fragments and pasted into one of the *Kyota* albums. The original *surimono* launched the bid of young Utaemon III (Shikan) to rival Rikan. Shikan's father Nakamura Utaemon I (1714–91) had been one of the great villain-role actors of his time. The imagery of two swords – a symbol of the samurai – is unexpected, since actors were officially ranked beneath the four-class system altogether. Perhaps it is implied that he comes from a samurai lineage. A crane motif, one of Utaemon's crests, decorates the sword-stand.

Shikan presents himself to Osaka in the print as the head of a troupe (*za-gashira*). He had been away acting in Nagoya and Kyoto for most of the previous year and returned to the city in the eleventh month, 1806, to prepare for his father's seventeenth memorial in 1807. That event is commemorated here with verses by Shikan himself, fellow actors Ogawa Kichitarō III (Eishi, 1785–1851), Nakamura Kashichi II (d. 1840) and Arashi Sangorō III (Raishi, d. 1838), and by the aristocratic poet–writer Tomi Doran. However, frustrated that he could not get top billing in Osaka, Shikan left for Edo in the third month, 1808, not to return until the eleventh month, 1812.

My late father was originally from Kanazawa in Kaga Province, and came to Kyoto to train as an actor. He managed eventually to gain many patrons in all three cities. Due to his fame I have been able to perform on the stage in minor roles. To thank him for his marvellous blessings to me, I would like to offer a memorial for him on this seventeenth anniversary of his passing by presenting these two swords that I brought from Kanazawa. With hands folded in front of the incense and flowers, I pray for his soul.

Nukazuku ya / nori no koe sumu / yuki no naka
Bowing deeply
The voice of the Buddha is clear
Amid the falling snow
SHIKAN (Nakamura Utaemon III)

In attendance at the Buddhist ceremony:

Uchiyorite / mukashi o kataru / hi-oke ka na
Gathered together
Around the brazier
Chatting of old times
EISHI (Ogawa Kichitarō III)

Kuchi-kiri no / dai-ichi kyaku o / kono hotoke
First to speak
As main guest
The departed soul
KASHICHI (Nakamura Kashichi II)

Remembering times past:

Omokage wa / nita to koso ie / ajiro-mori
Say that his image
Resembles him well
You who guard the wicker gate
RAISHI (Arashi Sangorō III)

Final poem:

Tsuwamono to / nokoru na o yo ni / shiki-busuma
As a soldier
His fame remains
The foundation
DORAN (of Higashiyama, Kyoto)

Shiki-busuma is the mattress under a futon. Utaemon I, known for his powerful portrayal of villain roles, is the strong foundation upon which the Utaemon name will flourish from generation to generation.

146 Twenty-fifth memorial for Nakamura Utaemon I

Spring 1815

Artist: Yamanaka Shōnen

Signature: Shōnen

Seal: Suiren

Surimono, colour woodblock with cut gold-leaf, 42.8 x 53.4 cm

Private Collection (Japan)

The image, which complements the poem, is a branch of plum blossoms and two sutra hand-scrolls. Utaemon III (Shikan)'s father Utaemon I (1714–91) was one of the great villain or rough-role (*jitsuaku*) actors of his time. Shikan offers a haiku to his father's memory:

Myōhō rengekyō / yome ya / hana ni tori
Chant the sutra
The warbler sings
Among the plum blossoms
SHIKAN

'Sutra-reading bird' (*kyōyomu-tori*) is a poetic name for the warbler (*uguisu*) and a conventional seasonal word for spring. It is said that the warbler's song sounds like 'hokkekyō', the chanting of the Lotus Sutra. Shikan suggests that the birds, too, are singing a memorial for his father. HI

147a Nakamura Utaemon III (Shikan) as Yojirō the monkey-trainer

PLAY *Sarumawashi kadode no hitofushi* at the Kado Theatre; third month, 1817

Artist: Hokkei (Shun'yō)

Signature: Shun'yō sha

Publisher: Hon'ya Seishichi

Ōban, colour woodblock, 38.6 x 25.9 cm

Private Collection (UK)

This should be compared to the print by Hokkei of Kichisaburō II (Rikan) in the same role (cat. 97), dated the eighth month, 1814. Shikan performed Yojirō to great success in Edo, as recorded in a print by Toyokuni I (cat. 147b).

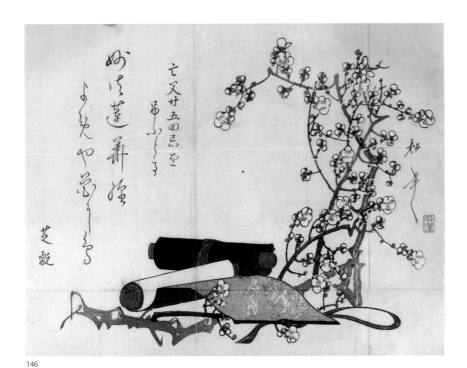

146

147b Nakamura Utaemon III (Shikan) as Yojirō the monkey-trainer

PLAY *Oshun Denbei* at the Nakamura Theatre (Edo); fifth month, 1808

Artist: Utagawa Toyokuni I (Edo)

Signature: Edo Toyokuni hitsu

Publisher: Moriya Jihei (Edo)

Censor's seal: Moriya Jihei

Ōban, colour woodblock, 33.7 x 23.2 cm

Ikeda Bunko Library (73)

This print is signed 'Toyokuni of Edo' and may have been aimed at the Kyoto–Osaka market as well as Edo buyers. Unusually the print is also dated with the month and year. Shikan had arrived in Edo for the first time in the third month of 1808. It is instructive to compare the Toyokuni and Osaka representations of Shikan in the same role (cat. 147a).

Matsudaira 1983, no. 81.

147a

147b

148

148 'Planting turnip seeds, wishing he'll return next spring'
Mata kuru haru suzuna no tanemaki
Ninth month, 1812
Artist: Utagawa Toyokuni I (Edo)
Signature: Utagawa Toyokuni ga
Publisher: Unknown
Horizontal *ōban*, colour woodblock, 25.2 x 36.9 cm
Victoria & Albert Museum, London (E.4842-1886)

The text, signed and sealed 'by Manki, a fan', says that all Edo has gathered, a force as strong as a waterfall, determined to stop Utaemon III (Shikan) from leaving; and that even though he must part, they pray he will come back down to Edo again and dance *Sanbasō* once more. The image shows Shikan and Nakamura Akashi performing the auspicious *Sanbasō* dance and is drawn to look like a votive painting at a shrine. A copy is also in *Kyota* (Kansai) 7.

Matsudaira in *Hizō ukiyo-e taikan*, vol. 4, pp. 241–2, no. 119.

149 Retirement of Bandō Hikosaburō III
Kado Theatre; ninth or tenth month, 1813
Artist: Niwa Tōkei
Signature: Tōkei sha
Seals: Tō, Kei
Surimono, colour woodblock with metallic pigment, 39.6 x 56.6 cm
Private Collection (Japan)

Nakamura Utaemon III (Shikan) worked in Edo from 1808 to the tenth month, 1812. His return, together with the great Edo star Bandō Hikosaburō III (Shinsui, Rakuzen, Hansōan Rakusen, 1754–1828), was a clever strategy to suggest Shikan's standing as the equal of the great Edo actor, and to establish his status as the rival of Rikan.

Hikosaburō performed his final roles in Edo from the seventh to the ninth month, 1811. His first performances in Osaka with Shikan were in the eleventh month, 1812. The two then performed together in both Kyoto and Osaka until the ninth month, 1813, when Hikosaburō declared that the performance would be his final in Osaka. Tōkei's *surimono* with imagery of a setting sun above autumn grasses is appropriate to the season and occasion.

The Osaka performances lasted through the tenth month and then switched to Kyoto. (Hikosaburō's teacher had been the great Onoe Kikugorō I [Baikō] who was originally from Kyoto. See his portrait of Kikugorō, cat. 64). Finally Hikosaburō took the tonsure and returned to Edo, where he led a life dedicated to Buddhism, with a sign on the door reading: 'No dustmen or actors allowed'.

The actors Nakamura Daikichi I (Hajō, 1773–1823) and Shikan contributed poems, together with the writer Kanazawa Issen (Nakamura Kashichi II, d. 1840?):

> After successfully completing his final performances in Edo, his home town, the great Hikosaburō has kindly come to perform for the final time in Osaka. Our gratitude for this blessing is impossible to express, deeper than Naniwa Bay.

Mi ni amari / aki ni amareru / nagori ka na
More than I could expect
One more autumn
To say farewell
HANSŌAN SHINSUI (Hikosaburō)

Ran no ka no / tōzakaru hodo / natsukashiki
Fragrance of the orchid
As it grows distant
We cherish it more
HAJŌ (Daikichi)

Kōbashiki / tsuyu ni ya kaze no / oki-miyage
The sweet smell
On the dew
A parting gift from the wind
SHIKAN (Utaemon)

Oshimarete / takigi ni majiru / momiji ka na
His parting regretted
Autumn leaves
Among the kindling wood
ISSEN (Kashichi)

Hikosaburō's pen name includes the character *maki* ('firewood').

Ushirokage / mise yo asa-giri / fukaku to mo
Let me see your parting figure
No matter how thick
The morning mist
SŌSHŌ (of Osaka)

The hawk knows the autumn has come and retires to the mountains to his hermitage Hansōan ['Hermitage among the low grasses']. Knowing how precious this occasion is, I have come to Naniwa [Osaka] to receive its blessings and say my farewell.

E ni kaite / iu koto nokose / aki no kaze
Leave us a painting
As a farewell
To the autumn wind
IPPONBŌ JŌAN (of Edo)

Another impression of the *surimono* is in *Kyota* (Waseda) 23: 58–9.

149

150 'Fan clubs toasting Shikan and Ebijūrō I'
Norikomi butai sakazuki

Seventh day, eleventh month, 1815
Parody flybill (*mitate banzuke*), woodblock,
19.6 x 30.1 cm
Waseda University Theatre Museum, Tokyo
(*Kyota* 26: 4)

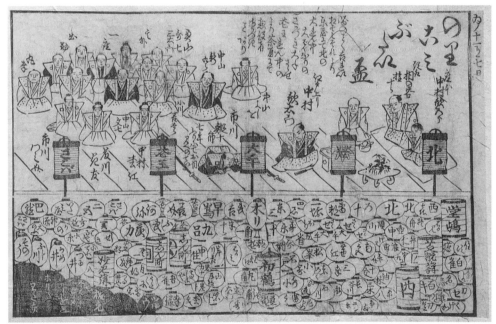
150

This celebrates the ritual of greeting new members of a troupe at the opening-of-the-season (*kaomise*) performance in the eleventh month – usually the beginning of a year-long contract for the actors. Ebijūrō had received his new name in Edo a few months earlier and is shown here returning with Shikan to Osaka. The pair kneel centre-stage with Ebijūrō bowing. To either side and behind are other members of the troupe. After various speeches are concluded, the fan-club members toast the actors. The five lanterns on poles at the front of the stage have the names or emblems of the major Kabuki fan clubs (right to left): Kita, Sasase, Ōte, Sakura and Zakoba. The smaller lanterns in the 'audience' represent neighbourhood groups.   MK

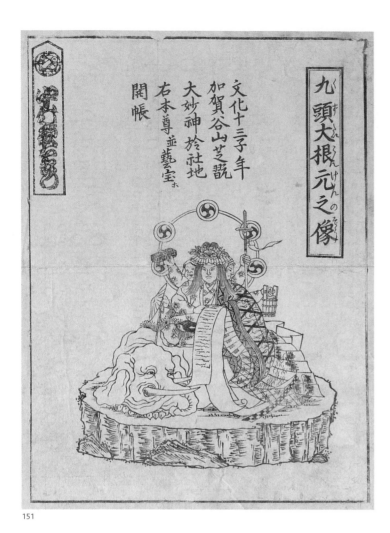

151

151 'Statue of the Nine-headed Great Deity'
Kuzu Daigongen no zō

1816
Parody flybill (*mitate banzuke*), woodblock,
31.4 x 22.6 cm
Waseda University Theatre Museum, Tokyo
(*Kyota* 26: 46)

A spoof flybill parodying the announcement of a special display of shrine treasures. The statue 'Great Deity Kagaya-san Shikan' will be revealed, together with 'the treasures of his art'. This ultimate statement of celebrity worship shows Shikan as a nine-headed deity, holding combined attributes of the nine quick-change dance roles which he has made famous.

152 'List of farewell gifts for Mr Nakamura Shikan'
Nakamura Shikanjō e senbetsu mokuroku

17th day, tenth month, 1819
Publisher: Tsutaya Chūgorō (Edo)
Parody flybill (*mitate banzuke*), woodblock,
25.9 x 58.4 cm (maximum)
Waseda University Theatre Museum, Tokyo
(*Kyota* 28: 60–61)

This was produced at the end of Shikan's final tour of Edo. The donors are most of the famous Edo actors of the day, and other fans. Gifts include 150 sake-cup stands (from Ichikawa Danjūrō), 150 'snake-eye' pattern umbrellas (from Sawamura Sōjūrō) and 130 Edo-style tobacco pouches (from Onoe Kikugorō). Shikan is feted as a superstar of Edo theatre.

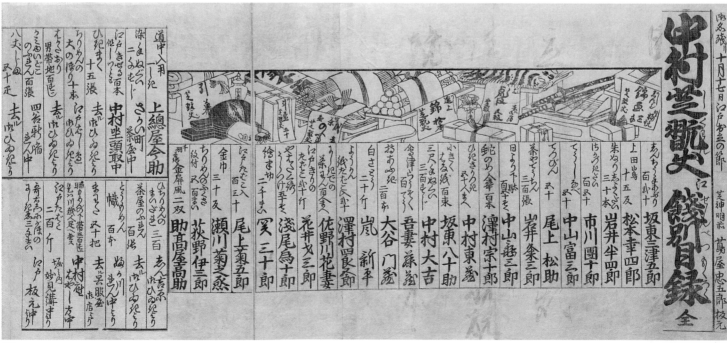

152

153 'Map of Shikan's kingdom'

Shikan koku no zenzu

c. Tenth month, 1819

Author: Akatsuki Kanenari

Surimono, colour woodblock, 19.3 x 25.7 cm

Waseda University Theatre Museum, Tokyo (*Kyota* 28: 62)

Nakamura Utaemon III (Shikan) returned from Edo for the last time at the end of 1819. In this map the coastline of the large 'island' in the centre takes the form of the first *uta* (song) character of the name Utaemon. The words are a riddle, and if followed around the map spell out a sentence meaning 'We can't wait to see Utaemon back again in Osaka'. The world of Utaemon is full of gold and wealth from his patrons. Map-making had mushroomed in the world of popular publishing during the eighteenth century and it was common for publishers to produce playful maps of Japan (see Yonemoto 2003).　　　MK

154 'Just how he [Shikan] looked, arriving back last night'

Sakuya kono ima iri sugata

Eleventh month, 1812

Multi-sheet pamphlet, woodblock, 18.4 x 28.3 cm (this page)

Waseda University Theatre Museum, Tokyo (*Kyota* 22: 67)

This ephemeral printed pamphlet, the pages now separated out, features Utaemon III (Shikan)'s return to Osaka after five years performing in Edo. A flotilla of boats fills the Yodo River and crowds throng the streets: the city's hero has returned. The text describes how the boats left Osaka and met Shikan halfway from Edo at the Ōi River, on the border between Suruga and Tōtōmi Provinces, then again at Ōtsu, and finally returned with him all the way to the Naka Theatre on Dōtonbori Canal in Osaka, bringing him for the opening-of-the-season (*kaomise*) performance in the eleventh month. The level of passion generated among the fans seems to be something like the welcome given The Beatles in London after their first successful tour of the USA, and Shikan is referred to as 'Great Saviour Deity' (*Yo-naoshi Daimyōjin*). The picture shows how grandstands were built along the route Shikan walked so that fans could view his progress. It is also reported that fan clubs fought over who would enjoy precedence to greet the actor, and that he had to step in to calm their anger. A popular ditty was sung to his bravery: 'Shikan wields the strength of the Edo rough actors [*aragoto*]: now that Shikan is back, we need nothing more.'　　　MK

153

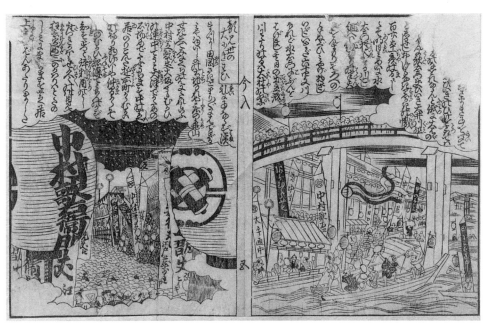

154

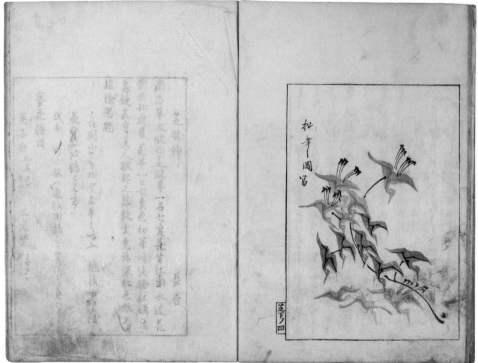

155a

155a Shikanjō
Shikan Album

Fifth month, 1814

Authors: Hamamatsu Utakuni and Baishiken Hakuō

Publisher: Kawachiya Tasuke

Hanshibon book, colour woodblock, 22.2 x 15.7 cm (covers)

The British Museum, London (SJ209)

155b Shikanjō
Shikan Album

Fifth month, 1814

Authors: Hamamatsu Utakuni and Baishiken Hakuō

Publisher: Kawachiya Tasuke

Chūbon book, colour woodblock, 2 vols, 18.2 x 12.9 cm (covers)

Waseda University Theatre Museum, Tokyo (i-13-17)

A book in praise of Nakamura Utaemon III (Shikan) by his fan-club members. It was published in the fifth month, 1814, as a farewell to Shikan when he left to tour Edo for the second time in his career. Poems of various types (*kyōka*, *hokku* and *kanshi*) by a wide range of people are interspersed with *surimono* illustrations. The sources for the book are primarily the two albums *Shikan shōsanjō* (cat. 7) and *Kyota kyakushokujō* (Kansai), vol. 7 (cat. 3). It is clear that a great many individuals participated in the publication, and it was evidently common for these literati and patrons to share information and actual items in the compilation of such albums and books.

Illustrated is a picture by Yamanaka Shōnen,

'Shikan grasses' (*Shikan-gusa*, cat. 155a), in which the leaves take the form of stylized cranes, Shikan's emblem. A fan painting by Shōnen of a similar design is found in *Kyota* (Kansai) 7 (see fig. 17 above). It was not unusual for an artist to compose a painting, and then for that design to be reused for a *surimono* and/or for a book illustration.

This collective creativity was stimulated by the performances of Kabuki actors and interaction with them, and poetry circles were a key element of these networks. Shikan was the most active and successful in stimulating creativity among his fans. We can imagine their enjoyment at gatherings at which Shikan joined in among the artists, poets and writers. Kawachiya Tasuke is known to have been a Shikan fan, and he was an active publisher of Kabuki-related materials, particularly titles which focused on Shikan himself. Such ephemeral pamphlets included *Hiiki hanamichi* (*Patrons on the Catwalk*) and *Hanashi no tsuru* (*Talk about the Crane [Shikan]*), as well as the book *Shikan-koku ichiran* (*Guide to Shikan's Kingdom*).

Shikanjō stimulated publication six months later of the rival book *Rikanjō* (cat. 119), compiled by Rikan's fans. The fact that this was also issued by Kawachiya Tasuke suggests that the publisher's eye for profit may have overcome his support for Shikan.

The original blocks for this title (cat. 155b) were cut in the smaller *chūbon* size. A larger format edition (cat. 155a), with its wider margins, was probably specially printed for a patron to use as gifts. YK

156 (Nakamura Utaemon kokyō e hare no) Nishiki-e sugata
Nakamura Utaemon's Return Home: Portrayed in Glorious Colour Print

Tenth month, 1812

Author: Hachimonsha Jishō

Publisher: Kawachiya Tasuke

Chūbon book, woodblock (two colour pages), 2 vols, 18.0 x 12.7 cm (covers)

Waseda University Theatre Museum, Tokyo (ro-3-393-1/2)

The book was published to welcome Utaemon III (Shikan) back to Osaka after his five-year tour in Edo performing at the Nakamura Theatre. It reviews the ninety-nine roles that he performed there. Shikan is presented as a star actor even in the bigger metropolis of Edo. The book belongs to the genre of comic fiction (*kokkei-bon*), with lively text aimed at a popular audience.

For a transcription see Tsuchiya 1979, pp. 247–6.

156

157a, b Nakamura Utaemon III (Shikan) performing a medley of dance pieces

PLAY *Sono kokonoe saishiki-zakura* at the Nakamura Theatre (Edo); third month, 1815

Artist: Utagawa Toyokuni I (Edo)

Signature: Toyokuni ga

Publisher: Yamamotoya Heikichi (Edo)

Censorship seal: *kiwame*

Ōban, colour woodblock, series of eight prints, 36.2 x 24.2 cm (a); 36.3 x 24.2 cm (b)

Waseda University Theatre Museum, Tokyo (001,0195-0202)

Utaemon III (Shikan) was a master at quick changes and at playing multiple roles during a day's performance. Here he is shown performing in Edo in 1815, in a medley of dance pieces in nine different roles, judged a great success. Each print also has a poem by the actor, signed with his pen name Shikan. Most of the same poems were used again for a series by seven Osaka artists recording performances exactly a year later, after Shikan's return to Osaka (cat. 159).

The first two, Shakkyō (a) and Fugen (b), are illustrated.

Shakkyō (Lion dance)
Hana ni kite / shishi no kurui no / kochō ka na
The butterfly alights on a flower
Amid the lion's
Whirling madness

Bodhisattva Fugen
Shirakumo to / itsuwaru yo ari / fugenzō
Disguised as
A cloud in the night
Bodhisattva Fugen [mountain cherry]

Kaji-mochi yakko (Ruffian holding a hammer) and Tsuki no tsuji-gimi (Lady of the night)
Ideshiro ya / otoko onna no / futari-mae
Taking turns
Dancing as a man
Then as a woman

Thunder-god
Mino-ichi ya / kaminari mon no / hana no kumo
At the market
By Asakusa's Thunder Gate
Clouds of blossoms

Asakusa Kannon Temple is situated at the centre of Edo's popular entertainment area.

Ama-goi Komachi (Komachi praying for rain)
Hi-ōgi no / kazashi mo shiraji / kami-biina
A paper doll
Doesn't know
How to hold a picture fan

Sake shop clerk
Michitose no / mimasu taru ya / momo no sake
Lasting for three thousand years
The three-measure cask
Of peach wine

Mimasu (a set of three square wooden rice measures) is the crest of the Ichikawa acting clan.

Old woman
Sono hana no / utsuroi yasushi / uba-zakura
The beauty of its flower
Easily fades
Early-blossoming cherry

Uba-zakura ('old woman cherry') is a type that blossoms before the leaves appear, and can also mean an older woman with lingering beauty.

Fumi-zukai musume (Young woman letter-writer)
Yabu iri no / ya no ji musubi ya / otoko-obi
Into the forest [Dressed for the holiday]
A man's sash
Tied a woman's way

Yabu-iri (literally 'into the forest') was a term for the holiday employees received at New Year and at the Obon Festival in late summer. Shikan holds a battledore, which is a traditional game at New Year.

The entire set is on the Waseda Theatre Museum website (www.waseda.ac.jp/enpaku).

157a

157b

158

158 Nakamura Utaemon III (Shikan)'s farewell performance at the Nakamura Theatre, Edo

Eighth month, 1815

Artist: Utagawa Kunisada I (Edo)

Signature: Gototei Kunisada ga

Publisher: Yamadaya Shōjirō (Edo)

Censorship seal: *kiwame*

Ōban, colour woodblock, triptych, 36.2 x 25.0 cm (right), 36.5 x 26.1 cm (centre), 36.3 x 24.9 cm (left)

Victoria & Albert Museum, London (E.5554-1886)

This print shows Utaemon III (Shikan) as the clever showman in nine different roles, his farewell performance at the end of three years working in Edo (see also cat. 148). He bows to the audience and offers a parting speech, explaining how much he regrets having to leave. One reason he offers is that his elderly mother is not well. The speech is presented as his final farewell, but two years later Shikan was back in Edo for another two-year stint.

Hizō ukiyo-e taikan, vol. 5, 1989, pp. 208–9, no. 2.

159a, b Nakamura Utaemon III (Shikan) performing a medley of dance pieces

PLAY *Sono kokonoe saishiki-zakura* at the Kado Theatre; third month, 1816

Artists: Ashiyuki, Ashisato, Utakuni, Ashihiro, Ashikiyo, Ashifune and Yoshikuni

Signatures: Ashiyuki ga, Ashisato ga, Utakuni ga, Ashihiro ga, Ashikiyo ga, Ashifune ga, Ashimaru aratame Yoshikuni ga

Publisher: Shioya Chōbei

Ōban, colour woodblock, set of eight prints, 35.6 x 23.8 cm (a), 38.5 x 26.5 cm (b)

The British Museum, London (1906.12-20.01139); Ikeda Bunko Library (4 prints A151, 1–4); Private Collection (Japan); Hendrick Lühl Collection (Germany)

The set of eight prints celebrates the triumphant return of Utaemon III (Shikan) to Osaka in 1815, after his second tour in Edo. The sequence of nine dance roles was the same he had performed to acclaim in Edo exactly one year earlier. The Edo artist Toyokuni's series of eight prints (cat. 157) was the model for this Osaka series, and all but one of the poems by Shikan are the same.

Some of the fundamental differences between Edo and Osaka actor-print production are evident in a comparison between the two series. Toyokuni, a professional artist working for a publisher, produced the entire Edo series himself. In Osaka, by contrast, seven different 'amateur' artists contributed designs for a collaborative production. Collaborative production (*gassaku*) was rare in Edo, but relatively common in Osaka. The artists were: Ashiyuki (2), Ashisato, Utakuni, Ashihiro, Ashikiyo, Ashifune and Yoshikuni.

The variant poem by Shikan is on the Yoshikuni (Ashimaru) print illustrated (British Museum, a):

Shakkyō (Lion dance)
Kaze no te o / karite arau ya / yanagi-gami
With the wind's helping hand
Shall I wash
This willow-like mane?

The second illustration is of Bodhisattva Fugen (Hendrick Lühl Collection, b).

Four other designs are illustrated in Ikeda 1999, vol. 3, no. 51, and Lühl 1998, p. 514.

159a

159b

160

160 Six *surimono* celebrating dance pieces by Nakamura Utaemon III (Shikan)

PLAY *Sono kokonoe saishiki-zakura* at the Kado Theatre; third month, 1816

Surimono, colour woodblock with metallic pigment, six prints, each approx. 17.7 x 12.1 cm

Victoria & Albert Museum, London (E.196/197/198/199/200/201-98)

These six *surimono*, drawn in the style of Ashikuni, are most likely from a set of eight representing the same dance sequence as Toyokuni's Edo series of 1815 (cat. 157) and the Osaka series by seven artists in collaboration (cat. 159). This is another example of a group of poets, artists and fans getting together to celebrate their favourite actor Shikan's return to Osaka. The poems are in different genres: one Chinese, two *kyōka* and three haiku. The identities of the poets are not known.

Illustrated is 'Ushiro-men', showing Shikan playing two roles – one male, one female – at once, with a mask on the back of his head.

**161 Ichikawa Ebijūrō I as Miura Arajirō (right)
and Nakamura Utaemon III (Shikan) as Sano
Genzaemon (left)**

PLAY *Yayoi ni hiraku ando no funahashi* at the
Kado Theatre; third month, 1816

Artists: Ashihiro (right) and Ashisato (left)

Signatures: Ashihiro ga, Ashisato ga

Publisher: Wataya Kihei (?)

Ōban, colour woodblock with metallic pigment,
diptych, 37.5 x 51.5 cm

Hendrick Lühl Collection (Germany)

The pair are competing huntsmen who both claim
the dead crane shot with arrows. Collaborative
diptychs and triptychs are rare in Edo publishing
but relatively common in Osaka, where amateur
artists worked together to contribute to Kabuki
culture and promote their favourite stars. Ashihiro
(worked *c*. 1813–24) and Ashisato (worked *c*.
1813–16) were each active for only short periods
and few of their prints survive. There was a burst
of activity by amateur artists in support of Shikan
upon his return to Osaka late in 1815.

Matsudaira 1997(c), no. 10.

**162 Ichikawa Ebijūrō I as Miura Arajirō (right)
and Nakamura Utaemon III (Shikan) as Sano
Genzaemon (left)**

PLAY *Yayoi ni hiraku ando no funahashi* at the
Kado Theatre; third month, 1816

Artist: Ashiyuki

Signature: Ashiyuki

Seal: Ashiyuki

Surimono, colour woodblock with metallic pigment
and cut gold-leaf, diptych, each approx. 38.4 x 52.8 cm

Nihon University Center for Information Networking,
Tokyo (*Shikanjō*)

The *surimono* (from vol. 4 of *Shikanjō*, cat. 6) celebrates the return to Osaka of Shikan and Ichikawa
Ebijūrō I, who had just received this new name in
Edo from Ichikawa Danjūrō VII. It depicts the two
actors as competing archers, both claiming the
prize. (See cat. 161 for another representation of
this scene.) This was part of a systematic re-
launching of Ebijūrō's career in Kyoto–Osaka as
the foil to Shikan and heir to the famous Edo
actor Danjūrō. There are fourteen haiku and eight
kyōka poems. Several poets such as Doran,
Jitokuken and Garaku appear in other *surimono* in

this catalogue. From the summer imagery we can
assume that the gathering from which this *surimono* was produced took place towards the end
of the run of the play, late in the fourth month.

Following is a selection of the poems (fig. 5):

Matsu uete / ka ni kuwarekeri / natsu no tsuki
The pine planted at New Year
Eaten by mosquitoes
Summer moon
SHIKAN (Utaemon)

The pine tree is associated with the crane, used
by Shikan on his crest.

Tsuru ni mi o / kaete hoshisa yo / hototogisu
How the cuckoo
Dreams of becoming
A crane
SHINSHŌ (Ebijūrō)

Kōhaku ni / saki-kurabetaru / botan ka na
One red, one white
How nice to compare
Peony blooms
KISHŌ

Peony is often used as a metaphor for a bloom-
ing actor.

162

Masurao no / yumi isamashiki / hakama ka na
How martial
The taut bow
And formal uniform
JURAKU

Juraku's poem complements the warrior image on the print.

Nani shite mo / haneru ya ebi no / na mo suzushi
The prawn just keeps
Jumping around
Even its name sounds cool
DORAN (of Kyoto)

Doran praises the lively performance by Ebijūrō, the 'prawn' (*ebi*) of the verse. By this time Doran had ceased to be a fan of Shikan.

Yumi to ya no / iu ni iwarenu / tsuru no ba no / futari o hikanu / mono tote wa nashi
With bow and arrow
No contest
At the crane hunt
Who would not
Back them both
JITOKUKEN

The *kyōka* poem above refers to the scene depicted, where the characters shoot down a crane. Comparing the two actors, one cannot help but praise them both.

Namanuruki / Arashi kurai wa / itowajina / ki mo futou saku / kono Edo-zakura
As for the tepid
Arashi (Rikan)
Don't even bother –
How grand it blossoms
This cherry from Edo
MŌKITEI FUSUI

There is no need to worry at all about that tepid Rikan, our Ebijūrō has blossomed as an actor after going to Edo.

Kyō Edo ni / shiru mo shiranu mo / nabikikeri / mazu yakusha de wa / Ōsaka no seki
Known or not known
In Kyoto and Edo
They have their charms
But an actor's ultimate test
Is the Osaka Barrier
HŌENTEI KABOKU

Actors may achieve fame in Kyoto and Edo, but the real test is whether they can make it on the Osaka stage (likened to the 'barrier' [*seki*], or guard-post, on the ancient highway leading to the city). The implication is that these two have succeeded.

163

163 Nakamura Utaemon III (Shikan) as Iruka Daijin

PLAY *Imoseyama onna teikin* at the Kado Theatre; eleventh month, 1815

Artist: Hokushū (Shunkō)

Signature: Shunkō ga

Publisher: Shioya Chōbei

Ōban, colour woodblock with metallic pigment and embossing, 37.1 x 24.9 cm

Private Collection (UK)

Iruka Daijin is one of the great super-villain roles in Kabuki. Originally a puppet play by Chikamatsu Hanji, first performed in 1771, *Imoseyama* was adapted for Kabuki and is still regularly performed. The play treats the struggle between Soga no Iruka (d. 645) and Fujiwara Kamatari (614–69) for control of Japan.

For another design relating to the same performance, see cat. 175.

164a

164b

164a Nakamura Utaemon III (Shikan) as Osode

PLAY *Yayoi ni hiraku ando no funahashi* at the Kado Theatre; third month, 1816

Artists: Ashikuni and Shikan

Signatures: Ashikuni sha, Shikan ga

Ōban, colour woodblock with metallic pigment and embossing, 37.4 x 25.1 cm

Ikeda Bunko Library (927-A20A)

Shikan appears in the role of Osode, wife of Yūsuke, seated with a brush and writing box, as if she has just done the ink painting on the screen. This painting within a painting is indeed by Shikan, as is the poem: he is thus presented here as actor, artist and poet combined. The similar phenomenon of actor-as-artist is seen in a Kunihiro print of Nakamura Matsue (Sankō), dating from the ninth month, 1824 (cat. 164b).

On the screen is depicted the famous monk–poet Saigyō (1118–90), who travelled extensively around Japan. A common subject in classical painting was to show him gazing at Mt Fuji in admiration.

Saigyō mo / Fuji minu tabi ya / tsuiri-gumo
Saigyō, too, will not see Fuji
On his journey
Rainy-season clouds
SHIKAN

164b Nakamura Matsue III (Sankō) as Osode

PLAY *Yayoi ni hiraku ando no funahashi* at the Kado Theatre; ninth month, 1824

Artists: Kunihiro and Sankō

Signatures: Kunihiro ga, Sankō ga

Publisher: Tenmaya Kihei

Ōban, colour woodblock with embossing, 37.9 x 26.3 cm

Private Collection (UK)

The woodblocks originally used to print a design of Nakamura Utaemon III (Shikan) eight years earlier (cat. 164a) are here partially plugged and re-carved to present Matsue in the same role as, and in similar vein to, his mentor. He is celebrated as both actor and artist.

168 Playbill for an opening-of-the-season performance (*Kaomise banzuke*)

PLAY *Shima-meguri tsuki no yumihari* at the Naka Theatre; eleventh month, 1808

Kaomise banzuke, woodblock, 35.6 x 48.2 cm

Bristol's City Museum & Art Gallery (Mb 4391/18)

The programme was based on a best-selling novel of adventure published in Edo, *Chinsetsu yumihari-zuki* (*Strange Tales of the Bow Moon*) by Takizawa Bakin (1767–1848), with illustrations by Hokusai, and is an early example of adapting this type of fiction for the Kabuki stage. Arashi Kichisaburō II (Rikan) was a big hit as the warrior strongman Tametomo. The Kabuki season begins in the eleventh (occasionally the twelfth) month of the year. This is not the usual Osaka format for a playbill but rather the Edo style, with an illustration of the actors in role at the bottom beneath their names. This was most likely because Bakin was a well-known Edo writer.

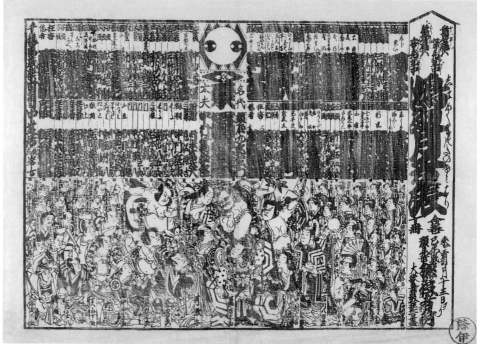

168

169 Playbill for an opening-of-the-season performance (*Kaomise banzuke*)

PLAY *Hirugaesu nishiki no tamoto* and *Kanadehon Chūshingura* at the Naka Theatre; eleventh month, 1812

Kaomise banzuke, woodblock, 35.0 x 49.1 cm

Artist's signature: Eshi Okayama Shigenobu hitsu ('from the brush of the artist Okayama Shigenobu)

Bristol's City Museum & Art Gallery (Mb 4391/19)

This was the all-important first performance in Osaka by Nakamura Utaemon III (Shikan), after his return from five years working in Edo. To mark the occasion the playbill is designed in the unusual Edo style, with depictions of the actors in their upcoming roles.

Shikan played seven roles in *Chūshingura*, which seems to have been put on from the twenty-first, towards the end of the month. There is a *surimono* representing him in these roles in *Kyota* (Waseda) 23: 7–9, on which a group of *kyōka* poets celebrate his performance. The actor Bandō Hikosaburō III also came from Edo with Shikan.

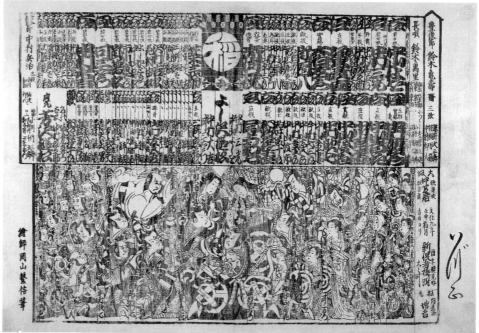

169

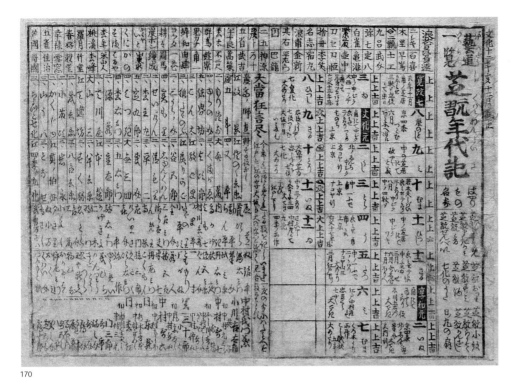

170

170 'Table of his artistry: Shikan year-by-year'
Geidō ichiran: Shikan nendaiki

Twelfth month, 1815

Parody flybill (*mitate banzuke*), woodblock,
22.0 x 30.7 cm

Waseda University Theatre Museum, Tokyo
(*Kyota* 25: 36)

A flybill containing a handy list of Shikan's fans,
his career year-by-year and his hit roles. This
was originally published in the fourth month,
1815. In the fifth month, 1815, a rival Rikan
version was published. Finally, both were reissued together in the twelfth month, 1815 (compare cat. 171). In 1820 the Shikan print was
updated substantially and reissued (*Kyota* 29:
46–7). MK

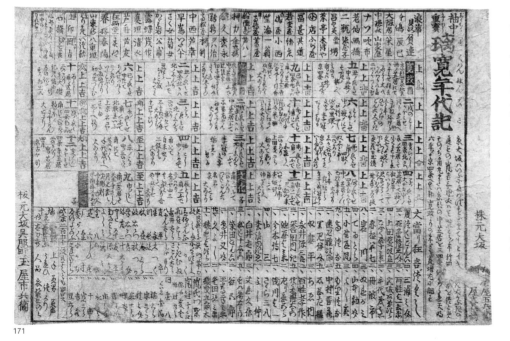

171

**171 'Precious treasure up your sleeve:
Rikan year-by-year'**
(Shūchū chōhō) Rikan nendaiki

Twelfth month, 1815

Publisher: Tamaya Ichibei

Parody flybill (*mitate banzuke*), woodblock,
21.8 x 32.5 cm

Waseda University Theatre Museum, Tokyo
(*Kyota* 25: 37)

The broadsheet print lists the names of Rikan's
fans (some of whom contributed poems to *surimono* elsewhere in this catalogue), gives an outline of his career year-by-year, and a list of his
hit roles. This was originally issued in the fifth
month, 1815, one month after the rival *Shikan
nendaiki* (cat. 170). Both were then reissued at
the same time in the twelfth month, 1815.

172

172 Nakamura Utaemon III (Shikan)

PLAY *Igagoe norikake gappa* at the Kado Theatre;
first month, 1816

Artist: Ashikuni

Signature: Ashikuni sha

Artist's seal: Unread

Surimono, colour woodblock with metallic pigment,
23.7 x 37.0 cm

Waseda University Theatre Museum, Tokyo
(*Kyota* 26: 18)

Shikan is represented as none other than a
feudal lord (*daimyō*), seated leaning on an arm-
rest (*kyūsoku*) and with an attendant kneeling
respectfully behind, holding his sword. The print
has articulated parts: at first glance it looks like
a set of closed sliding paper doors (*shōji*); these
then fold back to reveal Shikan seated in
grandeur. The portrait is accompanied by three
haiku, two *kyōka* and one Chinese poem. This
was the model for a competing Kunihiro *surimono* of Rikan in similar guise (cat. 173), published exactly one year later.

173 Arashi Kichisaburō II (Rikan) as the aristocrat Shigefusa

PLAY *Chigo ga fuchi hana no shiranami* at the
Naka Theatre; first month, 1817

Artist: Kunihiro

Signature: Kunihiro sha

Artist's seal: Unread

Surimono, colour woodblock with metallic pigment,
mother-of-pearl and embossing, 37.7 x 51.7 cm

The British Museum, London (1906.12-20.01131)

In the first month, 1817, Rikan was performing at
the Naka Theatre and Shikan at the nearby Kado
Theatre, both in the role of the boy acolyte
(*chigo*) Sutewakamaru. Here Rikan wears the
aristocratic costume of another role he played in
that performance, the elegant courtier Nagisa no
Chūnagon Shigefusa. He is depicted leaning on a
lacquered elbow-rest – which has been decorated by the printer with flakes of real mother-
of-pearl – while a pageboy kneels respectfully
behind displaying the courtier's sword.

The pose echoes a *surimono* print by Ashikuni
from exactly a year before (cat. 172), in which
Shikan was also shown seated with a servant
behind holding a sword. Poems by Shikan's
patrons on that print all praise his brilliance.
When considered together, these two lavish

surimono illustrate how the groups of supporters promoted rival images of the two superstars
as sophisticated aristocrats.

The eight haiku poems here are by amateur
poets, perhaps members of the Sakura (Cherry
Blossom) fan club that supported Rikan, and the
content of the poems shows the fervour of the
fan-club activities at this high point in the
rivalry between Rikan and Shikan. As was
common practice, nearly all have a flower or
plant image. Mandarin orange (*tachibana*) was
Rikan's crest and cherry blossom (*sakura*) was
associated with him as well, while plum (*ume*)
and pine (*matsu*) were associated with his rival
Shikan. The phrase 'even the crane has come' in
the third poem is most likely a reference to
Shikan, whose crest was a crane (*tsuru*).

Ichiju mite mo / kototaru hana no / arashi ka na
Just looking at one tree
Seeing its flowers is enough
As they flutter in the storm
SHUNBI

The Arashi Kichisaburō (Rikan) tree stands tall
and magnificent; all others bow before the
storm (*arashi*) of fluttering cherry blossoms.
There is no need to go to see other flowers
(Shikan).

Tachibana no / miki yori ha yori / haru no kaze
Mandarin orange tree
From its trunk, from its leaves
A spring breeze
SHŌZAN

Fresh winds of spring arise from Rikan (orange
tree) and his troupe of actors.

Tsuru mo kite / kono ikioi no / sakura mi ni
Even a crane has come
To join the throng
And gaze at the cherry blossom
JUNSHO

Even Shikan (crane) flies in, wondering at the
crowds flocking to see Rikan (cherry blossom).

Oboroyo ni / mitagae mo nashi / matsu kikoku
Night of mist and cloud
Impossible to mistake
Pine for wild orange tree
SANPŌ

Even in the night Shikan (*matsu*) cannot be
compared with Rikan (*kikoku* or *karatachi*, a type
of wild orange tree that mandarin orange trees
are grafted onto). This suggests a Chinese phrase
about how a mandarin orange tree (*tachibana*)
from south of the Yangtze River was trans-

173

planted north of the river and became a wild orange tree with inedible fruit (*karatachi*). The crane, Shikan's crest, is associated with pine trees.

> *Iu made mo / nashi konosetsu no / arashiyama*
> No need to say
> This is the season for
> Mt Arashiyama
> SHIYŌ

It is clear that this is the moment of (Arashi) Rikan's glory and victory over his rival, just as the spring cherry blossom is obviously splendid at Arashiyama in Kyoto.

> *Jitto shite / irarenu hana no / uwasa ka na*
> Unable to stay still
> Rumours of cherry blossom
> In the wind
> KOGYŌ

No-one can resist the talk of how good Rikan's (cherry blossom) performance is, just as no-one can stay at home when the cherries blossom.

> *Ume to iu / mono wa aredomo / sakurabito*
> Plum is fine
> But we love
> Cherry blossom best
> KOSHŪ

We have heard of an actor called Shikan (plum blossom), but we love Rikan (cherry blossom) best.

> *Taoredomo / nao sakaemase / chigo-zakura*
> Even if plucked,
> May you flourish even more
> Young cherry tree
> RIKAN

Chigo-zakura is a type of mountain cherry blossom and can also just mean 'boy'.

Rikan and Shikan were both playing young boys in rival productions at this time, and Rikan could be teasing Shikan, implying that the younger Shikan will have another time to blossom, since he was 'plucked' this time in the competition between them. Certainly a parody flybill (*mitate banzuke*) in *Kyota* (Waseda) 27: 18 comparing the two performances gives victory to Rikan over Shikan.

This *surimono* is also discussed and translated in Gerstle 2002.

174

174 Ichikawa Ebijūrō I as Matsugae Tetsunosuke

PLAY *Meiboku Sendai hagi* at the Kado Theatre; ninth month, 1816

Artist: Ashiyuki

Signature: Gigadō Ashiyuki

Artist's seal: Gigadō (hand-impressed)

Surimono, colour woodblock with metallic pigment, 36.0 x 49.5 cm

Private Collection (Japan)

This large-format *surimono* print celebrates the re-launch of Ichikawa Ebijūrō I (formerly Ichizō) as an Osaka star. He appears in the role of the strong and loyal Matsugae Tetsunosuke in the play *Meiboku Sendai hagi*, a tale about plotting for control of Sendai Castle, north of Edo (Tokyo). Matsugae tries to secure a list of conspirators that will incriminate some evil retain-

ers. This *surimono* depicts the scene where the villain Niki Danjō transforms himself into a rat to steal the document back from Matsugae.

Nakamura Utaemon III (Shikan) had originally arranged for Ebijūrō to go to Edo in 1808, following the death of Ebijūrō's teacher, Ichikawa Danzō IV. Ebijūrō returned to Osaka in 1815, after receiving his new name as a disciple of the most famous Edo actor, Ichikawa Danjūrō VII. Another *surimono* of the same year, which celebrates the return of Shikan and Ebijūrō, includes poems by two of the same poets that feature on this print (cat. 162).

Mi iri-yoki / aki o mimasu no / mondokoro
Magnificent harvest
A fine autumn view
The Ichikawa 'mimasu' crest
GARAKU

The harvest is a metaphor for Ebijūrō's maturing late in life and the word *iri* ('to enter') also refers to the audience of a performance. *Mimasu* is a pun meaning both the three-square (triple rice-measure) crest of the Ichikawa actor family and that the 'view is even better'. The overall flavour is obviously auspicious, wishing Ebijūrō success under his new name in Osaka.

The second poem is by 'Master of the Gigadō (Playful painting studio)', Ashiyuki himself:

Hakari uraru / miyo no tameshi ya / masu no ichi
Measure for measure
The standard for our age
And ruler of the market.
GIGADŌ ARUJI (Ashiyuki)

A *masu* is a square box, typically used for measuring rice; a stack of three *masu* of different sizes, each fitting inside the other, form the *mimasu* crest. Ashiyuki's poem picks up on the image of the *mimasu* crest and takes it for its literal meaning: we will be able to measure Ebijūrō's success as he seeks his fame on the Osaka stage again and comes to dominate the market by becoming number one, the standard (*tameshi*).

The third poem is by Shinshō, the pen name of the actor himself:

Okurezaku / hagi ni mo tsuyu no / megumi ka na
Late to bloom
May the dew on the bush clover
Grace me from above
SHINSHŌ (Ebijūrō)

Ebijūrō modestly professes that he does not yet deserve his new status as a Danjūrō disciple.

Kiku awase / tare mo yubi sasu / hana no kata
Chrysanthemum competition
All stare and point
At this flower's style
KIZAN

Kizan presents a final auspicious image of Ebijūrō arriving in full flourish at the theatre.

175 Ichikawa Ebijūrō I (Shinshō) as the fisherman Fukashichi

PLAY *Imoseyama onna teikin* at the Kado Theatre; eleventh month, 1815

Unsigned

Publisher: Unknown (Osaka)

Ōban, colour woodblock, 37.9 x 26.7 cm

Private Collection (UK)

The poem is by Shinshō, the pen name taken by Ebijūrō upon receiving his new stage name in Edo as a disciple of Ichikawa Danjūrō VII, earlier the same year. The print records his first performance in Osaka under this new name. The young actor is presented as 'the new Danjūrō', a master of Edo rough-style acting (*aragoto*). Striking a most forceful pose, the way he faces directly out at us is unusual in an Osaka print. Also, this may well be the earliest example of an Osaka *ōban* actor print that includes a poem.

Fukashichi, really the loyal retainer of Lord Fujiwara Kamatari, is in disguise as a lowly fisherman. He infiltrates the evil Iruka's palace to thwart his plans to usurp the government. This is a rough, but proud and loyal character, normally played by 'villain-role' (*jitsuaku*) specialists.

Fuyu no umi / aretaki mama ni / arenikeri
The winter sea
Rough it wants to be
Rough it always was
SHINSHŌ

For another design relating to the same performance see cat. 163.

175

176

176 Arashi Kichisaburō II (Rikan) as Akizuki Daizen

PLAY *Sono no yuki koi no kumidai* at the Naka Theatre; second month, 1816

Artist: Kunihiro

Signature: Kunihiro ga

Publisher: Wataya Kihei

Ōban, colour woodblock, 39.2 x 24.6 cm

Private Collection (UK)

Another front-facing portrait was produced by Hokushū for the same performance (Ikeda 1997, no. 54) and it would seem that both artists were responding to the anonymous print of Ichikawa Ebijūrō I issued three months earlier (cat. 175). On that occasion Ebijūrō had acted in the bombastic 'rough stuff' (*aragoto*) style of his Edo mentor Ichikawa Danjūrō VII. So perhaps Hokushū and Kunihiro are promoting Rikan as the superstar able to rival the newly minted Ebijūrō, just returned from his many years in Edo.

Daizen is the grand villain of this play, plotting to overthrow the government. In this print he is apparently in costume as a performer on a Noh stage, in the role of a lion dancer, with the customary large pine tree painted on the wall at the back of the stage behind him. Scowling grimly, he half kneels with most of the upper robes turned under around the waist. It seems that he is about to bear his stomach and stab himself with the point of a sword, to commit ritual suicide (*seppuku* or *harakiri*). He does not, however, kill himself in the play. The story does revolve around a famous sword, the treasure of an estate, which is defaced (see also the commentaries for cat. 177). An anonymous stencil print (cat. 178), dating from the same time as this performance, shows Rikan and Shikan (Utaemon) in a tug-of-war competition, both in the role of a lion dancer.

177 Arashi Kichisaburō II (Rikan) as Akizuki Daizen

PLAY *Sono no yuki koi no kumidai* at the Naka Theatre; second month, 1816

Artist: Hokkei (Shun'yō)

Signature: Kintarō Shun'yō sha

Artist's seal: Unread

Publisher: Shioya Chōbei

Ōban, colour woodblock with embossing, 36.6 x 25.1 cm

Private Collection (UK)

177

Akizuki Daizen was one of Rikan's successful roles (see also cats 176 and 177). The play was a variation on *Shin usuyuki monogatari*, a puppet play first performed in the fifth month, 1741, in which Daizen, a swordsman, murders his rival. For the Kabuki production of 1816 Rikan also played the loyal retainer Tsumahei. Hokkei, a great promoter of Rikan, was only active as an artist for a few years between about 1813 and 1818, and produced most of his prints for performances by Rikan's troupe.

In the collection of Ikeda Bunko Library this print is paired with another of Rikan in the role of Tsumahei to make a diptych (Ikeda 1998, vol. 2, no. 444). If this was indeed originally a diptych (and it would appear to be), then it is a rare example of a single actor shown in two different roles in the same design.

178 Shikan (right) and Rikan (left) in a 'neck-tugging' contest

PLAYS *Yayoi ni hiraku ando no funahashi* (Shikan) at the Kado Theatre, *Sono no yuki koi no kumidai* (Rikan) at the Naka Theatre; third month, 1816

Anonymous

Horizontal *ōban*, woodblock with stencil-printed colours (*kappazuri*), 26.7 x 38.9 cm

The British Museum, London (2003.8-18.01)

An imagined 'neck-tugging' (*kubi-hiki*) contest between Nakamura Utaemon III (Shikan) in the role of Shakkyō, the Lion Dancer (right, seated), and Arashi Kichisaburō II (Rikan) in the role of Akizuki Daizen (left, seated), with Ichikawa Monnosuke (from Edo) standing between them as the referee with his ceremonial fan. Ichikawa Ebijūrō I as Miura Arajirō (right, standing) backs Shikan, and Arashi Sangorō III (left, standing) as Dankurō supports Rikan. Shikan and Ebijūrō were performing at the Kado Theatre in *Yayoi ni hiraku ando no funahashi*; Rikan and Sangorō were performing at the Naka Theatre in *Sono no yuki koi no kumidai*.

Each eggs on his man (from right to left):

Ebijūrō: Don't give in.
Shikan: I'll not be defeated [shamed].
Monnosuke: Ready, steady, go!
Rikan: I'm as strong as a thousand men.
Sangorō: Don't give in!

The only other known impression of the print is in the *Kyota kyakushokujō* album in Waseda University Theatre Museum, Tokyo (*Kyota* 26: 45; Matsudaira [Waseda] 1995[c], vol. 4, no. 96).

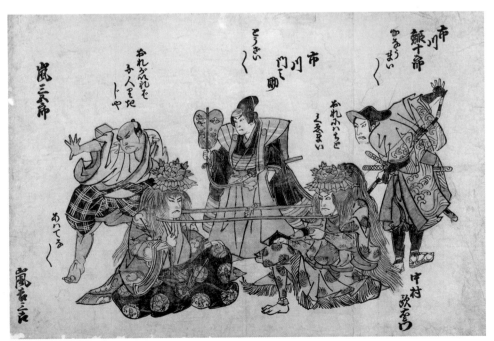

178

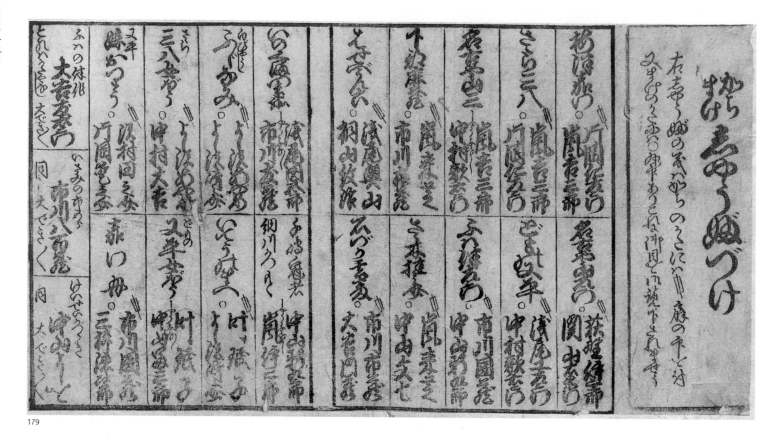

179

179 'Ranking of winners and losers'
Kachi-make shōbu-zuke

First month, 1808

Parody flybill (mitate banzuke), woodblock, 18.5 x 33.8 cm

Waseda University Theatre Museum, Tokyo (Kyota 20: 22)

Both Rikan and Shikan were performing the role of the outlaw hero Nagoya Sanza in variants of the same play for the New Year production. The text says that it was a draw between them, with no clear winner. This was the year that Shikan departed for Edo to try to make his name as a troupe leader, at the relatively young age of thirty.

180a 'Kado Theatre, Naka Theatre: winners and losers in the spring sumo bout'
(Kado shibai, Naka shibai) Haru no hana sumō no kachi-make (not illustrated)

First month, 1813

Parody flybill (mitate banzuke), woodblock

Waseda University Theatre Museum, Tokyo (Kyota 23: 27)

180b 'Sumo competition between the Kado and Naka Theatres'
(Kado-Naka) Sumō kachi-make

First month, 1813

Parody flybill (mitate banzuke), woodblock, 21.2 x 30.7 cm

Waseda University Theatre Museum, Tokyo (Kyota 23: 28)

Nakamura Utaemon III (Shikan) had returned two months earlier to Osaka to perform in the eleventh month, 1812, after five years touring in Edo. At the end of 1812 Rikan was performing in Kyoto, so the first head-to-head between the two stars had to wait until the New Year performances. The Kabuki media went into overdrive to promote the rivalry. In these two prints actors at each theatre are paired off for mock 'sumo wrestling bouts': Rikan and Shikan are said to have drawn in their competition. From 1813 onwards there was a tremendous increase in the production of Osaka actor prints and the standard format became the large ōban size.

Kabuki nenpyō (vol. 5, p. 513) has the transcription of another parody flybill for this performance, the original of which is unknown. This is fascinating because it is both a competition between the actors and between the theatres as well. The winner in each category is here shown underlined and in bold. Rikan was at the Kado, and Shikan at the Naka Theatre.

Kado (Rikan)		Naka (Shikan)
Play		Play
Actor's skill		**Actor's skill**
Actor's salary		Actor's salary
Male lead		Male lead
Female lead		**Female lead**
Dance		**Dance**
Costumes		Costumes
Seating	Draw	Seating
Theatre		**Theatre**
Front decorations		**Front decorations**
Male audience		**Male audience**
Female audience		Female audience
Saké		**Saké**
Food		Food
Free passes	Draw	Free passes
Boats		Boats

The text then goes on to describe the elaborate banners and decorations outside and inside each theatre, with the names of patrons and fan clubs.

Rikan was more popular among women, Shikan among men.

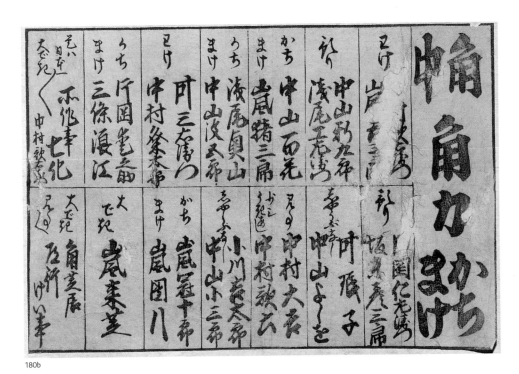

180b

181 'Parody sumo of the hits: neck-tugging between the hits, neck-tugging between the misses'
(*Atarimono kubihiki: ataranu mono kubihiki*)
Atarimono no mitate sumō

Fourth month, 1813

Artist's signature: Shūzan/Hideyama ga

Parody flybill (*mitate banzuke*), woodblock, 27.8 x 41.0 cm

Waseda University Theatre Museum, Tokyo (*Kyota* 23: 65)

'Neck-tugging' (*kubihiki*) is the equivalent of arm-wrestling or tug-of-war. Contestants have a rope or sash tied between their necks (see also cats 178 and 218). This is another example of an imagined competition between the Kado and Naka Theatres, and between Rikan and Shikan who were performing at each, respectively. Also it is quite clear that male fans support Shikan (right), while women rally behind Rikan (left).

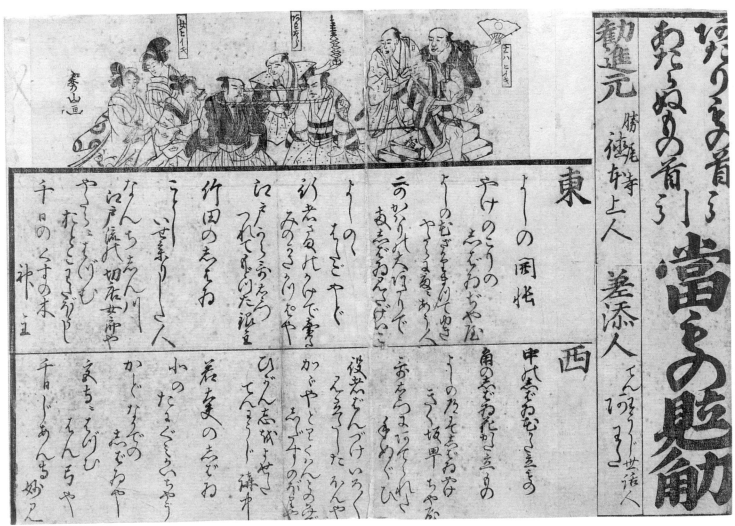

181

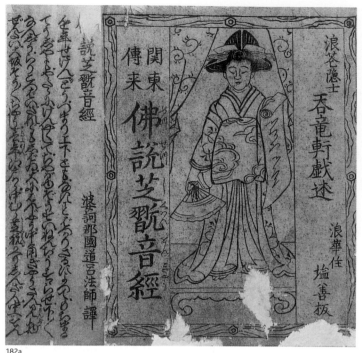

182a

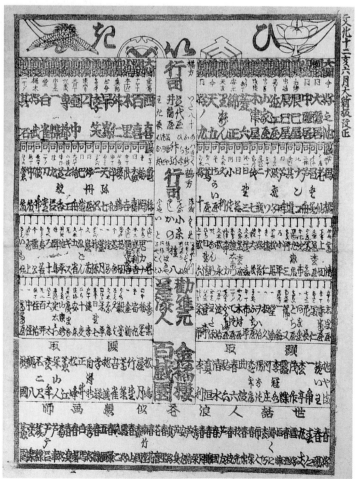

183b

182a 'Shikan sutra'
Bussetsu Shikannon kyō

c. Eleventh month, 1813

Author: 'Donryūken'

Publisher: Shio-Zen

Parody flybill (*mitate banzuke*), woodblock,
19.5 x 58.8 cm

Waseda University Theatre Museum, Tokyo
(*Kyota* 23: 67–8)

A parody of the *Kannon Sutra* (*Kannon kyō*), with
Nakamura Utaemon III (Shikan) as the Buddhist
deity. This genre of comic sutra parodies became
popular in Osaka around 1811. The text is a playful prayer of worship and describes his departure
from Edo and great success in Osaka on his
return.   MK

182b 'Comic display of temple treasures:
Rikan sutra'
(Odoke kaichō) Rikan kyō (not illustrated)

c. Twelfth month, 1813

Parody flybill (*mitate banzuke*), woodblock,
19.5 x 58.8 cm

Waseda University Theatre Museum, Tokyo
(*Kyota* 23: 69)

This Sutra parody was produced in response to
the *Shikannon kyō* (cat. 182a). It describes
humorously how Rikan left Osaka after Shikan
arrived and was a success in a Kyoto production.
It also describes how women love his performance and even dogs are wild about him.   MK

182c 'Tale of Quarrels'
Isakai hanashi (not illustrated)

1813

Parody flybill (*mitate banzuke*), 2 sheets, woodblock,
18.7 x 27.3 cm, 18.6 x 27.8 cm

Waseda University Theatre Museum, Tokyo
(*Kyota* 23: 69, 70)

Rikan and Shikan are presented as deities for
worship: Rikan for women, Shikan for men.   MK

184

183a 'Rikan–Shikan: sumo competition of their fans'
Rikan Shikan: hiiki sumō (not illustrated)

c. Late 1815

Parody flybill (*mitate banzuke*), woodblock,
47.0 x 34.6 cm

Osaka University (Daigaku-in Bungaku Kenkyū-ka
5-6-1-39)

The parody flybill (*banzuke*) ranks the rival fans
of Arashi Kichisaburō II (Rikan, right) and Nakamura Utaemon III (Shikan, left) like opposing
teams of sumo wrestlers.

183b Parody sumo: fans of the Mandarin Team versus fans of the Crane Team
Tachibana-kata, Tsuru-kata hiiki mitate sumō

Sixth month, 1815

Parody flybill (*mitate banzuke*), woodblock,
47.0 x 34.6 cm

Osaka University (Daigaku-in Bungaku Kenkyū-ka
5-6-1-40)

The parody flybill (*banzuke*) ranks the rival fans
of Arashi Kichisaburō II (Rikan, right, mandarin
crest) and Nakamura Utaemon III (Shikan, left,
crane crest) like opposing teams of sumo
wrestlers.

Across the bottom, affiliated to neither camp,
is a category 'Facilitators – Osaka Likeness
Artists' (*Sewanin Osaka nigao eshi*), the forty-
four Osaka actor-print artists active at the time
(see also pp. 47–8).

184 Nakayama Yoshio as Komurasaki (right) and Nakamura Utaemon III (Shikan) as Hirai Gonpachi (left)

PLAY *Beni murasaki aide some-age* at the Kado Theatre;
eighth month, 1816

Artists: Shunkin (right) and Shun'ei (left)

Signatures: Shunkin ga, Shun'ei ga

Publisher: Shioya Chōbei

Ōban, colour woodblock, diptych, 38.8 x 52.5 cm

Hendrick Lühl Collection (Germany)

Gonpachi is a dashing character, a former samurai who accidentally killed another man when he
was sixteen and fled to Edo, there to lead a life
of crime. Komurasaki is the beautiful courtesan
who loves him. Very few prints survive by these
two artists, both of whom seem to have been
active only in 1816.

185

185 Nakamura Utaemon III (Shikan) in twelve dance roles

PLAY *Matakaina jūni bake* at the Kado Theatre; third month, 1817

Artists: Kyōgadō Ashikuni and Shikan

Signatures: Ashikuni, Shikan

Two prints (each cut in half), woodblock with metallic pigment, 25.4 x 74.0 cm (right pair); 25.4 x 74.0 cm (left pair)

Waseda University Theatre Museum, Tokyo (*Kyota* 27: 21/22)

Each image of Shikan in a different dance represents a month of the year, as if painted on a pair of six-fold screens, and is accompanied by a poem by Ashikuni, Shikan or one of Shikan's fans. For the figures drawn by Shikan himself, his own face is modestly hidden. This *tour de force* print presents Shikan simultaneously as actor, dancer, poet and artist, and as the focus of a group of adoring poet-fans.

Illustrated is screen one with six roles (right to left): Courtesan (by Ashikuni), Mita Inari Festival (by Shikan), Shirozakeya (by Ashikuni), Yakko (by Shikan), Yanone (by Ashikuni) and the Ikakeya husband (by Ashikuni). The Edo courtesan's robe has a design of New Year decorations (see also cat. 186). A reveller returns from an Inari Festival with comic mask and large wooden paddle. *Shirozake* is a sweet, cloudy sake served at the Doll's Festival. Yakko were low-level samurai. They were known to perform witty dances and to have a dandy appearance. 'Yanone' is one of the 'eighteen favourite' Danjūrō plays, an auspicious dance piece. Soga Gorō sharpens a metal arrowhead for a huge arrow. Ikakeya were craftsmen who repaired metal pots. The term came to mean a man and woman walking out together.

One of the poet names is different on the impression in the Philadelphia Museum of Art, which also has the second set (screen two). Roger Keyes comments in detail on these six images

(Keyes and Mizushima, 1973, pp. 62–3, no. 11). The name 'Nihyō' (known as a fan of Shikan's rival Rikan) has been changed to '(woman) Koto'. From right to left the characters given in bold and the poems accompanying them are:

SCREEN ONE (right, illustrated)

Courtesan
Warubirenu / yanagi-gami ari / miyo no haru
Free-flowing
Her willow-like hair
Ah the peaceful spring
KYŌGADŌ ASHIKUNI

Mita Inari (Mita Inari festival)
Ukasarete / hito ni yoikeri / nigatsu-zora
Floating along
Drunk among the crowds
Spring sky
SHIKAN

Shirozakeya (Seller of sweet sake)
Hitokuchi wa / nanichō momo ni / hina no sake
How about a drink
Peach blossom and sweet sake
At the Doll's Festival
ASHIKUNI

Yakko (Rough dandy)
Kore hodo ni / me-saki atarashi / hatsu-katsuo
How fresh
Around the eyes
First bonito of the season
SHIKAN

Yanone ('Arrow-sharpening')
Utaemon / hiku ya satsuki no / ayame-gusa
Utaemon
Plucking him
Like iris in summer
ASHIKUNI

Ikakeya (Husband)
Yūdachi hare / toshiyori koi no / kowa takashi
The evening shower has cleared
An old loving couple
Cry out to one another
(RIGHT) UTAMARU

SCREEN TWO (left, not illustrated)

Ikakeya (Wife)
Asagao ya / mizu mo morasazu / kado ni saku
Morning glory
No water leaks through
Blooms at the gate [at the Kado Theatre]
KAKURENBO ('MR HIDE-N-SEEK')

Tōru (Courtier Tōru)
Ki-takasa wa / kumoi no ue yo / tsuki no tsuru
Feelings high
As the palace above the clouds
Crane in the moon
(WOMAN) KOTO

The crane is one of Shikan's crests.

Goze (Itinerant blind singer)
Aki-kaze wa / me ni mienu nari / koto no uta
Autumn wind
Invisible to the eye
The harp's song
KAKUHAN

Chongare (Mendicant dancer)
Igaguri no / hayashi me ni tatsu / shigure ka na
Chestnut burr
Sticks out in the forest
In the winter shower
ROSHŌ/ASHINAO

Musume (Young woman)
Mutsu de no / hana ni bai kake / yoi kiryō
At dawn
Twice the beauty of a snowflake
Makes a pretty bloom
KAKURENBO (AGAIN)

A dance in twelve quick changes, danced in the snow.

Kan U (Guan Yu) [Chinese poem]
One name of Shikan is 'Beautiful Beard'
In loyalty as firm as iron and gold.
His noble art is a wick's free swing,
The whir of an 82-*kin* Dragon Sword
(Offering congratulations for the third time)
KAKURENBO
(Trans. Roger Keyes)

Keyes and Mizushima 1973, pp. 62–3, no. 11.

186

186 Nakamura Utaemon III (Shikan) as a courtesan

c. 1820–25

Artist: Hokushū

Signature: Shunkōsai Hokushū

Artist's seal: Yoshinoyama (Mt Yoshino)

Hanging scroll, ink, colour and gold on silk, 103.8 x 38.1 cm

John C. Weber Collection, New York

Utaemon III (Shikan) was known for his ability to play a wide range of roles, including female characters. He played a courtesan in dance pieces several times in his career in Osaka between 1817 and 1825 (for example, cats 185 and 228). Here the woman poses with one sleeve held up to the mouth in a gesture of surprise and a long love letter unrolled in the other. The elaborate costume, with brocade sash tied prominently in front in the manner of courtesans, features a design for New Year festivities – pine, dwarf bamboo, red and white plum blossoms, and a large lobster with cut-paper decorations (*noshi*).

This is perhaps the most technically brilliant of the few paintings currently known by Hokushū, attesting to his thoroughly professional abilities as an artist; even though his primary profession was a merchant, possibly a lumber merchant (Matsudaira 1996[a], pp. 22–3). After having used the name Shunkō during his earliest period of activity, from about 1802 (fig. 13 above), the artist is thought to have begun to use the name Hokushū from the fifth month, 1818 (two paintings of Rikan, cats 100 and 101, seem to have been done just before this). The change of name seems to have been prompted by a visit to Osaka of the great Edo artist Katsushika Hokusai (1760–1849); according to one account Hokusai visited Osaka in 1812 and again late in 1817 or early in 1818 (see Iijima 1893, pp. 48–9; Keyes and Mizushima 1973, p. 26; Matsudaira ibid.). This would further explain the use on this painting, also on a print of Shikan as Yakanbei (dated to the fifth month, 1824; cat. 229a) and other works of a hand-impressed seal that reads 'Yoshinoyama' (Mt Yoshino) in tangled phonetic characters (*kana*). A similar, though not identical, seal is known to have been used by Hokusai during the period 1815–19 and if Hokushū briefly became a pupil during Hokusai's visit to Osaka, then the master may well have authorized him to use this Yoshino art name (*gō*).

Matsudaira lists eleven uses by Hokushū of the Yoshinoyama seal between 1818 and 1830 (ibid. pp. 23–5), not including either the present painting or cat. 229a. TC

188a

188b

187 Nakamura Utaemon III (Shikan) as Katō Masakiyo

PLAY *Hachijin shugo no honjō* at the Kado Theatre; ninth month, 1820

Artist: Hokushū

Signature: Shunkōsai Hokushū ga

Artist's seal: Hokushū

Ōban, colour woodblock with metallic pigment, 38.9 x 26.9 cm

The British Museum, London (2003.8-21.01)

A striking portrait of Shikan in the role of the Osaka hero Katō Masakiyo, crossing his eyes and grimacing for a dramatic 'stage pose' (*mie*). Masakiyo was the fictional name given by convention to warlord Katō Kiyomasa (1562–1611), who defied Tokugawa Ieyasu of Edo (known as Kitabatake in the play). Masakiyo sacrifices himself by drinking poison in an effort to save the heir of his lord Toyotomi Hideyoshi and Osaka Castle from the treacherous Ieyasu, who had earlier pledged to protect the Toyotomi clan.

The *kyōka* poem inscribed above reads:

*Sekaijū / kagayaku tsuki no / Kiyomasa wa /
janome o akete / araitaru gei*
Kiyomasa is the moon
Shining on the world
At midday:
An art of piercing insight
CHŌSOKUSAI FUMINARI
(Trans. Roger Keyes)

Shikan is the star whose magnificent art shines throughout the world. Among several puns is one on the bull's-eye (*janome*) crest, visible on the actor's sleeves.

For an imaginary double portrait by Hokushū of Shikan in this role, opposite Rikan in the role of Prince Koretaka, see cat. 188a, b.

Keyes and Mizushima 1973, pp. 68–9, no. 14.

188a, b Arashi Kichisaburō II (Rikan) as Prince Koretaka (right) and Nakamura Utaemon III (Shikan) as Katō Masakiyo (left)

PLAY *Toki ni saikō Ariwara keizu* at the Horie Theatre (Rikan); *Hachijin shugo no honjō* at the Kado Theatre (Shikan); ninth month, 1820

Artist: Hokushū

Signature: Shunkōsai Hokushū ga

Ōban, colour woodblock with metallic pigment (188a), 37.1 x 25.5 cm (188a), 37.8 x 25.5 cm (188b)

Ikeda Bunko Library (188a) (H359a); Hendrick Lühl Collection (Germany) (188b)

The print imagines Rikan and Shikan together even though they were performing at different theatres. Around this time patrons began in earnest to try to persuade the two rival actors to share the same stage.

Prince Koretaka (Rikan, right), in brocade dragon robes and holding up a gold court cap, is in the villainous role of an imperial prince who will stop at nothing to regain disputed succession to the throne. Katō Masakiyo (Shikan, left) is a samurai role, the hero here dressed in voluminous formal black robes with white 'snake's-eye' (*janome*) crest to receive Kitabatake (modelled on Tokugawa Ieyasu); for more on this performance see cat. 187.

188a (see also cover) is a special *surimono*-like impression, with metallic printing in brass to imitate gold; 188b is the normal printing in colour woodblock for general sale. Perhaps the special editions were printed at the request of patrons, who would then distribute them privately; alternatively, the patrons may have presented them to the actors to give as gifts.

Keyes & Mizushima 1973, pp. 66–7, no. 13.

189

189 Ichikawa Ebijūrō I (Shinshō) as Jūrō Sukenari (right), Arashi Kichisaburō II (Rikan, Kitsusaburō I) as Kudō Suketsune (centre) and Nakamura Utaemon III (Shikan) as Gorō Tokimune (left)

Mid-1821

Artist: Yoshikuni

Signature: Yoshikuni ga

Artist's seal: Yoshikuni (?) (hand-impressed)

Publisher: Wataya Kihei

Ōban, colour woodblock, triptych, 37.0 x 25.8 cm (right), 36.9 x 26.8 cm (centre), 37.0 x 25.8 cm (left)

The British Museum, London (1983.5-23.01, 60-62)

This is an 'imagined' (*mitate*) performance, with the three stars together as a dream cast in the perennial favourite play about the Soga brothers. Each actor is given his pen name (*haimyō*), rather than his stage name. At this time, patrons and artists were pushing to persuade the great rivals Rikan and Shikan to perform together.

The moor at the base of Mt Fuji was the setting for the famous vendetta attack of the Soga brothers Jūrō and Gorō against their father's murderer Kudō Suketsune. This was an actual historical incident of 1193, which took place during a hunting party of the Shogun Minamoto no Yoritomo. The tension between the characters is intense at the moment of confrontation: the brothers have waited eighteen years for the opportunity to avenge their father.

Matsudaira in *Hizō ukiyo-e taikan*, vol. 3, 1988, p. 266, no. 121.

190

190 Kataoka Nizaemon VII as Priest Gennō (far right) and Nakamura Utaemon III (Shikan) as Miuranosuke Yoshiaki (right), Arashi Koroku IV as Tamamo no Mae (centre), Ichikawa Ebijurō I as Kazusanosuke Hirotsune (left) and Arashi Kitsusaburō I (Rikan) as Abe no Yasunari (far left)

PLAY *Tamamo no Mae asahi no tamoto*; ninth month, 1821

Artist: Hokushū

Signature: Shunkōsai Hokushū ga

Publisher: Hon'ya Seishichi

Ōban, colour woodblock, triptych, 38.3 x 26.6 cm (right), 39.5 x 26.6 cm (centre), 39.4 x 26.0 cm (left)

The British Museum, London (2003.1-23.01)

This is an 'imagined' (*mitate*) performance, with actors from opposing troupes brought together as a dream cast for the featured play. Rival stars Shikan (right) and Rikan (left) are given equal prominence on either side of the composition. Intriguingly, no actor names are give, only roles.

The play, full of magic and supernatural elements, was originally written for the puppet theatre and first performed in Osaka in the first month, 1751. It was revised in the third month, 1806, again in Osaka. This revision was then made into a Kabuki play in 1813. Retired Emperor Toba is said to be suffering agonies

because of the malevolent influence of a fox spirit, which has travelled from India, through China to Japan. The evil fox has killed Princess Tama no Mae, taken the shape of her body and linked up with evil plotters. Miuranosuke and Kazusanosuke are sent by the court to subdue the fox. In fact, an elaborate plot is being conducted by Abe no Yasunari to overthrow the emperor and install his elder brother instead. Gennō is the priestly Buddhist name taken by Dairoku after he kills his own wife Oyana, after being taken over by the evil fox spirit.

191

191 (*Rikan Shikan*) *Hanakurabe nikan-banashi Rikan–Shikan: Contest of Flowers, Their Two Tales*

Second month, 1814

Author: Ikku Rōjin

Artist: Suga Shōhō

Publishers: Kagaya Yasuke and three others

Hanshibon book, woodblock, 2 vols, 18.7 x 12.8 cm (covers)

Kansai University Library, Osaka (913.69/I2/1-1/2)

This is an illustrated book in the 'comic story-telling' (*hanashi-bon*) genre. It divides into two volumes: the first, *Hanakurabe Shikan-banashi: ume no maki* (*Contest of Flowers, Shikan Tale, Plum Volume*), focuses on Nakamura Utaemon III (Shikan); the second, *Hanakurabe Rikan-banashi: sakura no maki* (*Contest of Flowers, Rikan Tale, Cherry Volume*), on Arashi Kichisaburō II (Rikan). The word *nikan* (the two 'kans') in the title refers to the *kan* character in each of their pen names. Shikan was always associated with plum and Rikan with cherry.

Illustrated is a portrait from the beginning of volume two of Rikan as the famous calligrapher Ono no Tōfū, one of his most popular roles (see also cats 116–18). The text is a riddle.

For a transcription of the book see Tsuchiya 1979, pp. 269–98.

192a *Yakusha nazokake ron*
Treatise on Actors and Riddles

First month, 1816

Author: Hachimonjiya Jishō

Publisher: Hachimonjiya Hachizaemon

Yoko kohon book, woodblock, 3 vols,
10.4 x 15.6 cm (covers)

Waseda University Theatre Museum, Tokyo
(*ro*-11-1469-1/2/3)

Actor critiques (*yakusha hyōbanki*) were regularly published by the Hachimonjiya firm from
the late seventeenth until the middle of the
nineteenth centuries. Performances by all the
top actors at the theatres of Kyoto, Osaka and
Edo were reviewed. These are an unparalleled
resource for theatre history.

This book has a section on Utaemon III
(Shikan)'s return to Osaka from Edo in the
eleventh month, 1815. It also discusses the events
organized by Shikan's fans to welcome him home.

192b *Yakusha meibutsu-awase*
Competition between Famous Actors
(not illustrated)

First month, 1817

Author: Hachimonjiya Jishō

Publisher: Hachimonjiya Hachizaemon

Yoko kohon book, woodblock, 3 vols,
10.4 x 15.2 cm (covers)

Waseda University Theatre Museum, Tokyo
(*ro*-11-1471-1/2/3)

This book gives critiques of the acting of Kichisaburō II (Rikan) and Utaemon III (Shikan) in
1816, during the period of their fiercest rivalry.

192c *Yakusha tōsen kagami*
Actors: Mirror of their Success (not illustrated)

First month, 1818

Author: Hachimonjiya Jishō

Publisher: Hachimonjiya Hachizaemon

Yoko kohon book, woodblock, 1 vol.,
10.4 x 15.3 cm (covers)

Waseda University Theatre Museum, Tokyo (*ro*-11-1477)

This book gives critiques of the acting of Kichisaburō II (Rikan) and Utaemon III (Shikan) in
1817, during the period of their fiercest rivalry.

193a *(Shibai ehon) Imose no kurumaki*
Theatre Picture Book: Hitched Pulley-wheels
(not illustrated)

1813

Artists: Ashikuni and Ashifune

Publishers: Kawachiya Tasuke and others

Hanshibon book, woodblock, 4 vols, 22. 0 x 15.5 cm
(covers)

Waseda University Theatre Museum, Tokyo
(*ro*-5-5344)

Cat. entries 193a–f describe fictionalized illus-

192a

trated playbooks (*e-iri nehon*), a genre which
flourished in Osaka from about 1800 to the
1860s. It was common practice in these to
imagine an ideal dream cast (*mitate*) of actors
for the roles. In most of the plays Arashi Kichisaburō I (Rikan) and Nakamura Utaemon III
(Shikan) are cast in opposing roles, even though
they did not actually perform together. Patrons
and fans wanted to see them side-by-side, but
Rikan seems stubbornly to have refused.

Arashi Kichisaburō II (Rikan) plays Ishioka Sazen
and Nakamura Utaemon III (Shikan) plays Kohama
Shinbei, in imagined opposition to one another.

193b *Kamikakete chikai no tsuma-gushi*
**Pledged before the Gods on a Fine-toothed
Comb** (not illustrated)

1815

Artist: Ashikuni

Publishers: Kawachiya Tasuke and others

Hanshibon book, woodblock, 4 vols (bound as 2),
22.5 x 15.3 cm

Waseda University Theatre Museum, Tokyo
(*ro*-5-00103)

Arashi Kichisaburō II (Rikan) plays the role of
Kaiya Zenkichi and Kanō Minshi is Oroku in this
illustrated Kabuki text. The play was written by
Nagawa Harusuke for Rikan and his troupe, and
was based on the final 'Nibugawa' section of
Takizawa Bakin's novel *Aoto fuji tsuna mori yōan*
(1812). Zenkichi is framed by his wife and her
lover, and faces the death penalty, but in the end
his lover of long ago, Oroku, saves him by revealing the truth. This *nehon* playbook, unusually,
has the same title as the original play, which
must have required the permission of the playwright and theatre (see cat. 126).

Ashikuni also designed a *surimono* (cat. 126),
celebrating a production of the same play in the
eighth month, 1814. There is a cut-out of the
two figures from this *surimono* in *Kyota*
(Waseda) 24: 44.

193c *Ken-mawashi sato no daitsū*
Party Games and Dandies of the Pleasure Quarter

1815

Artist: Ashikuni

Publishers: Kawachiya Tasuke and others

Hanshibon book, colour woodblock, 4 vols,
22.0 x 15.8 cm (covers)

Waseda University Theatre Museum, Tokyo (*ro*-5-363)

The play, by Nagawa Kunisuke (fl. 1789–1818)
and Shiba Shisō, was first performed in the
second month, 1802, at the Kita Theatre, Kyoto.
The book presents an imagined 'dream cast'
(*mitate*) of actors, led by rival stars Rikan and
Shikan. Illustrated are Kanō Minshi as the courtesan Takao (right), Nakamura Utaemon III
(Shikan) as Kōsai Tenzō (centre), and Arashi
Kichisaburō II (Rikan) as Imaki Denkichi (left).

Tenzō is an interpreter for the Korean Mission
at Nagasaki. Denkichi is in debt to him, as a
result of borrowing money to help his lord
ransom a favourite courtesan. As a return favour
Denkichi is asked by Tenzō to arrange for another
courtesan, Takao, to become his wife. Denkichi
reluctantly agrees, but then Tenzō explodes in
anger when he learns that Takao and Denkichi
are lovers. Tenzō then breaks all his promises and
thwarts all Denkichi's plans, taunting him until
Denkichi finally kills Tenzō and flees to Osaka. It
must have been very exciting for fans to imagine
Rikan and Shikan performing opposite one
another as enemies in such a lurid plot.

193d *Ehon kataki-uchi Ganryūjima*
Picture Book: Vendetta at Ganryūjima
(not illustrated)

1817

Artist: Ashikuni

Publisher: Kawachiya Tasuke and others

Hanshibon book, woodblock, 6 vols,
22.0 x 15.7 cm (covers)

Waseda University Theatre Museum, Tokyo (*ro*-5-1100)

193c

The text of a popular play first performed at the Ōnishi Theatre, Osaka, in summer, 1737. This version is based on the Kabuki play *Kataki-uchi nitō eiyūki* (1814), which belongs to the popular tradition of 'true tales' (*jitsuroku*), in which the details of incidents and scandals were handed down orally or passed on in manuscript form because their subjects would be censored if published.

Arashi Kichisaburō II (Rikan) is imagined playing the warrior hero Katō Masakiyo, opposite Nakamura Utaemon III (Shikan) as the master swordsman Miyamoto Musashi. Both actors had performed in *Kataki-uchi Ganryūjima* – Shikan performed Musashi in the third month, 1814, for example – but the two never appeared on stage together. The book includes the spoof 'playbill' of an imagined ideal cast for this play, drawn from the rival Kyoto–Osaka troupes. Ashikuni, a patron of Shikan, here brings Rikan into Shikan's orbit to perform with him in this fictional production.

193e *Ehon kogane no shachihoko*
Picture Book: Golden Dolphin Roof-Decorations
(not illustrated)

1820

Artists: Hokushū, Shuntei and Shun'yō

Signatures: Shunkō Hokushū ga, Shuntei ga, Shun'yō ga

Publishers: Kawachiya Tasuke and others

Hanshibon book, woodblock, 2 vols, 22.4 x 15.7 cm (covers)

Waseda University Theatre Museum, Tokyo (ro-05-00281)

The play, originally by Namiki Gohei, was first performed under the title *Keisei kogane shachihoko* (*Courtesans and Golden Dolphin Roof-Decorations*) at the Kado Theatre, Osaka, in the twelfth month, 1782. This fictional version imagines Rikan and Shikan performing opposite one another.

193f *Kuwanaya Tokuzō irifune-banashi*
Kuwanaya Tokuzō: Tale of Boats Entering Harbour (not illustrated)

1822

Author: Akatsuki Kanenari

Publishers: Kawachiya Tasuke and others

Hanshibon book, woodblock, 7 vols, 21.8 x 15.3 cm (covers)

Waseda University Theatre Museum, Tokyo (ro-5-276)

The book was published after the death of Arashi Kichisaburō II (Rikan, Kitsusaburō I), which occurred in the ninth month, 1821. Akatsuki Kanenari was a *kyōka* poet, literati figure and patron of both Rikan and Utaemon III (Shikan), and wrote books about both actors. There are three sets of illustrations of Rikan and Shikan together. The actors had finally agreed to perform together at the end of 1821, but this dream was never realized because of Rikan's untimely death.

194 'In all humility' (*Osorenagara*) (Arashi Rikan's name change from Kichisaburō II to Kitsusaburō I)

First month, 1821

Artists: Getchō and Ueda Kōchō

Signatures: Getchō, Kōchō

Artist's seal: Unread

Actor's seal: Rikan (hand-impressed)

Surimono booklet, colour woodblock, 20.6 x 56.0 cm (top), 20.6 x 55.8 cm (bottom)

Waseda University Theatre Museum, Tokyo (*Nishizawa Ippō harikomi-chō*, vol. 3)

We get a clear sense of Rikan's personality in this text of his speech on taking a new stage name. His favourite crest (*kaemon*) was the mandarin orange (*tachibana*), which can also be read 'kitsu' in a Sino-Japanese reading. He therefore created an entirely new stage name in his own image, something rarely done in Kabuki. Such hubris from the great actor had the result that his three major Osaka stage names would continue to flourish until the twentieth century: in the persons of Kichisaburō VIII (d. 1987), Kitsusaburō VI and Rikan V (d. 1920). This is an extraordinary legacy, considering that most Osaka names have either disappeared or have continued only after moving to Tokyo.

Rikan, precocious and bright, was selected to take the name of his father Kichisaburō instead of his elder brother Isaburō, by senior actors such as Arashi Hinasuke I, Sawamura Kunitarō I and Arashi Sangorō II. Here he returns his father's name to his nephew, Isaburō's son. We know that Kichisaburō's son Yoshisaburō had been an actor, but had decided to give up the stage. Rikan displays considerable acumen. He safely passes on the clan name, but simultaneously establishes the new name Kitsusaburō to permit someone to carry on the legacy of his own stage career.

'In all humility'

Thanks to the patronage of my fans I have been able to perform until after the age of fifty. My debt is deeper than the sea and higher than any mountain. However, over the last year or so I have not been well, and have not been able to perform to my satisfaction. I took time off to try to recuperate and when the illness seemed better, I would again take to the stage after encouragement from others. But I am afraid that my performances of late have not been pleasing to the audience, and I apologize for this. They say even the Buddha grows impatient after three affronts. If I were to continue to displease you time and again, all your warm affection would gradually dissipate and I would only

soil my family's name. Therefore, borrowing the wisdom of others and taking my patrons' advice, I have decided to withdraw from the stage and convalesce – before I defile my name – and to pass on this present name to Daisaburō, the son of my older brother Arashi Isaburō. I now pass my name Kichisaburō to him and take the name Kitsusaburō. However, I shall not abandon my responsibilities to the troupe and become just a doddering old man who grinds miso paste at temples. Therefore, I beg your continued favour and patronage for Kitsusaburō. Although this isn't the same as feeding both the cat and the mouse, I beg the favour of all of you from the north and south, east and west; we depend on your strength to support us.

May our patrons prosper for thousands upon thousands of generations, and may we see a thousand autumns and safely conclude our performance.

Arashi Rikan

There are two parts to the *surimono*; illustrated is the cover designed by Getchō, which says *Osorenagara* ('In all humility') in Chinese characters, and the text translated above. A second part (not illustrated), drawn by Ueda Kōchō, is of a mandarin orange branch with a chick taking its first steps. An impression is also in *Kyota* (Waseda) 29: 52–5.

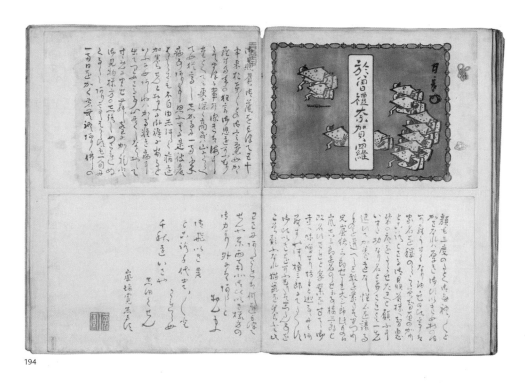

194

195 Arashi Kichisaburō II (Rikan) in the three roles of Sasaki Takatsuna (right), Miuranosuke Yoshimura (lower centre) and Sasaki Moritsuna (left)

First month, 1821

PLAY *Ōmi Genji senjin yakata*

Artist: Kunishige (Shigeharu)

Signature: Baigansai Kunishige ga

Surimono, colour woodblock with metallic pigment, 36.5 x 50.0 cm

Hendrick Lühl Collection (Germany)

Rikan first played the three roles depicted here to great success in 1805, at the time when he came to be acknowledged as the most prominent star in Osaka and head of a troupe. He performed the same three characters again to great acclaim in 1812, in both Osaka and Kyoto, and they were considered among his most famous roles. Takatsuna and Moritsuna were brothers on opposite sides of a civil war. Takatsuna, the elder and more forceful brother, has Moritsuna sacrifice Takatsuna's own son for the sake of his lord (see also cat. 196).

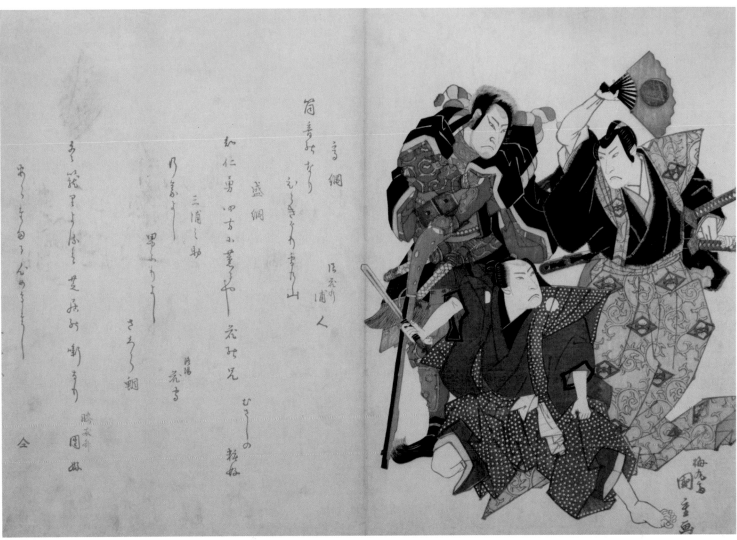

195

A version of this print is in the *Kyota* albums (Waseda, 18: 58), mistakenly placed in sequence for the year 1805. The figures have been cut out of the *surimono*, a common practice in the case of these albums. The earliest known prints by Kunishige (Shigeharu) in fact date from this year, 1821. The print is trimmed but from the last phrase we can deduce that the *surimono* was produced to celebrate Rikan's taking of the new stage name Kitsusaburō I, and his passing on of the name Kichisaburō to his nephew.

The poets are otherwise unknown Rikan fans. Their names seem to be playful inventions: Naniwa no Urabito (Osaka fisherman); Musashi no Shōkō (Edo-ite who loves grease paint);

Rakuyō Kashu (Guardian of flowers [actors] from Kyoto); and Shitsuyūsai Dankō (Man of many friends, fond of companionship). The first three poems address Rikan in each of his three roles:

'Takatsuna'

Tsutsu oto no / narihibikikeri / yuki no yama
The sound of a musket
Reverberates in
Snowy mountains
NANIWA NO URABITO

'Moritsuna'

Chi jin yū / yomo ni kaoru ya / hana no ani
Wisdom, compassion, bravery
Fragrance wafts in all directions
This plum blossom, first among flowers
MUSASHI NO SHŌKŌ

'Miuranosuke'

Gyōgi yoshi / otoko-buri yoshi / sakura-dai
Disciplined
Manly
The cherry bream
RAKUYŌ KASHU

Fuyu-gomori / yoru wa shibai no / hanashi nari
Tucked up in winter
Evenings spent
Talking of the stage
SHITSUYŪSAI DANKŌ

Aratamaru kokoro medetashi [trimmed]
Congratulations on this change of heart...

196

196 Arashi Kitsusaburō I (Rikan) as Sasaki Takatsuna

First month, 1821

PLAY *Ōmi Genji senjin yakata*

Artist: Hokushū

Signature: Shunkōsai Hokushū ga

Publisher: Hon'ya Seishichi

Ōban, colour woodblock with metallic pigment, 39.4 x 27.0 cm

The British Museum, London (2003.1-23.03)

Many prints were issued or reissued at the time when Rikan took the new name of Kitsusaburō I at the New Year performances in 1821. We have relatively few half-length (*ōkubi-e*) portraits of Rikan, and this is an 'imagined' (*mitate*) composition, recalling the role of Sasaki Takatsuna that he had performed to great success in 1805, 1806 and again in the tenth month, 1811, at the Osaka Kita-Shinchi Theatre. Rikan also acted the role of Sasaki Moritsuna, Takatsuna's brother. The pair are pitted against one another at the time of the siege of Osaka Castle in 1616. Takatsuna is the more ruth-

less and strategically brilliant of the two, and determines to sacrifice his own son for the military cause: it is Moritsuna who must kill the young boy. He poses determinedly here with the breastplate of his armour visible, and carrying a flintlock rifle.

Takatsuna ni / ataru arashi no / naruko ka na
The storm [Arashi] may strike
Takatsuna
As a clapper frightens off the birds
RYŪSHAKUTEI

'Storm' (*arashi*) is also Rikan's actor-family name. This role is also seen on a *surimono* by Kunishige (Shigeharu, cat. 195).

197 Arashi Kitsusaburō I (Rikan) backstage as Gofukuya Jūbei

First month, 1821

PLAY *Igagoe dōchū sugoroku* (*mitate*)

Artist: Shibakuni

Signature: Saikōtei Shibakuni ga

Ōban, colour woodblock with metallic pigment, 39.2 x 26.9 cm

Private Collection (UK)

The print celebrates Rikan's taking of a newly minted name, Kitsusaburō I, in the first month, 1821, and looks back to one of his successes in an earlier role. The actor takes one last look in his dressing-room mirror to check costume and makeup before going onstage, as the clothes merchant Jūbei, a role he had performed in the ninth month, 1818. The two strands of hair loose on his face might suggest the presentation of him as a 'sexy' actor. 'Kitsu', of the new name, is another reading for the character *tachibana* ('mandarin orange') – one of the actor's crests – here seen decorating the frame of the mirror, which is highlighted with metallic printing.

Rikan was involved with both haiku and *kyōka* poetry circles from his youth, and his poems were often included in printed anthologies and on *surimono*. His verses did not appear on commercial prints, however, until around this date: only months before the end of his life, as it transpired. This was in contrast to Shikan (Utaemon III) and his troupe, who from the end of 1815 regularly included poems on commercial prints.

The poem here is by the artist Shibakuni, or one of his friends:

Furumekita / shiuchi wa arashi / sapparito / tegiwa o miseta / gofukuya no yaku
His style is traditional
But what a storm [Arashi] he creates
How graceful his skill
In the clothes merchant role
SAIKATEI MEICHOKU

The artist Yoshikuni alluded to this image in his portrait of successor Rikan II (cat. 251) done one year later, after Rikan I's death.

For more on the play and this print see Keyes and Mizushima 1973, pp. 78–9, pl. 19.

198 Arashi Kitsusaburō I (Rikan)'s wigs for the famous roles of his career

1821

Artist: Hokushū

Signature: Shunkōsai Hokushū ga

Artist's seal: Hokushū

Publisher: Toshikuraya Shinbei

Carver: Kasuke

Ōban, colour woodblock with metallic pigment, 38.5 x 25.9 cm

The British Museum, London (2003.1-23.02)

One from a set of six similar designs issued in 1821 to celebrate Rikan's taking of the new name Kitsusaburō I. Fans loved to learn of the backstage life of their heroes and this series presented a wide range of Rikan's transformations into his hit roles.

Top right shows Rikan applying his makeup in an oblong mirror. Wigs for various roles are featured: bottom right, for instance, is the fierce warrior-monk Benkei (cat. 125). In the centre is Okitsu Jinzō, a character in Chinese dress, his hat done in fine metallic printing; see the Hokushū *surimono* cat. 130 for a portrait of Rikan in this role. Among the others roles are Takatsuna (cat. 196), Moritsuna, Matasuke (cats 101 and 129) and Noritsune. If carefully cut out, the 'wigs' and made-up faces could be placed over the face seen in the mirror, to imagine the actor in role more vividly.

The full set of six prints is in the Museum of Fine Arts, Boston (Bigelow Collection). See also Ikeda Bunko 1977, vol. 1, no. 90.

199 Reconciliation song of Arashi Kitsusaburō I (Rikan, right) and Nakamura Utaemon III (Shikan, left)

c. Sixth month, 1821

Artist: Yoshikuni

Signature: Yoshikuni ga

Publishers: Ariwaradō Chūbei and Toshikuraya Shinbei

Ōban, colour woodblock with metallic pigment, 35.9 x 25.1 cm

Private Collection (UK)

Patrons of the two superstars got together and agreed a strategy to persuade them to perform together again after more than fifteen years of rivalry, during which Rikan had steadfastly refused to perform with Shikan. Their efforts finally bore fruit, and this print celebrates the auspicious occasion when the two actors met, at the end of summer, 1821. An inset landscape vignette, inside a circular red 'Yoshi' (for Yoshikuni) cartouche, shows crowds thronging a bridge over the Ōkawa (Yodo) River in Osaka, enjoying summer fire-

199

works. Rikan's untimely death in the ninth month of the same year, however, shattered the fans' dream of a joint performance.

The treatment is reminiscent of Hokushū's print of the ninth month, 1820, which shows the pair performing together, even though they were acting at rival theatres (cover image; cat. 188). In Yoshikuni's print the summer cotton *yukata* robe of each actor is identical, with both their crests, mandarin and crane, printed onto the fabric together in a symbolic reconciliation pattern. Rikan holds the printed text of a song composed for the occasion entitled 'Crane and Mandarin, with second string tuned higher' (*Ni-agari tsuru tachibana*). Shikan tunes the strings of a *shamisen*, ready to accompany him. The final line is: 'All our past enmities have washed away in the Ōkawa River, how cool the summer breeze!'

200

200 Arashi Kitsusaburō I (Rikan) as Yorimasa

PLAY *Yorimasa nue monogatari* at the Kita Shinchi Theatre; eighth month, 1821

Artist: Hokushū

Signature: Shunkōsai Hokushū ga

Publisher: Toshikuraya Shinbei

Ōban, colour woodblock with metallic pigment, 38.7 x 26.5 cm

Victoria & Albert Museum, London (E. 4964-1886)

Rikan fell ill during this performance and died a month later, on the twenty-seventh day of the ninth month, 1821. Two states of the print are known: one with just the role given, implying that the actor was still alive (Birmingham Museums and Art Gallery, 580'29); and the other with the added inscription, seen here, that reads 'the last performance of his life' (*shōgai o-nagori kyōgen*). This was obviously sold as a memorial print.

The warrior-poet Minamoto no Yorimasa (Hyōgo-no-Kami, 1104–80), famous for his heroic killing of the *nue* monster that threatened the imperial palace in Kyoto, was one of Rikan's trademark roles.

201 Arashi Kitsusaburō I (Rikan) memorial as Nagai Genzaburō

After twenty-seventh day of the ninth month, 1821

PLAY *Kataki-uchi chikai no shigarami*

Artist: Kunihiro

Signature: Kunihiro ga

Publisher: Tenmaya Kihei

Ōban, colour woodblock with metallic pigment, 39.1 x 26.5 cm

Hendrick Lühl Collection (Germany)

Arashi Kichisaburō II (Rikan, Kitsusaburō I) died on the twenty-seventh day of the ninth month, 1821, at the peak of his career. Several memorial prints (*shini-e*) to him have survived. Images of the actor in their most popular roles were sometimes reissued to serve as a memorial, suitably annotated. Here the role is the samurai hero Nagai Genzaburō, dressed as a mendicant, flute-playing monk (*komusō*), which had been performed by Rikan to acclaim in the ninth month, 1812, at the Kado Theatre. The play was written for Rikan by Nagawa Harusuke. It was common to include a final testament poem by the actor:

Omokage ya / tsuki no nagori no / Koma-ga-ike
His visage lingers
Farewell to the moon
Above Koma Pond
RIKAN

202 Arashi Kitsusaburō I (Rikan) memorial
as Mashiba Hisayoshi

After twenty-seventh day, ninth month, 1821

PLAY *Kinoshita kage hazama kassen*

Artist: Hokushū

Signature: Shunkōsai Hokushū ga

Ōban, colour woodblock with metallic pigment,
37.0 x 25.9 cm

Victoria & Albert Museum, London (E.4965-1886)

The text is a eulogy from Rikan's rival Shikan:

> Last summer Rikan and I met and agreed to perform
> together in the play *Hazama kassen*, but
> unfortunately he passed away the end of autumn,
> taken away by a storm, and our dream was
> unfulfilled. I shall regret this all my days. I have
> many fond memories and when I heard about the
> publication of this memorial print, I offered this
> poem as a farewell:

202

*Sono hito no / nasu chō mashiba no / shiba shita ni /
hama no masago no / tsukinu omoide*
That fellow
Was a master at playing Mashiba
Now only memories of him
Beneath the brushwood
As many as sands on the shore
SHIKAN

Shikan praises Rikan's playing of the role of
Mashiba (Hideyoshi) in the play *Hama no
masago* (literally, 'sands on the shore'), also a
poetic epithet meaning 'myriad'.

Mashiba Hisayoshi was the fictional name for
the historical figure Toyotomi Hideyoshi
(1536–98) used in the popular theatre to get
around government censorship. He had risen
from being a farmer to become ruler of Japan,
making his final base Osaka Castle until his
death. Tokugawa Ieyasu had promised to support
his heir as ruler but overthrew the Toyotomi
forces in the Battle of Sekigahara in 1600. The
Tokugawa government did not permit plays
about recent historical incidents or individuals.

Keyes and Mizushima 1973, no. 200 illustrates
an impression with the actor's name, role and the
character *ko* ('deceased') printed in the top left corner
(Philadelphia Museum of Art). Other impressions are
in Schwaab 1989, no. 37, Ikeda Bunko 1997, vol. 1,
no. 105, and Matsudaira (Kōnan) 1997(c), no. 117.

201

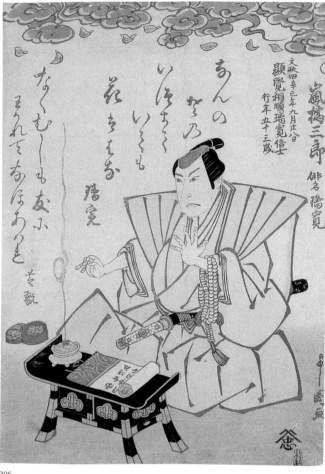

206

Rikan's rival Shikan also offers a memorial verse:

Naku mushi mo / tomo ni wakarete / nao aware
An insect that cries
Is even more sad
To lose a friend
SHIKAN

207 Nakamura Utaemon III (Shikan, left) dreaming of his dead rival Arashi Kitsusaburō I (Rikan, right) in the role of Yorimasa

After twenty-seventh day, ninth month, 1821
Artist: Nan'yōsai (Hokuga)
Signature: Okonomi ni tsuke Nan'yōsai ('Nan'yōsai, at special request')
Artist's seal: Hokuga
Surimono, colour woodblock with metallic pigment, 22.4 x 28.5 cm
Victoria & Albert Museum, London (E.193-1898)

This is a rare print. The only other recorded impression is in *Kyota* (Waseda) 30: 79. The text reads, in part:

[**Nan'yōsai:**] Shikan composed a poem on seeing in his dream at dawn the spirit of Rikan in his famous portrayal of the warrior Yorimasa, so I quickly composed this picture.
[**Shikan:**] Even the frost on the eaves has disappeared, as I return from my dream touched by the sun's morning light.

Utatane ni / tomo o ushinau / kotatsu ka na
Was it just a dream
That I lost my friend
Dozing by the heater?
SHIKAN

206 Arashi Kitsusaburō I (Rikan) memorial

After twenty-seventh day, ninth month, 1821
Artist: Yoshikuni
Signature: Yoshikuni ga
Publishers: Toshikuraya Shinbei and Ariwaradō Chūbei
Ōban, colour woodblock, 36.0 x 25.1 cm
Ikeda Bunko Library (Y51-146)

Rikan sits in formal attire, rosary on his arm, before a small table with a sutra; a billow of smoke rises from the incense that he has placed on the hot coals. It was conventional in a memorial print to depict the actor's robes in pale colours. The top right gives his posthumous Buddhist name and notes the exact day, month and year of his death. Rikan's death poem reads:

Nan no sono / itsu made ite mo / hana wa hana
How could we want
To live on forever
A flower is but a flower
RIKAN

Flower is often used in poems as a metaphor for an actor or for acting.

207

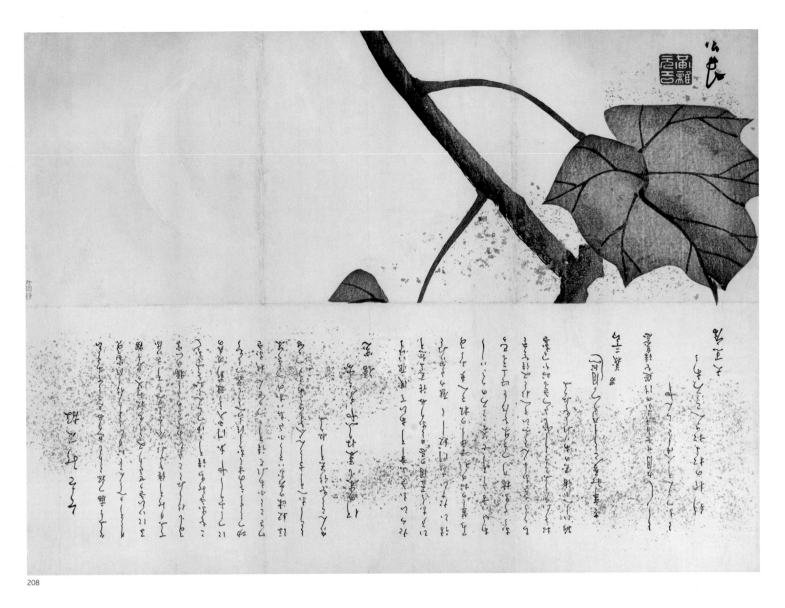

208

208 First memorial for Arashi Kitsusaburō I (Rikan)

Ninth month, 1822

Artist: Ueda Kōchō

Signature: Kōchō

Artist's seal: Unread

Surimono, colour woodblock with cut gold-leaf, 44.6 x 57.9 cm

Private Collection (Japan)

A branch is drawn without blossom or fruit and there is a faint bow moon in the sky. The memorial print was issued in the ninth month, 1822, one year after the actor's death. With a touch of sombre luxury, the paper has been sprinkled with fragments of cut gold-leaf. The prose text is by Rikan, followed by his final verse. His son Yoshisaburō and the poet Daikokuan (Kien) also contributed poems. It is clear that Rikan did not choose a successor for the Kitsusaburō name before he died; on the contrary, he asks those left behind to give the name to the best person possible, even if not from his own group (*shinso no sabetsu sara ni*):

'A Scrap of Paper'

Today my illness seems better than it has been of late. But I cannot hope to return to my former self. My family affairs are in the hands of my son, and as for my father's name, it is now with my nephew, so my nights are now free of worry. However, now that I have assumed the new name Kitsusaburō, I wonder who will carry it on, since my son has left the profession. I must have been evil always to have such worries. Although there are many in my troupe who have trained hard and blossomed, each has his own skill, and so to whom should I pass on this name? After I am gone, I ask that you use your discretion and choose the most suitable individual from wherever may be to graft the mandarin tree onto: someone who will preserve the name.

Nan no ki mo / sakae negau ya / ware wa tsuyu
Doesn't any tree
Wish to flourish
I am but dew
RIKAN

Another impression is in *Kyota* (Waseda) 31: 61, 62, 63.

209

209 First memorial for Arashi Kitsusaburō I (Rikan)

Ninth month, 1822

Artist: Sachō (?)

Signature: Sachō (?)

Artist's seal: Sachō (?)

Surimono, colour woodblock with cut metal-leaf, 34.6 x 75.2 cm

Private Collection (Japan)

This *surimono*, with its image of travellers being carried across a wide river on the shoulders of porters, served two purposes. It was a memorial one year after the death of Rikan, and at the same time a celebration of the rise of Arashi Kitsusaburō II (Tokusaburō II, Rikan II, Rikaku, 1788–1837) as the new Rikan who would become a star and rival of Utaemon III (Shikan) in the 1820s and 1830s. Twenty-three actors, including Shikan, and one poet (Daikokuan Kien, 1765–1834) contributed verses. The actors sign with their stage names and not their pen names; most likely this was meant as a promotion for Rikan II and distributed widely.

I [Kitsusaburō] humbly accept the bestowal of the name of the great Rikan, a lord among actors, and feel unworthy of this honour. I fear that I will not live up to the promise that others have seen in me. Now on this occasion of the first anniversary of his death, I hope that to hear his name mentioned again will serve as an offering to his memory. I thank the patrons from all over who have offered their support to me.

Tachibana no / na oba kazashi no / kikoku ka na
To take the name of
Mandarin orange –
A decorative Chinese mandarin perhaps
ARASHI KITSUSABURŌ (former Tokusaburō)

'Mandarin orange' (*tachibana*) was the symbol of Rikan I. Rikan II was unrelated to Rikan I and here says that he is an inferior version, perhaps the Chinese mandarin orange (*kikoku*). The two travellers on the right in the picture appear to be wearing white cotton robes decorated with a mandarin pattern in blue.

(Congratulatory words)
Sue shigere / kyō no ne-wake no / fūki-gusa
Long may it flourish
The peony that grows
From today's borrowed roots
OKAJIMA YOSHISABURŌ

Yoshisaburō was Rikan's son who had given up acting in his youth. The peony is often used as the metaphor for an actor.

Tada naranu / kaori fukumite / kiku no hana
No ordinary scent
Deep and powerful
This chrysanthemum
ARASHI ISABURŌ

Isaburō was Rikan's elder brother.

Yoku hikaru / momiji o omoe / hatsu momiji
First autumn leaves
Should remember autumn leaves
That next will shine
NAKAMURA UTAEMON (Shikan)

Shikan implies that Rikan II will become the new star to shine as Rikan I did in the past.

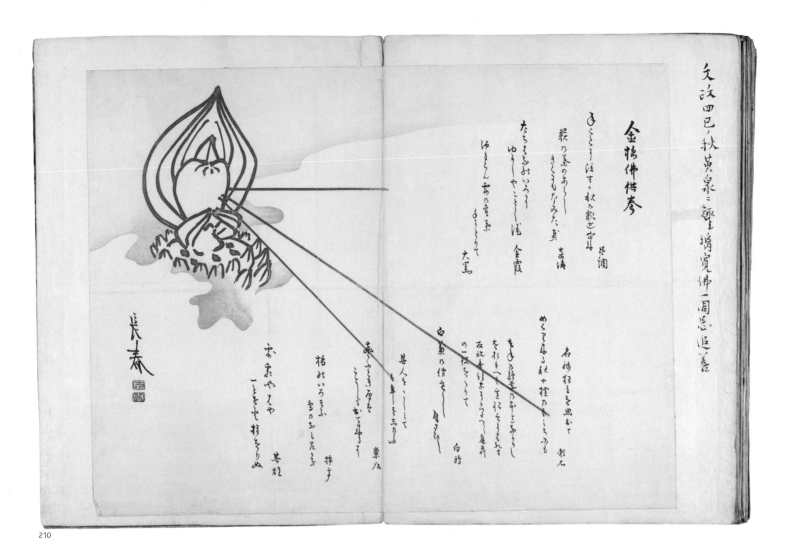

210

Kono michi no / na koso no seki zo / mamore aki
Protect this precious name
At barriers on the long road
Oh autumn
DAIKOKUAN

'*Nakoso no seki*' was a famous checkpoint on the highway in north Japan. Daikokuan urges Rikan II to live up to the new name and bring it honour in his future acting career.

Another impression is in *Kyota* (Waseda) 31: 48.

210 'Memorial service for the Golden Mandarin Buddha'
Kinkitsubutsu kuyō

Ninth month, 1822

Artist: Nakamura (?) Nagaharu (Chōshun)

Signature: Nagaharu

Artist's seals: Naga, Haru

Surimono, woodblock with metallic pigment, 39.0 x 50.3 cm

Waseda University Theatre Museum, Tokyo (*Nishizawa Ippō Harikomichō*, vol. 3)

A first memorial for Kitsusaburō I (Rikan), one year after his death. In this highly parodic image a golden mandarin (Rikan's crest) – two leaves brought together in a ritual gesture – takes the place of the Buddha on a lotus pedestal in paradise, radiating holy light. Rikan is thus the Buddha. Nine patrons offer haiku verses in his memory: Daikoku is the poet Kien, who contributed verses to several *surimono* related to Rikan and Shikan.

211a, b *Kikkōjō*
Album of Mandarin Orange Blossom Fragrance
ILLUSTRATED Arashi Rikan I in the role of Yorimasa (a)

ILLUSTRATED Arashi Rikan I bust portrait (b)

Ninth month, 1822

Artist: Ashiyuki

Signature: Gigadō Ashiyuki (a); Ashiyuki (b)

Artist's seal: Ashiyuki (hand-impressed) (a);
Ashiyuki (hand-impressed) (b)

Surimono, folding album in *chūban* format, colour
woodblock with metallic pigment and cut gold-leaf,
25.8 x 19.4 cm (covers)

Gerhard Pulverer Collection (Germany)

A first-year memorial album for Rikan, with
luxurious *surimono*-style printing. There are
three portraits by Ashiyuki of Rikan, a landscape,
and a large group of haiku and *kyōka* poems by
actors, artists, writers and many others, including several women; there is a total of seventy-
six verses, replete with autumn references.

The preface is signed Kyōgadō Ōzui, most likely
a patron or friend of the artist Kyōgadō Ashikuni,
who had died in 1818. Ashiyuki indicates that he
was a member of Ashikuni's 'Kyōgaren' ('... of the
Kyōga poetry group'), as do three other artists:
Yoshikuni, Ashinao and Shibakuni. *Kikkōjō* thus
represents a co-operative collaboration between
artists, poet-fans and actors to celebrate the life
and career of Rikan. The bridge across the river in
the landscape image appears to be the famous
one at Uji, and this seems to be confirmed by
references in the poems, suggesting that the
gathering for this memorial was held in that
town, just south of Kyoto.

The poems facing the bust portrait of Rikan
(illustrated, 211b) are all by actors (and one
playwright, Nagawa Harusuke), using their stage
names rather than pen names. This would seem
to indicate that the album was meant for wider
circulation than just among the inner circle of
participants. The double page of portrait and
poems may have been circulated separately as
well, as a single-sheet *surimono*. Kitsusaburō II is
listed under this newly acquired name.

The succession of Arashi Kitsusaburō II (later
Rikan II) to that name also took place at the
time of the first memorial to Rikan I in the ninth
month, 1822. The first image of Rikan as Yorimasa in *Kikkōjō* (illustrated, 211a) was the
model for a very similar *surimono*-like print by
Ashiyuki of Rikan II in the same role (cat. 247),
made for this succession. Ashiyuki would become
the most important artist-promoter of Rikan II.

Umoregi no / naka yori nioe / yama rindō
From within a buried tree
A fragrance wafts
Autumn bellflower
RIKAN (deceased)

211b

Sono hito no / kutsu ato yukashi / hagi no hara
How I miss
His footsteps
Field of bush clover
KOROKU (Minshi)

Kurenai no / aki ya kochō o / utsusu mizu
How deep red
The autumn
Butterfly reflected in the water
KITSUSABURŌ (Rikan II)

Sanbyaku rokujû nichi / wasuru ma mo naku / aki kurenu
Three hundred and sixty days
Never forgotten
The end of autumn
HARUSUKE

Shiragiku no / rippa ni sakite / kanashikere
The white chrysanthemum
Blooms magnificently
How sad
(Ōe) TSUYU (woman)

Mono omou / yo ya naki-tōru / tsuki no kari
Thinking of him
Cries through the night
Geese in the moonlight
(Hisayo) HAGIKO (woman)

Sasowarete / onaji aki shiru / hagi mi ka na
Enticed along by him
The same 'autumn' comes again
Shall I view the bush clover
(Uji) KOTAKE (woman)

Kinō made / hotaru narishi o / Uji no tsuki
Only yesterday
Fireflies along the river
Moon over Uji
ŌZUI

Hotaru tori / Uji ni ōgi o / nokoshikeri
Capturing fireflies
A fan left behind
Along the Uji River
(Kyōgaren) YOSHIKUNI

The folding-fan (*ōgi*) is an essential element in
Kabuki dance.

Nita kao no / araba dete min / aki no kure
For a face like his
I would go out to look
End of autumn
(Kyōgaren) SHIBAKUNI

Shibakuni here gives a clear sense of the fascination which an actor in performance had for the
amateur artist.

Hotarubi mo / itsushika kiete / Uji no aki
The firefly's glow
When did it disappear
Autumn in Uji
(Kyōgaren) ASHIYUKI

Hana wa hana / ano yo ya tsuki no / ōbutai
A flower [actor] is always a flower
In the next world
The moon your great stage
YACHIBŌ

Matsudaira in *Hizō ukiyo-e taikan* (Pulverer coll.), 1990,
p. 275, nos 338–43; another copy of the album, its
individual sheets divided, is in *Kyota* (Waseda) 30: 83–9.

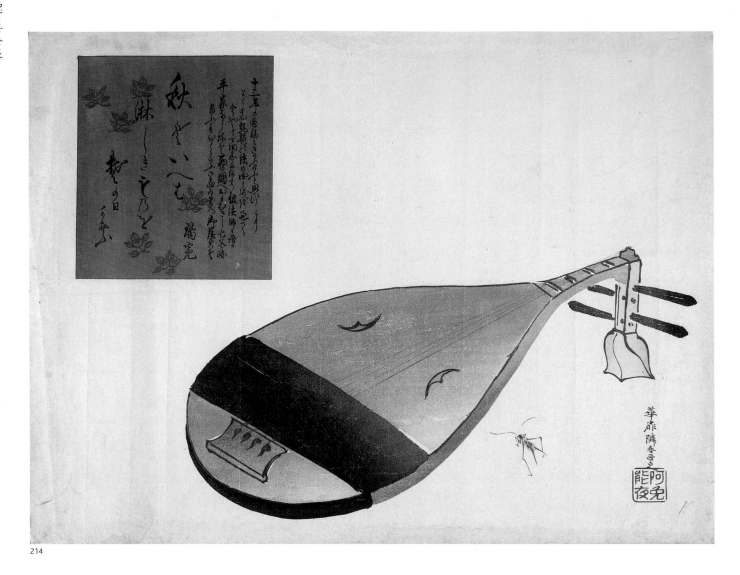

214

214 Seventeenth memorial for Arashi Kitsusaburō I (Rikan)

Ninth month, 1837

Artist: Rinshun

Signature: Hanatobira Rinshun kore [o] egaku

Seal: Amenoyo (?)

Surimono, colour woodblock with metallic pigment and embossing, 42.4 x 56.0 cm

Victoria & Albert Museum, London (E.3930-1916)

Arashi Rikan II offers a memorial *surimono* on the occasion of the seventeenth anniversary of the death of Rikan I, whom he calls his 'father' even thought they were not blood relations.

Aki to ieba / sabishiki mono o / sono hi ka na
Thinking of autumn
The saddest thing of all
Is that day
RIKAN (II)

Rikan I died on the twenty-seventh day of the ninth month, which by the lunar calendar is late autumn. The image is of a *biwa* (a kind of lute played with a plectrum) and a cricket.

215

215 'Bandō Mitsugorō III (second from right), Asao Okuyama II and Nakamura Karoku I (left) arriving in Osaka'
Nobori Bandō Mitsugorō, Asao Okuyama, Nakamura Karoku gakuya-iri no zu

First month, 1821
Artist: Yoshikuni
Signature: Jukōdō Yoshikuni ga
Publishers: Ariwaradō Chūbei and Toshikuraya Shinbei
Ōban, colour woodblock, diptych, 37.3 x 25.9 cm (right), 37.3 x 25.5 cm (left)
The British Museum, London (2003.8-22.01,1-2)

The Edo actors are welcomed to Osaka by verses from Akatsuki Kanenari and his poetry club. Kanenari was active in *kyōka* poetry and Kabuki circles. He was the editor of *Rikanjō* (cat. 119) and several illustrated playbooks (*e-iri nehon*; for example, cat. 193f).

The inscription reads as follows:

I was asked by my friend Yoshikuni to write a few words when we were out drinking.

Naniwa-zu ni / noboreru mitsu no / asahi kage / emi o fukumeru / yomo no yama yama
Coming to Osaka
These three actors
Reflect the morning sun
In all directions
Smiles across the mountains
AKATSUKI KANENARI

The poem celebrates Mitsugorō III.

Kozo no shiori no / michi o tagaede / nao fukaku / wakete mezurashi / okuyama no hana
Broken twigs to guide
No mistaking the path
Even more deeply has he explored
How delightful the blossoming Okuyama
Deep in the mountains
AKATSUKI SHONICHIREN, MAMA NO KAWANARI

The poem celebrates the return of Okuyama from Edo, suggesting that he has blossomed into a marvellous actor after his experience there.

Emi fukumu / yama no hitai no / murasaki wa / akeyori hito no / ki o tsudou sora
Smiles cover the mountains
His peaked forehead
Covered in purple
A sky to entice the crowds
Even before dawn
KŌKUSAI FUMINARI

This celebrates Karoku, who is a female role specialist (*onnagata*) and therefore by custom wears a purple scarf to hide his forelock shaven in the mature male manner.

216

216 'Picture of backstage at a theatre in Dōtonbori, Osaka'
Ōsaka Dōtonbori shibai gakuya no zu
c. 1821
Artist: Kunisada (Edo)
Signature: Gototei Kunisada ga
Publisher: Nishimuraya Yohachi (Edo)
Censorship seal: *kiwame*
Ōban, colour woodblock, triptych, 36.4 x 25.4 cm (right), 36.3 x 26.0 cm (centre), 36.5 x 23.5 cm (left)
Victoria & Albert Museum, London
(E.5995, 5996, 5997-1886)

The triptych print shows a fictionalized coming together of Edo and Osaka actors in dressing rooms located on two floors backstage in an Osaka theatre, seen as if with the walls partly removed. (The name of the theatre is not specified, but the emblems of two Osaka fan clubs, Sasase and Ōte, are prominent on the low 'balcony' railings between the floors.) As a long text at the top of the centre sheet by the Edo publisher Nishimuraya Yohachi (Eijudō) explains, triptychs of backstage scenes in the Edo theatres by the (Edo) artist Kunisada that he had published in

an imposing checked and padded costume of the character Matsuōmaru, for the favourite play *Sugawara denju tenarai kagami* (*Sugawara's Secrets of Calligraphy*). He is respectfully greeted by the figure second from the right on the centre sheet, who wears the black *haori* jacket with the mandarin crest that identifies him as the Osaka star Rikan. Rikan is clearly named on the print as Arashi Kitsusaburō [I], the stage name he only used from the New Year, 1821, until his untimely death in the ninth month of that same year. This suggests the approximate date of Kunisada's triptych.

Other celebrities to point out are Rikan's rival Shikan, the other great Osaka star, who kneels in front of the mirror holding a fan, in the room on the upper level on the right sheet. The dressing room on the lower level in the left sheet is shared by Edo star Iwai Hanshirō V, seated on the black wig box in the costume of the character Umeōmaru, and just to his right, chatting, the Osaka female role specialist (*onnagata*) Sawamura Kunitarō II.

Female fans were strictly forbidden to enter the backstage areas of the theatres and so they must have been particularly keen to scrutinize detailed depictions such as these. Bearing in mind, however, that Osaka rivals Shikan and Rikan never appeared in the same theatre together, and that Edo stars Kōshirō and Hanshirō are not recorded as having performed these roles during their Osaka tour, it is certain that Kunisada here presents a highly fictionalized and entertaining 'compendium' scene. Artist and publisher are saying primarily to a curious Edo public back home: if you happened to be in and around the theatres of Osaka in the spring (?) of 1821, these are the kind of scenes you might have witnessed backstage. TC

Keyes and Mizushima 1973, pp. 70–71, no. 15;
Hizō ukiyo-e taikan, vol. 5, 1989, pp. 215–16, no. 22;
Izzard 1993, no. 34.

earlier years (actually 1812–13) were a great success with the public. Building on that success, he issued this view as a souvenir of Kunisada's recent visit to Osaka. Another advertisement under the title, top right, promises further views of the front of house, including the stage, in a book by the author Ryūtei Tanehiko (1783–1842). The book *Shōhon-jitate* was indeed published in 1822, with illustrations by Kunisada of the Edo actors in Osaka in vols 5 and 6.

Following on from the Osaka star Utaemon III (Shikan)'s three successful tours to Edo, leading Edo actors made the unusual decision late in 1820 to pay a return visit to Osaka as a group. All of the main Edo stars who went to Osaka and many of the supporting actors, too, are depicted alongside their Osaka hosts in Kunisada's triptych, and each actor is clearly named. Beginning with the right sheet, on the lower level, Bandō Mitsugorō III, third from the right, returns from the bath wearing a cotton robe and with a towel draped over his shoulder and is about to enter his room. To his left, Matsumoto Kōshirō V is already dressed in wig and

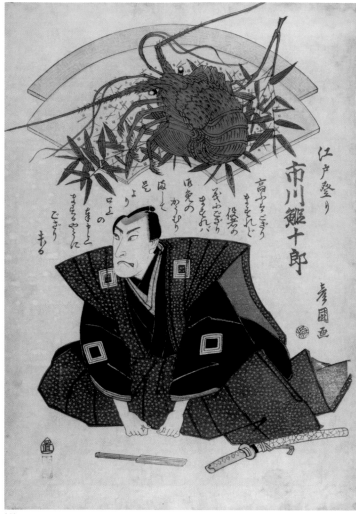

219

219 'Ichikawa Ebijūrō I returns from Edo'
Edo nobori Ichikawa Ebijūrō

Eleventh month, 1821

Artist: Hikokuni

Signature: Hikokuni ga

Publisher: Hon'ya Seishichi

Censorship seal: *kiwame*

Ōban, colour woodblock, 38.7 x 26.3 cm

Hendrick Lühl Collection (Germany)

The text is the beginning of a formal speech asking for the audience's renewed patronage, after the actor has been so long away from Osaka. The image of the giant lobster (*ebi*) and bamboo is auspicious, and reflects the names of both the actor *Ebi*jūrō and his mentor *Ebi*zō (Ichikawa Danjūrō VII), head of the most famous Edo acting family. Ebijūrō, a specialist in rough character and villain roles (*jitsuaku*), is presented in the manner of an Edo 'rough-style' (*aragoto*) actor. After the death of Rikan in the ninth month of 1821, Utaemon III (Shikan) most likely asked Ebijūrō to return to Osaka for the new season to shore up the number of star actors.

220 'Picture of Nakamura Utaemon III (Shikan) and his son Nakamura Komanosuke enjoying the cool in Hyakkien Garden'
Hyakkien teizen nōryō no zu, Nakamura Utaemon, segare Nakamura Komanosuke

c. Sixth month, 1821

Artist: Yoshikuni

Signature: Yoshikuni ga

Publisher: Ri

Printer: Toyo

Ōban, colour woodblock, 37.0 x 25.8 cm

The British Museum, London (1983.5-23.01, 95)

A scene imagined in Shikan's Hyakkien garden in summer (Hyakkien was one of Shikan's artistic names [*gō*]). The actor is presented as a cultivated gentleman at leisure in his garden, enjoying the evening cool with his young adopted son Komanosuke (Shikan III, 1810–47).

221 'Nakamura Sankō's speech on joining the troupe at the opening-of-the-season performance'
Nakamura Sankō kaomise zatsuki kōjō
Eleventh month, 1821
Artist: Yoshikuni
Signature: Jukōdō Yoshikuni ga
Publishers: Wataya Kihei and Ariwaradō Chūbei
Ōban, colour woodblock, 37.0 x 25.8 cm
The British Museum, London (1983.5-23.01, 98)

Nakamura Sankō (Matsue III, Tomijūrō II) kneels respectfully to make a speech from the stage to the audience at the Kado Theatre. The occasion is his return from Edo to join the troupe for the opening-of-the-season (*kaomise*) performances in the eleventh month, 1821. The same design was adapted for a later performance at the Kita Theatre, Kyoto, in the eleventh month, 1823 (Matsudaira [Kōnan] 1997[c], no. 255). Printed above is the text of his speech; the poem is by the actor, using his pen name Shōhotei Sankō. The actor had recently begun to use his pen name Sankō as his acting name as well.

Matsudaira in *Hizō ukiyo-e taikan*, vol. 3, 1988, pp. 268–9, no. 128.

221

222

222 Nakamura Utaemon III (Shikan) as Sankichi the tobacconist (right) and Ichikawa Ebijūrō I as Saitō Kuranosuke (left)

PLAY *Keisei somewake tazuna* at the Naka Theatre; first month, 1822

Artist: Hokushū

Signature: Shunkōsai Hokushū ga

Publisher: Hon'ya Seishichi

Ōban, colour woodblock with metallic pigment, diptych, each sheet approx. 37.6 x 25.7 cm

The British Museum, London (1906.12-20.01118)

Two 'serpent' diptychs (see also cat. 223) cele-brated the premier of this play, the first written

by Shikan himself – using his writer's name Kanazawa Ryūkoku – along with several other authors, including Nagawa Harusuke and Hamamatsu Utakuni. Ebijūrō (left) plays the villain, who conjures up the giant serpent, and Shikan (right) is the hero. Shikan did not have a great reputation as a playwright. There is a famous story that during the first reading of a text to the troupe by the playwrights, the expe-rienced writer Nagawa Harusuke became so angry about the bad construction of the play that he tried to stab Shikan (*Nihon koten bun-gaku daijiten*, vol. 2, p. 350).

Cats 222 and 223 depict the same scene, but this one by Hokushū is more striking and unusual as an actor print. Hokushū dares to represent the hero Shikan (right) as a smaller figure of the pair, half hidden behind the stage-prop grass at the corner. In contrast, Yoshikuni (cat. 223) places Shikan grandly as the star in the centre, like most actor prints. By this innova-tive technique, Hokushū successfully highlights the massive serpent and the tense atmosphere in the scene.

Matsudaira in *Hizō ukiyo-e taikan*, vol. 3, 1988, p. 259, no. 110.

223

223 **Ichikawa Ebijūrō I as Saitō Kuranosuke (right) and Nakamura Utaemon III (Shikan) as Sankichi the tobacconist (left)**

PLAY *Keisei somewake tazuna* at the Naka Theatre; first month, 1822

Artist: Yoshikuni

Signature: Yoshikuni ga

Publisher: Toshikuraya Shinbei

Ōban, colour woodblock, diptych, each approx. 36.1 x 24.8 cm

Hendrick Lühl Collection (Germany)

See the commentary to cat. 222.

224

224 'Picture of a general rehearsal in the major Kabuki theatres at Dōtonbori, Osaka'
Naniwa Dōtonbori ō-kabuki butai sō-geiko no zu

c. Eleventh month, 1822

Artist: Yoshikuni

Signature: Naniwa Jukōdō Yoshikuni ga ('Jukōdō Yoshikuni of Osaka', left sheet)

Publishers: Izumi-Ri and Sōshiya

Ōban, colour woodblock, triptych, 37.5 x 26.2 cm (right), 37.5 x 25.6 cm (centre), 37.3 x 24.9 cm (left)

The British Museum, London (2004.6-19.02)

A rehearsal by an imagined grouping of all the major stars of Osaka Kabuki who performed in the top theatres in the Dōtonbori theatre district at about the end of 1822, a year after the death of Arashi Kitsusaburō I (Rikan). They represent the two rival troupes who would nor-

mally be performing in competition at the Naka and Kado Theatres.

Reading from the right, from back to front, the actors are named:

Right: Arashi Koroku IV, Asao Kuzaemon I, Arashi Kichisaburō III, Asao Gakujūrō I and Ichikawa Ebijūrō I

Centre: Kataoka Nizaemon VII, Arashi Danpachi I, Nakamura Utaemon III (Shikan) and Kiriyama Monji III

Left: Nakamura Karoku I, Arashi Kitsusaburō II (later Rikan II), Hyakumura Shikazō I, Ogawa Kichitarō III, Arashi Tomisaburō II and Ōtani Tomoemon II

An advertisement to the left of the title, top right, promises views of the dressing rooms, but these do not seem to have been published.

Compare also the Edo artist Kunisada's view of backstage (cat. 216).

25

225 Nakamura Utaemon III (Shikan) as Kanda Yogorō (right), Nakamura Sankō I as the courtesan Kashiwagi (centre), and Ichikawa Ebijūrō I as Teraoka Hei'emon (left)

PLAY *Ōishi-zuri sakura tanzaku* at the Naka Theatre; third month, 1822

Artist: Hokushū

Signature: Shunkōsai Hokushū ga

Publishers: Toshikuraya Shinbei, Izutsuya Denbei, Hon'ya Seichichi and Yamaichi

Ōban, colour woodblock, triptych, 36.0 x 25.2 cm (right), 36.0 x 26.1 cm (centre), 36.0 x 25.5 cm (left)

Ikeda Bunko Library (187-H388A-1/2/3)

The text for this play is unknown, but it is most likely a variant on the *Chūshingura* (forty-seven *rōnin*) vendetta theme because of Teraoka Hei'emon, well known to that story (see also cat. 40). Although there is a clear notation that this is a triptych print, each sheet has a different, striking repeat-pattern in yellow as the background, like a printed cotton fabric. In addition, each has a *kyōka* poem by a fan, including one by the artist Umekuni:

Ōiri o / totta to tachimi / shikan yori / hoka e hiiki wa / metta ni yaran zo
A smash success
Only standing room
Nobody but Shikan
Never support
Another
SHIYŪ

Ryōhō no / tachi-e no ume ni / uguisu no / sono sankō o / hikanu no wa nashi
On either side
A plum branch
In the middle a song thrush
Who would not be
Charmed?
UMEKUNI

Hyōban o / totta to date no / tatemono wa / ge ni senryō no / shinshō zo yoshi
Great reviews
This dandy star
Truly he is
Shinshō worth
A thousand gold coins
TANTORŌ

Shinshō is the pen name of the actor Ebijūrō.

232 Nakamura Utaemon III (Shikan)'s 'farewell performance' as Kumagai no Jirō Naozane

PLAY *Ichinotani futaba gunki* at the Kado Theatre; third month, 1825

Artist: Hokushū

Signature: Shunkōsai Hokushū ga

Artist's seal: Hokushū (hand-impressed)

Publishers: Wataya Kihei and Kakuseidō (hand-impressed seal)

Ōban, colour woodblock with metallic pigment, 38.1 x 25.8 cm

Gerhard Pulverer Collection (Germany)

Kumagai is a fierce warrior who for complex reasons must kill his own son in order to save the life of Atsumori, a young warrior of the same age. Here he wears full battle armour, with a large balloon of cloth (*horo*) behind the shoulders to snag arrows. This is one from a set of 'summer-fan' (*uchiwa*) portraits of Shikan performing a medley of roles for his retirement production. He held retirement performances (*issei ichidai*) in the third month in Osaka and again in the fifth month in Kyoto. Utaemon, however, continued to perform in Kyoto and Sakai during 1825 and 1826. He returned in the seventh month of 1826 to perform again in Osaka until his death in 1838.

This impression is brilliantly embellished with metallic printing in brass and tin. Another, possibly earlier, state with no metallic pigments has the inscriptions 'Last retirement performance of hit plays' (*Issei ichidai atari kyōgen*); also an additional publisher's mark (Chū), an engraver's seal (Zakoba); and a different hand-impressed seal (Ariwaradō) on the handle of the fans.

See Schwaab 1989, p. 110, no. 80.

233 Nakamura Utaemon III (Shikan)'s 'farewell performance' as Kumagai no Jirō Naozane

PLAY *Ichinotani futaba gunki* at the Kado Theatre; third month, 1825

Artist: Hokushū

Signature: Shunkōsai Hokushū ga

Artist's seal: Hokushū (hand-impressed)

Publisher: (Hon'ya Seishichi)

Ōban, colour woodblock with metallic pigment, 38.0 x 25.7 cm

Gerhard Pulverer Collection (Germany)

Kumagai was a rugged warrior on the Genji side of the civil war between the Heike (Taira) and the Genji (Minamoto) in the late twelfth century. He killed the young Heike warrior Atsumori and later, repenting, became a Buddhist monk to pray for the souls of the Heike dead. In Bunraku puppet plays and Kabuki he sacrifices his own son to save the life of the aristocratic Atsumori, in order to repay a debt to Atsumori's mother

232

who had helped him and his wife after a scandal. Kumagai is one of the great Kabuki roles; the actor must portray the agony of having to kill his own son while at the same time trying to appear calm to let no one else, not even his wife, know what he has done.

Artist Hokushū created a set of five bust portraits in fan-shapes for Shikan's retirement performances (cats 232 and 234–6). This is a deluxe impression with metallic (brass) printing in the dragon design on Kumagai's robe. The seal after Hokushū's signature is hand-impressed, and there is no seal of the commercial publisher Hon'ya Seishichi, suggesting that this edition was not put on public sale. An impression without so much metallic pigment, with no artist's seal, and with the publisher's mark of Hon'ya Seishichi is in the collection of the Birmingham Museums and Art Gallery (573'29).

234

234 Nakamura Utaemon III (Shikan)'s 'farewell performance' as Gotobei

PLAY *Yoshitsune koshigoe jō* at the Kado Theatre; third month, 1825

Artist: Hokushū

Signature: Shunkōsai Hokushū ga

Artist's seal: Hokushū

Publisher: Hon'ya Seishichi

Ōban, colour woodblock with metallic pigment, 38.6 x 25.8 cm

Gerhard Pulverer Collection (Germany)

This is one of a series of five bust portraits in the shape of a fan that Hokushū designed for Utaemon III (Shikan)'s retirement. The text says that this is one of his great roles (*atari-kyōgen*). The play is one version of the story of the fall of Osaka Castle transposed much earlier into the twelfth-century world of General Minamoto no Yoshitsune and the Genpei Civil War. Gotobei is the central figure, a powerful and clever warrior who is sought after by opposing sides. His son, daughter and wife get caught up in the turbulent events.

235

236

235 Nakamura Utaemon III (Shikan)'s 'farewell performance' as Osono

PLAY *Hikosan gongen chikai no sukedachi* at the Kado Theatre; third month, 1825

Artist: Hokushū

Signature: Shunkōsai Hokushū ga

Artist's seal: Hokushū

Publisher: Akashidō (hand-impressed seal)

Ōban, colour woodblock with metallic pigment, 37.8 x 25.8 cm

Gerhard Pulverer Collection (Germany)

One of a series of five bust portraits in the shape of a fan that Hokushū designed for Utaemon III (Shikan)'s retirement performances: the inscription reads 'Final lifetime hit-play' (*issei ichidai atari kyōgen*; see also cats 233–4 and 236). These are among the finest works in Hokushū's oeuvre. Here

Shikan plays Osono, displaying his famous versatility in female dance roles. Osono is a strong character who is seeking to avenge the murder of her father by Kyōgoku Takumi (cat. 236).

236 Nakamura Utaemon III (Shikan)'s 'farewell performance' as Kyōgoku Takumi

PLAY *Hikosan gongen chikai no sukedachi* at the Kado Theatre; third month, 1825

Artist: Hokushū

Signature: Shunkōsai Hokushū ga

Artist's seal: Hokushū

Publishers: Ariwaradō Chūbei (hand-impressed seal), Wataya Kihei and Goichi

Ōban, colour woodblock with metallic pigment, 36.8 x 25.1 cm

Victoria & Albert Museum, London (E.1321-1922)

One of a series of five bust portraits in the shape of a fan that Hokushū designed for Utaemon III (Shikan)'s retirement performances: the inscription reads 'Final lifetime hit-play' (*issei ichidai atari kyōgen*). Here Shikan plays Takumi, a villainous murderer who is pursued by Osono (cat. 235) seeking revenge for her father's death.

Keyes and Mizushima 1973, no. 30; Matsudaira in *Hizō ukiyo-e taikan*, vol. 5, 1989, p. 264, no. 149.

240

241

239 Arashi Kitsusaburō II (right) and Ichikawa Ebijūrō I (left)

Eighth month, 1825

Artist: Ashiyuki

Signature: Gigadō Ashiyuki ga

Publisher: Wataya Kihei

Ōban, colour woodblock, 37.0 x 25.8 cm

The British Museum, London (1983.5-23.01,10)

In the light of Utaemon III (Shikan)'s retirement announcement, Arashi Kitsusaburō II (later Rikan II) and Ichikawa Ebijūrō I present themselves as new rivals in a speech at the Kado Theatre. Each asks the patrons for continued support. Their bristling body language and glaring eyes project them as fierce competitors.

240 Nakamura Utaemon III (Shikan) as Ishikawa Goemon (right) and Ichikawa Ebijūrō I as Mashiba Hisayoshi (left)

PLAY *Kinoshita kage hazama kassen* at the Naka Theatre; seventh month, 1826

Artist: Ashiyuki

Signature: Gigadō Ashiyuki ga

Publisher: Wataya Kihei

Ōban, colour woodblock, 37.0 x 25.8 cm

The British Museum, London (1983.5-23.01,42)

The performance marked the return of Utaemon III (Shikan) to Osaka after his supposed 'retirement' the year before. The text is the dialogue from the play in which Goemon, the famous outlaw, confronts Hisayoshi (Hideyoshi), the most powerful warlord in the land. See cat. 260 for a commentary on these two historical-legendary figures and their fierce rivalry in the world of the theatre.

241 Nakamura Utaemon III (Tamasuke, Shikan) memorial

After the twenty-fifth day, seventh month, 1838

Artist: Sadanobu

Signature: Hasegawa Sadanobu ga

Publisher: Tenmaya Kihei

Ōban, colour woodblock with metallic pigment, 37.2 x 25.5 cm

Victoria & Albert Museum, London (E.12309-1886)

The inscription says of Utaemon III (Shikan) that this was 'the last performance of his life' (*shōgai o-nagori kyōgen*) and gives his posthumous Buddhist name and age at death, sixty-one. The roles performed were Shindō Saemon (right) and Kajiwara Heizō (left). Shikan had taken the final stage name Tamasuke in the first month of 1836 when Shikan II succeeded to become the

fourth holder of the Utaemon name. Shikan's death marked the end of an era for Osaka Kabuki. Only a few years later in 1742 the Tenpō Reforms would crack down on popular culture across the land and Kabuki felt its blow severely. The closure of smaller theatres, ban on actor prints and exiling of Ichikawa Danjūrō VII from Edo and Nakamura Tomijūrō II from Osaka all made clear the government's determination to punish 'extravagance' by commoners in the two cities. In retrospect Shikan was fortunate to have matured as an actor just at the time of the heyday of actor prints in Osaka. His enthusiasm for and cultivation of influential patrons certainly contributed to a great flourishing of Kabuki culture during his long career.

242

242 'Snow scene in Osaka south of the river'
Naniwa kōnan yuki-geshiki

c. Eleventh month, 1825
Artist: Ashiyuki
Signature: Gigadō Ashiyuki sha
Publisher: Wataya Kihei
Ōban, colour woodblock, triptych, each sheet
approx. 37.0 x 25.8 cm
The British Museum, London (1983.5-23.01, 1-3)

The 'south of the river' of the title seems to refer in this case to the Dōtonbori theatre district in the south of Osaka. Matsudaira Susumu has identified the precise location as Aiaibashi Bridge over the Dōtonbori Canal, with Nihonbashi Bridge in the distance, which means that the theatres are situated along the canal bank to the right.

Crossing the snow-covered bridge is a line-up of the star actors of the day performing in Kyoto–Osaka (from the right): Sawamura Kunitarō II, Ichikawa Danzō V, Onoe Kikugorō III, Nakamura Utaemon III (Shikan I), Nakamura Sankō I (Matsue III), Asao Kunigorō III, Nakamura Karoku I, Arashi Koroku IV, Arashi Kitsusaburō II and Ichikawa Ebijūrō. A noticeable absence is Nakamura Shikan II, who changed his name from Tsurusuke in the eleventh month, 1825, at a performance in Kyoto. Utaemon III (Shikan I) had officially retired from the stage in Osaka at this time, but continued to perform in Sakai and Kyoto. Onoe Kikugorō III had come from Edo to perform in Kyoto in the eleventh month, 1825. Thus the line-up of actors is ideal rather than actual.

Matsudaira in *Hizō ukiyo-e taikan*, vol. 3, 1988, p. 261, no. 114.

243

243 Nakamura Utaemon III (Shikan, left) introduces Arashi Kitsusaburō II (later Rikan II, right) as successor to Rikan I

Ninth month, 1822

Artist: Hokushū

Signature: Shunkōsai Hokushū ga

Artist's seal: Hokushū

Publishers: Izutsuya Denbei, Yamaichi

Ōban, colour woodblock, diptych, 37.3 x 25.8 cm (right), 37.1 x 26.5 cm (left)

Private Collection (UK)

A year after the death of Arashi Rikan I (Kichisaburō II, Kitsusaburō I) Arashi Tokusaburō II (1788–1837) was recalled from Edo to become Arashi Kitsusaburō II (later Rikan II). He was originally a student of Rikan's elder brother Isaburō, but was also supported by Utaemon III (Shikan), who most likely arranged for him to go to Edo from the eleventh month, 1820, to further his training and increase his experience. A print by Kunisada (cat. 244) shows a performance by Tokusaburō in Edo. Rikan had not chosen his successor before he died and this

print gives the impression that Shikan was influential in the choice.

The composition presents Kitsusaburō II as the incarnation of the deceased Rikan, depicted in his final role as Yorimasa (cat. 200) in the circular cartouche, top right. Quite unlike his appearance in the earlier Kunisada print, Hokushū here recreates Kitsusaburō II in the image of the great Rikan. The one clear distinction between the generations is the manner of drawing Kitsusaburō II's eyes. He was known as 'Big-eyes' and his eyelids are drawn with an extra line to indicate a double fold. We are presented with portraits of both actors to make the comparison. Rikan looks down from above, acknowledging his successor.

The text is the speech given on stage at the Naka Theatre at the name-taking ceremony (*shūmei kōjō*). Shikan first introduces Kitsusaburō II as the worthy successor of Rikan. It was the first time that Kitsusaburō had performed at the top level in Osaka, and Shikan presents this also as the first memorial for Rikan, begging patrons to offer their support to the new actor. Kitsusaburō

then modestly begins by saying that he is unknown to most of the audience since he has been away performing in Edo for the last few years. He refers to Rikan as his teacher-master (*shishō*) and relates how sad he was to hear of his death when he was far away in Edo, and how rudderless he felt after returning to Osaka without the great actor as his guide. He states that he first refused to accept the new name, feeling unworthy of the honour, but then modestly accepts the mantle, asking for the help of other actors and patrons to enable him to develop into a worthy successor. He concludes with a *kyōka* poem:

*Shiratsuyu no / megumi o ukete / iroka naki /
ogi mo chigusa ni / majiru kono-goro*
Receiving the blessing of
Sparkling dew even an
Unattractive reed
Can now mingle with
Beauteous wildflowers
ARASHI KITSUSABURŌ II
(Trans. adapted from Charles Dunn)

Dunn 1984, p. 84.

244

245

244 Arashi Tokusaburō II as Yakko Yadahei

PLAY *Saruwaka hisago gunki* at the Nakamura Theatre (Edo); eleventh month, 1820

Artist: Kunisada (Edo)

Signature: Gototei Kunisada ga

Publisher: Matsumura Tatsuemon (Edo)

Censorship seal: *kiwame*

Ōban, colour woodblock, 35.8 x 24.0 cm

Private Collection (UK)

When this portrait of Arashi Tokusaburō II (1788–1837) as the street tough Yadahei was drawn the actor had just arrived in Edo from Osaka. He performed at the Nakamura Theatre regularly in varied roles until the seventh month, 1822, when he was recalled to Osaka to succeed to the name Arashi Kitsusaburō II (later Rikan II) in the ninth month (cat. 243). Edo artist Kunisada seems to have created Tokusaburō in the image of Nakamura Utaemon III (Shikan). Indeed, it was most likely Shikan who had arranged for Tokusaburō to perform with the leading Edo actor Ichikawa Danjūrō VII, as well as with the Osaka

actor Ichikawa Ebijūrō I, who was also in Edo in 1820. There is a striking contrast in appearance between the portrait drawn here by Kunisada and those done of the same actor by Osaka artists such as Hokushū (cat. 243).

The poem is written from Tokusaburō's perspective as he ventures in the cold of winter from Osaka to Edo:

Yuki no michi / kokoro moto naku / ayumikeri
On the snowy road
Unsure of my way
I stumble along
JUKAKU (Tokusaburō)

245 Arashi Kitsusaburō II (later Rikan II) as Minamoto no Yorimasa

PLAY *Yorimasa nue monogatari* at the Naka Theatre; ninth month, 1822

Artist: Yoshikuni

Signature: Yoshikuni ga

Publishers: Izumi-Ri and Hon'ya Seishichi

Ōban, colour woodblock, 37.0 x 25.8 cm

The British Museum, London (1983.5-23.01,76)

The text states that this is the occasion of the first memorial for Arashi Kitsusaburō I (Rikan I), and that Arashi Tokusaburō has succeeded to the name Arashi Kitsusaburō II (later Rikan II), upon his return from Edo. Yorimasa was one of Rikan I's most famous roles and he was due to perform it when he fell ill and died. It was common for successors to a name to perform the trademark roles of their predecessors. This would have been a very important performance for Kitsusaburō II, as he would have been under great scrutiny from critics and patrons.

246 Arashi Kitsusaburō II (later Rikan II) as Minamoto no Yorimasa (right) and Sawamura Kunitarō II as Ayame no Mae (left)

PLAY *Yorimasa nue monogatari* at the Naka Theatre; ninth month, 1822

Artist: Kunihiro

Signature: Kunihiro ga

Publisher: Tenmaya Kihei

Ōban, colour woodblock, 36.0 x 27.0 cm (right), 36.2 x 25.3 cm (left)

Hendrick Lühl Collection (Germany)

The depiction of Kitsusaburō II (later Rikan II) as Yorimasa here is almost a mirror image of the Hokushū print of Rikan I in the same role, in the eighth month, 1821 (cat. 200). Kunihiro seems to be portraying Kitsusaburō II virtually as the reincarnation of Rikan I.

247 Arashi Kitsusaburō II (later Rikan II) as Minamoto no Yorimasa

PLAY *Yorimasa nue monogatari* at the Naka Theatre; ninth month, 1822

Artist: Ashiyuki

Signature: Ashiyuki

Artist's seals: Ashi, Yuki (hand-impressed)

Surimono, colour woodblock with metallic pigment and embossing, 36.9 x 25.4 cm

Private Collection (UK)

This *surimono*-like actor print of Kitsusaburō II (later Rikan II) was part of the campaign to promote him as the heir to Rikan I. Ashiyuki follows quite closely one of his own memorial images of Rikan I in the same role in the album *Kikkōjō* (cat. 211a). The poems are by Kitsusaburō (using his pen name, Rikaku) and Ashiyuki:

O-kashira mo / shirade ugomeku / namako ka na
Head and tail both
Wriggle oblivious
Like a sea slug
RIKAKU

Kitsusaburō is being modest about his attempts to imitate Rikan I, famous in this role. *Namako* (a sea slug or sea cucumber) is a winter metaphor often used by actors to refer to their unpolished skills.

Tegiwa yoki / tsugiki zo fuyu no / tamatsubaki
With marvellous technique
A branch well grafted in winter
The camellia will flourish
ASHIYUKI

Kitsusaburō was not related by blood to Rikan, but rather a disciple of Isaburō, Rikan's older brother (hence 'grafted'). *Tamatsubaki*, the poetic name for a camellia, is a symbol of long life.

246

247

248

248 Arashi Kitsusaburō II (later Rikan II) as Sasaki Kurando

PLAY *Keisei shina sadame* at the Naka Theatre; first month, 1823

Artist: Ashiyuki

Signature: Gigadō Ashiyuki

Artist's seal: Ashiyuki

Publishers: Izumi-Ri and Hon'ya Seishichi

Ōban, colour woodblock with metallic pigment and embossing, 37.0 x 25.8 cm

The British Museum, London (1983.5-23.01,35)

The composition recalls, in mirror image, the Kunihiro *surimono* of Rikan I with his young sword-bearer (cat. 173) from 1817. Kitsusaburō II (later Rikan II) is once again presented as the incarnation of his predecessor. The poem is by the actor himself, using his pen name Rikaku:

> *Katawara ni / iro hazukashi ya / yabu tsubaki*
> Standing alongside
> Ashamed of its colour
> Wild camellia
> RIKAKU

Kitsusaburō II compares himself humbly to Rikan I, whose crest was the mandarin orange and in whose shadow he stands.

249a

249b

249a Sawamura Kunitarō II as Ayame no Mae (right) and Arashi Kitsusaburō II (later Rikan II) as Hyōgo-no-kami Yorimasa (left)

PLAY *Yorimasa nue monogatari* at the Naka Theatre; ninth month, 1822

Artist: Hokushū

Signature: Shunkōsai Hokushū ga

Artist's seal: Hokushū

Ōban, colour woodblock with metallic pigment, 37.0 x 25.0 cm

Victoria & Albert Museum, London (E.14735-1886-34)

249b Sawamura Kunitarō II as Ayame no Mae (right) and Arashi Kitsusaburō II (later Rikan II) as Hyōgo-no-kami Yorimasa (left)

PLAY *Yorimasa nue monogatari* at the Naka Theatre; ninth month, 1822

Artist: Hokushū

Signature: Shunkōsai Hokushū ga

Artist's seal: Hokushū

Publisher: Yamaichi (?)

Ōban, colour woodblock, 37.3 x 25.8 cm

Hendrick Lühl Collection (Germany)

Two impressions of the same design, the first in deluxe, *surimono*-style with metallic printing in tin and brass, and poems by the actors and a certain Shōkokuan. The second is ordinary colour woodblock, for commercial release. This was another design used for promotion of the new 'Rikan'.

An impression in Kōnan Women's University has the seal of the publisher Yamaichi.

Schwaab 1989, p. 94, no. 59.

250 Nakamura Utaemon III (Shikan) as Ishikawa Goemon (right) and Arashi Kichisaburō III as Goemon's son Goroichi (left)

PLAY *Kama-ga-fuchi futatsu-domoe* at the Naka Theatre; ninth month, 1822

Artist: Yoshikuni

Signature: Yoshikuni ga

Publishers: Izumi-Ri and Hon'ya Seishichi

Ōban, colour woodblock, 37.0 x 25.8 cm

The British Museum, London (1983.5-23.01,63)

Utaemon III (Shikan), in the role of the master thief Goemon, here demonstrates his support for young Arashi Kichisaburō III, Rikan I's nephew, who had succeeded to this name one year earlier. On the stone shrine lantern in the background is a message from Kichisaburō III's cousin Yoshisaburō, the son of Rikan I: 'Offering by Okajimaya Yoshisaburō of Osaka Shimanouchi' (Okajimaya is the name of the Kichisaburō stage-clan [*yago*]). Yoshisaburō had given up the acting profession and pronounces support for his cousin as successor to his father's name.

253 Arashi Kitsusaburō II (later Rikan II) as Satomi Isuke (right) and Fujikawa Tomokichi II as Taruya Osen (left)

PLAY *Meisaku kiriko no akebono* at the Kita Theatre (Kyoto); seventh month, 1826

Artist: Ashiyuki

Signature: Gigadō Ashiyuki ga

Publisher: Hon'ya Seishichi

Ōban, colour woodblock, 37.0 x 25.8 cm

The British Museum, London (1983.5-23.01,19)

The inscription states that the pair were a great hit in Kyoto. This play by Chikamatsu Tokuzō was first performed in the eighth month of 1801 at the Naka Theatre, with Arashi Rikan I in the role of Isuke. It was based on a real murder incident only a month earlier in the area between Kyoto and Osaka of a young woman called Osen during the early autumn Obon festival of ancestral spirits. Her story was then tied to the character Isuke from another play of 1777 about turmoil in a samurai estate after a precious

254

253

heirloom sword is stolen. Isuke is ordered to investigate its whereabouts. He knows Osen from their childhood when her father helped him, but he must kill her out of loyalty to his lord. He is then killed. Kitsusaburō II (Rikan II) revived this play of his predecessor to great acclaim. In 1828 he acceded to the name Rikan II and become the rival of Utaemon III (Shikan).

Matsudaira in *Hizō ukiyo-e taikan*, vol. 3, 1988, pp. 261–2, no. 116.

254 Ichikawa Ebijūrō I as Ukisu no Iwamatsu (right), Arashi Kitsusaburō II (later Rikan II) as farmer Jūsaku (middle), Arashi Kitsuzō as Jūkichi and Sawamura Kunitarō II as Jūsaku's wife Okinu (left)

PLAY *Keisei kakehashi monogatari* at the Naka Theatre; fifth month, 1827

Artist: Ashiyuki

Signature: Gigadō Ashiyuki ga

Publisher: Wataya Kihei

Ōban, colour woodblock, triptych, each sheet approx. 37.0 x 25.8 cm

The British Museum, London (1983.5-23.01,15-17)

This is another of the so-called 'Osaka courtesan' (*keisei*) plays for which a popular plot was recast to give the female role specialists (*onnagata*) more prominence (see also cats 256–7). No details survive of this production. The characters – the farmer Jūsaku, his wife, child and another – pose on the shore, with Mt Fuji dwarfed by a huge rising sun on the distant horizon. For most of its history the print was bound into an album which has helped to preserve magnificently its brilliant colours. The combination of pink and blue seen in the sky here is particularly characteristic of Osaka prints at this time.

Matsudaira in *Hizō ukiyo-e taikan*, vol. 3, 1988, p. 263, no. 120.

255a Arashi Rikan II memorial
(not illustrated)

After the thirteenth day of the sixth month, 1837

Artist: Kunihiro

Signature: Kunihiro ga

Artist's seal: Naniwa Kunihiro

Publisher: Tenmaya Kihei

Ōban, colour woodblock, 35.8 x 25.1 cm

Waseda University Theatre Museum, Tokyo (016-1707)

The print records the final testament verse of Rikan II, who died at the peak of his career just under the age of fifty:

> *Mida tanomu / toki ni hiraku ya / hasu no hana*
> Calling on Amida
> Let it bloom now
> Lotus flower
> ARASHI RIKAN (II)

Illustrated in Matsudaira (Waseda) 1995(c), vol. 4, no. 579.

255b Arashi Rikan II memorial

After the thirteenth day of the sixth month, 1837

Artist: Tessai (Utagawa Nobukatsu)

Signature: ōju Tessai sha ('drawn by Tessai at special request')

Artist's seal: Unread

Ōban, colour woodblock with metallic pigment, 37.2 x 25.0 cm

Private Collection (UK)

A group of Kabuki fans and amateur poets commemorates the death of the actor Arashi Rikan II (Kitsusaburō II, Tokusaburō II). The memorial portrait, as if painted on a round fan, depicts the actor in lay-Buddhist robes, holding a rosary. An incense burner fills the composition with fragrant smoke, subtly gradated by the printer in exquisite, *surimono*-like technique.

There are sixteen memorial haiku in total. The group has taken care to fashion the poems into a linked sequence, with many associations between them. Korin, whose poem is given prominence on the fan next to Rikan's portrait, was most likely the editor (see the final poem below).

> *Arashi ni nabiku / murasaki no / kumo no mine*
> Purple clouds
> Drawn by the storm [Arashi]
> At the peak
> SHIYŪ

Amida Buddha arrives on purple clouds to meet the dying person and lead them to Paradise.

> *Soko ga gokuraku / susumi-goro / arashi kuru*
> In Paradise
> Just as it cools
> A storm appears
> KITSUMARU

It is summer in Paradise – the actor died in late summer – and the approaching storm (Arashi) is Rikan.

> *Kukuri-zaru / hasu no utena e / yaru mai zo*
> The monkey crawls
> Up to the lotus calyx [throne]
> 'No one's gonna beat me!'
> SHARIN

Monkeys are associated with actors, and a *kukuri-zaru* is a kind of stuffed monkey-toy. The final line is also common in Kyōgen plays, where at the end of the farce a character says 'You'll not get away with it!' Here the image evoked is of the actor Rikan ruling in Paradise, atop the lotus calyx (or lotus throne), symbol of Buddhist rebirth into the Pure Land above the murky swamp of this world.

> *Tachibana mo / hasu no kaori e / makikomare*
> Mandarin orange
> Be enveloped too
> In lotus fragrance
> HIKIO

The mandarin orange is one of Rikan's crests. The sequence of poems has now arrived at a lotus in Paradise, and Rikan is at peace.

> *Tachibana no / mon natsukashimi / doyō-boshi*
> Mandarin crest
> Evoking memories
> His robes hung out to air
> DONNI

The focus is shifted back to this world, and those left behind, while retaining the mandarin image. *Doyō-boshi* was an end-of-summer custom of hanging clothes out to air.

> *Tachibana mo / ima wa uchiwa ni / ka o todome*
> Mandarin orange
> Capture its fragrance too
> With your fan
> GOTE

Fans were used to draw fragrances towards the face: here the imagery in the print itself is evoked.

> *Senryō to / hometeru natsu no / yū arashi*
> Fêted as an actor
> Like a summer evening storm [Arashi]
> Worth a thousand in gold
> BUNCHŌ

Memories are of Rikan taking the stage by storm. It was common to praise an actor as being worth a salary of a thousand gold pieces – an enormous amount. The biggest stars did in fact command such huge salaries.

> *Goku wa kurai / raku wa kinen ni / nokoru natsu*
> Unparalleled his rank
> Remembering with pleasure his skill
> At the final summer curtain
> HAKURYŪ

Now we are among a group of fans recalling the actor in performance. The poem turns on wordplay: *gokuraku* is Paradise, but *goku* alone also refers to the 'superlative' ranking in the actor-critique books. *Raku* means pleasure or love, and is also used as an abbreviation for the final day (*senshūraku*) of a two-month stage-run.

> *Rikan ta zo / hasu ni doyomeku / hime-botoke*
> Is that Rikan?!
> All around the lotus
> Female buddhas clamour
> HAIGYOKU

Back in Paradise Rikan's arrival has set many female hearts aflutter as they gather around to admire their hero.

> *Tachibana no / hanagata chirasu / natsu no kaze*
> Mandarin blossom
> Scattering its youthful charm
> In a summer breeze
> KASHU

Rikan retained his erotic appeal even as an older man: not a storm this time, but a smooth and enticing summer breeze.

> *Hōō e / iza tamuke baya / kirinsō*
> Come let us offer
> Prayers for the phoenix
> 'Kylin flowers' are here
> GYOKUSEN

Phoenix, kylin (*kirin*), turtle and dragon are four mythical creatures of Chinese lore. *Kirinsō* is the plant 'orange stonecrop', which has yellow-orange flowers in summer. *Kirin* is a metaphor for the best person imaginable; phoenix is a metaphor for the arrival of a prince.

> *Tonda koto / kiri yori saki e / ōtori chiri*
> How strange
> The phoenix falls first
> From the paulownia
> KURONDO (?)

Rikan is the grand phoenix, the best actor: phoenixes were thought to live in paulownia trees. Perhaps this refers to the fact that Rikan II, although much younger than Utaemon III (Shikan I), has died before him. (Utaemon in fact died the following year.)

The poem within the fan reads as follows:

In the style of *Haifū yanagidaru*

> *Gokuraku mo / arashi de hazumu / bon-gawari*
> In Paradise too
> All delight at the storm [Arashi]
> As good as Bon Festival
> KORIN

Haifū yanagidaru was a multi-volume collection of light, limerick-like verses (*senryū*) published serially between 1765 and 1838. The Bon (Obon) Festival in the middle of the seventh month (early autumn) is when the dead spirits return to be welcomed by their families. The poem implies that all those in Paradise are fans of Rikan, and that his arrival is as good as going back home at festival time. A pun may be intended on 'bon-gawari', which could mean the stage revolves and Rikan appears in his full glory.

Another impression is in Kokuritsu Gekijō 1991, vol. 10, no. 05134.

N/A

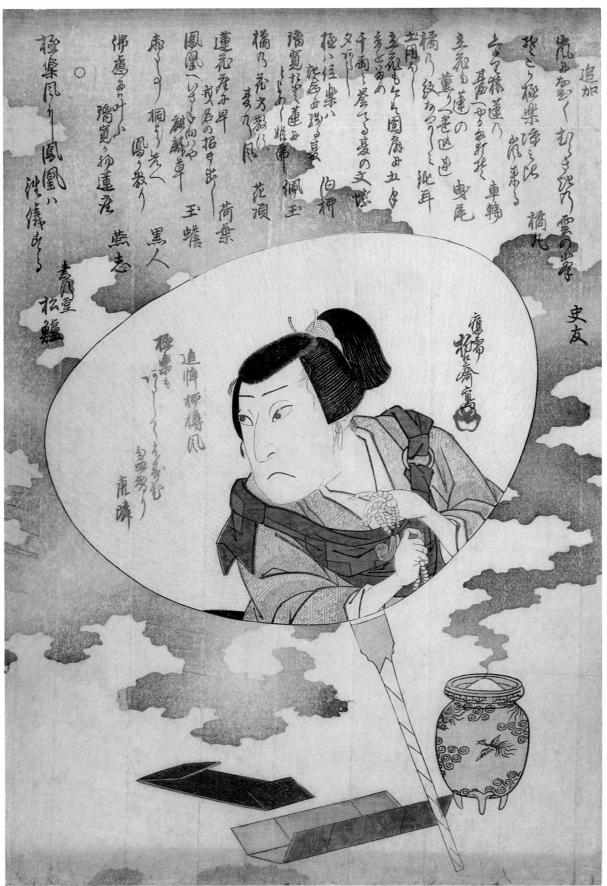

256

256 Sawamura Kunitarō II as Shinkurō's wife Shigarami (right), Nakamura Karoku I as Shōkurō's wife Kochō (centre), and Fujikawa Tomokichi II as Katsumoto's wife Nagisa (left)

PLAY *Keisei ōmonguchi* at the Kado Theatre; first month, 1823

Artist: Hokushū

Signature: Shunkōsai Hokushū ga

Publisher: Toshikuraya Shinbei

Ōban, colour woodblock with metallic pigment, triptych, 37.8 x 25.7 cm (right), 38.0 x 26.2 cm (centre), 38.2 x 26.1 cm (left)

Gerhard Pulverer Collection (Germany)

'Courtesan' (*keisei*) plays were usually performed at the New Year. Older plays were rewritten usually with a courtesan in a prominent role and with other female characters given high-profile roles. This triptych print highlights the three female specialist (*onnagata*) stars of the troupe. The

text of this play does not survive, but it was based on the Kabuki play *Ōmon-guchi yoroi-gasane* by Namiki Sōsuke, first performed in Osaka at the Ōnishi Theatre in the twelfth month, 1743. In this play Shinkurō and Shōkurō are the protagonists of a long and complicated tale, in which Shokuro plans an insurrection and revenge against Shinkurō, who had killed Shōkurō's father. The actors are cast as the wives of the protagonists who are in conflict. Here Karoku in the centre is in opposition to the other two. Shifting the focus away from the men and onto the loyal wives offered *onnagata* actors an opportunity to show off their dance and martial arts skills. Matsudaira 1999, p. 144 quotes a section of *Yakusha shinji-kurabe*, a critique published a year later in the first month, 1824, that describes the encounter in the darkness (*danmari*) of the three *onnagata* as magnificent and 'an excellent scene, perfect for the artists'.

Hokushū skilfully links the composition with a stream flowing across the background and willow tresses cascading from above. There is also an unusual and effective suggestion of illumination: the lantern held up by the crouching figure of Nagisa, on the left, shines on Kochō, in the middle, and she turns her face from the glare. The scene is otherwise set in darkness and the bands of black-and-white stripes in the background, suggesting sudden flashes of light from the jostling lanterns, creates dramatic tension between the figures.

An instructive comparison can be made with cat. 257, where the same performance is depicted by three different artists with poems by patrons. As might be expected, each actor, artist and poet is featured more independently, the link between the three panels not nearly as strong as in this Hokushū version.

257

257 Fujikawa Tomokichi II as Nakai Ohana (right), Nakamura Karoku I as Shōkurō's wife Kochō (centre), and Sawamura Kunitarō II as Shinkurō's wife Shigarami (left)

PLAY *Keisei ōmonguchi* at the Kado Theatre; first month, 1823

Artists: Ashiyuki (right), Yoshikuni (centre) and Kunihiro (left)

Signatures: Ashiyuki ga, Yoshikuni ga, Kunihiro ga

Publishers: Toshikuraya Shinbei, Izutsuya Denbei and Tenmaya Kihei (Kunihiro)

Ōban, colour woodblock, triptych, 37.4 x 25.5 cm (right), 38.2 x 26.3 cm (centre), 39.0 x 26.5 cm (left)

Hendrick Lühl Collection (Germany)

Production of a print through collective effort (*gassaku*) – here three artists, four poets and three publishers – was more common in Osaka than Edo. Kunihiro is thought to be the artist persona of the publisher Tenmaya Kihei, and here

he prints his own composition. Cat. 256 shows the same scene by the single artist Hokushū.

> *Iro fukaku / miru tabi mashinu / hana no tomo*
> Deeply colourful
> Better each time
> This 'friend of flowers'
> FUJIN

Hana no tomo ('friend of flowers') is alternatively read *Kayū*, the pen name of the actor Tomokichi. *Iro* ('colourful') has strong connotations of 'sexy'.

> Nakamura Shikin [Karoku] performing Kochō, the little butterfly, reminded me of [the Chinese legend of] Zhuang Zi's dream of butterflies of long ago.

> *Yume ni sae / mitemo ureshiki / kochō ka na*
> Such joy even to
> See it in my dream
> Little butterfly
> SHARYŪ

> *Kara made mo / na o ba ageha no / kochō ka na*
> His fame reaches China
> Riding the wings of
> Little butterfly
> KAKUICHI

Sawamura Kitō [Kunitarō], too, as the courtesan of Naniwa Bay, was a magnificent success.

> *Tachi-narabu / naka ni sugurete / ume kaoru*
> Even in such company
> It stands out alone
> Scent of the plum blossom
> ROKUMATSU

Naniwa (Osaka) is associated with plum blossom.

258

258 Nakamura Tsurusuke I (Shikan II) as the fox Tadanobu

PLAY *Yoshitsune senbon-zakura* at the Ōnishi Theatre; fourth or fifth month, 1824

Artist: Umekuni

Signature: Umekuni

Surimono, colour woodblock with metallic pigment, 16.7 x 24.6 cm

Victoria & Albert Museum, London (E.213-1898)

The Jukōdō poetry group led by artist Yoshikuni was active in its promotion of the actor Tsurusuke; here members Masakuni, Yoshikuni and Shishō (Tsurusuke himself) contribute poems to a small *surimono*, otherwise unrecorded. Nakamura Utaemon III (Shikan) first noticed Tsurusuke's dancing talents during his first tour of Edo, when Tsurusuke was still a youth. Shikan took the promising young actor into his troupe, brought him back to Osaka and eventually adopted him as his successor. Tsurusuke was promoted as a rising star around the time of Shikan's retirement in 1825.

The play, one of the most popular, was originally composed for the Osaka puppet theatre in 1747 and then immediately adapted for Kabuki. Tadanobu is one of the great dance roles in Kabuki. The historical Satō Tadanobu (1161–86) was a retainer of the Minamoto general Yoshitsune and remained loyal to him after Yoshitsune's brother Yoritomo turned against him and had him hunted down. In the play Tadanobu accompanies Shizuka Gozen, Yoshitsune's lover, in a flight for safety, and their journey (*michiyuki*) is a dance piece. Shizuka carries a hand drum, which is stretched with fox skins. The offspring of the pair of foxes to whom these skins belonged magically changes himself into Tadanobu, in order to be close to his parents. The actor had to alternate skilfully between the human (Tadanobu) and fox characters, with some quick costume changes. This became one of Tsurusuke's trademark roles.

石川五左門
中村鶴助

260

type of role in Kabuki, allowing the actor to present a lively performance with great verve and masculine sex appeal, occasionally with chest bared.

The Ōnishi in Osaka was a 'middle theatre' (*chū-shibai*) where younger actors vied to rise in the ranks and transfer to the two major troupes, usually at the Kado and Naka Theatres. Edo artists only portrayed actors of the top rank, but in Osaka artists freely made prints of whichever actor they admired, and by so doing promoted their fame and celebrity.

260 Nakamura Tsurusuke I (Shikan II) as Ishikawa Goemon

PLAY *Kinmon gosan no kiri* at the Onishi Theatre; third month, 1825

Artist: Yoshikuni

Signature: Yoshikuni ga

Publisher: Hon'ya Seishichi

Ōban, colour woodblock, 39.1 x 26.5 cm

The British Museum, London (1983.5-23.01,104)

Ishikawa Goemon (1558–94), the most famous thief in Japanese history, was later transformed into the fictional character of a Chinese warrior who seeks revenge against Toyotomi Hideyoshi for the death of his father. The play by Namiki Gohei was a great success and parts of it have been performed regularly in Kabuki ever since, particularly the scene at the grand gate of Nanzenji Temple in Kyoto, portrayed here. Hisayoshi (the fictional name for Hideyoshi) confronts Goemon.

In this particular scene, atop the imposing gate of Nanzenji Temple, a hawk alights before Goemon, holding a torn-off sleeve with a message written in blood. It is the testament of Sō Sokei, a retainer of the twelfth Ming Emperor who had come to Japan as an emissary but was imprisoned by Hisayoshi. Eventually released, he married a Japanese woman and had two sons. His plot to overthrow Japan was discovered by Hisayoshi, however, and the note is his final testament before execution. Goemon realizes, because of the mention of a rare incense Ranjatai, that Sokei is his father, and plots to kill Hisayoshi.

At this time Tsurusuke was playing big roles in the 'middle theatres' (*chū-shibai*) of Osaka, in preparation for his accession to the name Shikan II, to be inherited from Utaemon III (Shikan) in the eleventh month, 1825. Tsurusuke had to prove himself able to project the power of the legendary-historical figure Goemon, and thereby complete this rite of passage as an aspiring actor. Colour prints such as this were essential tools in the promotion of an actor to stardom.

259 Nakamura Tsurusuke I (Shikan II) as Yakko Ranpei

PLAY *Hana-goromo iroha engi* at the Ōnishi Theatre; ninth or tenth month, 1824

Artist: Yoshikuni

Signature: Jukōdō Yoshikuni ga

Publishers: Wataya Kihei and Ariwaradō Chūbei

Printer: Zakoba

Ōban, colour woodblock with metallic pigment, 37.1 x 26.0 cm

Victoria & Albert Museum, London (E.13825-1886)

Tsurusuke glares out of the picture, hand on the hilt of his sword, threatening to draw. The portrait is presented as if a padded-fabric picture (*oshi-e*) on a battledore (*hagoita*), used as a type of New Year decoration. It is very likely that Yoshikuni copied this idea from the Edo artist Utagawa Kunisada (1786–1864), who did an almost identical series in Edo *c*. 1823, *Tōsei oshi-e hagoita* (*Modern Cloth-Picture Battledores*). Kunisada visited Osaka briefly in 1821.

Yakko ('street tough') was a brash and brave

261

262 Nakamura Tsurusuke I (Shikan II) as Sanbasō

PLAY *Kotobuki shikisan* at the Kado Theatre; third month, 1825

Artist: Tamikuni

Signature: Tamikuni ga

Artist's seal: 'Mi'

Surimono, colour woodblock with metallic pigment, 18.4 x 25.3 cm

Victoria & Albert Museum, London (E.182-1898)

This is a *surimono* version of the dance performance depicted in cat. 261, privately produced in support of Tsurusuke. Artist Tamikuni was a member of Yoshikuni's Jukōdōsha haiku poetry group. Tsurusuke is featured as both actor and poet:

> *Manaita ni / i-ari ya namako / chijimikeru*
> On the cutting board
> Does the sea slug know
> As it curls up?
> SHISHŌ (Tsurusuke)

'Sea slug' (*namako*), sometimes translated more appealingly as 'sea cucumber', is often modestly used by young actors to describe themselves: clumsy and not yet fully coordinated, ready for the chop by critics.

Roger Keyes has suggested that Tamikuni was an early name used by Hirosada (Keyes 1984, p. 89).

261 Nakamura Tsurusuke I (Shikan II) as Sanbasō

PLAY *Kotobuki shikisan* at the Kado Theatre; third month, 1825

Artist: Yoshikuni

Signature: Yoshikuni ga

Ōban, colour woodblock, 37.0 x 25.8 cm

The British Museum, London (1983.5-23.01,84)

Tsurusuke performed this auspicious dance for Utaemon III (Shikan)'s retirement performances at the Kado Theatre. Sanbasō was originally a ritual dance in Noh and other theatrical traditions. In Kabuki it was further developed into a full and lively dance. Yoshikuni actively promoted Tsurusuke as a rising star in the Shikan camp by producing prints himself, and by encouraging other members of his Jukōdōsha poetry group to design prints and *surimono* of the young actor.

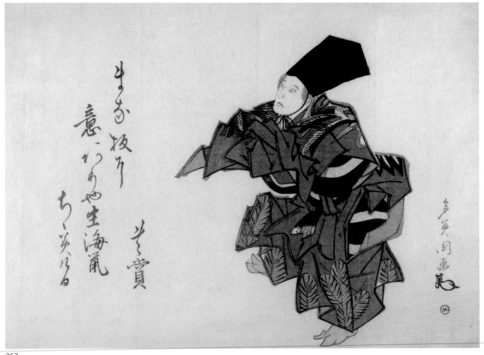

263 Nakamura Tsurusuke I (Shikan II) as Miyamoto Musashi

PLAY *Kataki-uchi Ganryūjima* at the Naka Jizō Theatre
(Ise); fourth month, 1825

Artist: Yoshikuni

Signature: Baito (Ume no Miyako) Jukōdō Yoshikuni ga
('by Jukōdō Yoshikuni of Osaka')

Ōban, colour woodblock, 37.0 x 24.7 cm

Bodleian Library, Oxford University (Nipponica 354–19)

Artist Yoshikuni and his Jukōdōsha haiku group
offer poems in support of Nakamura Tsurusuke I
(later Shikan II and Utaemon IV) on his tour to
Ise, where he performed the role of the famous
swordsman Miyamoto Musashi. Their poems are
inscribed on the votive panel (*ema*) at which the
actor gazes. He is dressed in travelling clothes
and sports large paired swords. The votive
plaque to the right features two more swords,
which it says are an offering 'from Miyamoto
Musashi', who, historically, lived from 1584 to
1645 and is known to have travelled all around
Japan learning the art of swordsmanship.

The Yoshikuni poetry group was active in the
promotion of Tsurusuke as the successor to
Utaemon III (Shikan). The text makes this clear:
'The Jukōdō poetry group offers this to the
shrine celebrating the performance of Nakamura
Tsurusuke [Shishō] at Ise in the role Miyamoto
Musashi'. The sequence of poems is by Umekuni,
Masakuni, Fujikuni, Toshikuni and Yoshikuni. All
of these individuals also produced actor prints.

Botan sakite / hoka ni hana naku / omoikeri
The peony blooms
Other flowers
Pale in comparison
UMEKUNI

Tsurusuke is the peony blossom that dominates
the landscape.

Hana yori to / hito mo iikeri / wakaba-yama
Even more than as a flower [actor]
He is a fine man
This 'Young-leaf' Mountain
MASAKUNI

Koromogae / sate sate koruki / tachii ka na
A change of robe
Heralds the summer
He stands lightly
FUJIKUNI

Home-goe no / doyomi-aikeri / ōya-kazu
Cries of praise
Echo all together
Hails of arrows [poems]
TOSHIKUNI

Hototogisu / ikanaru hito mo / kiku ki nari
The cuckoo's song
Everyone wants
To hear
YOSHIKUNI

263

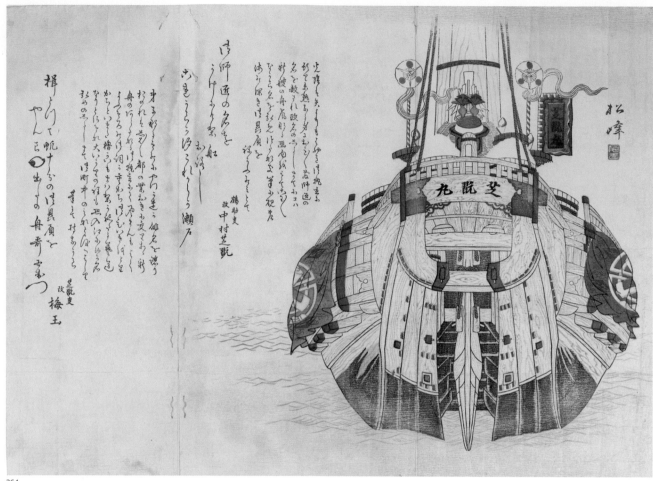

264

264 'Shikan ship'
Shikan-maru
Eleventh month, 1825
Artist: Suga Shōhō
Signature: Shōhō
Artist's seal: Hyakubyaku (?)
Surimono, colour woodblock with metallic pigment, 43.8 x 59.2 cm
Private Collection (Japan)

A great sea-going ship, decorated with festive offerings and purple curtains bearing the actor's crest, is seen from the stern setting off on a voyage. With its large rudder forming the beak, it almost looks like a brooding crane – another of the actor's emblems – facing towards us. For this *surimono* celebrates the succession of Nakamura Tsurusuke I to the name Nakamura Shikan II, which made him the artistic heir of Nakamura Shikan I (Utaemon III). Simultaneously Utaemon, who had recently retired from the stage, changes his pen name from Shikan to Baigyoku. The artist Suga Shōhō (1790–1851) was a pupil of Niwa Tōkei.

Shikan II asks his patrons to help him become an actor worthy of the illustrious name:

Goshishō no / na o kakenikeri / funa-oroshi / kore kara ga shio / kore kara ga seto
My great teacher
Has bestowed his name on me
Now to launch the boat
First upon the tide
Then to face the narrow straits
(Tsurusuke, now renamed) NAKAMURA SHIKAN II

Finally, Utaemon III asks all his fans to support the young Shikan II and the others in his troupe:

Kaji totte / ho jūbun no / go-hiiki o / yanra medeta no / funa utaemon
Taking the rudder
Sails fully unfurled
Patrons applaud
Cheering on the launch
Of the Utaemon fleet
(Shikan, now renamed) BAIGYOKU

The print is also in *Kyota* (Waseda) 35: 10–11.

265 'Actors of today parody the Six Immortals of Poetry'
Tōsei yakusha mitate rokkasen
c. First month, 1827
Artist: Yoshikuni
Signature: Toyokawa Yoshikuni ga
Publisher: Hon'ya Seishichi
Ōban, colour woodblock, 37.8 x 25.2 cm
Hendrick Lühl Collection (Germany)

Six top stars of the moment are cast as the 'Six Immortals of Poetry' (Rokkasen), an imagined (*mitate*) cast. The five male roles are depicted clockwise from the top, followed by the single female role, Komachi, in the centre:

Rikaku (Arashi Kitsusaburō II) as Bun'ya no Yasuhide

Baigyoku (Nakamura Utaemon III) as Priest Kisen

Shikan (Nakamura Shikan II) as Ariwara no Narihira

Shikō (Ichikawa Danzō V) as Ōtomo Kuronushi

Shinshō (Ichikawa Ebijūrō I) as Priest Henjō

Sankō (Nakamura Matsue III) as Lady Komachi

See the description of this play in cat. 38. Other representations are by Shigeharu, cat. 273, and Hokuei, cat. 274.

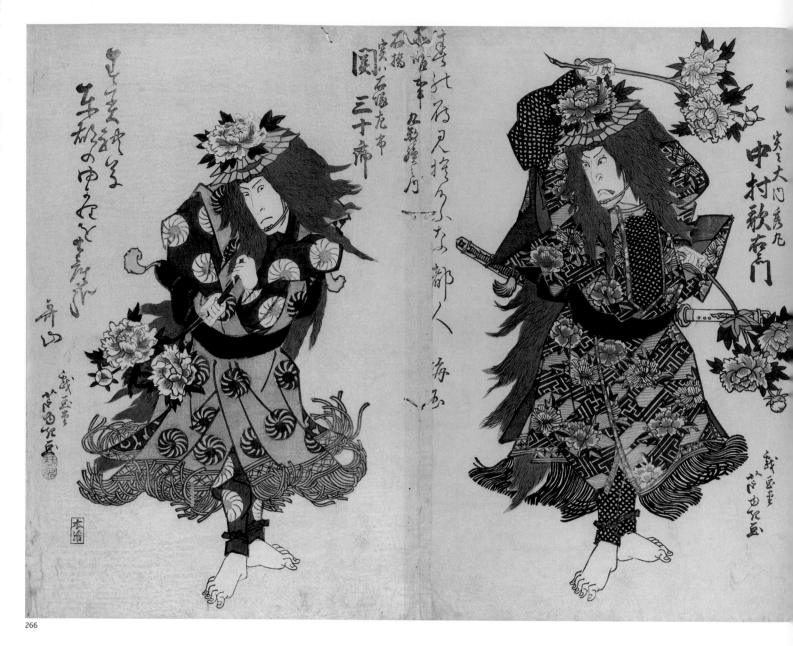

266

266 Nakamura Shikan II as Shakkyō (actually Satake Shinjūrō, right), Nakamura Utaemon III (Shikan I) as Shakkyō (actually Ōuchi Hidemaru, centre) and Seki Sanjūrō II as Shakkyō (actually Ishizuka Sa'ichi, left)

PLAY *Imayō mitsu no shishi-gashira* at the Kado Theatre; first month, 1827

Artist: Ashiyuki

Signature: Gigadō Ashiyuki ga

Artist's seal: Ashiyuki (hand-impressed)

Publisher: Hon'ya Seishichi

Ōban, colour woodblock, three from a set of nine prints, 37.8 x 25.7 cm (right), 37.9 x 25.6 cm (centre), 37.8 x 25.5 cm (left)

Victoria & Albert Museum, London (E.2857-1886)

These are the three 'lion' roles from a set of nine prints of actors performing this play (a complete set is illustrated in Ikeda Bunko, vol. 1, 1997, no. 261). *Shakkyō* was a dance piece that Kabuki adapted from the Noh theatre. The story goes back to a Chinese legend about father and son lions. The father lion (with white mane) throws his son (with red mane) down a ravine as a test of his mettle in order for him to prove himself as a lion. The dance ends auspiciously when the young lion returns. The poems are by the actors themselves. Sanjūrō II (1786–1839), whose rise was supported by Utaemon III (Shikan I), had just returned from Edo the previous month. He is given pride of place among the five actors appearing in the set, with three images (the largest number) and three poems (pen name Kazan). Other actors included in the set are Sawamura Kunitarō II and Nakamura Matsue III, who each contribute a single verse.

His final testament is the verse:

Jitsuaku no / suguranu mi mo / shinite yuku /
michi wa yugamanu / saihō gokuraku
Although I played
Crooked villains
The path I take in death
Is straight
To the Western Paradise
SHINSHŌ

267c Ichikawa Ebijūrō I memorial print (shini-e)
(not illustrated)
After the sixteenth day, seventh month, 1827
Artist: Hokushū
Signature: Shunkōsai Hokushū
Seal: Hokushū
Ōban, colour woodblock, 38.9 x 26.3 cm
Hendrick Lühl Collection, Germany

Final testament verse:

Saihō no / sora arigatashi / bon no tsuki
The western sky
How delightful
The moon at Obon Festival
SHINSHŌ

Nakamura Utaemon III writes that they were like brothers and offers a parting verse:

Kata ude o / mogarete naku ya / kirigirusu
One arm
Torn off, crying
A grasshopper
BAIGYOKU

Illustrated in Ikeda Bunko 1997, vol. 1, no. 17.

267a Ichikawa Ebijūrō I memorial as the bandit Tanseki (actually Tamashima Kōbei)
(not illustrated)
After the sixteenth day, seventh month, 1827
PLAY *Keisei kakehashi monogatari*
Artist: Ashiyuki
Signature: Gigadō Ashiyuki ga
Publisher: Wataya Kihei
Ōban, colour woodblock, 39.0 x 26.4 cm
Hendrick Lühl Collection (Germany)

The Obon Festival, in the seventh month, welcomed ancestral spirits back home from the other world, and then saw them off again with bonfires or fires floated on streams (*okuri-bi*).

In this memorial print (*shini-e*) Ebijūrō I is shown in one of his best-loved roles, as Tanseki. Ebijūrō was a villain- or rough-role (*jitsuaku* or *kataki-yaku*) specialist.

The actor's final testament poem reads:
Okuri-bi to / tomo ni kieyuku / tabiji ka na
Will I disappear
Together with the ritual flames
For the spirits at Obon
SHINSHŌ
Illustrated in Ikeda Bunko 1997, vol. 1, no. 269.

267b Ichikawa Ebijūrō I memorial print (shini-e)
After the sixteenth day, seventh month, 1827
Artist: Hokushū
Signature: Shunkōsai Hokushū
Seal: Hokushū
Publishers: Tenmaya Kihei, Izutsuya Denbei
Carver: Kasuke
Ōban, colour woodblock, 38.0 x 26.0 cm
Hendrick Lühl Collection, Germany

267b

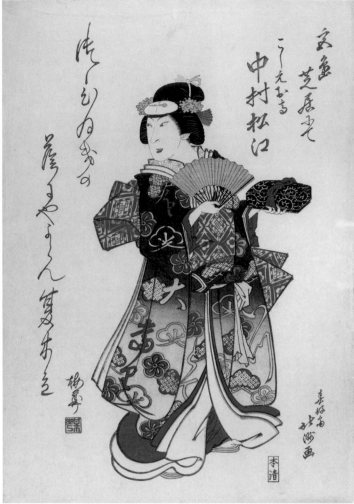

268

269

268 Nakamura Matsue III (Tomijūrō II) as the servant Otaka

PLAY *Gishinden* at the Miyajima Shrine; sixth month, 1828

Artist: Hokushū

Signature: Shunkōsai Hokushū ga

Publisher: Hon'ya Seishichi

Poet's seal: Baika

Ōban, colour woodblock, 39.4 x 27.1 cm

Private Collection (UK)

This is a companion to cat. 269: the two sheets can be viewed as a diptych. Both relate to a touring performance at the Itsukushima Shrine, Miyajima (modern Hiroshima Prefecture). The poem is by the actor himself:

> *Go-hiiki no / kage ni ya yoran / natsu kodachi*
> Thanks to the grace
> Of patrons we gather
> In the shade of summer trees
> BAIKA (Matsue)

This compliments the imagery in the companion print of the moon's rays: the 'shade' of the patrons, soothingly cool in summer, has made the trip possible. Such poetic imagery is also

quite sensual and erotically suggestive. The costume is extravagant even for the serving woman (*koshimoto*) of a high-ranked person; the lettering woven into the fabric reads: 'A great hit every time' (*itsumo ō-atari*).

269 Nakamura Matsue III (Tomijūrō II) as Akoya

PLAY *Genpei nunobiki no taki* at the Miyajima Shrine; sixth month, 1828

Artist: Hokushū

Signature: Shunkōsai Hokushū ga

Publisher: Hon'ya Seishichi

Poet's seal: Baika

Ōban, colour woodblock, 37.5 x 25.7 cm

Birmingham Museums and Art Gallery (583'29)

This is a companion to cat. 268: the two sheets can be viewed together as a diptych. Nakamura Matsue III is in the role of the courtesan Akoya, as part of the special touring performances staged at the Itsukushima Shrine, Miyajima Island. The poem is by Matsue himself:

> *Arigataya / tsuki no megumi no / umi suzushi*
> Grateful for
> The blessing of the moon
> Over a cool sea
> BAIKA (Matsue)

The poem seems to refer to the pleasant memories of the time spent with his patrons on the shore at Miyajima Island (Hiroshima Bay) in late summer. Performances at places like Miyajima must have required the financial backing of patrons, as acknowledged by the poem on the previous print. Matsue was known for his extravagant costumes: the artist Hokushū spares no efforts in creating a luxurious kimono, with spreading pampas grasses under a silver moon (on the shoulder), and a white fox, seemingly alive, done in a manner whereby parts of the textile design project in appliqué technique (*nuitori*). Doubtless there were particular wealthy patrons who indulged Matsue's desires for such sensual apparel.

270 Nakamura Utaemon III (Shikan I) as farmer Gosaku (really Ishikawa Goemon, right) and Ichikawa Danjūrō VII (Hakuen) as Saeda Masaemon (left)

PLAY *Keisei setsugekka* at the Kado Theatre; first month, 1830

Artists: Shigeharu (right) and Hokushū (left)

Signatures: Ryūsai Shigeharu, Shunkōsai Hokushū ga

Artist's seal: Unread (right)

Publisher: Hon'ya Seishichi (?)

Carver: Kasuke (hand-impressed)

Ōban, colour woodblock with metallic pigment, diptych, 38.2 x 50.6 cm

Hendrick Lühl Collection (Germany)

The diptych is lavishly produced in *surimono* style, with especially fine carving and special metallic printing – the work of Kasuke the 'carver of *surimono*' (*surimono hori Kasuke*), as announced in the hand-impressed seal, bottom right. Utaemon III, in disguise as the farmer Gosaku, humbly performs obeisance before the great Edo actor Danjūrō, in the role of a proud samurai, Saeda Masaemon. Danjūrō VII toured in Kyoto–Osaka during 1829–30 due to a fire at the theatre in Edo where he had been scheduled to perform. He would make several later tours to Osaka, notably during his long period of enforced exile from Edo during the Tenpō Reforms, from 1842 to 1849.

The poems are by the two actors:

Performing together with Danjūrō

Iro usuki / tera kara hirakan / fuyu no ume
Faint in colour
From the temple grounds
A plum in winter
BAIGYOKU (Utaemon)

Plum is associated with Osaka and is also the 'Bai' of Utaemon's pen name. The actor is being modest: his 'flower' on stage pales in comparison.

Nagori nani / haru zo yakusha mo / uruu ka na
Another farewell performance
This spring even actors
Get an extra month
ICHIKAWA SHICHIDAIME HAKUEN (Danjūrō)

In the first year of the new Tenpō era (1830) an extra 'intercalary' (*uruu*) month was officially added after the third month, a relatively common practice used to regulate the lunar calendar. Danjūrō is suggesting that he is happy to have this extra month and would like to stay longer.

Other impressions have the mark of the publisher Hon'ya Seishichi.

271a

271b

271a Nakamura Utaemon III (Shikan) as Ikyū and Ichikawa Hakuen (Danjūrō VII) as Sukeroku

PLAY *Sukeroku yukari no Edo-zakura* at the Kado Theatre; third month, 1830

Artist: Shunpu (Hokumyō)

Signature: Shunpu ga

Publishers: Tenmaya Kihei and Izutsuya Denbei

Koban, colour woodblock with metallic pigment and embossing, 16.4 x 11.0 cm

Victoria & Albert Museum, London (E.210-1898)

271b Arashi Rikan II as Tsumahei and Sawamura Kunitarō II as Magaki

PLAY *Shin Usuyuki monogatari* at the Kado and Naka Theatres; first month, 1829

Artist: Shunpu (Hokumyō)

Signature: Shunpu ga

Publishers: Tenmaya Kihei and Izutsuya Denbei

Koban, colour woodblock with metallic pigment and embossing, 16.2 x 11.6 cm

Victoria & Albert Museum, London (E.208-1898)

A pair of beautifully produced *surimono*-like prints in the small *koban* format. *Koban* of this kind were not generally published in Edo. The first showing Utaemon and Danjūrō is from an actual performance. The second seems to be an 'imagined' (*mitate*) performance by Rikan (Naka) and Kunitarō (Kado). Rival theatres, Naka and Kado, put on the same play in competition, but with different titles.

272 Ichikawa Hakuen (Danjūrō VII) as Katsuma Gengobei (right) and Nakamura Matsue III (Tomijūrō II) as Kikuno (left)

c. Sixth month, 1829

PLAY *Godairiki koi no fūjime*

Artist: Shigeharu

Signature: Ryūsai Shigeharu

Seal: Unread

Publisher: Hon'ya Seishichi

Ōban, colour woodblock, 24.1 x 36.5 cm

Birmingham Museums and Art Gallery (493'26)

Danjūrō is listed in a playbill as having performed this role briefly at the Kita Theatre, Kyoto, at the beginning of the third month, 1829. Matsue, however, is not listed alongside

272

him. This is, therefore, a good example of the creation of an imagined (*mitate*) 'dream cast' print, in this case pairing the Edo male star with an Osaka female specialist. In this famous play by Namiki Gohei, Gengobei murders his courtesan lover Kikuno.

Extensive use is made in the print of the vivid chemical pigment Berlin (Prussian) blue, which seems to have been suddenly adopted for commercial printing in both Edo and Kyoto–Osaka at about this time. The surface of the print is heavily abraded, but the design is otherwise unrecorded.

273 Nakamura Shikan II and Nakamura Baika as the Six Immortal Poets (Rokkasen)

PLAY *Rokkasen sugata no saishiki* at the Kado Theatre; first month, 1834

Artist: Shigeharu

Signature: Ryūsai Shigeharu ga

Artist's seal: Ryūsai (hand-impressed)

Carver: Kasuke

Ōban, colour woodblock with metallic pigment, 36.7 x 25.4 cm

Gerhard Pulverer Collection (Germany) (1664)

Shikan II plays all five male roles among the six famous classical poets; Baika (Matsue IV, 1814–35) plays the single female role (Komachi). Shikan II had returned from Edo in the last month of 1833, and here is being promoted as the successor to Utaemon III (Shikan I). Arashi Hinasuke I had first starred in this dance play in 1789; it was a *tour de force* for an actor to play five roles in one production. Shikan promotes the personae of elegant and cultivated courtier-poets. See also cats 38 and 274.

273

274a

274b **Nakamura Shikan II as Ariwara no Narihira** (not illustrated)

PLAY *Rokkasen sugata no saishiki* at the Kado Theatre; first month, 1834

Artist: Hokuei

Signature: Shunbaisai Hokuei ga

Artist's seal: Shunbai

Publisher: Hon'ya Seishichi

Oban, colour woodblock, from a set of six, 37.4 x 25.6 cm

Birmingham Museums and Art Gallery (277'29)

Illustrated in Keyes and Mizushima 1973, no. 47.

274c **Nakamura Shikan II as Kisen Hōshi** (not illustrated)

PLAY *Rokkasen sugata no saishiki* at the Kado Theatre; first month, 1834

Artist: Hokuei

Signature: Shunbaisai Hokuei ga

Artist's seal: Shunbai

Publisher: Wataya Kihei

Ōban, colour woodblock with metallic pigment, from a set of six, 37.2 x 25.0 cm

Gerhard Pulverer Collection (Germany) (1327,4)

Illustrated in Keyes and Mizushima 1973, no. 47.

274d

274a–d Nakamura Shikan II (Utaemon IV) and Nakamura Baika (Matsue IV) as the Six Immortal Poets (Rokkasen)

Shikan II had returned from a tour of Edo in the first month, 1834. This performance and publication was aimed at reasserting his position as Utaemon III's successor and as the rival of Arashi Rikan II.

274a Nakamura Baika as Ono no Komachi

PLAY *Rokkasen sugata no saishiki* at the Kado Theatre; first month, 1834

Artist: Hokuei

Signature: Shunbaisai Hokuei ga

Publisher: Hon'ya Seishichi

Artist's seal: Shunbai

Ōban, colour woodblock with metallic pigment, from a set of six, 37.4 x 25.5 cm

Birmingham Museums and Art Gallery (570'29)

274d Nakamura Shikan II as Sōjō Henjō

PLAY *Rokkasen sugata no saishiki* at the Kado Theatre;
first month, 1834

Artist: Hokuei

Signature: Shunbaisai Hokuei ga

Publisher: Tenmaya Kihei

Seal: Shunbai

Oban, colour woodblock with metallic pigment,
from a set of six, 37.2 x 25.1 cm

Gerhard Pulverer Collection (Germany)

The remaining two designs from the six show
Shikan II as Bun'ya no Yasuhide and Shikan II as
Kisen Hōshi. Both are illustrated in Keyes and
Mizushima 1973, no. 47.

　See cats 38, 265 and 273 for other representations and more about this play.

**275 Fiftieth memorial for Nakamura
Tomijūrō I: Nakamura Tomijūrō II (Matsue III)
as Shirotae, Genzaemon's wife**

PLAY *Kaikei yuki no hachi no ki* at the Naka Theatre; ninth
month, 1837

Artist: Sadanobu

Signature: Hasegawa Sadanobu ga

Publisher: Hon'ya Seishichi

Ōban, colour woodblock with metallic pigment,
37.6 x 25.3 cm

Private Collection (UK)

Tomijūrō II is here presented as a superstar of
his generation, the equal of the legendary
Tomijūrō I who had died fifty years earlier. This
evocation of the acting lineage of the great
Tomijūrō I (Keishi) takes us right back to the era
of the beginning of Osaka actor prints. Matsue
III had succeeded to the name Tomijūrō II in
1833, most likely with the support of his
mentor, Utaemon III (Shikan). However, he was
only born in 1786, the year of Tomijūrō I's death,
and thus in fact had no direct connection with
his great predecessor.

　The print also records Tomijūrō II's celebrated
love of luxurious costumes. Such opulence would
lead to his expulsion from Osaka only a few years
later in 1842, during the Tenpō Reforms that
cracked down on actors' extravagant lifestyles
and closed many small theatres. There was also a
ban on actor prints that lasted for some five years
– until about 1847 – and dealt a severe blow to
the buoyancy of Kabuki culture.

275

276 Rojū leading a hand-clapping chant

Eleventh month, 1823

Artist: Kunihiro

Signature: Kōnantei Kunihiro ga

Publisher: Tenmaya Kihei

Ōban, colour woodblock with metallic pigment, 37.9 x 25.7 cm

Private Collection (UK)

Rojū of the Sasase fan club uses wooden clappers to lead ritual hand-clapping and chanting by club members. The chant was accompanied (*ai no te*) by the tune from the song *Yachiyo jishi*, often used in Kabuki. The occasion is the opening-of-the-season (*kaomise*) performance at the Naka Theatre in the eleventh month, 1823, the stage set with peonies and a red-lacquered railing for the performance of *Futatsu chōchō kuruwa nikki*. Earlier that year in the summer the arrival of a pair of male and female camels in Japan had created a popular sensation when put on show in the Kita-Shinchi area of north Osaka. The text relates this, and the new chant contains many comic puns on the word 'camel' (*rakuda*). Rojū has even had a costume made for the occasion with camels around the hem and his name embroidered into the fabric at the shoulders. Thus the fan-club leader takes to the stage to become star performer, and the artist Kunihiro awards him further celebrity status through the publication of an 'actor' print.

Matsudaira 1999, p. 18 discusses this rare print in more detail.

277 'Seki Sanjūrō from Edo joining the theatre troupe'
Edo Seki Sanjūrō zatsuki hikiai no zu

Twelfth month, 1826

Artist: Ashiyuki

Signature: Gigadō Ashiyuki ga

Publisher: Wataya Kihei (?)

Ōban, colour woodblock, 37.7 x 25.8 cm

Private Collection (UK)

Sanjūrō returned to Osaka in the twelfth month, 1826, after nineteen years away performing in Edo. He kneels and modestly bows to the fans

277

from the stage at the Kado Theatre, part of a ritual of welcoming an actor back to Osaka for the opening-of-the-season (*kaomise*) performance. This was when all the actors contracted to the troupe for the coming year were introduced. In his speech, quoted above, Sanjūrō thanks everyone and requests their continued patronage. A fan standing on the stage holds wooden clappers with which to lead the ritual hand-clapping and chanting. He and all the other fans wear matching costumes and headgear emblazoned with the name of the Sakura (Cherry) fan club ('cherry' is written with characters that mean 'king of flowers').

The print is discussed in detail in Matsudaira 1999, pp. 12–13.

278

279

278 Nakamura Karoku I returns to Osaka

Eleventh month, 1832

Artist: Hokuei

Signature: Shunkōsai Hokuei ga

Publisher: Hon'ya Seishichi

Ōban, colour woodblock, 36.3 x 25.0 cm

Hendrick Lühl Collection (Germany)

Nakamura Karoku I here returns to perform at the Naka Theatre in Osaka after five years away performing in Edo. He had performed at the Kado Theatre with Utaemon III in the eighth month of that year, but here he is contracted to the rival troupe of Arashi Rikan II. A female-role specialist (*onnagata*), he kneels in costume on the stage at the Naka Theatre, bows to the audience and introduces himself for the coming season. The text of the speech is quoted above. The fan standing on the stage wears the special headgear of the Sakura fan club, and is dressed in a colourful costume with a peony and stone bridge motif that relates to the Kabuki dance *Shakkyō* (Stone Bridge). He carries wooden clappers with which to lead ritual hand-clapping and chanting, and introduce Karoku.

This print and the phenomenon of the elaborate rituals of Osaka Kabuki fan clubs it represents are further discussed in Matsudaira 1999, pp. 12–13.

279 Iwai Shijaku and his 'servant' Yasuke

c. 1834

Artist: Hokuei

Signature: Shunbaisai Hokuei ga

Publisher: Hon'ya Seishichi (?)

Ōban, colour woodblock, 37.5 x 25.2 cm

National Museums of Scotland, Edinburgh (1877-745-35-8)

Immediately striking is the prominence given to the 'servant' (*ochobo*) Yasuke, who walks behind the Edo actor Shijaku carrying his sedge hat, and the relatively realistic manner in which his portrait is drawn. Matsudaira (1999, pp. 53–6) suggests that Yasuke must have been a patron who commissioned the artist Hokuei to immortalize his moment of glory with the famous actor Shijaku, who performed in Osaka from 1832 to 1835.

Ochobo was a term in Kyoto–Osaka pleasure quarters for girls of around thirteen or fourteen who served courtesans. Calling this grown man an *ochobo* would seem to imply that he is Shijaku's servant, perhaps even in a sexual sense.

280 Four amateurs performing skits (*niwaka*) as courtesans

c. 1835

Artist: Sadanobu

Signature: Ōju Hasegawa Sadanobu ga
('drawn by Hasegawa Sadanobu at special request')

Artist's seal: Tokuhei

Publisher: Tenmaya Kihei

Ōban, colour woodblock with metallic pigments, four-sheet print, each approx. 37.0 x 24.7 cm

Bodleian Library, Oxford University
(Nipponica 354-1/2/3/4)

Four Osaka men perform as grand, extravagantly dressed courtesans (*oiran*) from the Yoshiwara Quarter of Edo, in a Kabuki-style skit (*niwaka*). Their courtesan names – Nangyoku, Negoto (illustrated), Shinchō (fig. 2 above) and Sanki – appear in a round cartouche in the top corner of each print that represents *niwaka*, that is, double (*ni*) ring (*wa*) plus the written syllable *ka*. We can imagine that these four (and maybe others) rented a theatre for their special performance. It was common at this time for amateur performers of the theatrical arts of chanting (*gidayū*, *nagauta*, *tokiwazu*) and dance to have recitals in the grounds of temples or shrines open to the public, and even to charge fees, which were then donated (*kishin*) to the temple or shrine. The four have made the full 'cross-over' from patron to performer, and are now immortalized in print. The use of the term *ōju* (or *motome ni ōjite*, 'by special request') next to the artist's signature suggests that Sadanobu was specially commissioned to produce the set.

The padded surcoat (*uchikake*) worn by each performer has 'her' courtesan name woven into the hem. As attested by the texts above, the skits were full of low-level, puerile humour with lots of references to bodily functions. Another set of prints is known by Sadahiro that features three of these same fellows: Nangyoku, Shinchō and Sanki (Sumai 2001, no. 71). In this second set they perform different roles and the text is the dialogue between the three characters.

All four prints are illustrated in Matsudaira 1997(b), no. 175.

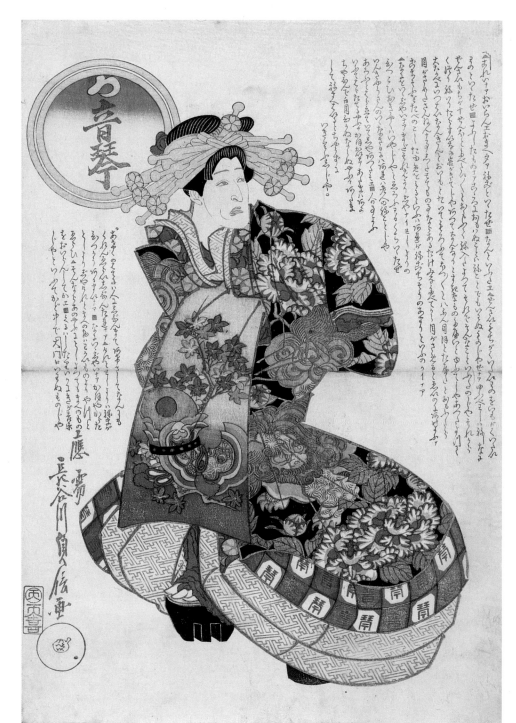

280

281

281 Edo strong man (right) versus Osaka strong man (left)

Third month, 1825

Artists: Yoshikuni (right) and Ashiyuki (left)

Signatures: Naniwa Yoshikuni ga ('Yoshikuni of Osaka'); motome ni ōjite Ashiyuki ga ('Ashiyuki by special request')

Seals: Yoshi (right), unread (left)

Publishers: Hon'ya Seishichi (right) and Wataya Kihei (left)

Ōban, colour woodblock, 36.6 x 24.8 cm (right), 36.6 x 24.9 cm (left)

National Museums of Scotland, Edinburgh (1887-745-45b.12-13)

A rare pair of prints that celebrates the winners of a competition for strong men to lift rice bales: the best from Edo (Kimura Yogorō, twenty-four years old, right) and the best from Osaka (Yaegaki Yatarō, left). Each gets his moment of fame. An inscription, top left on the right sheet, reads: 'A picture of the strong men who were a great hit and achieved great acclaim in the fields of Naniwa Shinchi in Osaka' (Ōsaka Naniwa Shinchi nogawa ni oite ō-atari dai-hyōban chikaramochi no zu).

A flybill has also survived which records this event. See Setsuyō kikan in Funakoshi 1926–30, vol. 6, pp. 313–22. Another print of Kimura Yogorō by Ashiyuki in this series is in Matsudaira (Kōnan), 1997(c), no. 339.

282

282 Sawamura Gennosuke II (Sōjūrō V) as Dote no Oroku (right) and Kataoka Ichizō I as Kimon no Kihei (left)

PLAY *Osome Hisamatsu ukina no yomiuri* at the Wakatayū Theatre (Osaka); third month, 1828

Artist: Kunihiro

Signature: Kunihiro ga

Publishers: Tenmaya Kihei (right) and Hon'ya Seishichi (left)

Ōban, colour woodblock, diptych, 37.5 x 25.8 cm (right), 37.9 x 26.0 cm (left)

Private Collection (UK)

The play was originally written by Tsuruya Nan-boku and performed at the Morita Theatre, Edo, in 1813, but it came to be more popular in Osaka than in Edo (at least until the late nine-teenth century). Oroku and Kihei are Edo low-lifers who extort money for a living, and Oroku

is one of the first 'bad woman' (*akuba, dokufu*) heroines in Kabuki. At this point in the play the pair are down on their luck and out of money. Previously they had worked in a samurai resi-dence, but were evicted when their clandestine affair was discovered. The text is from the char-acters' dialogue in the play. Imitating Kabuki declamation (*kowa-iro*) was a common hobby, so some purchasers of the print undoubtedly acted this out:

> Oroku: I used to work in the women's quarters at the Chiba residence and serve Lady Takekawa. She was always saying that she would get me married off to a nice, well-off fellow. I didn't listen to her. I pleaded that I already had something going with you, who worked for Mr Yachūda, and finally we had to flee together. We've been through all sorts of ups and downs since we ran off. It's been hard.

> Kihei: Now, now, take it easy. You know that it's best for us both if the master agrees with our plans. If we get into a real fix, I can always beg money from my master, Mr Yachūda. But he can be difficult to handle sometimes.

> Oroku: That may be so, but lately I hear you've been spending time with courtesans, drinking a lot, and gambling. You've always been a gambler, but it's no good. If you gamble too much, it'll get you in the end.

> Kihei: But if I just stick to a proper job, I won't be able to drink the best saké!

This is a good example of an artist featuring promising young stars from the 'middle the-atres' (*chū-shibai*, in this case the Wakatayū Theatre) and raising their stature by means of his prints. This was not the practice in Edo, where only actors in the top three theatres were depicted in prints.

BIBLIOGRAPHY

Reference should also be made to the extensive bibliography in Keyes and Mizushima 1973. For bibliographies of the writings of Matsudaira Susumu, see *Andon* nos 72–3, 2002; also Kitagawa 2002 (a).

Akama Ryō. *Edo no engekisho – Kabuki-hen*. Tokyo, Yagi Shoten, 2003

Akita Kiyoshi. *Kamigata-ban kabuki kankei ichimai-zuri kō*. Osaka, Seibundō, 1999

Aoki Shigeru. 'Sanse Utaemon no "seiha"'. *Ronshū kinsei bungaku 2: Kabuki*. Tokyo, Benseisha, 1991, pp. 16–92

Aoki Shigeru. 'Chū shibai saikō'. *Chikamatsu Kenkyūjo kiyō*, vol. 13, December 2002, pp. 23–31

Asano Shūgō. *Tōshūsai Sharaku (Artists' Japan* 11). Tokyo, Dōmeisha Shuppan, 1992

Asano Shūgō and Clark, Timothy. *The Passionate Art of Kitagawa Utamaro (d. 1806)*. London, British Museum Press and Tokyo, Asahi Shinbun, 1995

Azabu Bijutsu Kōgeikan, eds. *Shibai-e ni kabuki o miru – Honolulu Academy of Arts, James A. Michener Collection*. Tokyo, 1990

Brandon, James R., *et al. Studies in Kabuki*. Honolulu, University of Hawaii Press, 1978

Brandon, James R. and Leiter, Samuel L. *Kabuki Plays on Stage*, vols 1–4. Honolulu, University of Hawaii Press, 2002

Calza, Gian Carlo. *Ukiyoe: Il Mondo Fluttuante*. Milan, Palazzo Reale and Electa, 2004

Carpenter, John T. '"Twisted Poses": The *Kabuku* Aesthetic in Early Edo Genre Painting', in *Kazari: Decoration and Display in Japan, 15th–19th Centuries*, ed. Nicole Coolidge Rousmaniere. London, British Museum Press, 2002(a), pp. 42–9

Carpenter, John T. 'Edo actors in Osaka prints: *Surimono* by Ukiyo Utayoshi'. *Andon* 72–3, October 2002(b), pp. 95–101

Chiba-shi Bijutsukan, ed. *Edo no surimono – suijin-tachi no okurimono*. Chiba, 1999

Chiba-shi Bijutsukan, ed. *Chiba-shi Bijutsukan shozō ukiyo-e sakuhin sen*. Chiba, 2001

Clark, Timothy. 'Kunisada and Decadence', in *Modern Japanese Art and the West*, ed. Meiji Bijutsu-shi Gakkai. Tokyo, 1992(a), pp. 89–100

Clark, Timothy. *Ukiyo-e Paintings in the British Museum*. London, British Museum Press, 1992(b)

Clark, Timothy. 'Katsukawa Shunshō and the Revolution in Actor Portraiture', *Orientations*, June 1992(c), pp. 53–4

Clark, Timothy and Ueda Osamu. *The Actor's Image: Print Makers of the Katsukawa School*. Art Institute of Chicago and Princeton University Press, 1994

Clark, Timothy. 'Utamaro's Portraiture'. *Proceedings of The Japan Society (London)* 130, winter 1997, pp. 2–30

Clark, Timothy. 'Flowers of Yoshiwara: Iconography of the Courtesan in the Late

Edo Period', in *Kazari: Decoration and Display in Japan, 15th–19th Centuries*, ed. Nicole Coolidge Rousmaniere. London, British Museum Press, 2002, pp. 64–73

Clark, Timothy. 'Some Portraits of *Kyōka* Poets by Kitao Masanobu'. *Orientations*, February 2004, pp. 36–41

Clark, Timothy. 'Frilly Undergarments: Some Paintings by Hokusai's Pupils', in *Hokusai and His Age*, ed. John Carpenter. Amsterdam, Hotei Publishing, 2005, pp. 76–91

Daichō o Yomu Kai, ed. *Bakin no 'Yakusha meisho zue' o yomu*. Osaka, Izumi Shoin, 2001

Dōmoto Kansei. *Kamigata engekishi*. Tokyo, Shunyōdō, 1944

Dunn, Charles. 'Episodes in the career of the kabuki actor Nakamura Utaemon III, including his rivalry with Arashi Rikan I'. *Modern Asian Studies* 4, no. 4, 1984, p. 84

Dunn, Charles and Torigoe Bunzō. *The Actors' Analects*. New York, Columbia University Press, 1969

Earle, Ernst. *The Kabuki Theatre: Japan's Spectacular Drama*. London, Secker and Warburg, 1956

Engeki Hakubutsukan Yakusha-e Kenkyūkai, eds. *Zōho Kokon yakusha nigao-e taizen*. Tokyo, Waseda Daigaku Tsubouchi Hakushi Kinen Engeki Hakubutsukan, 1998

Enomoto Yūsai. 'Ryūkōsai-ha no kenkyū (Nagasawa Ingyō no hakken)'. *Ukiyo-e geijutsu* 8, December 1964, pp. 36–9

Fiorillo, John. 'Drama in the Surimono-style Prints of Hokuei'. *Impressions* 20, 1998, pp. 60–77

Fiorillo, John and Ujlaki, Peter. 'Ryūsai Shigeharu: "Quick change" dances in the Utaemon tradition'. *Andon* 72–3, October 2002, pp. 115–35

Forrer, Matthi. *Stars from the Stage in Osaka: Early 19th-century Japanese Kabuki Prints*. Bergeyk, Society for Japanese Arts, 1994

Funakoshi Seiichirō, ed. *Naniwa sōsho*, 17 vols. Osaka, Naniwa Sōsho Kankōkai, 1926–30

Funakoshi Seiichirō, ed. *Naniwa sōsho keiroku*. Osaka, Naniwa Sōsho Kankōkai, 1930

Geinōshi Kenkyūkai, ed. *Nihon shomin bunka shiryō shūsei*, vol. 14. Tokyo, Sanichi Shobō, 1975

Geinōshi Kenkyūkai, ed. *Nihon shomin bunka shiryō shūsei*, vol. 15. Tokyo, Sanichi Shobō, 1976

Genshoku ukiyo-e daihyakka jiten. 11 vols. Tokyo, Taishūkan, 1980–2

Gerstle, C. Andrew, ed. *Eighteenth-Century Japan: Culture and Society*. London, Curzon, 1989

Gerstle, C. Andrew. 'Amateurs and the theatre: The so-called demented art of *gidayū*'. *Senri Ethnological Studies* 40, 1995, pp. 37–57

Gerstle, C. Andrew. 'Representing Rivalry and Transition in Kabuki'. *Andon* 72–3, 2002, pp. 52–64

Gerstle, C. Andrew. 'Osaka Kabuki Actor Prints: Artists as Patrons', in *Masterful Illusions: Japanese Prints in the Anne van Biema Collection*, ed. Ann Yonemura. Washington, D.C., 2002

Gerstle, C. Andrew. 'Kabuki ni miru suta-no taikō to sedai keishō – nidaime Arashi Kichisaburō tai sandaime Nakamura Utaemon no baai'. *Kokugo Kokubun* 72, 3 March 2003(a), pp. 574–95

Gerstle, C. Andrew. 'The Culture of Play: Kabuki and the Production of Texts'. *Bulletin of SOAS* 66, no. 3, 2003(b), pp. 358–79

Gidayū nenpyō, 6 vols. Tokyo, Yagi Shoten 1979–90

Gondō Yoshikazu. 'Kamigata kabuki no suitai – sono geiin ni tsuite no ichi kōsatsu'. *Bungaku* 55, 4 April 1987, pp. 212–20

Gookin, Frederick W. 'A Master Artist of Old Japan, Katsukawa Shunshō'. Chicago, 1931 [mimeographed]

Gotō Kenji. *Haikai surimono zufu* (*Nihon shoshigaku taikei*, vol. 66). Tokyo, Seishōdō, 1992

Grove Art Online 2004

Gunji Masakatsu. *Kabuki – yōshiki to denshō*. Tokyo, Gakugei Shorin, 1976

Haga Noboru. 'Osaka kabuki no shakaiteki kiban – shakai hendō to bunka ninaosha to no kanren o chūshin ni shite', in *Kinsei shakai no seiritsu to hakai*, eds Osaka Rekishi Gakkai. Tokyo, Yoshikawa Kōbunkan, 1976, pp. 37–80

Hájek, Lubor. *Holzschnitte aus Kamigata: Hirosada*. Prague, Artia, 1959

Hamada Giichirō, ed. *Ōta Nanpo zenshū*. 20 vols. Tokyo, Iwanami Shoten, 1987–90

Hamada Keisuke. 'Kokkeibon to shite no gekisho'. *Bunkyō kokubungaku* 24, December 1989, pp. 74–90

Hanyū Noriko. 'Arashi Rikan to Maruha kyōka – *Tsukinami no gaen* e no sanka'. *Naruo setsurin* 11, December 2003, pp. 1–11

Hanyū Noriko. 'Ryūkōsai, Shunchōsai, Tōkei to kyōka – Maruha kyōka saakuru e no sanka'. *Mukogawa kokubun* 63, March 2004, pp. 28–37

Haruyama Takematsu. 'Ryūkōsai to Shōkōsai – Naniwa nishiki-e no kenkyū'. *Tōyō bijutsu* 12, July 1931, pp. 1–42

Hattori Yukio, ed. *Shibai gakuya zue* (*Kabuki no bunken*, vol. 5). Tokyo, Kokuritsu Gekijō, n.d.

Hattori Yukio, ed. *Shibai kinmō zui* (*Kabuki no bunken*, vol. 3). Tokyo, Kokuritsu Gekijō, 1969

Hattori Yukio, ed. *Ukan sandai zue* (*Kabuki no bunken*, vol. 4). Tokyo, Kokuritsu Gekijō, 1971

Hattori Yukio. *Edo no shibai-e o yomu*. Tokyo, Kōdansha, 1993

Hayashi Yoshikazu. 'Shini-e kō (1) – Shini-e no hasseiki to sono tenkai'. *Ukiyo-e geijutsu* 45, August 1975(a), pp. 3–15

Hayashi Yoshikazu. 'Shini-e kō (2) – Hachidaime Ichikawa Danjūrō seppuku jiken'. *Ukiyo-e geijutsu* 46, November 1975(b), pp. 3–21

Herwig, Arendie and Henk J. *Heroes of the Kabuki Stage*. Amsterdam, Hotei Publishing, 2004

Hida Kōzō. *Kamigata gakugeishi sōkō*. Tokyo, Seishōdō Shoten, 1988

Hida Kōzō. 'Nishizawa Ippō harikomi-chō'. *Engeki kenkyū* 21, March 1997, pp. 137–52

Hino Tatsuo. *Edojin to yutopia*. Tokyo, Asahi Shinbunsha, 1977

Hizō ukiyo-e taikan, ed. Narazaki Muneshige. 13 vols. Tokyo, Kōdansha, 1987–90

Ihara Toshirō. *Nihon engekishi*. Tokyo, Waseda Daigaku Shuppanbu, 1904

Ihara Toshirō. *Kinsei Nihon engekishi*. Tokyo, Waseda Daigaku Shuppanbu, 1913

Iijima Kyoshin. *Katsushika Hokusai den*. 2 vols. Tokyo, Hōsūkaku, 1893

Iizuka Tomoichirō. *Kabuki saiken*. Tokyo, Daiichi Shobō, 1926

Ikeda Bunko, ed. *Shibai banzuke mokuroku*, vol. 1. Osaka, 1981

Ikeda Bunko, ed. *Shibai banzuke mokuroku*, vol. 2. Osaka, 1984(a).

Ikeda Bunko, ed. *Kamigata yakusha-e shūsei*, vol. 1. Osaka, 1997

Ikeda Bunko, ed. *Kamigata yakusha-e shūsei*, vol. 2. Osaka, 1998

Ikeda Bunko, ed. *Shibai banzuke mokuroku* vol. 3. Osaka, 1999

Ikeda Bunko, ed. *Kamigata yakusha-e shūsei*, vol. 3. Osaka, 2001

Ikeda Bunko, ed. *Kappazuri no sekai*. Osaka, 2002

Ikeda Bunko, ed. *Kamigata yakusha-e shūsei*, vol. 4. Osaka, 2003

Ishii Kendō. *Nishiki-e no hori to suri*. Kyoto, Unsōdō, 1929

Itsuō Bijutsukan and Kakimori Bunko, eds. *Buson – botsugo 220-nen*. Kyoto, Shibunkaku, 2003

Iwasaki Haruko. 'The World of Gesaku: Playful Writers of Late Eighteenth Century Japan'. PhD thesis, Harvard University, May 1984

Iwata Hideyuki. 'Meiji no ko-shashin 1–13'. *Kabuki – kenkyū to hihyō* 18–30, 1996–2003

Iwata Hideyuki. 'Yakusha-e nendai kōshō ni okeru mondaiten'. *Ikeda Bunko kanpō* 12, April 1998(a), pp. 9–11

Iwata Hideyuki. 'Yakusha-e no ryūsei (1) – Edo-e', in *Kabuki bunka no shosō* (*Iwanami kōza: Kabuki, Bunraku* no. 4), ed. Torigoe Bunzō. Tokyo, Iwanami Shoten, 1998(b), pp. 145–72

Iwata Hideyuki. '*Mitate* in Actor Prints: Anticipation and Juxtaposition'. *Atomi-Gakuen Joshi-Daigaku kokubun-gakkahō* 30, March 2002, pp. 134–18

Izzard, Sebastian. 'Kunisada's Journey to Osaka', *Ukiyo-e geijutsu* 59, 1978, pp. i–iii

Izzard, Sebastian. *Kunisada's World*. New York, Japan Society, 1993

Kabuki hyōbanki shūsei (1st series). 11 vols. Tokyo, Iwanami Shoten, 1972–7

Kabuki hyōbanki shūsei, daini-ki (2nd series). 11 vols. Tokyo, Iwanami Shoten, 1987–95

Kabuki nenpyō, ed. Ihara Tōshirō. 8 vols. Tokyo, Iwanami Shoten, 1956–63

Kaguraoka Yōko. 'Kamigata kabuki shiryō ten – Sandaime Utaemon no shūhen' [pamphlet]. *Engeki Hakubutsukan* 75, March 1996

Kaguraoka Yōko, 'Kankyaku no shiten (4) – hiiki to kankyaku', in *Kabuki bunka no shosō* (*Iwanami kōza: Kabuki, Bunraku no. 4*), ed. Torigoe Bunzō. Tokyo, Iwanami Shoten, 1998, pp. 121–44

Kaguraoka Yōko. 'Kandai-bon *Kyota kyakushokujō* ni tsuite'. *Kokubungaku* 78, March 1999(a), pp. 287–99

Kaguraoka Yōko. 'Shikan-jō seiritsu to sono shūhen'. *Geinōshi kenkyū* 145, April 1999(b), pp. 1–13

Kaguraoka Yōko. 'Teuchi no fukkatsu'. *Geinō konwa* 12, May 1999(c), pp. 74–82

Kaguraoka Yōko. 'An'ei-ki no hiiki renchū'. *Bungaku* 1, no. 5, September–October 2000(a), pp. 124–33

Kaguraoka Yōko. 'Sandaime Utaemon hiiki no giga surimono'. *Kokubungaku* 81, November 2000(b), pp. 99–109

Kaguraoka Yōko. 'Sandaime Utaemon hiiki to shuppan'. *Kabuki – kenkyū to hihyō* 26, December 2000(c), pp. 150–9

Kaguraoka Yōko. 'Sandaime Utaemon hiiki no harikomichō'. *Geinōshi kenkyū* 153, April 2001, pp. 1–10

Kaguraoka Yōko. *Kabuki bunka no kyōju to tenkai – kankyaku to gekijō no naigai*. Tokyo, Yagi Shoten, 2002

Kaguraoka Yōko. 'Shibai no uwasa, yakusha no kansen', in *Edo bunka to sabukarucha*, ed. Watanabe Kenji. Tokyo, Shibundō, 2005, pp. 169–76

Kakimori Bunko, ed. *Haikai ichimai-zuri*. Ikeda, Kakimori Bunko, 1991

Kano Kaian. *Kyōka jinmei jiten*. 1928, repr. Tokyo, Shinsei Seihon Kabushikigaisha, 1978

Kansai Daigaku Toshokan, ed. *Osaka bungei shoqaten: Kinsei kara kindai e*. Osaka, 1994

Kansai Daigaku Toshokan, ed. *Ōsaka gadan mokuroku*. Osaka, 1997

Kasuya Hiroki and Kabuki Nenpyō Kenkyūkai, eds. *Nihon-daigaku Sōgō Gakujutsu Jōhō Sentā shozō DVD-ban Kabuki banzuke shūsei* [DVD]. Tokyo, Yagi shoten, 2004

Katō Sadahiko. 'Haikai "surimono" jijō – bunseki Kamigata o chūshin ni'. *Edo bungaku* 16, October 1996, pp. 64–82

Kawai Masumi. 'E-iri nehon *Yakusha hama no masago* o megutte'. *Osaka Joshidai bungaku* 54, 2003, pp. 12–24

Keyes, Roger S. and Mizushima, Keiko. *The Theatrical World of Osaka Prints. A Collection of Eighteenth and Nineteenth Century Japanese Woodblock Prints in the*

Philadelphia Museum of Art. Philadelphia Museum of Art, 1973

Keyes, Roger S., ed. *Hirosada, Osaka Printmaker*. Long Beach, The University Art Museum, 1984(a)

Keyes, Roger. *Japanese Woodblock Prints: A Catalogue of the Mary A. Ainsworth Collection*. Oberlin, OH, Allen Memorial Art Museum, 1984(b)

Keyes, Roger. 'Tani Seikō and his circle'. *Andon* 72–3, October 2002, pp. 12–26

Keyes, Roger. 'Kyōka surimono no kinjitō'. *Siren* (Bulletin of the Chiba City Museum of Art) 5, March 2002, pp. 7–21

Kikuchi Akira. 'Kabuki no ema'. *Ukiyo-e geijutsu* 89, April 1987, pp. 8–12

Kikuchi Sadao. 'Shodai Utagawa Toyokuni ni tsuite', in *Ukiyo-e shūka*, vol. 15. Tokyo, Shūeisha, 1980, pp. 204–14

Kikuchi Sadao. *Toyokuni* (*Ukiyo-e hakka*, vol. 6). Tokyo, Heibonsha, 1985

Kinsei Nihon fūzoku ehonshū. Tokyo: Rinsen Shoten, 1979–81

Kinryūzan Sensōji, ed. *Ema zuroku*, Tokyo, 1978

Kira Sueo. 'Tashoku-zuri no rekishi to haikai ichimai-zuri o megutte'. *Edo bungaku* 25, June 2002(a), pp. 1–5

Kira Sueo. 'Saitanchō, e-baisho, tashoku-zuri e-baisho'. *Edo bungaku* 25, June 2002(b), pp. 29–59

Kishi Fumikazu. 'Kamigata yakusha-e kō – "Suijin" to shite no nigao eshi'. *Kamigata bijutsu no 19-seiki*. Osaka Daigaku bungakubu, 1999, pp. 5–17

Kitagawa Hiroko. 'Osaka no homekotoba'. *Ikeda Bunko kanpō* 3, April 1993(a), pp. 9–10

Kitagawa Hiroko. 'Ikeda Bunko shozō Osaka no homekotoba nishu'. *Engeki Kenkyūkai kaihō* 19, June 1993(b)

Kitagawa Hiroko. 'Tenmei-ki no Naka no shibai no ezukushi'. *Ikeda Bunko kanpō* 4, October 1993(c), pp. 16–18

Kitagawa Hiroko. 'Yakusha ehon no nagare'. *Ukiyo-e geijutsu* 114, January 1995(a), pp. 3–9

Kitagawa Hiroko. 'Nishiki-e ni miru sandaime Bandō Mitsugorō no jōhan'. *Ikeda Bunko kanpō* 8, October 1995(b), pp. 21–3

Kitagawa Hiroko. 'Arashi Kichisaburō to Nakamura Utaemon no wakai'. *Ikeda Bunko kanpō* 12, April 1998, pp. 14–16

Kitagawa Hiroko. 'Kamigata yakusha-e *Sono kokonoe saishiki-zakura* – Hisorufu [J.H. Gisolf] korekushon kara'. *Ikeda Bunko kanpō* 15, October 1999(a), pp. 6–8

Kitagawa Hiroko. 'Kamigata kabuki ni okeru Kyō to Ōsaka – yakusha-e o tegakari toshite'. *Kōnan bungaku* 46, March, 1999(b)

Kitagawa Hiroko. 'Shinshū Kamigata yakusha-e – Hokuei ga *Kinmon gosan no kiri* – hanmoto Watahei no arata naru kokoromi'. *Ikeda Bunko kanpō* 16, April 2000, pp. 14–16

Kitagawa Hiroko. 'Matsudaira Susumu Sensei ryaku nenpu – gyōseki mokuroku'. *Chikamatsu Kenkyūjo kiyō* 12, March 2002(a), pp. 43–56

Kitagawa Hiroko. 'Notes on the *sumizuri* actor prints of Kyoto'. *Andon* 72–3, October 2002(b), pp. 27–33

Kitagawa Hiroko. 'Kamigata ni okeru yakusha-e shuppan no shosō'. *Ukiyo-e geijutsu* 146, 2003, pp. 58–68

Kokuritsu Gekijō (Chōsa Yōseibu Shiryōka), eds. *Kamigata shibai-e ten zuroku – Miyako, Osaka no meiyū-tachi, Ikeda Bunko shozō*. Tokyo, 1985

Kokuritsu Gekijō (Chōsa Yōseibu Shiryōka), eds. *Shibai hanga tō zuroku*. 11 vols. Tokyo, 1979–2000

Kokuritsu Gekijō (Geinō Chōsa-shitsu), ed. *Kabuki haiyū myōseki binran – dai niji shūtei-ban*. Tokyo, Nihon Geijutsu Bunka Shinkōkai, 1998

Kominz, Laurence R. *The Stars who Created Kabuki: Their Lives, Loves and Legacy*. Tokyo, Kōdansha, 1997

Kondo, Eiko. *Protagonisti del Palcoscenico di Osaka*. Bologna, Centro Studi d'Arte Extremo-Orientale, 2001

Kunstmuseum Düsseldorf, eds. *Die Osaka Meister: Japanische Farbholzschnitte des 19. Jahrhunderts*. Düsseldorf, Kunstmuseum, 1966

Kuroda Genji. *Kamigata-e ichiran*. Kyoto, Satō Shōtarō Shōten, 1929

Kyoto Bunka Hakubutsukan, ed. *Miyako no kabuki ten*. Kyoto, 1991

Lefebvre, Henri, trans. Donald Nicholson-Smith. *The Production of Space*. Oxford, Blackwells, 1991

Leiter, S. ed. *Kabuki Reader: History and Performance*. Armonk NY, M.E. Sharpe, 2002

Lühl, Hendrick. *Helden, Schurken, Kurtisanen: Das Japanischer Kabukitheater des 19. Jahrhunderts in Holzschitten der Osaka Meister*. Unna, Kreis Unna, n.d.

Lühl, Hendrick. *Osaka-Holzschnitte*. Dortmund, 1982

Lühl, Hendrick. *Wellenblumen: Theater-Holzschnitte aus Osaka*. Dusseldorf, 1998

Lühl, Hendrick. '*Ireki* in Osaka actor prints'. *Andon* 72–3, October 2002, pp. 65–94

Masukawa Kōichi. *Sugoroku II*. Tokyo, Hōsei Daigaku Shuppankyoku, 1995

Matsudaira Susumu. 'Shunkōsai Hokushū – Kamigata no yakusha-e (1)'. *Baika Joshi Daigaku bungakubu kiyō* 4, December 1968, pp. 65–112

Matsudaira Susumu. 'Gigadō Ashiyuki – Kamigata no yakusha-e (2)'. *Kansei Daigaku kokubungaku* 43, March 1969(a), pp. 29–44

Matsudaira Susumu. 'Shunbaisai Hokuei – Kamigata no yakusha-e (3). *Baika Joshi Daigaku bungakubu kiyō* 5, December 1969(b), pp. 63–106

Matsudaira Susumu. 'Ganjōsai Kunihiro – Kamigata no yakusha-e (4). *Osaka no kenkyū* 5, August 1970(a), pp. 33–69

Matsudaira Susumu. 'Jukōdō Yoshikuni – Kamigata no yakusha-e (5)'. *Baika Joshi Daigaku bungakubu kiyō* 7, December 1970(b), pp. 1–31

Matsudaira Susumu. 'Kamigata ukiyo-e' in *Edo jidai zushi* vol. 3: *Osaka*. Tokyo, Chikuma Shobō, 1976

Matsudaira Susumu. 'Ryūsai Shigeharu – Kamigata no yakusha-e (6). *Baika Joshi Daigaku bungakubu kiyō* 13, February 1977(a), pp. 55–98

Matsudaira Susumu. 'Kamigata yakusha-e ni miru nisei Arashi Rikan no ninki – Dōtonbori 1822–1837'. *Geinōshi kenkyū* 57, April 1977(b), pp. 20–35

Matsudaira Susumu. 'Hiiki renchū ni tsuite – Dōtonbori 1789–1829'. *Kinsei bungei* 30, March 1979, pp. 70–80

Matsudaira Susumu, ed. *Hokushū to Toyokuni – Kamigata Edo yakusha-e meishō ten*. Osaka, Ikeda Bunko, 1983

Matsudaira Susumu. *Kamigata yakusha-e ten – Bakufu no meishō Hirosada*. Osaka, Ikeda Bunko, 1984(a)

Matsudaira Susumu. 'Hiiki renchū (Theatre Fan Clubs) in Osaka in the Early Nineteenth Century'. *Modern Asian Studies* 18, no.4, 1984(b), pp. 699–709

Matudaira Susumu. 'Kabuki Theatre in Osaka and the Tenpō Reforms', in *Hirosada: Osaka Printmaker*, ed. Roger S. Keyes. Long Beach, The University Art Museum, California State University, 1984(c), pp. 26–31

Matsudaira Susumu. *Kamigata shibai-e ten zuroku*. Tokyo, Kokuritsu Gekijō, 1985

Matsudaira Susumu. 'Chū shibai no yakusha-e'. *Kabuki – kenkyū to hihyō* 4, December 1989

Matsudaira Susumu. 'Kamigata yakusha-e no hankei (fu, hosoban mokuroku)'. *Kōnan kokubun* 37, 1990(?)

Matsudaira Susumu. 'Kamigata yakusha-e no shoki'. *Kokugo to kokubungaku* 68, June 1991, pp. 1–14

Matsudaira Susumu. 'Shunkin ga Kamigata yakusha-e nimai-tsuzuki'. *Ikeda Bunko kanpō* 1, April 1992, pp. 17–18

Matsudaira Susumu. 'Nakamura Sankō shūmei surimono ni tsuite'. *Ikeda Bunko kanpō* 3, April 1993, pp. 15–16

Matsudaira Susumu. 'Dai'ei Hakubutsukan shinshū Kamigata yakusha-e jō ni tsuite'. *Kōnan Joshi Daigaku kenkyū kiyō* 30, March 1994(a), pp. 23–44

Matsudaira Susumu. 'Kamigata yakusha-e shuppan no ichi sokumen – Bunsei yonen Arashi Kichisaburō no baai'. *Kabuki – kenkyū to hihyō* 14, December 1994(b), pp. 16–26

Matsudaira Susumu. 'Kamigata shibai hiiki to yakusha-e'. *Kōnan Joshi Daigaku kenkyū kiyō* 32, 1995(a), pp. 1–24

Matsudaira Susumu. 'Jūdai no ninki yakusha Nakamura Tamashichi'. *Ikeda Bunko kanpō* 8, October 1995(b), pp. 18–20

Matsudaira Susumu, ed. *Zenki kamigata-e (jō) – shibai-e zuroku* 4. Tokyo, Tsubouchi Memorial Theatre Museum, Waseda University, 1995(c)

Matsudaira Susumu, ed. *Zenki kamigata-e (ge) – shibai-e zuroku* 5. Tokyo, Tsubouchi Memorial Theatre Museum, Waseda University, 1995(d)

Matsudaira Susumu. 'Kimura Mokurō to Shikanjō seiritsu no haikei', in Kobayashi Tadashi ed., *Nikuhitsu ukiyo-e taikan*, vol. 10. Tokyo, Kōdansha, 1995(e), pp. 240–5

Matsudaira Susumu. 'Hokusai to Kamigata ukiyo-e'. *Hokusai kenkyū* 21, September 1996(a), pp. 5–30

Matsudaira Susumu. 'Kamigata shibai hiiki to yakusha-e'. *Kōnan Joshi Daigaku kenkyū kiyō* 32, March, 1996(b)

Matsudaira Susumu, ed. *Kōki Kamigata-e – shibai-e zuroku* 6. Tokyo, Tsubouchi Memorial Theatre Museum, Waseda University, 1997(a)

Matsudaira Susumu. *Shodai Hasegawa Sadanobu hanga sakuhin ichiran*. Osaka, Izumi Shoin, 1997(b)

Matsudaira Susumu. *Kōnan Joshi Daigaku Toshokan shozō Kamigata nishiki-e zuroku*. Kōbe, Kōnan Joshi Daigaku, 1997(c)

Matsudaira Susumu. 'Kappazuri no yakusha-e ni tsuite'. *Ikeda Bunko kanpō* 11, October 1997(d)

Matsudaira Susumu. 'Yakusha-e no ryūsei (2) – Kamigata-e', in *Kabuki bunka no shosō* (*Iwanami kōza: Kabuki, Bunraku* no. 4), ed. Torigoe Bunzō. Tokyo, Iwanami Shoten, 1998(a), pp. 173–94

Matsudaira Susumu. 'Tenpō kaikaku igo no Kamigata-e no mondaiten'. *Ikeda Bunko kanpō* 10, April 1998(b), pp. 15–17

Matsudaira Susumu. *Kamigata ukiyo-e no saihakken*. Tokyo, Kōdansha, 1999

Matsudaira Susumu. *Kamigata ukiyo-e no sekai*. Osaka, Izumi Shoin, 2000

Matsudaira Susumu and Nagata Seiji. 'Taidan – Kamigata-e ni tsuite'. *Nihon no ukiyo-e bijutsukan*, vol. 3. Tokyo, Kadokawa Shoten, 1996, pp. 154–61

Matsuyama Kaoru. 'Ehon butai ōgi ni tsuite'. *Engeki kenkyū* 15, March 1991, pp. 95–120

Matsuzaki Hitoshi. '*Shinpan yakusha homekotoba* – ei'in, honkoku to chūkai'. *Nihon bungaku kenkyū* 27, November 1991

Miyoshi Teiji. *Osaka jinbutsu jiten*. Osaka, Seibundō, 2000

Mizuta Kayano. 'Kamigata yakusha-e kenkyū 1989–1999'. *Geinōshi kenkyū* 145, April 1999

Mori Senzō, *et al.*, eds. '*Ochiba no shita-gusa* (1827)', in *Zoku Nihon zuihitsu taisei*, vol. 9. Tokyo, Yoshikawa Kōbunkan, 1980, pp. 89–93

Moriya Takeshi. 'Kinsei no chōnin to yūgei'. *Rekishi kōron* 59, no. 10, October 1980

Moriya Takeshi. *Genroku bunka – yūgei, akusho, shibai*, Tokyo, Kōbundō, 1987

Morris, Mark. 'Group Portrait with Artist: Yosa Buson and His Patrons', in *Eighteenth-Century Japan: Culture and Society*, ed. C. Andrew Gerstle. London, Curzon, 1989, pp. 87–105

Munemasa Isoo and Asakura Haruhiko, eds. *Kyoto shorin nakama kiroku*. (*Shoshi shomoku shiriizu* 5) 6 vols. Tokyo, Yumani Shobō, 1977–80

Mutō Junko. 'Torii-ha no yakusha nigao – Torii Kiyoshige ni chūmoku shite', in *Ukiyo-e no genzai*, ed. Yamaguchi Keizaburō. Tokyo, Bensei Shuppan, 1999, pp. 71–97

Nagatomo Chiyoji. 'Bakufu Osaka no bunka saron'. *Bungaku* 1, no. 5, September–October 2000, pp. 144–8

Nagatomo Chiyoji. *Edo jidai no shomotsu to dokusha*. Tokyo, Tokyodō Shuppan, 2001

Nakade, Akifumi. *Watakushi no kamigata-e monogatari kappazuri hen*. Osaka, Nakao Shōsendō, 2003

Nakade Akifuki and Ujlaki, Peter. 'A brief overview of Kamigata stencil prints'. *Andon* 72–3, October 2002, pp. 34–51

Nakamura Nakazō (III). *Temae miso*, ed. Gunji Masakatsu. Tokyo, Seiabō, 1969

Nakano Mitsutoshi. 'Higashiyama Rōbaikutsu shujin Doran – Kaseiki ichi kyōshin no fūryū seikatsu' in *Edo bungaku kenkyū*, ed. Jinbo Kazuya. Tokyo, Shintensha, 1993, pp. 582–600

Nakano Mitsutoshi. *Shoshigaku kōgi Edo no hanpon*. Tokyo, Iwanami Shoten, 1995

Nakano Mitsutoshi. 'Hōreki-Meiwa no Kamigata'. *Bungaku* 1, no. 5, September–October 2000, pp. 91–3

Nakao Chōken. *Kinsei itsujin gashi*, in *Nihon kaigaron taisei*, ed. Kimura Shigekazu, vol. 10. Tokyo, Perikansha, 1998

Nakauchi Chōji and Tamura Nishio, eds. *Nihon ongyoku zenshū*, vol. 3: *Kiyomoto zenshū*. Tokyo, Nihon Ongyoku Zenshū Kankōkai, 1928

Nakayama Mikio. *Kabuki-e no sekai*. Tokyo, Tokyo Shoseki, 1995

Newland, Amy Reigle. *Time Present and Time Past, Images of a Forgotten Master: Toyohara Kunichika 1835–1900*. Leiden, Hotei Publishing, 1999

Newland, Amy Reigle, ed. *The Commercial and Cultural Climate of Japanese Printmaking*. Amsterdam, Hotei, 2004

Nihon Hōsō Kyōkai, eds. *Engeki gedai yōran*. Tokyo, 1971

Nihon Keizai Shinbun (Osaka Honsha Jigyōbu), eds. *Kamigata ukiyo-e nihyakunen ten*. Osaka, 1975

Nihon koten bungaku daijiten. 6 vols. Tokyo, Iwanami Shoten, 1983–5

Nihon Koten Bungakukai, eds. *E-iri haisho shū* (*Nihon koten bungaku ei'in sōkan*, vol. 31). Tokyo, Kichōbon Kankōkai, 1986

Nikuhitsu ukiyoe taikan. 10 vols. Tokyo, Kōdansha, 1994–6

Nishijima Atsuya. *Kinsei kamigata kyōka no kenkyū* (*Kenkyū sōsho*, vol. 90). Osaka, Izumi Shoin, 1990

Nishizawa Ippō. *Denki sakusho – kyōgen sakusho* (*Shin gunsho ruiju* series, vol. 3). Tokyo, Kokusho Kankōkai, 1906

Nojima Jusaburō, ed. *Kabuki jinmei jiten*. Tokyo, Nichigai Associates, 1988

Noma Kōshin, ed. *Kenkadō nikki, honkoku-hen*. Osaka, Kenkadō Nikki Kankōkai, 1972

O'Connell, Sheila. *London 1753*. London, British Museum Press, 2003

Ogata Tsutomu. *Za no bungaku*. Tokyo, Kadokawa Shoten, 1973

Ogata Tsutomu, eds. *Haibungaku daijiten*. Tokyo, Kadokawa Shoten, 1995

Ogawa Kendō. 'Chirizuka monogatari', in *Enseki jisshu*, ed. Ichijima Kenkichi, vol. 1. Tokyo, Naigai Insatsu, 1907

Ogita Kiyoshi. 'Shikan setsuyō hyakugi-tsū kō'. *Baika Joshi Daigaku bungakubu kiyō* 27, December 1992, pp. 47–87

Ogita Kiyoshi. 'Kieta shūmei – Meijin sekisan wa yondaime Utaemon?' *Osaka geinō konwa kai*, December 1993, pp. 63–8

Ogita Kiyoshi. 'Sandaime Utaemon no "kodomo"'. *Ukiyo-e geijutsu* 113, 1994, pp. 12–13

Ogita Kiyoshi. 'Kyoto kaomise no nigiwai – Shikan, Rikan no jidai kara'. *Geinōshi kenkyū* 130, July 1995, pp. 25–46

Ogita Kiyoshi. 'Makimura Shiyō-shi no Shikan-kō shiryō ni tsuite'. *Osaka geinō konwa kai*, May 1996, pp. 55–62

Ogita Kiyoshi. *Kamigata kabuki kankei ichimai-zuri kō*. Osaka, Seibundō, 1999(a)

Ogita Kiyoshi. '*Shikan setsuyō hyakugi-tsū* – chūshaku (1)'. *Baika Joshi Daigaku bungakubu kiyō* 33, December 1999(b), pp. 25–47

Ogita Kiyoshi. 'Jitsuyō-sekken seishin to tomo ni – kinsei kōki Osaka shuppan bunka no hito-tokushitsu'. *Bungaku* 1, no. 5, September–October 2000(a), pp. 114–23

Ogita Kiyoshi. '*Shikan setsuyō hyakugi-tsū* – chūshaku (3)'. *Baika Joshi Daigaku bungakubu kiyō* 34, December 2000(b), pp. 69–86

Ogita Kiyoshi. '*Shikan setsuyō hyakugi-tsū* – chūshaku (2)', in *Maeda Tomiyoshi sensei taikan kinen ronshū – Nihongo Nihon bungaku no kenkyū*. Ōtsu, 2001(a), pp. 89–98

Ogita Kiyoshi. '*Shikan setsuyō hyakugi-tsū* – chūshaku (4)'. *Baika Joshi Daigaku bungakubu kiyō* 35, December 2001(b), pp. 65–85

Ogita Kiyoshi. '(*Shōsan gagen*) Rikanjō ni tsuite', *Chikamatsu Kenkyūjo kiyō* 12, March 2002, pp. 9–26

Okamoto Masaru. 'Aichi Kyōiku Daigaku zō no haikai ichimai-zuri'. *Edo bungaku* 25, June 2002, pp. 60–79

Ōkubo Jun'ichirō, 'Sansei Toyokuni bannen no shokan to yakusha ōkubi-e'. *Museum* 478, January 1991, pp. 25–39

Osaka Furitsu Nakanoshima Toshokan, eds. *Osaka hon'ya nakama kiroku*. 18 vols. Osaka, 1975–93

Osakajō Tenshukaku, eds. *Nishiki-e ni miru Naniwa fūbutsu-shi – Shodai Hasegawa Sadanobu botsugo 100 nen kinen*. Osaka, 1980

Osakajō Tenshukaku, eds. *Nanki korekushon sōmokuroku*, 2 vols. Osaka, 1982, 1992

Osaka Shiritsu Bijutsukan, eds. *Kinsei Ōsaka gadan*. Kyoto, Dōhōsha, 1983

Osaka Tosho Shuppangyō Kumiai, eds. *Kyōhō igo Osaka shuppan shoseki mokuroku*. Osaka, 1936

Ōtani Tokuzō ed. *Kinsei Osaka geibun sōdan*. Osaka, Osaka Geibun Kai, 1973

Riccar Art Museum, eds. *Katsukawa-ha no yakusha-e ten*. Tokyo, 1992

Royal Academy of Arts, eds. *The Dawn of the Floating World, 1650–1765: Early Ukiyo-e Treasures from the Museum of Fine Arts, Boston*. London, 2001

Sasaki Jōhei. 'Ōkyo and the Maruyama-Shijō School', in *Ōkyo and the Maruyama-Shijō School of Japanese Painting*, eds St Louis Art Museum, St Louis, 1980

Sasaki Jōhei and Sasaki Masako. *Maruyama Ōkyo kenkyū*. 2 vols. Tokyo, Chūō Kōron, 1996

Schwab, Dean J. *Osaka Prints*. New York, Rizzoli International Publications, 1989

Shindō Shigeru. *Gototei Kunisada – yakusha-e no sekai*. Tokyo, Gurafikku-sha, 1993

Shindō Shigeru. 'Edo Toyokuni hitsu sandaime Nakamura Utaemon'. *Ikeda Bunko kanpō* 6, October 1994, pp. 6–8

Shindō Shigeru. 'Edo Toyokuni hitsu sandaime Nakamura Utaemon (hoi)'. *Ikeda Bunko kanpō* 9, April 1996, pp. 14–16

Shiomura Tsutomu. 'Aru kinsei Osakajin no shōgai keihi keisan'. *Bungaku* 1, no. 5, September–October 2000, pp. 105–13

Shirane, Haruo. *Traces of Dreams: Landscape, Cultural Memory, and the Poetry of Bashō*. New York, Columbia University Press, 1998

Shitamura Naoya, ed. *Kabuki jiten*. Tokyo, Heibonsha, 1983

Smith, Henry D. (II). *Kiyochika – Artist of Meiji Japan*. Santa Barbara Museum of Art, 1988

Sotheby's (London). *Catalogue of Highly Important Japanese Prints, Illustrated Books and Drawings, from the Henri Vever Collection*, part 1 (auction cat.). 1974

Sotheby's (London). *Kabuki in Japanese Prints from the Collection of the Late Prof. H.R. Kühne* (auction cat). 11 June 1993

Sumai Museum, eds. *Kamigata yakusha-e no sekai*. Osaka, 2001

Suwa Haruo. 'Kamigata yakusha-e no genryū – shinshutsu kohan yakusha-e hachi-zu o megutte'. *Kokka* 1186, September 1994, pp. 21–30

Suzuki Jūzō. '*Byōsui kiga* (Hokusai-Ryūkōsai gappitsu) to *Gekijō gashi* (Ryūkōsai ga)'. *Ukiyo-e geijutsu* 13, December 1966, pp. 40–4

Takahashi Hiroko. *Sandaime Nakamura Utaemon no onnagata gei*. Tokyo, Mitsuki Shobō, 1993

Takahashi Noriko. *Kusazōshi to engeki – yakusha nigao-e sōshiki o chūshin ni*. Tokyo, Kyūkō Shoin, 2004.

Takasugi Shio. 'Niwa Tōkei kenkyū joron'. *Ukiyo-e geijutsu* 145, January 2003, pp. 49–55

Takasugi Shio. 'Niwa Tōkei kenkyū joron – denki kenkyū o chūshin ni'. *Fukuoka Daigaku daigakuin ronshū* 36, no. 1, September 2004, pp. 225–42

Takei Kyōzō. 'Goshippu no tōjō', in *Edo bunka to sabukaruchā*, ed. Watanabe Kenji. Tokyo, Shibundō, 2005, pp. 160–8

Tanahashi Masahiro. 'Kibyōshi sōran, zenpen'. *Nihon shoshigaku taikei* 48, no. 1. Tokyo, Seishōdō, 1986

Tatekawa Enba. *Kabuki nendaiki*. Tokyo, Kabuki Shuppanbu, 1926

Tinios, Ellis. 'How to Draw Actor Portraits: An Introduction to Toyokuni's *Yakusha nigao haya-geiko*'. *Andon* 32, 1989, pp. 168–74

Tinios Ellis. *Mirror of the Stage: The Actor Prints of Kunisada*. Leeds, The University Gallery, 1996

Tinios, Ellis. 'The Kunisada-signature Half-length Actor Portraits of Utagawa Kunisada', typescript list, 2005 [available in the Japanese Section, Department of Asia, The British Museum]

Torigoe Bunzō *et al.*, eds. *Kabuki to bunraku* (*Iwanami kōza*). 10 vols. Tokyo, Iwanami Shoten, 1998

Tsuchida Mamoru. 'Kinsei no Osaka kabuki', in *Osaka no geinō*. Osaka, Mainichi Hōsō, 1973, pp. 1–52

Tsuchida Mamoru, ed. *Kamigata geibun sōkan*, vol. 4: *Kamigata yakusha ichidaiki shū*. Tokyo, Yagi Shoten, 1979

Tsugane Norio. 'Kabuki yonhyakunen to iu toshi'. *Kabuki – kenkyū to hihyō* 32, 2004, pp. 155–61

Ukiyo-e geijutsu (*Yakusha-e tokushū 1*) 112, July 1994(a)

Ukiyo-e geijutsu (*Yakusha-e tokushū 2*) 113, November 1994(b)

Ukiyo-e geijutsu (*Yakusha-e tokushū 3*) 114, January 1995

Ukiyo-e shūka. 18 vols. Tokyo, Shūeisha, 1979–87

Ukiyo-e taika shūsei. 20 vols. Tokyo, Taihōkaku, 1931–2

Ukiyo-e taisei. 12 vols. Tokyo, Tōhō Shoin, 1930–1

Van Doesburg, Jan. *Osaka kagami*. Dodewaard (Netherlands), Huys den Esch, 1985

Van Doesberg, Jan. 'Osaka tattoos'. *Andon* 72–3, October 2002, pp. 102–14

Waseda Daigaku Tsubouchi Hakushi Kinen Engeki Hakubutsukan, eds. *Zuroku*. 2 vols. Tokyo, 1978

Waseda Daigaku Tsubouchi Hakushi Kinen Engeki Hakubutsukan, eds. *Kabuki ema*. Tokyo, 1986

Yamamoto Takashi. 'Yakusha nigao-e to Ōsaka honya nakama – yomihon *Hōshū take no Fushimi* ikken to sono haikei', in *Yomihon kenkyū shinshū*, eds Yomihon Kenkyūkai, vol. 1. Tokyo, 1998, pp. 55–71

Yamamoto Takashi. 'Bun'un Tōzen to Osaka shoshi shōkō'. *Bungaku* 1, no. 5, September–October 2000, pp. 134–43

Yamanouchi Chōzō. *Nihon nanga shi*. Tokyo, Rokkyō Shuppan, 1981

Yonemoto, Marcia. *Mapping Early Modern Japan: Space, Place, and Culture in the Tokugawa Period, 1603–1868*. Berkeley, University of California Press, 2003

Yoshida Teruji. '*Ehon butai ōgi* no kenkyū'. *Yoshida Teruji choshaku shū – Ukiyo-eshi to sakuhin*. Tokyo, Rokuen Shobō, n.d.

Yoshida Teruji. *Kabuki-e no kenkyū*. Tokyo, Rokuen Shobō, 1964

CONCORDANCE OF NAMES
with page numbers where those names appear

KABUKI ACTORS
(from Kokuritsu Gekijō 1998)

Names in bold are actors specially featured in the current exhibition.

ARTISTS

PLAYS

LIST OF CONTRIBUTORS

ENTRIES

All entries are by C. Andrew Gerstle,
except those credited with initials to the following authors:

Timothy Clark (TC) (British Museum)

Barbara Cross (BC) (SOAS)

Hideyuki Iwata (HI) (Atomi University)

Yōko Kaguraoka (YK) (Ehime University)

Hiroko Kitagawa (HK) (Ikeda Bunko Library)

Masae Kurahashi (MK) (Waseda University Theatre Museum)

Hiroyuki Sakaguchi (HS) (Osaka City University)

Kōichi Sawai (KS) (Osaka Museum of History)

Akiko Yano (AY) (SOAS)

ASSISTANCE IN PREPARING THE CATALOGUE

Ryō Akama (Ritsumeikan University)

Keizō Akeo (Ashiya City Art Museum)

Alan Cummings (SOAS)

Noriko Hanyū (Mukogawa Women's University)

Kumiko Hayashi (Kyoto Tachibana University)

Fumiko Kobayashi (Hōsei University)

Mavis Pilbeam (British Museum)

Makiko Tsuchida (SOAS)

Yōko Uchida (Waseda University Theatre Museum)

LIST OF LENDERS

Art Research Centre, Ritsumeikan University, Kyoto

The Ashmolean Museum, University of Oxford

Birmingham Museums and Art Gallery

Bodleian Library, University of Oxford

Bristol's City Museum & Art Gallery

The British Library, London

The British Museum, London

Cambridge University Library

Chiba City Museum of Art

Dōmyōji Tenmangū Shrine, Osaka Pref.

The Fitzwilliam Museum, University of Cambridge

Freis Collection, USA

C. Andrew Gerstle

Kōzō Hida

Ikeda Bunko Library, Osaka

Scott Johnson

Kansai University Library, Osaka

Sadahiko Katō

Hendrick Lühl

Mukogawa Women's University, Nishinomiya

National Museum of Scotland, Edinburgh

Nihon University Center for Information Networking, Tokyo

Osaka City University Media Center

Osaka Museum of History

Osaka University

Gerhard Pulverer

School of Oriental & African Studies Library, University of London

Ellis Tinios

Peter Ujlaki

Victoria & Albert Museum, London

Waseda University The Tsubouchi Memorial Theatre Museum (Waseda University Theatre Museum), Tokyo

John C. Weber